ARCHAEOLOGY AND THE BIBLE

THE BEST OF BAR

Volume One
Early Israel

Archaeology and the Bible
THE BEST OF BAR

VOLUME ONE

Early Israel

•

EDITED BY

HERSHEL SHANKS
& DAN P. COLE

BIBLICAL ARCHAEOLOGY SOCIETY
WASHINGTON, D.C.

Library of Congress Catalog Card Number: 90-81697
ISBN 0-9613089-5-8 (Volume One)
ISBN 0-9613089-3-1 (Set)

Printed and bound in the United States of America
Copyright ©1990
Biblical Archaeology Society
3000 Connecticut Avenue, NW
Washington, DC 20008

Table of Contents

Introduction ix

SECTION A

The Terrain of Abraham and Moses — Beer-sheba and the Sinai Wilderness   1

Beer-sheba of the Patriarchs 2
  Ze'ev Herzog
  (**BAR**, *November/December 1980*)

Fifteen Years in Sinai 20
  Itzhaq Beit-Arieh
  (**BAR**, *July/August 1984*)

The Route Through Sinai—Why the Israelites
Fleeing Egypt Went South 50
  Itzhaq Beit-Arieh
  (**BAR**, *May/June 1988*)

After Words 60

SECTION B

In the Time of the Judges — A Visit with an Early Israelite Family; Evidence for Early Biblical Cult Sites   63

A Visit with Ahilud 64
  Joseph A. Callaway
  (**BAR**, *September/October 1983*)

Has Joshua's Altar Been Found on Mt. Ebal? .76
  Adam Zertal
  (**BAR**, *January/February 1985*)

Joshua's Altar—An Iron Age I Watchtower 94
  Aharon Kempinski
  (**BAR**, *January/February 1986*)

How Can Kempinski Be So Wrong! 95
  Adam Zertal
  (**BAR**, *January/February 1986*)

Queries and Comments 106
  Aharon Kempinski, Anson F. Rainey and Michael P. Thompson
  (**BAR**, *July/August 1986*)

Bronze Bull Found in Israelite "High Place"
From the Time of the Judges 108
    Amihai Mazar
    (**BAR**, *September/October 1983*)

Two Early Israelite Cult Sites Now Questioned 116
    Hershel Shanks
    (**BAR**, *January/February 1988*)

After Words 121

SECTION C

The Citadel of Lachish Bears the Scars of Biblical Wars   123

Answers at Lachish 124
    David Ussishkin
    (**BAR**, *November/December 1979*)

Destruction of Judean Fortress Portrayed
In Dramatic Eighth-Century B.C. Pictures 148
    Hershel Shanks
    (**BAR**, *March/April 1984*)

Defensive Judean Counter-Ramp Found
At Lachish in 1983 Season 166
    David Ussishkin
    (**BAR**, *March/April 1984*)

The Mystery of the Unexplained Chain 175
    Yigael Yadin
    (**BAR**, *July/August 1984*)

Lachish—Key to the Israelite Conquest of Canaan? 178
    David Ussishkin
    (**BAR**, *January/February 1987*)

Queries and Comments 200
    (**BAR**, *May/June 1987*)

After Words 201

SECTION D

Arad—An Israelite Border Fortress   203

Arad—An Ancient Israelite Fortress
With a Temple to Yahweh 204
    Ze'ev Herzog, Miriam Aharoni and Anson F. Rainey
    (**BAR**, *March/April 1987*)

After Words 224

SECTION E

Bringing Iron and Water from the Rock—
Two Emerging Technologies in Ancient Israel   227

**How Iron Technology Changed the Ancient World—
And Gave the Philistines a Military Edge** 228
James D. Muhly
(**BAR**, *November/December 1982*)

How Water Tunnels Worked 244
Dan Cole
(**BAR**, *March/April 1980*)

After Words 266

SECTION F

Voices from the Biblical Dust—
Inscriptions from the Israelite Period   269

Fragments from the Book of Balaam Found at Deir Alla 270
André Lemaire
(**BAR**, *September/October 1985*)

Did Yahweh Have a Consort? 284
Ze'ev Meshel
(**BAR**, *March/April 1979*)

Who or What Was Yahweh's Asherah? 296
André Lemaire
(**BAR**, *November/December 1984*)

**Jeremiah's Scribe and Confidant Speaks
From a Hoard of Clay Bullae** 306
Hershel Shanks
(**BAR**, *September/October 1987*)

**Yadin Presents New Interpretation
Of the Famous Lachish Letters** 314
Oded Borowski
(**BAR**, *March/April 1984*)

The Saga of Eliashib 318
Anson F. Rainey
(**BAR**, *March/April 1987*)

After Words 322

Contributors 323

Introduction

This series of volumes is not meant to present simply the "Best of BAR" (as *Biblical Archaeology Review* has come to be called). The objective has been to group together thought-provoking articles on related themes from different periods of Biblical history. As such, the volumes also serve as an excellent introduction to Biblical archaeology at its exciting, often controversial, best. Each volume contains a series of articles selected and organized as a coherent, progressive whole. The first volume focuses on Israel during the period of the Hebrew Bible; the second, on the world of the New Testament. Subsequent volumes will cover other discrete areas.

The series has been designed to serve the interests and needs of both the general reader and the student of Biblical studies and archaeology.

Each volume covers a range of recent scholarly discoveries and interpretations. The reader will also become familiar with the process of archaeological discovery and interpretation, as well as with some of the problems involved in that process.

Archaeology holds a natural fascination for most of us. It allows us to retrieve from the dusty earth some personal reminders of our own past. Uncovering an ancient artifact somehow brings us into contact with our distant ancestors, especially when it connects us with the Bible.

But archaeology involves more than a mere nostalgic diversion—like spending a rainy afternoon rummaging through a box of childhood mementos. Sometimes the excitement comes from retrieving a better understanding of our past. In this way, we better understand ourselves. That **BAR** tries to foster this understanding perhaps explains why it has become such a popular journal over the past fifteen years, with over a quarter million readers, and why an increasing number of teachers have been using its articles in their classrooms.

The attraction of having a series of such articles in a single volume is obvious. No need to fight over a single library copy. No need to worry about back-issue availability. It's OK to mark up your own copy to use for future reference. You may even want to read unassigned articles.

And for the general reader: You can read articles grouped together in a meaningful way.

Occasionally, as in volume two of the series—*Archaeology in the World of Herod, Jesus and Paul*—articles from **BAR**'s sister publication, *Bible Review* (**BR**), will provide useful supplements to the selections drawn from **BAR.**

The pictures here appear in black and white, while in the original most were in color. Unfortunately, only by using black-and-white reproduction could the price of the volumes be kept within reasonable limits.

Readers will note that the articles within each volume have been arranged as much as possible in accord with the chronological development of Biblical history. Brief introductions to each section call attention to the implications of the articles for Biblical understanding and to the way particular articles illustrate facets of the archaeological process or issues of scholarly interpretation. Supplementary After Words follow the articles and call attention to matters more readily discussed after the articles have been read, occasionally adding follow-up comments by readers, or by the authors, in subsequent issues of **BAR**.

For those interested in pursuing a subject further, additional related articles in **BAR** and **BR** have been listed in For Further Reading at the end of each topical section. In most instances, the back issues containing these articles are still available and may be purchased individually from the Biblical Archaeology Society.

The rest is up to you. We hope you enjoy it.

A Word About Volume I

The topics included in this volume of *Archaeology and the Bible* have in common an interest in reconstructing the character of ancient Israel, the community from which the Hebrew Bible emerged. Beyond that, they have been selected to provide a deliberate diversity—a sense of scope in both Biblical history and in the archaeological enterprise.

In terms of the Biblical drama, the articles range from the Genesis stories of Abraham at Beer-sheba to inscriptions of the time of Jeremiah to the last days of Judah before its fall to the Babylonians.

In the archaeological materials considered, the articles range from wilderness worship sites to domestic dwellings, from major citadels to border outposts, from huge tunnels hewn from bedrock to tiny scraps of barely visible writing.

In reflecting different facets of the archaeological process, the articles range from interpretation of single subjects to the reconstruction of whole aspects of culture and technology by drawing on materials uncovered at a number of sites; from the use of archaeological clues to reconstruct ancient geography and settlement patterns to puzzling over enigmatic pictures and one-sentence texts in reconstructing ancient religious ideas.

To make this volume easier to use, we have made two changes in the articles. References to colors in captions have been deleted, since all illustrations are now black and white. References to particular pages within the articles have been changed to correspond to the pagination of this volume. When an article in a specific issue is mentioned it will appear like this if it is included here: May/June 1980 p. 42 [112]. The page number in brackets is the page where the article will be found in this volume.

Acknowledgment

Like all the projects of the Biblical Archaeology Society, *Archaeology and the Bible* was produced by the devoted and careful efforts of numerous members of our staff. Our special thanks for these volumes go to Carol Andrews, Steven Feldman, Lauren Krause, Susan Laden, Suzanne F. Singer and Judith Wohlberg.

The Terrain of Abraham and Moses—
Beer-sheba and the Sinai Wilderness

Here we look at recent archaeological investigations at the edge of the Negev, on ancient Canaan's southern fringe and in the wilderness farther south in the Sinai Peninsula.

These articles deal with two important early periods in Biblical sacred history: the activities of the patriarchs Abraham, Isaac and Jacob at Beer-sheba as recounted in Genesis and the Exodus flight of Moses and his followers from Egypt to the wilderness of Sinai.

As Ze'ev Herzog indicates in "Beer-sheba of the Patriarchs," scholars disagree about the most likely date for the period of the patriarchs and some even doubt the historicity of the Genesis accounts altogether. Herzog's article, based on discoveries made in excavations at Beer-sheba, adds a dramatic contribution to the ongoing debate.

Before reading this article, you may wish to read the Genesis references to the patriarchs' associations with Beer-sheba to see how much or how little can be inferred from them about the character of the Beer-sheba settlement (Genesis 21:25-34, 22:19, 26:23-33, 46:1-5).

Quite apart from Herzog's arguments concerning the dating of Abraham, his article provides a good example of the kinds of physical evidence derived from excavation of an early Iron Age town site and of the sharp shifts that can occur over a couple of centuries. In this case, five closely overlaid strata of remains during a two-century period (c. 1150-950 B.C.*) reveal several dramatic changes.

The second and third articles in this section, by Itzhaq Beit-Arieh, turn our attention farther south. In "Fifteen Years in Sinai," Beit-Arieh summarizes the extensive evidence for shifting patterns of ancient occupation in this seemingly hostile wilderness, as gleaned by Israeli archaeologists during 1967-1982. His report reflects the importance of surveying archaeological remains over a broad geographical area. This has been a fairly recent development in Near Eastern archaeology and is yielding significant results. Often the data gathered from an isolated site are too scrappy and ephemeral to interpret, or they may give a misleading impression. By accumulating data from an entire region, a clearer picture emerges of changing patterns of habitation and social structure during different periods.

In the final article of this section, Beit-Arieh draws upon recently acquired knowledge of ancient Sinai settlement patterns to address anew the question posed by numerous scholars over the past century and a half: What is the most likely route for Moses and the Hebrew slaves to have taken in their flight from Egypt? (See Exodus 12:29-39, 13:17-17:13, 19:1-2; Numbers 10:11-12,33-20:1, summarized in Numbers 33:1-36.)

In his article, Beit-Arieh helpfully provides a chart showing the conclusions of 16 major scholars concerning the location of the sacred mountain of the Exodus.

---

* Some of the articles reprinted here use the designation B.C.E. (Before the Common Era), the scholarly, religiously neutral term that corresponds to B.C.

Beer-Sheba of the Patriarchs

By Ze'ev Herzog

THE FINDINGS OF ARCHAEOLOGISTS sometimes seem to confirm the Biblical text. At other times, the excavation results present a problem.

Perhaps the best known case of the latter is Jericho. Most scholars date the Israelite conquest of Canaan to the Late Bronze Age, to a time (13th century B.C.) when, according to Jericho excavator Kathleen Kenyon, there was *no* settlement at Jericho, let alone a city whose walls could be trumpeted down. According to the Bible, the next city to fall to the Israelites, was Ai. There is a problem in this case too. Professor Joseph Callaway, who excavated Ai, found no settlement from that period.

We have encountered a somewhat similar problem at Beer-sheba* with respect to the Patriarchal Age. The problem is even more complicated because scholars disagree wildly as to the date of the Patriarchal Age.

The well-known American scholar, William F. Albright, placed the Patriarchal Age in what archaeologists call MBI or Middle Bronze I. He was supported by the famous Hebrew Union College archaeologist, Nelson Glueck. They reasoned, largely on the basis of Glueck's surface surveys done in the area south of the Biblical Negev, that the patriarchal stories preserve descriptions of conditions in the Negev which correspond only to archaeological remains from MBI. Albright dated this period from the 21st to 19th centuries B.C.

This view has now been almost totally abandoned because the Biblical references to the Patriarchal Age reflect an urban civilization with frequent allusions to kings and cities: Bethel, Gerar and Hebron appear prominently in the patriarchal narratives, and a number of other cities are mentioned too. Because there appear to

---

* Beer-sheba is sometimes spelled Beer-sheva because that is the way it is pronounced in modern Hebrew. We use "b" instead of "v" because it is the customary spelling of the English Bible.

have been no towns in Palestine in MBI, it is no longer tenable to regard this period as the Patriarchal Age. Many scholars have now shifted the date of the Patriarchal Age to MBII (c. 19th to 16th centuries B.C.). In the Bible the patriarchs are portrayed as pastoralists on the fringes of an urban society. According to many scholars, the urban society of MBII fits this picture admirably.

However, a number of other dates, both later and earlier, have also been defended, and two important books[1] have recently suggested that there was no Patriarchal Age, that the stories were composed during the Israelite monarchy or even the exilic period without reference to historical fact.

It is fair to say that there is no more perplexing question among Biblical scholars than the date of the Patriarchal Age[2]—there is even a question as to whether such an age ever occured. It is into this maelstrom that we must now introduce the evidence from Beer-sheba.

As reflected in patriarchal narratives, Beer-sheba is the

Yohanan Aharoni, *Excavation Director on site at Beer-sheba. Until his death in 1972, Aharoni led the Institute of Archaeology at Tel Aviv University.*

4

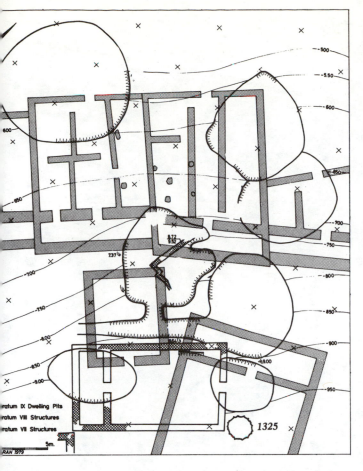

Stratum IX Dwelling Pits
Stratum VIII Structures
Stratum VII Structures

5m.

RAN 1979

1325

A model of the earliest *Iron Age I settlement at Beer-sheba (Stratum IX) is seen on the preceding page. Dwelling pits were cut into the rock on the slope of the hill and above the well. (The well is the small hole at the bottom of the slope.) Some of the pits were covered by beams and branches; others were protected by fabric or leather (at top of hill). Channels connected the pits and served as entrance lanes (lower center of slope). Huts or tents were probably erected in the open spaces between the pits.*

The plan on this page shows the pits of Stratum IX as rounded areas, some of which were reused in Stratum VIII. Three strata of Beer-sheba are superimposed in this plan. At the bottom is a building from Stratum VIII (with hatched lines) which was built over some pits from the earlier level. Above the pits at the top of the plan are some of the four-room houses which ringed the site in Stratum VII. Each of these four-room houses has a broad room at the bottom (forming the outside wall of the settlement) and three long rooms (sometimes subdivided) extending into the settlement from the broad room. These houses were entered from inside the settlement. Note that some structures in Stratum VII were built outside the circumvallation of houses, on the slope leading to the well (marked 1325).

most important center in the Negev during this period. Abraham dwelt at Beer-sheba (Genesis 22:19). Abraham and Abimelech entered a convenant at Beer-sheba (Genesis 21:32). Abraham planted a tamarisk tree at Beer-sheba (Genesis 21:33). The Lord spoke to both Isaac and Jacob at Beer-sheba (Genesis 26:23; 46:1). Beer-sheba is also the site of some famous wells: Abraham's well at Beer-sheba was seized by Abimelech's men (Genesis 21:25. Isaac's servants dug a well at Beer-Sheba also (Genesis 26:25).

Tel Beer-sheba, the site of the ancient city, is located on a hill overlooking the Wadi Beer-sheba about two and one half miles east of the modern city of Beer-sheba. The mound itself covers only two and one half acres.

Beer-sheba was excavated during eight seasons (1969-1976) by a team from Tel-Aviv University's Institute of Archaeology under the direction of the late Professor Yohanan Aharoni. Most of the dig was devoted to uncovering the great, fortified, Israelite city dating to the United Monarchy of King David (his reign being dated from 1000 B.C.) and, later, to the kingdom of Judah (980-701 B.C.). This period of time is called Iron Age II by archaeologists.

During Iron Age II, Beer-sheba was a rich and powerful urban city, surrounded by a massive circular wall containing an impressive gate through which one passed into the city. A circular street parallel to the wall allowed easy access to the carefully planned metropolis. Large storehouses to the right of the city gate accommodated commercial activity. An imposing governor's residence looked out on a plaza inside the gate. Cultic centers provided for the city's religious needs.

In this article, however, we are interested in the Beer-sheba of earlier periods. During the last three seasons of excavation (1974-1976), an effort was made to go below Beer-sheba of Iron Age II to find patriarchal Beer-sheba. A considerable part of the site was dug down to bedrock in order to find the earliest settlements at Beer-sheba. This effort revealed four earlier occupational strata (Strata VI through IX) which I am pleased to describe for **BAR** readers in the first published summary of this phase of our excavation.

I must tell you at the outset that these strata cover the 250 to 300 years immediately prior to the fortified Israelite city of the United Monarchy—from about 1250 B.C. to about 1000 B.C. Essentially the pre-urban occupation of the site was found. There was, however, *nothing* from an earlier period except a few Chalcolithic (4th millennium

B.C.) sherds: no evidence was found of habitation at Beer-sheba before about 1200 B.C. (the beginning of Iron Age I) which is several hundred years after the latest date scholars proposed for the Patriarchal Period.

The Iron I settlements at Beer-sheba were preserved mostly on the southeastern slope of the mound, the lowest part of the natural hill underlying the tell. To prepare for the construction of the later, fortified, Israelite (Iron Age II) city, during the latter part of King David's reign, the top of the hill was leveled. This not only gave a solid base for the new city, but also destroyed almost all earlier remains. The southeastern part of the mound where the topography was lower escaped such destruction.

Although we dug from Stratum VI down to Stratum IX (and then hit bedrock) I shall describe the strata in reverse order—from the lowest and earliest stratum to the latest and highest.

The earliest occupation at Beer-sheba (Stratum IX) was represented only by seven large pits about 22 to 25 feet in diameter. The pits are irregular in shape though most may be described as roughly round. Some of the pits are almost 10 feet deep: These we assume were used as granaries. Other pits, between three and four feet deep, were used for habitation.

The best preserved dwelling pit consists of three separate areas. A cave cut into the conglomerate rock which formed the side of the pit provided partial shelter from the elements. Niches cut into the rock at the rear of the cave contained two storage jars (one of whose lid was still on) which had been left in the niches. A second area which effectively enlarged the cave was formed by a wall in the middle of the pit and extending part of the way across it. This wall and the natural rock wall opposite it on the other side of the pit could have supported a roof built of beams, branches and clay. Although the cave floor was paved with rounded limestone slabs, the floor of the area behind the wall, on the side away from the cave, was raised by fill, creating a kind of terrace. The occup-

Crisscrossed by excavated areas, *Tel Beer-sheba is seen here from the air. In the background is the expedition camp which housed up to 300 students and staff. Structures of Stratum II (destroyed by Sennacherib in the late 8th century B.C.) are being reconstructed. The Western Quarter (1) is at left, the Governor's Place (2) is in the center, and the City Gate (3) and the storehouses (4) are on the right. Note the "brick factory" (5) on the edge of the tel in the foreground where sun-dried mud bricks are manufactured to use in reconstruction.*

ants came to the terrace, no doubt, to escape the oppressive heat in the lower parts of the pit or to catch the afternoon breeze. The pit's third dwelling area, in addition to the terrace and roofed areas, was probably an open court. There the floor was even lower than in the cave.

Several accumulated layers of ashen soil on the court floor contained large quantities of pottery sherds, pieces of charred wood and many bones, indicating that the pit had been used for the long period of time.

A lengthy corridor-like trench had been cut adjacent to this dwelling pit: An opening was cut into the corridor creating an entrance into the dwelling pit. One end of the corridor led to another dwelling pit.

We think that the entire settlement of this stratum covered about 2,990 sq. yds., approximately the area of half a football field. If so, it probably contained about 20 dwelling pits and 10 granaries and would have housed from 100 to 140 people.

Stratum IX was not destroyed by violence. It was abandoned then reused, new structures were added to the old. The pottery leads us to believe this stratum had been occupied in the 13th and 12th centuries B.C.

In Stratum VIII, which dates to the 11th century B.C., we found houses for the first time. The pit dwellings continued to be used, although with a raised floor, in most of the area in which they were built.

The houses of Stratum VIII had mud brick walls built on a stone foundation. A typical house of this stratum measured about 44 feet by 25 feet. It had only the internal wall along the back of the house creating a broad room about 9 feet wide and 25 feet long which was apparently the dwelling room. The remainder of the house was an open courtyard. This appears to be a variation of the later 4-room Israelite house which also had a broad room in back, but in which the remainder of the house was divided into three long rooms. In the later Israelite house only the middle room was used as an open courtyard.

Like Stratum IX, Stratum VIII was abandoned rather than destroyed. The pottery suggests that the same people who lived in Stratum VIII built Stratum VII at the end of the 11th century B.C. Stratum VII was the first fortified settlement at Beer-sheba.

Prior to building the settlement of Stratum VII, a substantial leveling operation was carried out during which the pits of the previous strata were filled. The new settlement shows a first attempt at planned development. About halfway down the slope, a chain of houses was built, each house sharing its side walls with its neighbors. The backs of the houses formed a fortification wall around the city. The houses were entered from inside the settlement further up the hill.

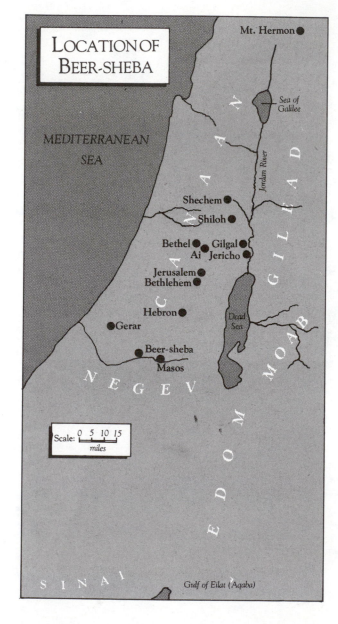

LOCATION OF BEER-SHEBA

Mt. Hermon

Sea of Galilee

MEDITERRANEAN SEA

Jordan River

Shechem

Shiloh

Bethel Gilgal
Ai Jericho

Jerusalem
Bethlehem

Hebron

Gerar

Dead Sea

Beer-sheba

Masos

NEGEV

Scale: 0 5 10 15
miles

SINAI

Gulf of Eilat (Aqaba)

A plan of the first fortified *settlement at Beer-sheba (Stratum VII) dating to Iron Age I in the early 11th century B.C. The individual houses were arranged in a belt to provide defense. The large open courtyard could be filled at night by herds of sheep and goats. Some houses also existed outside the main belt, mostly near the well. The solid black areas represent walls actually found. The other walls are reconstructed on the basis of the excavated walls. Note the two rooms on either side of the gate (marked X). These rooms extend beyond the outer line of the settlement and were probably protective towers. Below, an isometric reconstruction illustrates the possible three-dimensional appearance of Stratum VII which we have just examined in the plan. In the isometric reconstruction it is evident that the houses on the right, are built on a slope which descends to the well (marked 1325).*

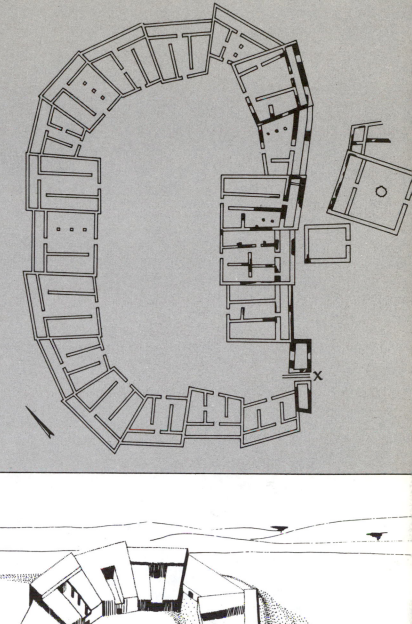

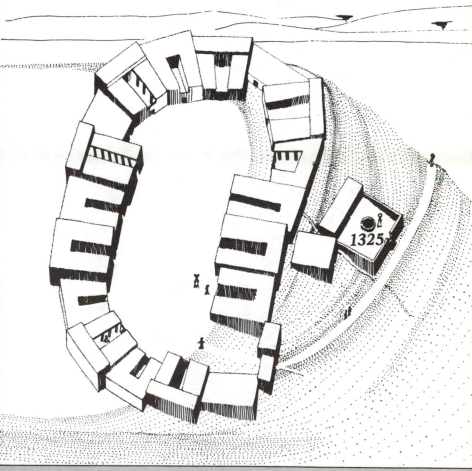

If the Patriarchal Age is represented at all at Beer-sheba, it must be the very modest villages from the 13th to 11th centuries B.C.

The dwellings were typical Israelite 4-room houses composed of the broad room in the back from which three long rooms (often subdivided) extended. The broad rooms of the ring of houses adjacent to one another, formed a kind of casemate wall around the settlement. That was exactly what the builders had intended.

This casemate-like fortification formed of the back rooms of houses also appears elsewhere. A group of similarly fortified settlements has been found in surveys and excavations in the central Negev mountains, south of Beer-sheba.[3] The sites of Hatira, Refed, Har-Boqer and also Atar Haroah[4] seem to share a similar planning concept with Beer-sheba VII. Based on the chronology and stratigraphy of Beer-sheba VII it is possible now to date the Negev sites with similar plans to the late eleventh B.C.

This type of casemate-like fortification probably was the prototype for the true casemate walls of the Iron Age II period. However, in terms of town planning, there is a major difference between the true casemate wall which surrounds a "fortified-city", and the arrangement of houses we found in Beer-sheba Stratum VII which we call a "fortified-settlement". In fortified-settlements the houses are the dominant unit: the defensive aspect is a result of the arrangement. In the true fortified-city, the city-wall is the dominant unit, preplanned in a continuous line, to which houses are often secondarily attached.

Settlements fortified with a ring of houses, like Beer-sheba, had different town plans from later cities with true casemate walls. The center of the fortified settlement at Beer-sheba and other similar sites was a large open courtyard without structures, other than the ring of houses; additional houses were also built outside the ring. In the later fortified-cities protected by true casemate

walls, houses were built over the entire central part of the site, and none were built outside the wall. And, finally, the tendency in fortified-cities was to build a water system within the walls, while in a fortified-settlement the water system was left outside a ring of houses.

The foundation walls of Stratum VII were made of uncut boulders collected from wadis (dry river beds). The rocks were placed in two or three lines in each course, and cemented to each other by a clay mortar and small stones. The superstructure was mud brick.

Although we uncovered only five of the houses in the ring, we have reconstructed the entire ring containing 18 houses. The inner court of the settlement measured about 80 feet by 160 feet. The city's entrance was on the south. Two rooms, probably protective towers, projected outside the settlement's outer line on either side of the gate.

Why did the residents of Stratum VII feel it necessary to fortify this settlement? As I previously noted, similar fortification systems had sprung up throughout the Negev at about this time. The most likely explanation for these fortifications is that the settlements were threatened by the powerful Amalekites who dominated the Negev during the early part of King Saul's reign (1 Samuel 15). Beer-sheba, which was on the southern border of the fledgling Israelite kingdom, was probably fortified by King Saul at the end of the 11th century B.C. during wars against the Amalekites.

Although Beer-sheba appears in the patriarchal narratives as the most important settlement in the Negev during the period before the Israelite monarchy, Beer-sheba appears from excavation results to have been more like a small village consisting of a few dwelling pits and houses. Another ancient site, known today as Tel Masos, lies 8 miles east of Beer-sheba and was far more impressive than Beer-sheba during the same period. To begin with, Masos, an enormous area forty times larger than Beer-sheba, was far better built. There is also evidence of its having had widespread trade connections.

The excavator of Tel Masos, Aharon Kempinski (following a suggestion of Yohanan Aharoni) contends that Tel Masos should be identified with Biblical Hormah* and that the city was settled peacefully by the southern tribes of Israel. If this were true, Beer-sheba would have to be regarded as a minor satellite of Masos.

A more probable suggestion has recently been made by Professor Moshe Kochavi of Tel Aviv University. Kochavi has suggested that Tel Masos is not Israelite at all but is rather Ir-Amalek, the city of the Amalekites. If this is true — and it seems quite likely — then Beer-sheba of Strata IX — VIII was simply a small Judean village on the southern border, just across from Israel's strongest enemy, the Amalekites. This easily explains why a fortified settlement was built at Beer-sheba in Stratum VII in the late 11th century B.C. At the time King Saul, in the course of his wars against the Amalekites, would have needed to fortify his settlements near the enemies' cities. It follows that, after Saul defeated the Amalekites, he would have built a series of fortified settlements further to the south to protect Israel against future Amalekite incursions, and those we find at Hatira, Refed, Har-Boqer and Atar Haroah.

Stratum VI at Beer-sheba must be understood in the context of Stratum V which was a royal urban center built by King David in the latter part of his reign.[5]. King David's city was a carefully planned town covering the entire mound. Preceding it was a short-lived city of Stratum VI. This settlement was a puzzle until we interpreted it in the light of Stratum V.

In Stratum VI, the line of houses that had protected the settlement against the Amalekites in Stratum VII was neglected and even dismantled; the back rooms of some houses were removed and the remaining rooms were subdivided. There was no attempt to plan the town.

In Stratum VI, only one new building of any substance was constructed: a three room house with a broad room in back and the large space in front divided into two rooms by a row of pillars. One room was an open court, the other was used for storage. Stairs led up to a flat roof.

We finally decided that Stratum VI could be interpreted only as a camp for the construction of Stratum V. When King David decided to build a royal urban center at Beer-sheba to replace King Saul's fortified settlement of Stratum VII, the Stratum VII population had to be evacuated and a large-scale leveling operation undertaken. The lowest part of the mound was filled, the top part was removed, building stones were gathered and transported, and hundreds of thousands of clay bricks were

* Numbers 14:45, 21:3; Deuteronomy 1:44; Judges 1:17; 1 Samuel 30:30.

The horned altar *from Beer-sheba. Corresponding to the Biblical description of such altars, the horns are one piece. However, contrary to Biblical requirements, the Beer-sheba altar is made of hewn stones, not "unhewn stones, upon which no man has lifted an iron tool" (Joshua 8:30-31). Yohanan Aharoni suggested that the Biblical proscription may have applied to iron tools, but not bronze ones.*

The altar was found dismantled and in secondary use in later walls. Aharoni dated the altar to the 8th century B.C., the Iron Age II city of the Divided Monarchy. Note the snake carved into the lower right corner of the altar.

Cooking jugs, *black juglets, iron blade sickles and shells help date Stratum VI to the early tenth century B.C.*

Buckets of fill *pulled up by a winch gradually expose the more than 100-foot-deep rock-cut shaft of the ancient well of Beer-sheba. So far, the bottom of the well, that is, water-level, has not been reached. Seen around the top of the well are some of the stones which line the upper 20 feet of the shaft.*

Another ancient well near Beer-sheba is represented (above) in a lithograph from about 1800. The deeply furrowed stones, marked by ropes pulling against them, were a clear feature at this earlier time although they are no longer present today.

manufactured. The single sizeable structure which we excavated in Stratum VI was probably built for the Commander of the Works. Most of the work force lived in tents or huts outside the mound. Perhaps some supervisors squatted in the abandoned houses of Stratum VII and quickly built subdividing walls to create temporary quarters. Probably the area of Stratum VII and Stratum VI was the last part of the city built in Stratum V, and the very last part of Stratum VI to be used for Stratum V was the Commander's house.

Having brought the story back to the Beer-sheba of King David, we may now return to the question of the Patriarchal Age at Beer-sheba. If the Patriarchal Age is represented at all at Beer-sheba, it must be the very modest villages of Strata IX and VIII from the 13th to

11th centuries B.C. In the former, the dwellings were pits; in the latter there were some houses, in addition to the reused dwelling pits. In Stratum VII the fortified ring of houses defended the settlement against the Amalekite threat during King Saul's reign. Stratum VI was the building camp for King David's royal urban city which was Stratum V. So the only possible Patriarchal Age settlement is Strata VIII and IX. Except for a few Chalcolithic potsherds, there is no evidence whatever of any earlier habitation at Tel Beer-sheba.

How can we explain this apparent contradiction between the archaeological evidence and the historical tradition preserved in the Bible?

One way is by rejecting the historicity of the Biblical tradition. Indeed, some scholars have used evidence from

Beer-sheba to support their view that there was no Patriarchal Age, that the Biblical stories are aetiological —that is, composed during the Israelite monarchy for the purpose of creating a history for the new state.

Another possibility is to reject the identification of Tel Beer-sheba with the site of Biblical Beer-sheba. But Tel Beer-sheba is the only fortified mound in the vicinity of Roman and modern Beer-sheba, and its modern Arabic name, Tell es-Saba, preserves a clear linguistic element of Beer-sheba. So this is not a very likely explanation.

Another explanation, first offered by Yohanan Aharoni, is to move the Patriarchal Age forward to the 13th or 12th century B.C., the dates of Stratum IX and VIII. In other words, the patriarchal stories concerning Beer-sheba should be regarded as originating at the end of the second millennium B.C. during the so-called settlement period. This is the explanation to which I incline.

A final suggestion relates to an ancient well which has been located in the center of the eastern slope of the mound just outside the ring of houses that fortified the city in Stratum VII. The well, uncovered in excavations, is obviously a very ancient one and is located in a very unusual place: It was cut on the hill and not lower down in the wadi. Therefore it had to be four times deeper than a well dug at the base of the hill. The shaft of this well on the hill was hewn from solid rock and the upper part is strengthened by a stone lining. We believe this well was dug during the period of Stratum VIII or IX, and therefore provides additional evidence regarding the dating of the Patriarchal Age at Beer-sheba. That none of the walls built on the site were cut by the well establishes that it was incorporated into the very first settlement and that, in later phases, the houses were built at locations relative to the existence and use of the well. We attempted to clean the well and examine the debris deposited in it. Technical problems prevented us from going deeper than about 100 feet and reaching the well's earliest deposits.

Unfortunately, we cannot conclusively settle the many

A dwelling pit *of the 13th-12th centuries B.C. (Stratum IX) cut into conglomerate rock. The floor of the cave was paved with flat stones. At the top is a later wall from the 11th century B.C. (Stratum VII) which was built on layers of fill.*

Walls of the royal storehouses *are part of the Iron Age II city from the time of the Israelite monarchy. To reach earlier levels the archaeologists dug between these walls so as not to destroy the upper levels. Beneath the storehouses they found deep pits which were used as granaries and shallower pits which were used as dwellings. These pits were in use in earlier levels of Iron Age I (Stratum IX and Stratum VIII) and may be glimpsed here between the storehouse walls.*

On the eastern slope *of Tel Beer-sheba Iron Age I levels (Strata IX-VI), from about 1250-1000 B.C. were uncovered. The excavation of these strata was restricted to limited and separate spaces between the walls of later Iron Age II cities which dominate the picture. Here we may identify structures from these later Iron Age II cities: (1) the city-gate; (2) storehouses; (3) the outer gate of Stratum V; (4) the water channel of Stratum II. Note also (5) the location of the well outside the fortified city.*

questions regarding the existence or the dating of the Patriarchal Age on the basis of the evidence from Beer-sheba. For that we must await the vast accumulation of evidence from sites throughout the Near East. But it is tempting to conclude that this well was—whether in the 13th century B.C. or at some earlier time—the "Well of the Oath" where Abraham and Abimelech made their convenant (Genesis 21:32).

(The study summarized in this article was carried out during the academic year 1977/1978 at the University of Pennsylvania in Philadelphia where the author spent his sabbatical leave from the Institute of Archaeology at Tel Aviv University. Dr. Herzog wishes to express his appreciation to the Oriental Studies department and the Ancient History Program for their kind hospitality and the Penn-Israel program of the University of Pennsylvania whose contribution made possible this research.)

[1]John Van Seters, *Abraham is History and Tradition*, Yale University Press, New Haven and London, 1975.

T.L. Thompson, *The Historicity of the Patriarchal Narratives*, Berlin and New York, 1974.

[2]See also:

Nahum M. Sarna, "Abraham in History", **BAR** December 1977, p.5.

John Van Seters, "Dating in Patriarchal Stones," **BAR** November/December 1978, p.6.

William H. Stiebing, Jr., "When Was the Age of the Patriarchs?". **BAR** June 1975, p. 17.

[3]See: Ze'ev Meshel, *History of the Negev in the Time of the Kings of Judah*, Ph.D Dissertation, Tel Aviv, Israel, 1974 [Hebrew].

[4]Rudolph Cohen, "Atar Haroah," *Atiqot* 6, 1970, pp. 6-27.

[5]See "King David as Builder," **BAR,** March 1975, p. 13.

Fifteen Years in SINAI

Israeli Archaeologists Discover a New World

Itzhaq Beit-Arieh

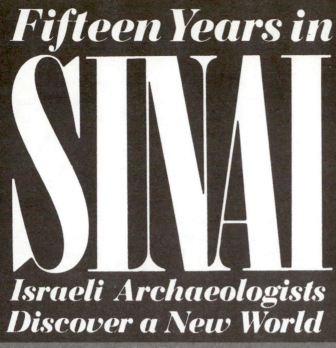

Preceding page: *Saint Catherine's monastery, dwarfed by the shade-blackened slope of Jebel Musa, the traditional site of Mt. Sinai. A faint track leads from the 1,400-year-old monastery to the vast open plain called El Raha. On this plain, tradition says, the Children of Israel camped while Moses communed with God on the mountain. The distant cluster of white tents in the plain belongs to Egyptian soldiers who were stationed in Sinai in 1964 when this photograph was taken.*

WE WERE DRIVING SOUTH, along the Gulf of Suez, heading for our excavation site when our jeep broke down. Fortunately, it happened on a paved road, before we turned onto the desert track that would take us to a desolate site in the interior of the Sinai Peninsula, still 65 miles away. We had another bit of good luck—a Bedouin mechanic from a nearby village offered to help. A friendly fellow, he happily engaged us in conversation.

"I've heard about you," he said.

"Oh?"

"Yes. You're the Israelis who are digging for gold in the hills near Jebel* Musa.

"No, no," I said, but before I could go on, he interrupted.

"Yes, yes," he smiled, "I know you've already found lots of it. The story has gotten around."

*Jebel means mountain in Arabic.

The face of Sinai, *aged but timeless, is personified by the Bedouin, who have called the peninsula home for thousands of years. Today most of the 80,000 Bedouin in Sinai live near the Mediterranean coastal city of El 'Arish.*

We tried to explain but to no avail. Our transparently false "cover story" as to what we were "really" digging for simply convinced him of our unbelievability. How could we expect him to believe that we would take so much time and go to all this trouble and expense in order to find a few chips of flint, some broken pieces of pottery and a few courses of an ancient wall?

We drove off in our sturdily repaired jeep, leaving our Bedouin mechanic convinced that the rumors he had heard about our search for gold were true.

Naturally, we were not prospecting for gold, nor did we find any. But during our 15 years of excavation in Sinai, we have found simple, unimpressive structures and artifacts that to us are worth far more than gold. These scientific treasures reveal a score of vanished civilizations that once made Sinai their home.

On most popular maps, the Sinai Peninsula is almost blank—as if there was nothing there. If you look closely, you might find a settlement or two on the Mediterranean coast and a mark to indicate the location of the traditional site of Mt. Sinai in the southern part, but little else. The truth now, as it was in ancient times, is far different.

Between 1967 and 1982, when Sinai was under Israeli control, Israeli archaeologists literally put the peninsula on the map. Before that it was a kind of *tabula rasa*; we wrote on a clean slate—or practically so.

True, there had been the early travelers and explorers whose often accurate accounts stirred centuries of readers—from Egeria in the fourth century to the German scholar Carl Richard Lepsius in the middle of the 19th century. Some archaeological work had also been conducted here. For example, in 1905 Sir William Flinders Petrie explored the Egyptian temple with its hieroglyphic inscriptions at Serabit el-Khadem in south central Sinai, and he also recorded other inscriptions in the earliest known alphabetic script found in the nearby turquoise mines. Later expeditions continued to study this temple and its inscriptions. In northern Sinai, the French archaeologist Jean Clédat excavated from 1910 to 1924 at Tel Farama (ancient Pelusium) on a branch of the Nile. Also in northern Sinai, Petrie dug near Sheikh Zuwaid, classical Anthedon. Israeli archaeologists had access to Sinai for a short time in 1956, and they too rushed in to do as much as possible in those few months.

But all these expeditions in the aggregate barely scratched the surface—if you will forgive the pun—certainly in comparison with Israeli activity during the 15 years Sinai was administered by Israel.

Flaunting her wealth *but hiding her face, a Bedouin woman wears the* hijab *(veil) traditional for married Moslem women.*

Ending abruptly at its southern edge in sandstone cliffs, the Tih Plateau stretches across the midsection of the Sinai peninsula. Virtually treeless, the plateau epitomizes the "great and terrible wilderness" described in Deuteronomy 8:15. But archaeologists were surprised to find cisterns, wells, potsherds and flint implements at what must have been seasonal camps here and there in this seemingly barren environment.

Between 1967 and 1982, dozens of Israeli expeditions mapped, explored and sometimes excavated hundreds of ancient settlements and cemeteries scattered throughout this vast region. Sinai's hot, dry climate, its inaccessible mountain terrain, and its isolation from civilization made it a working laboratory for Israeli scholars of various disciplines—zoologists, botanists, geologists and, above all, archaeologists.

Israeli archaeologists were in a sense pioneers, surveying and excavating the unknown and reexamining the known or partially known. Much of the latter had been covered with sand, and in some cases even the location of the sites had been forgotten.

After 15 years of work in the field and preliminary analysis of our findings, we now have a far clearer picture of human activity in Sinai, going back to the dawn of civilization. We are also beginning to understand how the peninsula related to the two lands it borders—the Land of Egypt on the east and the Land of Israel on the north.

Much of the material on which my brief sketch here is based is still unpublished. The remainder of the material is available primarily only in technical preliminary reports and brief notes in Hebrew scientific journals. I have been personally involved in uncovering many of the finds, but a great part of the discoveries reported here were made by my colleagues, who have kindly made available to me the results of their work.

To most people, Sinai is known as the Biblical wilderness where the Children of Israel wandered for 40 years before reaching the Promised Land. It is indeed a vast peninsula, covering over 40,000 square miles. It is bounded on the north by the Mediterranean and narrows as one proceeds south to form a triangle with its apex at the Red Sea. Two fingers of the Red Sea border it on either side—the Gulf of Suez on the west and the Gulf of Eilat or Gulf of Aqaba on the east.

The popular view of Sinai is that it is one vast homogeneous wilderness. But nothing could be further from the truth. Its geological structure as well as its climate varies greatly.

In the southern point of the Sinai triangle there rises a massif of rugged granite mountains composed of magnificently colored tiers of red, gray and black metamorphic and igneous rock cut by deep gorges that serve as the main routes across the peninsula. Here are the highest peaks of the peninsula—Jebel Musa, 9,000 feet above sea level (see p. 44), and Jebel Serbal, 6,900 feet above sea level, another leading contender among the dozen or more peaks that vie for identification as the site where Moses received the Tablets of the Law. This mountainous region in southern Sinai is comparatively rich in perennial springs and now supports a population of about 15,000 Bedouin.

The barren Tih Plateau stretches across the middle part of the peninsula. In Bedouin folklore, this area is associated with the wanderings of foreign tribes in the remote past—hence its name, the desert of the *Tih*, which means wanderings. Proceeding from north to south on the plateau, limestone hills begin to rise above the broad tableland in the north. As one proceeds south on the plateau, the hills become almost imperceptibly higher until they culminate in Jebel et-Tih and Jebel el-'Igma at the southern end of the plateau. The plateau ends abruptly in steep sandstone crags. The Tih is practically devoid of water and vegetation. Accustomed as we were to finding remains of human occupation in harsh, inhospitable areas, it still came as a surprise to discover numerous flint implements from various periods lying amongst the black-and-white gravel (*hammada*) of the Tih Plateau.

Between the lofty granite mountains in the south and the chalky cliffs at the southern end of the Tih Plateau is a narrow strip of Nubian sandstone that contains the richest mineral resources in the peninsula. Here, in ancient times, turquoise and manganese were mined. The population in this area clustered around a number of verdant oases like Abu Rodeis and Bir Nasb, which are dotted with date palm groves, orchards and small gardens. The present Bedouin population of this area is about 10,000.

In the northwestern hill region of the peninsula, a number of small peaks rise from 2,300 to 3,500 feet above sea level. Very little water falls here, supporting a correspondingly sparse population.

The other areas of the peninsula are the coastal strips—covered with sandstone, marl and shifting sand dunes. These border the Gulf of Suez on the west, the Gulf of Eilat on the east and the Mediterranean Sea on the north. The underground water level is high enough to be reached by wells bored from the surface, so these areas are capable of sustaining a comparatively large number of people, concentrated in fishing villages and small centers that supply services to the population. The coastal strip in the north covers considerably more territory than those on the east and west and consequently is more heavily populated.

The Sinai peninsula belongs to the same climatic zone as the deserts of Libya, Egypt and Arabia (Saharo-Arabian

Wresting a scanty crop of dates *from parched soil, Bedouins living near this small oasis continue virtually unchanged a lifestyle begun by their ancestors millennia ago. The name of this nomadic people derives from the Arabic word* ba'adiya, *which means desert.*

zone). Annual precipitation in Sinai rarely exceeds 60 millimeters, except along the Mediterranean littoral. During some years, the rain does not come at all. Such a harsh climate tolerates little vegetation except in oases and wadi* beds. In the wadis, low shrubs and thorny trees like the acacia sustain themselves on the rare floodwaters that burst upon the peninsula during the winter.

The Bedouin inhabitants of Sinai aggregate about 80,000. Most of them are concentrated around El 'Arish, the informal "capital" of the peninsula, located on the northern coast. The rest of the Bedouin are scattered in tribes living along the coasts, in the main wadis and in and around oases.

Despite the harsh living conditions, which have prevailed for millennia, Sinai has always been inhabited.

---

*A wadi is a dry riverbed that may be filled once or twice a year by winter floods.

Abundant archaeological remains testify to the presence of people in Sinai throughout the ages. Each period of settlement has its special characteristics.

It is remarkable that one of the best-understood periods in Sinai is also the most ancient. Professor Ofer Bar-Yosef of the Hebrew University of Jerusalem led an expedition that investigated both the northern and southern parts of Sinai, from which most of our material regarding prehistory comes. His expeditions found evidence of a nomadic society in Sinai as early as the Late Paleolithic period (32,000-28,000 B.C.). We don't even have a name for the people who inhabited the Sinai peninsula at that time, but they lived in northern Sinai in the barren (at least today) hills around Jebel Maghara and Jebel el-Lagama, not far from such rich water sources as Bir Gafgafa. They continued to inhabit this area into the Epipaleolithic period, which lasted until about 8000 B.C. Bar-Yosef discovered many of these nomads' old campsites, where they left their surprisingly sophisticated flint implements. Most were scrapers and knives. But archaeologists also found tiny rectangular or trapezoidal flint blades known as "microliths," which could have been mounted end-to-end in a wooden haft—long since decayed, of course. The result would have been a large cutting tool like a sickle.

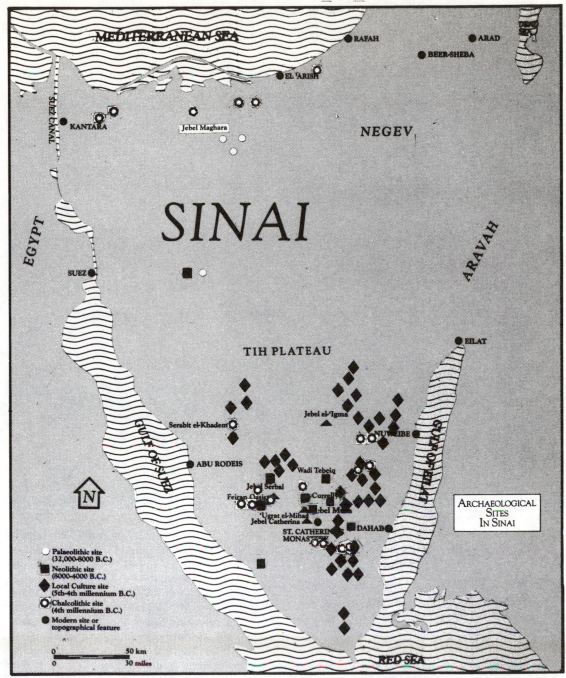

MEDITERRANEAN SEA

● RAFAH
● ARAD
● BEER-SHEBA

DEAD SEA

● EL 'ARISH

SUEZ CANAL

● KANTARA

Jebel Maghara

NEGEV

EGYPT

SINAI

● SUEZ

ARAVAH

TIH PLATEAU

● EILAT

GULF OF SUEZ

Serabit el-Khademi ◎

Jebel el-'Igma ▲

NUWEIBE

● ABU RODEIS

Wadi Tebeiq

GULF OF EILAT

N

Jebel Serbal
Feiran Oasis
Curreli
'Ugrat el-Mihad
Jebel Catherina
Jebel Musa
ST. CATHERINE
MONASTERY
● DAHAB

ARCHAEOLOGICAL
SITES
IN SINAI

○ Paleolithic site
(32,000-8000 B.C.)

■ Neolithic site
(8000-4000 B.C.)

◆ Local Culture site
(5th-4th millennium B.C.)

◎ Chalcolithic site
(4th millennium B.C.)

● Modern site or
topographical feature

0   50 km
0   30 miles

RED SEA

This flint (or lithic,* as the scholars call it) industry was already well-known to us from sites in the Negev highlands of southern Israel. The flint styles are the same, so we may assume that they were made by people of the same culture. Probably the Negev group gradually expanded south into northern Sinai. From their tools and the remains of their settlements, we can deduce that they were nomadic groups of hunters and food gatherers who encamped in small groups of not more than a hundred or so people.

These nomadic people seem to have come to northern Sinai from the Negev; other groups came to Sinai from North Africa. The earliest evidence for expansion from the area that was to become Egypt is from the period known as "Neolithic Pre-Ceramic B" (8000-5500 B.C.). The hunters from this period are well-known from their characteristic flint tools, previously found in the Nile Valley and Morocco. As we have seen, the Late Paleolithic people who came from the Negev in the north settled in northern Sinai. The neolithic newcomers who came from what was later to become Egypt settled in southern Sinai.

Even some of the stone dwellings of these Neolithic people have survived. A typical settlement lies in the Wadi Tebeiq, near the new road from the Gulf of Eilat to about 40 km north of Santa Catherina. The settlement

*Lithic means stone; hence the name Paleolithic for the period when this flint stone culture predominated.

covers about 750 square feet and consists of more than 20 interconnected circular structures built of unworked stone blocks. Some of these building blocks are quite large, in several cases over ten feet around. The excavators concluded from the amount of stone rubble in the debris that the stone portions of the walls were fairly low. The upper parts of the walls and the roofs must have been constructed of lighter materials, such as mudbrick and mud-

Round burial houses, *called* nawamis *by the Bedouin, dot the southern and eastern Sinai landscape. In the* namus *at left, discovered at Wadi Sawawin, a woman was buried in the fourth millennium B.C. wearing wrist and ankle bracelets.*

The walls of each namus, *about seven feet high, originally sloped inward to form a beehive shape. Many have been found with their roofs intact. Bedouin legend holds that these oddly shaped structures were built by the Israelites during their wanderings in the desert to protect themselves from a plague of* nawamis *(Arabic for mosquitoes) set upon them by heaven. The* nawamis *stand today as the oldest intact roofed structures in the world.*

plastered branches. The dwellings had doorsills of flat stone slabs and fire pits with hearths. Grinding stones, stone bowls, Red Sea shells, a few goat bones and a large variety of flints, including arrowheads, awls, drills, scrapers and various types of blades were found in the houses. At 'Ugrat el-Mihad, a few kilometers north of Jebel Catherina, the excavators found the same lithic assemblage, but they did not find the same kind of dwellings. Instead they uncovered six large oval-shaped structures that they assume were not roofed, since the remains of their walls were very low and there was not enough stone rubble around them to imagine that they ever stood much higher. The floors were paved. Perhaps these structures were sunken storage silos.

The fourth millennium B.C. is known to archaeologists as the Chalcolithic period. Etymologically, the name refers to the copper widely used by these people who lived more than 5,000 years ago. In Sinai, however, it was not copper that these people were mining but the rich veins of turquoise in the southwestern sector of the peninsula; these Chalcolithic people, as we shall see, were the first to exploit the turquoise mines.

In Israel, the Chalcolithic period is often referred to as the Ghassulian culture, after the site of Ghassul in the Jordan Valley where this culture was first identified. The "Ghassulians" from the Chalcolithic period have now been identified at numerous sites in northern Sinai. A survey conducted by the Ben-Gurion University of the Negev and directed by Professor Eliezer Oren found over 700 ancient sites from all periods strung along the main routes between Egypt and Canaan in the area between Rafah and the Suez Canal in northern Sinai. Over 100 of these sites included remains from the Ghassulian culture of the fourth millennium B.C.

At none of these sites, however, were any architectural remains uncovered. The pottery sherds that dated the sites and the occupational levels were typical of temporary encampments, and the archaeologists think they may have been wayside stations on the main route between Canaan and Egypt. Many of the sherds came from pots and jars that we recognize as having originated in either Egypt or Canaan.

As we already mentioned, Ghassulian culture in Sinai was confined almost exclusively to the northern coast. Intensive surveys elsewhere in Sinai failed to uncover other Chalcolithic sites—with one interesting exception.

At the foot of the mountain on which Serabit el-Khadem is located in south-central Sinai, we discovered a small Ghassulian settlement. I directed the excavation of this site, which turned out to be a work camp for miners employed in the famous turquoise mines of Serabit. It thus appears that these Chalcolithic people were the first to identify and exploit this mineral wealth that was later to assume such importance to the Egyptians.

In the ancient world, turquoise was highly prized. The rich deposits of semiprecious stone lying in the wadi embankments in this area are the only source of turquoise in the entire eastern Mediterranean. In and around this small Chalcolithic site, we found unpolished gems, hematite hammers to quarry the turquoise-bearing blocks of sandstone, flint blades to extract the turquoise nodules,

grinding stones to polish the gems, and large quantities of Ghassulian pottery (see p. 38).

We know from pottery sherds originating in Canaan that the Sinai "Ghassulians" had extensive contact with the north, but very few turquoise artifacts have turned up in Chalcolithic levels of excavations anywhere in Canaan. By contrast, at Egyptian sites, and particularly in tombs, considerable turquoise has been found. So we assume that most of the turquoise mined in Sinai at this time was exported to Egypt. Yet there is no evidence whatever—not even a few Egyptian sherds like those found in Chalcolithic sites in northern Sinai—that the Egyptians themselves were involved in these mining operations. As we shall see, 700 years later during the Third Dynasty (around 2600 B.C.), the Egyptians actually operated the mines and left temples to Hathor, mistress of the turquoise, to prove it. But in the Chalcolithic period the Egyptians were not involved. The Chalcolithic miners from Canaan were apparently independent entrepreneurs who sold their product on the Egyptian market.

Another phenomenon that belongs to the same chronological period—but not to the same culture—is the nawamis. These are beehive-shaped structures built of sandstone slabs or metamorphic cobbles. Found only in southern and eastern Sinai, they appear to have been built in clusters, each cluster lying several kilometers from its nearest neighbor. The nawamis are between 10 and 20 feet in diameter and approximately 7 feet high. Their walls curve inward towards the top to form a corbeled roof supported by a large stone slab. It is amazing that many of these roofs are still intact after thousands of years! Nawamis means mosquitoes in Arabic. The Bedouin call these curious structures nawamis because, according to local legend, they were built by the Israelites during their sojourn in the wilderness to protect themselves against mosquito attacks.

In fact, the nawamis are burial structures. Early Sinai explorers examined them and even excavated a few. The first comprehensive study of these tombs occurred in the early 1970s, when an expedition led by Ofer Bar-Yosef of the Hebrew University and Avner Goren, Archaeological Staff Officer for Sinai at the time, excavated a field of 24 nawamis in the Haggag Valley about 20 miles inland from Nuweibe on the Gulf of Eilat. Later, Goren excavated nawamis in eight other fields.

Each namus (singular of nawamis in one Bedouin dialect) contains several burials. Presumably these are members of the same family or clan. Sometimes the burials are what scholars call primary, and sometimes secondary. A primary burial is an interment immediately after death. A secondary burial is an interment of bones only, reburied after the flesh has decayed. The bones from these nawamis are now being studied by a team from the Tel Aviv University School of Medicine. Many characteristics of the bones conform to the Gracile Mediterranean type found in Israel. These similarities may give some hint of the origin of the *nawamis* population, about whom we know so little. The funeral offerings in the *nawamis* included shell bracelets, faience beads, flint tools, and juglets, as well as tools made of bone and copper—all reflecting contacts with both Canaan and Egypt.

When I first began writing this article for **BAR**, I included the *nawamis* phenomenon in my discussion of the Early Bronze Age rather than the Chalcolithic period, because the best scholarly guess then was that the *nawamis* were built in Early Bronze Age I, or EB I (3150 B.C. to 2850 B.C.). Very recently, however, in one of the *nawamis* burials, we found two juglets from what is known as the Naqada I* period in Egypt. Since this period parallels our Chalcolithic period, we now have some solid basis on which to date these tombs to the Late Chalcolithic period, or from about 3400 B.C. to 3150 B.C.

Each *namus* has a short entrance corridor, constructed of upright stone slabs, which invariably faces the setting sun. Some scholars suggest, because of the westward orientation of the tomb entrances, that these people shared the Egyptian belief that the soul journeys to the west after death; this strengthens the possibility of an Egyptian origin for them.

Whoever these people were, there is no doubt that they had a highly developed culture and were capable of constructing the architecturally sophisticated *nawamis* with corbeled roofs. *Nawamis* could not have been the work of nomadic desert tribes. Whether or not the builders of the *nawamis* came from Egypt or from the Asian continent, however, is still unknown.

Elsewhere in Sinai, especially in the eastern and southern sectors, there may be other fourth-millennium sites, representing a local culture, among the hundreds of poor, small settlements discovered by Israeli expeditions. But these settlements cannot be dated securely. The kinds of flint tools found—there is no pottery—cannot be used as chronological indicators because the same forms were used for hundreds and even thousands of years. Several scholars believe that some of these flint tools should be dated to the fourth millennium, but as yet there is no scholarly consensus.

The Early Bronze Age (3150 B.C. to 2200 B.C.) witnessed a population explosion all over the Near East. This occurred in Sinai as well, particularly in the southern part of the peninsula and in the northern coastal strip.

The Early Bronze Age is subdivided into three periods,

*Named after the site where this culture was first identified.

Canaanite
PIONEERS
in Sinai — The Early Bronze Age

During the Early Bronze Age, *Canaanite pioneers migrated to Sinai, where they built small clusters of stone houses (opposite) in the midst of a vast granite landscape. The author discovered more than 40 of these settlements in southern Sinai dating to the Early Bronze Age II (2850 to 2650 B.C.). So small they could not be considered villages or even hamlets, each settlement of 5 to 20 families had a corresponding number of dwelling units spaced about 100 feet apart.*

A dwelling unit consisted of as few as two rooms or as many as 20 rooms surrounding a courtyard (plan, opposite below). The rooms were built slightly below ground level and were entered by a short flight of steps, as the photo below of a house in a settlement near the Feiran Oasis illustrates. Other features visible in the photo that are typical of these houses are a central roof-support pillar and benches against the walls.

The houses and the tools and utensils they contained (see pp. 32-33) strongly resemble houses and implements found at the EB II city of Arad—evidence that the EB II Sinai settlers were closely related to the EB II people in the north.

ITZHAQ BEIT-ARIEH

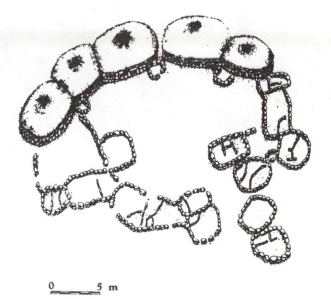

ITZHAQ BEIT-ARIEH

0 _____ 5 m

31

AVRAHAM HAI

AVRAHAM HAI

AVRAHAM HAI

Like clam shells *washed up on an ancient shore, 13 flint fan scrapers emerge from the earth under the patient hands of excavators at Nabi Salah (opposite, above). Above are two of the fan scrapers, cleaned up by excavators. An abundance of storage jars (opposite, far left) like those found at Early Bronze II Arad turned up at the contemporaneous southern Sinai settlements. Other finds included copper ax heads (opposite, below), a stone pendant (right), and an array of mother-of-pearl "buttons" (below).*

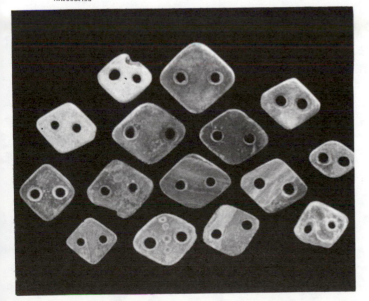

each with its own characteristics. Early Bronze Age I (3150 B.C.-2850 B.C.), or simply EB I, which corresponds to the proto-Dynastic period in Egypt, is represented by small unfortified settlements along the northern coast of Sinai. Here, an expedition sponsored by Ben Gurion University of the Negev collected both Canaanite and Egyptian pottery. As in the preceding Chalcolithic period, these small settlements undoubtedly marked the route between Egypt and Canaan. Traders were apparently already exploiting the economic resources (olive oil and wine) of southern Canaan, as they would so extensively in the following period (EB II). No other EB I sites have been found in Sinai except a large village in Wadi el-Fugiya in central Sinai, 30 miles east of Ras es-Sudar, discovered by Beno Rothenberg's expedition.[1]

One of the most surprising discoveries of my expedition (the Ophir Expedition) in southern Sinai was a whole series of settlements from the Early Bronze Age II (2850 B.C.-2650 B.C.). Six were excavated, but more than 40 additional sites were identified by surveys, all in the massive granite mountains in the heart of the peninsula.

Each of these small settlements consisted of from one to five dwelling units about 100 feet apart. Each dwelling unit was made up of from 10 to 20 interconnected rooms surrounding a large central courtyard. Some smaller dwelling units had only one or two rooms linked to a stone fence around the courtyard. Apparently one of the rooms was actually the dwelling and the other was an auxiliary chamber, perhaps for storage or sleeping. The floors of these auxiliary chambers, although usually paved, are slightly higher than ground level. Because most of the walls are low enough for a person to step over—as we deduced from the small amount of stone rubble around them compared to the quantity of rubble on both sides of the collapsed walls of the dwellings—we concluded that they must have been workrooms or storage rooms, perhaps protected from the sun by a tent-like covering of hides.

Each of these units was probably occupied by a single large or small family, according to the unit's size. The main room was of the "broadroom" type—wider than long, with the entrance through one of the long walls. In effect each unit was, in architectural terms, a "one-room house." All the entrances face the central courtyard of the settlement. The floors of the main rooms are about a foot and a half lower than the courtyard floor. You descend one to five steps from the courtyard to the house.

Each roof was supported by a pillar in the center of the room opposite the entrance. The pillar was either a monolith or a stack of several stone drums. Stone benches lined the walls, and in the corners of the rooms were cooking hearths or small storage bins.

The architecture of these dwelling units is important

because it helps us identify these peoples' place of origin. Exactly the same type of one-room house was built in Canaan in the Early Bronze II period. Such Canaanite houses are especially abundant at Arad, then a large fortified royal city in the Negev; indeed, Arad was the largest city in southern Canaan.

The similarity between the pottery found in these EB II sites in Sinai and at Arad confirms the relationship. In the Sinai sites some of this pottery appears to have been made locally, but a great deal was imported from Canaan. Whether made locally or imported, the same kinds of vessels turned up at our Sinai sites as in Strata III to I (the Early Bronze Age strata) at Canaanite Arad—*pithoi* (large storage jars), platters, red-slipped bowls and little loop-handled cup-bowls.

The rare fragments of First Dynasty Egyptian vessels we found in the Sinai sites only emphasized that the Canaanite relationship, especially with Arad, was the overwhelmingly important one.

In addition, we found flint tools (mostly scrapers and perforators), pendants and beads made of a local greenish stone, and over 80 different species of Red Sea shells. Of special importance were a number of copper tools, mainly axes and awls, produced from local ores.

It appears that these EB II people in Sinai were Canaanites from the southern part of the country, perhaps from Arad itself. They built themselves settlements modeled after the houses they had known in Canaan and continued to maintain close contacts with their homeland to the north.

The diet of the EB II people consisted of milk, cheese and meat produced by their flocks of goats or sheep. Based on the relative quantities of bones found in the excavations, the goats far exceeded the sheep. In addition, these Sinai settlers apparently ate cereals, probably imported from Canaan. These pioneers adapted themselves very well to the desert environment and seem to have learned how to exploit its economic potential.

But the question remains: What prompted these people to leave the cities of southern Canaan and migrate over 400 miles to this remote wilderness? The biggest reason was probably copper. In every site we excavated, we found copper tools and copper ores. In two sites we found crucibles, lumps of refined copper and casting molds. In our

Pharaoh Sekhemkhet *smites an Asiatic prisoner. Carved on a high cliff above Wadi Maghara, this relief is a near-duplicate of another found just 115 feet away. Nearby, at Serabit el-Khadem, the Pharaoh's miners toiled to extract precious blue turquoise. Sekhemkhet, far left, wears the crown of Upper Egypt. The other two standing figures also depict this Pharaoh, who reigned from 2648 to 2642 B.C. In the center depiction, Sekhemkhet wears the crown of Lower Egypt with the long feather curling forward.*

survey we came across three sites with evidence of copper production—smelting ovens sunk into the ground with lumps of ore and slag strewn about, and pieces of clay piping that must have been part of a bellows. These sites lie very close to an ancient copper mine, and chemical analysis has shown that this mine was the source of the ores and slags we found. Copper—the major component of bronze—was extremely valuable in those days before people learned to create a fire hot enough to melt iron. (See "How Iron Technology Changed the Ancient World—And Gave the Philistines a Military Edge," by James D. Muhly, **BAR**, November/December 1982.) It is thus not difficult to understand Sinai's attraction to these EB II settlers. They were probably "colonists" from royal Canaanite cities; the "mother city" of our Sinai settlements was very likely the powerful city-state of Arad. Since we found so little evidence of an Egyptian presence anywhere in Sinai at this time, we may assume that the Pharaohs had no interest in the region then. Only after another two or three centuries would Egypt's economic interest in Sinai become aroused, as we shall see. In the meantime, Canaan had the peninsula and its valuable mineral resources all to herself.

Egyptian interest in Sinai began in about 2650 B.C. during the Third Dynasty. What attracted the Egyptians was not copper, but turquoise, that semiprecious blue-green stone from which artisans made amulets, scarabs,

Text continues on p. 40

Egyptian
PHARAOHS
Mine Sinai's Turquoise

The Egyptian goddess Hathor (below), was called the "Lady of the Turquoise" in inscriptions at Serabit el-Khadem, a 2,800-foot-high plateau in south-central Sinai, famous for its turquoise mines. Patroness of the Serabit mines, Hathor was often depicted in statues or reliefs as a cow or with cow's ears. Hathor was the only goddess to whom the Egyptians dedicated a temple in Sinai.

Temple of Hathor, at *Serabit el-Khadem. Located at the eastern end of the plateau, this temple began in about the 19th century B.C. in a small cave. Later, two rooms were added, dedicated to the local god, Sopdu (plan, below).*

For more than half a millennium, the temple grew, with the addition of a great court and a single-file series of spacious chambers. In these chambers, numerous stelae were erected, such as those shown here and on pp. 35 and 38, bearing reliefs and hieroglyphic inscriptions. The inscriptions described in great detail the mining expeditions sent from Egypt by each successive Pharaoh, ending with the expedition of Rameses VI (1151-1143 B.C.). Most of the temple expansion was ordered by Queen Hatshepsut (1473-1458 B.C.) and Pharaoh Thutmose III (1479-1425 B.C.).

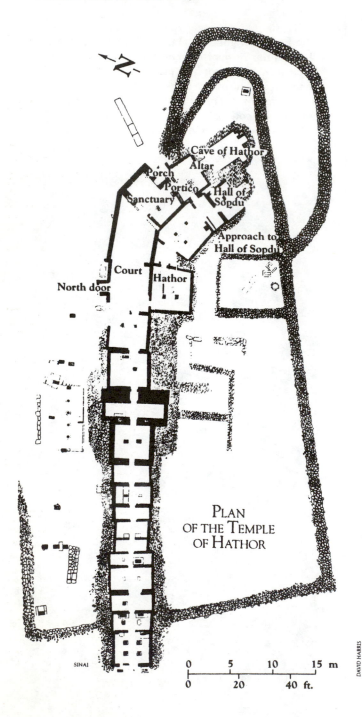

Cave of Hathor
Altar
Porch
Portico
Sanctuary
Hall of Sopdu
Approach to Hall of Sopdu
Court
Hathor
North door

PLAN OF THE TEMPLE OF HATHOR

SINAI

0	5	10	15 m
0	20		40 ft.

© HELFRIED WEYER

AVRAHAM HAI

Propped up among the ruins of Serabit el-Khadem by modern investigators, stelae (above) from the temple of Hathor recall the ancient Egyptian cult. In the large rectangular stela, left, a king of the XIX-XX Dynasty (1307-1070 B.C.) offers two small vases to a deity; the deity originally appeared to the right of the king but has been broken off. A female figure following the king wears emblems of Hathor: a sun disk and sacred asp on her headdress and a sistrum (rattle) in each hand.

Turquoise mines at Serabit el-Khadem yielded a new treasure to modern investigators—tools of the mining trade. Chalcolithic-period finds included unpolished stones (left) and a hammer (below) for quarrying the sandstone with its rich veins of turquoise.

AVRAHAM HAI

Passing through the entrance to Mine L (below), archaeologists discovered a stone air chamber of a foot bellows (above) and stone molds (right, center) for casting ax heads and a chisel. Nearly 40 such molds came to light in the mine, the largest hoard of molds ever found anywhere in the Near East.

A wall painting (right, above) decorating the 15th-century B.C. tomb of Vizier Rekhmire in Egypt illustrates the proper technique for using a foot bellows. Workers melting copper close valves of the bellows with their heels and fill leather air bags fitted on the bellows by stepping off and lifting the bags with leather straps.

AVRAHAM HAI

HERSHEL SHANKS

Earliest ALPHABET

A Canaanite Invention— Preserved in Sinai Mines

The earliest alphabet—from which all other alphabets in the world are derived—was invented in Canaan in the late 18th or early 17th century B.C. This alphabet consisting of pictographs is referred to by scholars as the proto-Canaanite alphabet. Only a few short inscriptions in this alphabet have been found in Canaan, however. Most of the inscriptions in this alphabet were discovered in or near the turquoise mines at Serabit el-Khadem in Sinai and date to a few hundred years after the initial invention. The Sinai version of this alphabet is called proto-Sinaitic and is identical to proto-Canaanite.

Shown here in a drawing and photographs is the longest of the proto-Sinaitic inscriptions, found on the wall of Mine L at Serabit (see p. 39). The photographs have been aligned with the corresponding letters drawn by William Foxwell Albright based on an earlier tracing from the rock wall. Each letter-pictograph stands for the first sound of the Semitic word for the object represented. It is easy to see several recognizable objects, such as the ox head (1, 11, 20, 23), the snake (2), the fish (7), the water sign (9, 14, 18, 21) and the two heads (22, 24). The sound equivalent for each pictograph is shown in the chart. For example, the ancient Semitic word for fish was *dag*. Therefore the fish symbol stands for the sound "d" as in the Hebrew letter *dalet*. Similarly, a snake is *nahash*, standing for the "n" sound as in the Hebrew letter *nun*.

The meaning of the proto-Sinaitic inscriptions is uncertain, although most scholars agree on the identity of the letters. William Foxwell Albright deciphered the inscription illustrated here: "Thou, O Shaphan, collect from 'Ababa eight(?) minas (of turquoise). Shimea, groom of the chief of the car[avaneers(?)]."

Recently, in the same mine, another inscription was discovered incised on a stone plaque. This inscription bears two clear symbols: on top, the ox head, symbol for the *'alef*; on the bottom the crooked staff, symbol for the *lamed*. Read as *El*, the word is the name of the principal north Semitic deity of those times and one of the names of God that appear in the Hebrew Bible.

and necklaces for Pharaohs and nobles. We have no doubts about the Egyptian presence because the mining expeditions left evidence behind, and it is still there. Maghara means cave in Arabic; that is the name the Bedouin have given to this area in southwest Sinai because of what they took to be caves in the steep sides of the wadi embankments.* In fact, these "caves" are Egyptian mine shafts from the Old Kingdom, formed when the ancient miners followed the blue-green veins of turquoise into the cliffs above the wadis here.

*It is not the wadi that is called Maghara, although it has come to be called so popularly. There are several wadis in this region, only one of which is called—sometimes—Maghara.

Remains of expedition camps, including a number of buildings, have come to light in some places along the scarps of the wadis. Of special interest are the many stone reliefs and inscriptions that provide a secure dating for the Eygptian mining activity. Sir Flinders Petrie hewed about 40 of these reliefs and inscriptions out of the cliffs in 1905 and sent them to the Cairo Museum. Much of this material had been found by early 19th-century explorers of Sinai. But a good deal of what these explorers had found was lost or forgotten by the 1970s. Israeli archaeologists and surveyors launched a comprehensive program of rediscovery.

One curious rediscovery was a relief of Pharaoh Sekhemkhet (the third king of the Third Dynasty, who

PHONETIC VALUE	SCHEMATIC FORMS	EARLY LETTER NAMES	MEANING OF NAMES
'	𐤀	'alp-	ox-head
b		bêt-	house
g		gaml-	throw-stick
d		digg-	fish
ḏ		?	?
h		hê(?)	man calling
w		wô (waw)	mace
z	?	zê(n-)	?
ḥ		ḥê(t-)	fence(?)
ḫ		ḫa( )	hank of yarn
ṭ	?	ṭê(t-)	spindle?
y		yad-	arm
k		kapp-	palm
l		lamd-	ox-goad
m		mêm-	water
n		naḥš-	snake
s̀	?	(šamk-?)	?
c		'ên-	eye
ḡ		ḡa( )	?
p		piʾt-(?)	corner?
ṣ/z		ṣa(d-)	plant
ḍ	?	?	?
q		qu(p-)	?
r		naʾš-	head of man
ś/ṯ		tann-	composite bow
š		?	?
t	+	tô (taw)	owner's mark

reigned from 2648 B.C. to 2642 B.C.) carved on one of the high cliffs above Wadi Maghara (see p. 34); this relief was found near an almost identical relief that was well-known to scholars. Professor Raphael Giveon, an Egyptologist from Tel Aviv University who studied both reliefs, has plausibly suggested that the duplication was required by the inscribers' errors. Omitted from the newly rediscovered relief, which must have been carved first, were some of the titles of the head of the mining expedition. Moreover, the carvers did not carve this important person's image in high enough relief. Consequently, he ordered them to do the job a second time, and this time to include all his titles and to carve his handsome picture in high relief.

During the Middle Kingdom, in the 12th Dynasty (1991 B.C. to 1786 B.C.), the Egyptians moved their turquoise mining operation to the rich veins of Serabit el-Khadem, a famous site in west-central Sinai. They continued to operate these mines for at least eight centuries thereafter, during the New Kingdom and up to the reign of Rameses VI (1191-1134 B.C.). At Serabit, the Egyptians left some of the most magnificent ruins in all of Sinai. Near the mines, on a mountain plateau, the Egyptians built a temple dedicated to the goddess Hathor, who among her other epithets was known as the "Lady of the Turquoise." Originally the shrine to Hathor was only a cave where the goddess was worshipped in the 12th Dynasty (1991 B.C.-1786 B.C.). Then a portico was built in front of the cave. Next, a magnificent temple was built in front of the portico. Countless mining expeditions thereafter rebuilt and added chamber after chamber—ablution halls, courtyards, pylons, and room after room in an extended string, entered from a sacred way that eventually reached 230 feet, lined with stelae* and statues. The walls of the temple and the stelae are covered with hundreds of hieroglyphic inscriptions. It is a breathtaking sight. The latest of the rooms and the last addition to the sacred way date to about 1140 B.C., thus providing an almost complete series of Egyptian inscriptions from the time of the 12th Dynasty to the 26th Dynasty.

The ruins of Serabit were first discovered by Carsten Niebuhr, a member of an early Danish expedition, in 1762. Later they attracted the attention of numerous scholars, the most famous of whom was Sir Flinders Petrie, who explored the site in 1905. In 1935 the Czech scholar Jeroslav Černy made a study of Serabit and later, together with Sir Alan H. Gardiner and T. E. Peet, published many of the hieroglyphic inscriptions.

Professor Raphael Giveon, Egyptologist of the University of Tel Aviv, restudied the site and found numerous inscriptions that were either unknown or had been "lost" or forgotten. One was an inscription of Thutmoses IV (1425 B.C.-1417 B.C.) that had been "lost" since 1859; Giveon rediscovered it about half a mile southeast of the temple. The inscription in fact turned out to be much longer than the previous publication of it had indicated. It contained a kind of appendix consisting of a so-called private text of an overseer, which was dedicated to Princess Wadjoyet, one of the daughters of Thutmoses IV.

Giveon's expedition also discovered three reliefs depicting Hathor in her Egyptian form as a sacred cow. Another such relief had been discovered by Černy in 1935. Together the four reliefs show that Hathor was worshipped at

---

*Stelae are upright stone slabs or pillars bearing inscriptions or sculptural designs.

Serabit el-Khadem not as a Canaanite goddess—as some scholars had maintained—but (at least in these reliefs) as an Egyptian deity.

The scholars who contend that Hathor was also worshipped as a Canaanite deity at Serabit rely on some of the most fascinating archaeological materials ever discovered—the so-called proto-Sinaitic inscriptions.

E. H. Palmer discovered the first proto-Sinaitic inscription in 1869. Petrie found about ten more in 1905 in the temple area, and the rest were discovered on stone slabs near two of the mineshafts, apparently scratched there by the miners.

Unlike the hieroglyphic inscriptions, the proto-Sinaitic inscriptions are written in an alphabetic script probably invented under hieroglyphic influence. The script represents the earliest form of the Semitic alphabet—from which all other alphabets are derived.

Scholars still do not agree on what these inscriptions say, but in general they agree on the identity of most of the letters. However, the meaning of one word that appears repeatedly in the proto-Sinaitic inscriptions is universally undisputed. Not until ten years after Petrie's discovery of the proto-Sinaitic inscriptions was this word deciphered—by Sir Alan Gardiner, one of the great Egyptian linguists of modern times. That single word is l-b-'*-l-t or l-'ba-al-at. It means: "to Baalat," the female form of the Semitic god Baal.

This word suggests to many scholars that some of the miners themselves worshiped Ba'alat in the form of the Egyptian deity Hathor. The miners' use of a Semitic alphabet indicates that they were Semites rather than Egyptians. In a few Egyptian inscriptions at Serabit, Asiatics or 'Amu are mentioned as participating in the Egyptian expeditions. One inscription refers to a certain Khebdedem, "the brother of the governor of Retjenu." (Retjenu is the Egyptian term for Canaan.) These Egyptian inscriptions confirm the presence of Semites at the site. In our opinion, the proto-Sinaitic inscriptions were undoubtedly written by Asiatics working there as free men, perhaps even as specialists, such as coppersmiths and the like, attached to the Egyptian mining expedition. It is obvious that whatever their status, they were literate and used an acrophonic** alphabet. This alphabet, although very closely related to Egyptian hieroglyphics, was nevertheless a departure from the complicated system that the Egyptians used in writing their own language. This alphabet may well have originated in Canaan itself.

In and around Serabit el-Khadem, the Ophir Expedition, which I directed, has made discoveries that are extremely useful in a number of respects, perhaps most important in dating the proto-Sinaitic inscriptions to the late 16th and early 15th centuries B.C.

Inside one of the mines (Mine L, which is the most famous because it is there that the longest proto-Sinaitic inscription was found), my expedition discovered more than 40 casting molds for bronze mining axes and other tools. A number of ceramic crucibles, some with a thin film of copper residue still adhering to them, were also found inside the mine. A unique stone bowl with a large spout was at first a puzzle. What was it used for? We finally decided it was the base of the air chamber of a bellows, probably originally fitted with a leather bag and pumped by foot, like similar instruments depicted on Egyptian wall paintings. All this equipment—the molds for mining tools, the crucibles, the bellows—indicates that metalsmiths were included in the mining work force. Their function was to melt down broken tools and to recast new ones on the spot. In our metallurgical laboratories at Tel Aviv University we cast a few axes in gypsum from the ax molds. These axes and the bellows we found turned out to be similar to those common in Egypt at the beginning of the New Kingdom (16th-15th centuries B.C.), as depicted in dated wall reliefs in Egypt. Together this material is of great assistance in dating the mining operations.

Another important bit of dating evidence we discovered was a sherd of bichrome ware, a type of pottery produced only in this period.

In Mine L we also discovered a stone plaque bearing the letters alef and lamed in proto-Sinaitic script, which spell 'El, the principal north Semitic deity at the time. 'El is also a common name for God in the Hebrew Bible.

In a mine about a kilometer southeast of Mine L, Benjamin Sass and Judith Dekel discovered two previously unknown proto-Sinaitic graffiti,* thereby increasing the corpus of proto-Sinaitic inscriptions by about ten percent! Perhaps this will help us one day to decipher fully the proto-Sinaitic inscriptions.

Inside this mine we found a faience bowl from the beginning of the New Kingdom. Outside were some more crucibles and another foot-operated bellows, identical to what we had found in Mine L. All these artifacts establish that the Egyptians were most active at Serabit el-Khadem during the New Kingdom (1550 B.C.-1100 B.C.).

In my chronological catalogue of the remains at Serabit

---

*This inverted apostrophe is the scholarly symbol for the Hebrew letter 'ayin, a guttural sound unknown to English, produced by tightening the throat.

**Acrophonic indicates that the sound of the alphabetic sign was the first sound in the object depicted. For example, a picture of a house, pronounced beth, had the phonetic value b.

*Graffiti are drawings or writing scratched, cut or written on a wall or a rock.

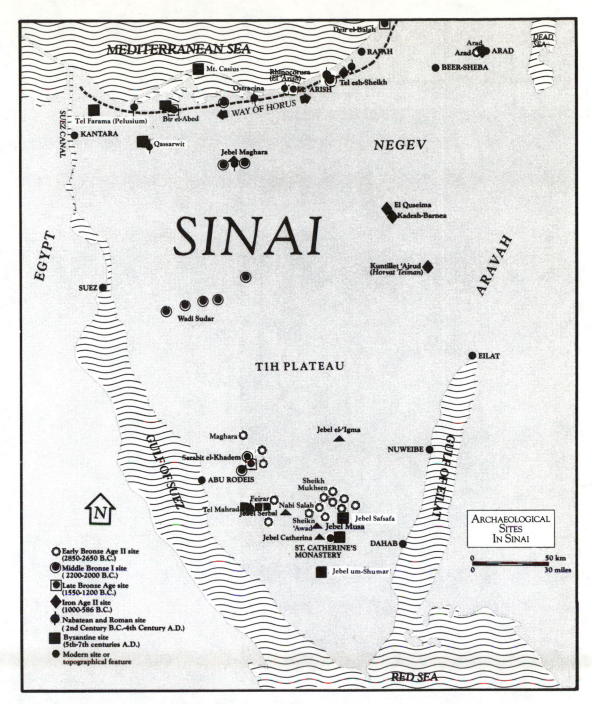

Archaeological Sites in Sinai map, including:

MEDITERRANEAN SEA

Mt. Casius — Deir el-Balah — RAFAH — Arad — ARAD — BEER-SHEBA

Rhinocorura (El 'Arish) — Ostracina — EL 'ARISH — Tel esh-Sheikh

WAY OF HORUS

Tel Farama (Pelusium) — Bir el-Abed

SUEZ CANAL — KANTARA — Qassarwit — Jebel Maghara

NEGEV

EGYPT

SINAI

El Quseima — Kadesh-Barnea

Kuntillet 'Ajrud (Horvat Teiman)

ARAVAH

SUEZ — Wadi Sudar

EILAT

TIH PLATEAU

GULF OF SUEZ

Maghara — Jebel el-'Igma — NUWEIBE — GULF OF EILAT

Serabit el-Khadem — Sheikh Mukhsen

ABU RODEIS — Feirar — Nabi Salah — Jebel Safsafa

Tel Mahrad — Jebel Serbal — Sheikh 'Awad — Jebel Musa

Jebel Catherina — DAHAB

ST. CATHERINE'S MONASTERY

Jebel um-Shumar

ARCHAEOLOGICAL SITES IN SINAI

0 — 50 km
0 — 30 miles

RED SEA

Legend:
○ Early Bronze Age II site (2850-2650 B.C.)
◉ Middle Bronze I site (2200-2000 B.C.)
▣ Late Bronze Age site (1550-1200 B.C.)
◆ Iron Age II site (1000-586 B.C.)
● Nabatean and Roman site (2nd Century B.C.-4th Century A.D.)
■ Byzantine site (5th-7th centuries A.D.)
● Modern site or topographical feature

N

el-Khadem, I got a little ahead of myself. But I didn't want to interrupt the exciting story of Serabit, even though the proto-Sinaitic inscriptions date to the Late Bronze Age (1550 B.C.-1200 B.C.). Let us go back for a moment now to some Sinai remains from the Middle Bronze Age I (2200 B.C.-2000 B.C.). **BAR** readers already know about the mysterious MB I people described by Rudolph Cohen in the July/August 1983 issue. Many MB I settlements were found in the Negev highlands in southern Canaan; traces of such settlements have also been found in northern Sinai. The houses consist of clusters of circular rooms separated by narrow open spaces or lanes, very unlike the EB II units of interlinked houses surrounding a large courtyard. Cohen suggests that the MB I settlers came out of Sinai and migrated into Canaan. My own view is the reverse. The MB I culture did not originate in Sinai but came from the opposite direction—from the north—and (with one exception) did not reach southern Sinai. Thus I believe the MB I settlements along Wadi Sudar represent the boundary of the southward migration of these nomadic Negev highlanders.

Moreover, I also disagree with Cohen in his effort to link these MB I people to the earlier Early Bronze II (EB II) people. Not only is their geographical dispersal in Sinai different, but they had entirely different architectural concepts: The MB I people had round, above-ground houses joined together like a cluster of grapes; the EB II people built sunken bench-lined broadrooms linked together in a

circle or oval around a large, common courtyard.

According to the generally accepted scholarly chronology, the Israelite Exodus from Egypt occurred at the end of the Late Bronze Age, in about the 13th century B.C. For this reason, the Late Bronze Age (1550-1200 B.C.) in Sinai is of special interest.

Except for the turquoise mining and the associated temple at Serabit, the archaeological remains in Sinai from the Late Bronze Age are confined to the Mediterranean littoral in the extreme north. Then, as now, a major international "highway" followed the coastline and formed the main artery connecting Egypt with Canaan and the lands to the north. In Late Bronze Age Egyptian inscriptions this highway was called "the Way of Horus." In recent years, literally hundreds of sites have been discovered on this highway in northern Sinai, mostly by the Ben-Gurion University of the Negev Expedition headed by Eliezer Oren. Among these sites were several Egyptian forts or depots to supply the caravan trade. These forts were concentrated along the stretch of road extending between the eastern Nile Delta and El 'Arish. One of the larger forts was excavated at a site called Bir el-'Abed (the well of the Servant [of God?]). Built of mudbrick, the fort measured about 125 feet square. Nearby was a large silo that still contained remnants of grains—a vivid illustration of the function of these forts in the Egyptian military system during the reign of Seti I (1318 B.C.-1304 B.C.).

Another stronghold in this network of forts was discovered somewhat further north, in the Gaza Strip near Deir el-Balah. Associated with this fort was an unusual cemetery in which the dead were buried in large clay coffins with strange faces molded on the coffin lids. A number of the coffins and the settlement where they were manufactured have been excavated by Hebrew University archaeologist Trude Dothan (see "Excavating Anthropoid Coffins in the Gaza Strip," **BAR**, March 1976, and "What We Know About the Philistines" by Trude Dothan, **BAR**, July/August 1982). Other Egyptian military posts along this highway are probably still buried under the sand dunes. Still others may no longer be preserved even underground.

But what of the rest of Sinai at the end of the Late Bronze Age? This is the time of the Exodus from Egypt, and according to the Bible, the Israelites dwelt in Sinai for 40 years, spending much of this time wandering in the wilderness. It was then, supposedly, that the tablets containing the Ten Commandments were given to the Israelites on one of Sinai's mountains. But which mountain? And what about the route of the Exodus? For centuries Biblical scholars, pilgrims and archaeologists have been searching for traces of the Israelites throughout the peninsula, trying to identify the route the Israelites followed and the location of the Mountain of God.

Although there are dozens of theories, none is supported by archaeological evidence. And much as we had hoped otherwise, our recent explorations have not advanced us toward a solution. Nowhere in Sinai did we or our colleagues find any concrete remains of the stations on the Exodus route, nor even small encampments that could be attributed to the relevant period. Neither did we discover anything that would help us identify the Mountain of God. So the enigma—and the challenge—remain.

Some scholars attribute the lack of archaeological evidence of the Israelites in Sinai to the theory that their vessels were made of wood, leather, gourds or other perishable materials. Other scholars suggest that the stations on the Exodus route mentioned in the Bible, with the exception of one or two sites in the Nile Delta, have been either covered over and obliterated by the desert sands or washed away by erosion. On the basis of our thorough surveys, however, we find it difficult to accept these arguments. There are thousands of ancient sites in Sinai, many of them predating the Exodus. The people who lived at many of these sites used pottery vessels, and the broken pottery sherds survived and have been discovered on the spot. Indeed, frequently they are found lying exposed on the surface after thousands of years. The notion that the Israelites had only vessels of perishable materials during their 40 years of wandering is most unlikely. If the poor indigenous nomads of the peninsula produced pottery vessels throughout the ages, there is no reason to suppose that the Israelites fleeing from the Land of Goshen had no pottery. Indeed, the Israelites in Goshen, who complained so bitterly when Pharaoh's overseers wouldn't supply straw to temper the clay of the bricks they were forced to produce and demanded that they go out and gather it themselves while still fulfilling their production quotas (Exodus 5:6-19), undoubtedly knew quite a lot about the composition of clays for various types of ceramic wares. If they knew straw was needed to make bricks, then they must have known that grits were needed to make clay cooking pots.

And so the riddle continues unsolved. But as a result of the intensive surveys conducted in the high mountains of south-central Sinai (the traditional location of Mount Sinai), we must conclude that no new ethnic element arrived there during the Late Bronze Age. Nor, in light of the Egyptian forts in the northern route, is it likely that the Israelites followed the Way of Horus along the Mediterranean coast. Indeed, the Bible itself tells us that they did not go by this route which, in the Bible, is called the Way of the Philistines (Exodus 13:17).

The only archaeological evidence of human settlement in Sinai at this time is in the north, near the Mediterranean coast. Central and southern Sinai are archaeological blanks for this period. Traces of what may be Israelite occupation have been found around the springs of Kadesh-Barnea (this region belongs geographically to the Negev highlands, but politically it is part of Sinai), but even these traces date to about the beginning of the Iron Age II (tenth to ninth centuries B.C.) at the earliest. Yet, according to the Bible, Kadesh-Barnea was the religious and administrative center of the Israelites on the eve of their penetration into the Promised Land in the 13th century B.C. But nothing was found to confirm their presence here at that time. An expedition directed by Professor Moshe Dothan excavated the remains around the springs, including the fort at 'Ain el-Qudeirat, during a brief season in 1956; then from 1976 to 1982 Rudolph Cohen of the Israel Department of Antiquities led ten seasons of excavation here. The remains of three superimposed forts were uncovered, each built on the ruins of its predecessor, but the earliest fort dates from about the tenth century B.C. (See "Did I Excavate Kadesh Barnea?" by Rudolph Cohen, **BAR**, May/June 1981.) These forts served as outposts on the desert fringes of Israel's United Monarchy (ninth century B.C.) and during the Kingdom of Judah (eighth century B.C. to 586 B.C.) and continued in use till the end of the Second Temple period (70 A.D.). These forts protected the borders and guarded the roads crossing Sinai. But from the period before the tenth century, there is nothing.

About 35 miles south of Kadesh-Barnea, on a hillock known as Kuntillet 'Ajrud (*Horvat Teiman* in Hebrew), an eighth-century B.C. site has produced some of Sinai's most startling finds. The major building at the site was probably a caravansary for travelers or a guard station to protect the desert track from the Nile Delta to Eilat. What makes this site unique are dozens of inscribed and painted plaster fragments found in the debris and on the walls of the main building by Ze'ev Meshel of Tel Aviv University's Institute of Archaeology. Originally, the walls must have been decorated with colorful murals and numerous inscriptions. Some of the texts are in Hebrew and others are in Phoenician script. Also excavated were large storage jars called *pithoi* which were likewise decorated with painted scenes and covered with inscriptions. A large stone bowl is beautifully inscribed in Hebrew on its rim: "[Belonging] to 'Obadyau son of 'Adnah, may he be blessed by Yahwe(h)." (See "Did Yahweh Have a Consort?" by Ze'ev Meshel, **BAR**, March/April 1979.)

Many of the names mentioned in these inscriptions end in what scholars call a theophoric suffix. Names in ancient times had meanings and were compressed or abbreviated sentences. Often a name of God was used as the final element in the name. Even today ancient names like Nathaniel and Daniel preserve the name of the God *El*, a name often used in the Hebrew Bible for God. The Israelite God Yahweh (or Jehovah in its Germanized form) was compressed into -*yo* or *ya* or *yahu*. In the eighth century B.C., -*yahu* was the common theophoric suffix in the southern kingdom of Judah, as in *Uzziyahu*; -*yo* was used in the northern kingdom of Israel, as in *Uzzyo*. At Kuntillet 'Ajrud, names ending in both -*yo* and *yahu* were found. According to Meshel, this shows that this outpost had ties not only with the southern kingdom of Judah but also with the northern kingdom of Israel; and the Phoenician inscriptions suggest ties with Phoenicia itself. The vessels themselves resemble the wares of the northern kingdom more closely than they do those of Judah, another indication of a northern connection. An inscription mentioning "Yahweh [of] Shomron [i.e. Samaria]" was probably written by a traveler from Samaria.

According to Pirhiya Beck of Tel Aviv University, who studied the drawings on the *pithoi*, they are the work of two or three rather incompetent, probably local artists who were nevertheless familiar with most of the motifs of the Syro-Phoenician artistic, religious and symbolic repertoire. The drawings look almost as if they had been reproduced from a pattern book. One of these motifs, a cow and her suckling calf, is almost identical to a scene depicted on some of the ivories found at Shalmaneser's palace in Nimrud. Other drawings appear to have been influenced, both by the popular and by the traditional art of the Sinai and Arabian deserts. For example, in one drawing we see a procession of schematically drawn people, each of whom has hands upraised in a gesture of adoration; in another is a lyre player and two pictures of the Egyptian dwarf god Bes. It will be years before these drawings are fully understood.

We have suggested that the building at this site was a caravansary or a guard station. But it probably had a religious function as well. Perhaps a group of priests from the northern kingdom of Israel lived here to provide a way station or stopover for pilgrims going to and coming from the sacred mountains of Sinai. Phrases in the inscriptions like "blessed of Yahweh" and "blessed be his day" seem to echo a religious ritual. Certain architectural elements of the building, like a small narrow room with benches at the building's entrance where many dedicatory offerings were found, are also evidence that the building had a religious function in addition to serving as an ancient version of a hotel and roadside fort.

In 1981 another expedition headed by Meshel excavated an Israelite fort that had been discovered a few years earlier on a high peak near Quseima, west of Kadesh-Barnea. It is one of the largest strongholds of the 11th-10th centuries B.C. on the road to Eilat. Unfortunately, no inscriptions or drawings were found here.

Settlements from the Persian (520 B.C.-332 B.C.), Hellenistic (332 B.C.-37 B.C.) and Roman (37 B.C.-324 A.D.) periods have long been known on the ancient highway from the eastern Delta along the northern coast. Others have been more recently discovered. The expedition headed by Eliezer Oren excavated several of these sites, including a large, fortified Egyptian enclosure south of Pelusium that dates to the sixth century B.C. The enclosure is about 600 feet square. The many Greek vessels found in the fort testify to an occupation by a Greek population under the aegis of the Egyptian monarchs of the 26th Dynasty.

The Persian conquest of Egypt in 525 B.C. is reflected in settlements, caravansaries and cemeteries along the coast. The rich finds include decorated Attic wares, amphorae for wine and clay burial masks; they confirm the historical sources that describe the prosperity of the region during Persian and Hellenistic times. No doubt this prosperity was due in no small part to the reciprocal trade between Egypt and her neighbors.

Among the Early Roman sites discovered were a number of Nabatean cities. The Nabateans were famous merchant traders who controlled the incense and spice traffic at the time. The largest and most important of their cities on the Mediterranean coast of Sinai was Qassarwit. Originally excavated in 1911 by Jean Clédat, Qassarwit was reexcavated in 1975-1976 by Eliezer Oren, who uncovered a series of most impressive Nabatean temples. I won't say more about these because Oren himself is preparing an article for **BAR** on this subject.

Hundreds of Nabatean inscriptions have been carved on the cliffs and rocks of southern Sinai, particularly in Wadi Mukattab (which is Arabic for "the canyon of writings or inscriptions") on the road to Serabit el-Khadem. Although these inscriptions have been known since the last century, they were only recently collected in a corpus published by Avraham Negev of the Hebrew University. His volume contains 2,743 entries, including numerous inscriptions that were previously unknown and unpublished. From the personal names, the occupations mentioned and the distribution of the inscriptions along the desert routes, Negev has concluded that in the second to third centuries A.D., large communities of Nabateans lived in the Negev and Sinai. They probably exploited the ancient turquoise and copper mines and worshipped on the heights of the sacred mountains like Jebel Musa and Jebel Serbal, where they erected stelae inscribed with the names of their priests.

During the Roman period, the Mediterranean littoral of Sinai prospered and flourished. This too will be described in a forthcoming **BAR** article by Oren.

In the Byzantine period, the center of action returned to southern Sinai, especially around Jebel Musa and the oasis in the Wadi Feiran, where, from the fourth century A.D. on, pilgrims sought out sacred sites in the mountains. This area became a center of Byzantine monasticism—in the sixth century, St. Catherine's monastery was built at the foot of Jebel Musa by the Emperor Justinian himself. An Israeli expedition headed by Israel Finkelstein of Bar-Ilan University and Uzi Dahari of the Santa Catherina Field School of the Society for the Protection of Nature in Israel has surveyed and excavated a number of these monastic complexes. In them, the archaeologists discovered scores of chapels, praying niches and hermitages. They also investigated the ways in which the monks developed intensive horticulture in little plots, how they prepared the soil for cultivation, how they built irrigation networks of aqueducts, dams and reservoirs, and how they planted a variety of crops. The archaeologists also found wine presses and trampling floors where the monks made their wine.

I have tried to convey here the broad range of Israeli archaeological exploration in Sinai, which had previously been a kind of *terra incognita*. This research has demonstrated that the Sinai peninsula teemed with human activity throughout the ages, from the prehistorical periods to our own day. There were periods of relatively intensive settlement and periods of sparse habitation. Most of the time, Sinai was inhabited by an indigenous population, although on occasion outsiders from neighboring lands extended their settlements into the peninsula. The northern coastal strip has been from time immemorial the major thoroughfare between Africa and Asia. With the exception of sites in this area of the peninsula, however, not a single site in Sinai has been continuously inhabited. The difficult terrain, the inhospitable desert climate and the lack of rainfall have molded the character of Sinai's people. This harsh environment taught them to prefer one or another site at certain times and at other times to migrate from one place to another. This harsh and frequently awesome environment undoubtedly also conditioned their deep spiritual experiences, of which all of western civilization is the legatee. ▨

[1]Rothenberg, Professor of Archaeology at Tel Aviv University, first excavated in Sinai in 1956. His major survey of the Sinai peninsula began in 1967 and continued until 1978.

THE ROUTE THROUGH SINAI

Why the Israelites Fleeing Egypt Went South

ITZHAQ BEIT-ARIEH

Can modern ecology and ethnology help to establish the route of the Exodus? I believe they can.

The Bible clearly identifies by name the stops along the Exodus route (Numbers 33:5-37). The area settled by the Israelites in Egypt is consistently identified as Goshen (Genesis 45:10, 47:1,4), which surely lay in the eastern Nile Delta. The Israelite rallying point for the Exodus was Raamses, one of the store cities in the eastern Nile Delta that the Israelites had built for Pharaoh (Exodus 12:37; Numbers 33:3,5); that is where the Exodus began.

Later the Israelites arrived at Kadesh-

WERNER BRAUN

Precariously perched *7,500 feet above sea level, a small chapel marks the summit of Jebel Musa, the mountain traditionally identified as Mt. Sinai. Built in 1934 by the Greek Orthodox monks of St. Catherine's monastery, who live at the foot of Jebel Musa, the chapel occupies the site of an earlier church, supposedly erected in the sixth century A.D. by the Byzantine emperor Justinian.*

In the background, dry streambeds called "wadis" mark out a sinuous route through the mountains—the type of route that the Israelites probably followed.

Kadesh-Barnea *from the air. A green ribbon in a barren landscape, Kadesh-Barnea was the end point of the Israelites' Exodus trek. Moses sent out from here 12 men "to spy out the land of Canaan" (Numbers 13:17), and later, after the Amalekites and Canaanites had repulsed the Israelites in their first attempt to take the Promised Land, the Israelites returned to Kadesh-Barnea to continue their 40 years of wandering.*

The small stream that serves as the lifeblood of this oasis flows from a spring, one of four springs in the region, at lower center. Tel Kadesh-Barnea (Tell Ein el-Qudeirat), in the open area at center, to the right of the crook in the stream, contains the remains of three fortresses, one atop the other, the earliest dating to the tenth century B.C. Despite the lack of archaeological evidence from the time of the Exodus, generally thought to be at least 300 years earlier, nearly all scholars agree that Ein el-Qudeirat is Kadesh-Barnea; it fits the geographical requirements well, and the name was preserved at a nearby spring called Ein Qadis, where another Israelite fort was discovered by Yohanan Aharoni. No such agreement can be found, however, on the question of how the Israelites got to Kadesh-Barnea—what route they took on the Exodus. In a new examination of this old question, author Itzhaq Beit-Arieh uses ecological and ethnographic clues to trace the Israelites' most probable route.

Barnea (Numbers 33:36; Deuteronomy 1:19). There they spent "many days" (Deuteronomy 1:46). From Kadesh-Barnea the Israelites attempted to, and finally did, enter Canaan.

With almost no dissent, scholars are agreed that Kadesh-Barnea is to be identified with the modern site of Ein el-Qudeirat.* Located at the confluence of two, important, ancient desert routes in northeastern Sinai and adjacent to the most abundant spring in northern Sinai, Ein el-Qudeirat also fits the geographical markers for Kadesh-Barnea in the Bible. Indeed, Ein el-Qudeirat has no real competition as the site of Kadesh-Barnea. There is also a tell at Ein el-Qudeirat (formerly Tell el-Qudeirat and now called Tel** Kadesh-Barnea), but thus far it has yielded no remains earlier than the tenth century B.C., hundreds of years after the Exodus. And this, of course, remains a problem.

Having located the beginning point and the end point of the Israelites' wilderness trek, it remains only to determine how the wanderers got from point A to point B. That, however, is easier said than done.

The Bible mentions several sites where the Israelites arrived shortly after leaving Raamses. From Raamses, they went to Succoth (Exodus 12:37; Numbers 33:5). From there, they went to Etham "on the edge of the wilderness" (Numbers 33:6). From Etham, they turned back and camped at Migdol (Numbers 33:7). These and a few other sites mentioned in this passage are no doubt also in the eastern Nile Delta, and scholars have suggested a number of candidates for these sites.

The problems for scholars really begin, however, after the Israelites entered the desert. The Israelites started with a three-day journey into the wilderness of Etham, arriving at Marah. From there, they went to Elim and

* See Rudolph Cohen, "Did I Excavate Kadesh-Barnea?" **BAR**, May/June 1981.

** A tel or tell is an artificial mound formed by accumulated remains. "Tel" is the spelling used in Hebrew site names; "tell" is the spelling used in Arabic site names.

from there to the Reed Sea by the wilderness of Sin. Next came Dophkah, then Alush and on and on, one site after another (Numbers 33).

And we have no idea where these sites are. They simply cannot be located on the ground with any confidence. That is why we have so many proposed routes for the Israelites' wilderness wandering.

To have validity at all, any suggested route must follow what I call the tracks of Sinai. Except along the Mediterranean coast, the roads or trackways of Sinai run—and have run from time immemorial—along the dry streambeds called "wadis." Most ancient settlements were built beside these wadis,[1] not only for the obvious reason of ease of communication with other settlements, but also because the available water resources were located mostly in the wadi beds, rather than on the high mountain uplands.

Four principal routes for the Exodus have been suggested by scholars.

The first and shortest is the northern route, along the Mediterranean Sea—the "way of the sea," first mentioned by that name in Isaiah 9:1 (8:23 in Hebrew). Since the Roman period, this route has been known in Latin as the Via Maris. The ancient Egyptians, at least in the reign of Seti I (1313-1301 B.C.), used it for military campaigns against the northern countries and called it "the way of Horus." The Bible refers to it also as the "way of the Philistines," but goes on to state explicitly that this was not the route taken by the Israelites after they left Egypt:

"Now when Pharaoh let the people go, God did not lead them by way of the land of the Philistines, although it was nearer; for God said, 'The people may have a change of heart when they see war, and return to Egypt.' So God led the people roundabout, by way of the wilderness at the Sea of Reeds" (Exodus 13:17-18).

Proceeding from north to south, the next candidate for the Exodus route through Sinai is the Way of Shur. This appears to have been the route taken by the patriarchs on their way to the land of Goshen (Genesis 16:7, 25:18). This route probably led from the area of Kadesh-Barnea via Jebel Halal, Bir Haseneh and Bir Gafgafa to the area of the modern town of Ismailia. The route passed between lakes where the Egyptians had constructed a fortification line called "Shur Mitzrayim," the Wall of Egypt, to protect the Delta and to control the movement of nomads coming from the other side.

Another possibility is the Way of Seir (Deuteronomy 1:2). This route probably led from the Gulf of Suez, via Eilat, to the mountain of Seir in the land of Edom, in southern Jordan.† Today, this route is known as the

† Another view (held by Zvi Ilan and supported by some other scholars) is that the mountain of Seir is not located in Jordan, but in east central Sinai close to the Negev Highlands. According to this view, this route starts in the Temed area and goes north via the Wadi Watir, the Wadi Shaireh and Jebel Shaireh (notice the similarity between the Arabic name Shaireh and the Hebrew name Sinai) to Kadesh-Barnea (see dashed line on map). In this view, Horeb/Sinai should be located in the area of Temed because "there are 11 days' journey from Horeb by the way of Mount Seir unto Kadesh-Barnea" (Deuteronomy 1:2).

"Darb el Haj," or Way of the Celebrants, because caravans of Moslem pilgrims travel along it on their way to Mecca for the observance of the *haj* (pilgrimage). In Biblical times it was named after its destination, the Mountain of Seir, or Edom.

The final and most southerly possibility is "the way to the hill country of the Amorites" (Deuteronomy 1:19). This route led from Mount Horeb in the south (wherever that is) to Kadesh-Barnea.

If we accept a southern location for Mt. Sinai, then this way is related to the second half of the Exodus journey—"From Horeb we went through all that great and terrible wilderness" (Deuteronomy 1:19).* This route would proceed (along the Gulf of Eilat) to Ezion-Geber (Numbers 33:16-35) and, via "the way to the hill country of the Amorites," to Kadesh (-Barnea) (Numbers 33:36). This segment is referred to in the Bible as "the way of the wilderness of the Red Sea" (Exodus 13:18).

At least theoretically, each of these routes is a

* The mountain of God is called both "Horeb" and "Sinai" at different places in the Bible (see, for example, Exodus 3:1 and Deuteronomy 1:6 for "Horeb"; and Exodus 19:20, 34:29 for "Sinai").

possibility. How do we decide among them?

Mt. Sinai was of course a critical stop along the route; if we could locate the mountain where God gave Moses the Ten Commandments, that could well be determinative of the route through the Sinai.

But, as we all know, the location of Mt. Sinai is in dispute and is a matter of speculation at best. Some scholars locate it deep in southern Sinai. Others go in the other direction and place it in the Negev Highlands. Still others place it in central Sinai; and others in north central Sinai. One scholar (Emmanuel Anati) argues that it is a site in the central Negev; another (Frank Moore Cross) that it is in Arabia. For those who wish to pursue the matter further, I have listed in the chart on pages 58-59 the various mountains that have been proposed, their locations and the scholars who support each location (with citations to their work).

It is interesting that of all the sites proposed for Mt. Sinai, only two have remains of human presence in ancient times.

One, proposed by the Italian scholar Emmanuel Anati, is the site known as Har Karkom, located in the central Negev Highlands, about 70 miles southwest of

AVINOAM DANIN

Jebel Serbal, *featuring distinctive multiple peaks, stands about 6,825 feet above sea level (see map on p. 59). As early as the second century A.D., Christian anchorites, living isolated lives of prayer and contemplation, believed Jebel Serbal was Mt. Sinai. This identification lasted until the early sixth century, when Jebel Musa supplanted Jebel Serbal as the traditional location. Nevertheless, some scholars have favored Jebel Serbal as the holy mountain (see chart on pp. 58-59).*

found.[2] These have been dated generally (due to a lack of specific finds) to the fifth or fourth millennium B.C. They are contemporary with the sanctuary recently excavated in Bika'at Uvda (on the fringes of the Arava, about 30 miles north of Eilat), also dated to the fifth millennium B.C. The remains discovered on the Har Karkom massif are also from this period, extending to as late as the third millennium B.C. So Har Karkom can hardly be Mt. Sinai and thus affords no assistance in locating the route of the Exodus.

The other site proposed for Mt. Sinai where human remains have been found is Serabit el-Khadem.[**] At Serabit el-Khadem, turquoise deposits were exploited by the ancient Egyptians during the Middle and New Kingdom periods (c. 1991-1190 B.C.).[3] At the beginning of the Middle Kingdom, a sanctuary dedicated to the Egyptian goddess Hathor was built here and was continually expanded over the centuries.

A number of very early alphabetic inscriptions (dated to about 1500 B.C.) have been found at Serabit el-Khadem in the mine area, rather than in the sanctuary area. Known as Proto-Sinaitic inscriptions, this pictographic-alphabetic script seems to have been used for a Semitic-Canaanite language.[4] Other examples of this script from an even earlier time (c. 1600 B.C.) have also been found in Canaan!

In addition, several pictures of what appear to be Semites were engraved on stelae in the Serabit el-Khadem sanctuary, and some of the names written on it in hieroglyphics are also Semitic.

Clearly, Semites were present at this Egyptian mining operation.

Some scholars have suggested that an Egyptian religious tradition sanctified Serabit el-Khadem, and that this religious tradition was somehow passed on to the Israelites. In that way, Serbit el-Khadem provided the model for Mt. Sinai.

Few scholars and fewer laymen are likely to be convinced by this speculation, however. Moreover, at the time of the Exodus, whether in the 13th century B.C. or in the 15th century B.C., Egyptian turquoise mining in the Sinai was at its most intensive. As we are told in the Egyptian dedication stelae of the Serabit el-Khadem sanctuary, Egyptian army escorts guarded the mines and the mining personnel. It is therefore highly unlikely that at this time the Israelites would have experienced a theophany here. Serabit el-Khadem is not Mt. Sinai.

We must admit that we can get no help in locating

Beer-Sheva and 50 miles northwest of Eilat. Anati recently published a sumptuously illustrated book titled *The Mountain of God,* concerning his recent investigation of this massif, and even earlier reported to **BAR** readers on his findings.[*] I do not wish to comment at length on Professor Anati's interpretation of certain structures discovered on this massif, except to note that his interpretation seems to me to strain the limits of my strictly archaeological approach. However, the most important point in connection with the problem we are exploring in this article is that most of the remains at Har Karkom date to the third millennium B.C., far too early for anyone's (except Anati's) reckoning of the Exodus. Moreover, those architectural elements at Har Karkom that Anati interprets as "cultic" are found in parallel forms at other mountain sites both in Eastern Sinai and in the Negev itself. At one mountain site in the Negev—Hasham el-Tarif—located some 40 miles southwest of Eilat, the remains of a number of sanctuaries, most of them open-air sanctuaries, were

* See Emmanuel Anati, "Has Mt. Sinai Been Found?" **BAR,** July/August 1985.

** From 1971 to 1982 I headed an archaeological expedition, on behalf of the Institute of Archaeology of Tel Aviv University, that investigated the archaeology of southern and eastern Sinai.

the Exodus route by trying to locate Mt. Sinai.

Let us therefore look at the ecological and ethnological picture of Sinai to see what guidance we can find.

The entire Sinai peninsula covers over 23,000 square miles. I would like to concentrate, however, on the nearly 2,900 square-mile area of south central Sinai.

Geologically, south central Sinai is part of the Arabian-Nubian massif. The highest peaks reach 8,200 feet above sea level. The mountain landscape is broken and cut by ravines and gullies. Some of these wadis are only a few yards wide; others are 500 feet wide and more.

As noted earlier, these wadis, or at least the wider ones, provide convenient natural passages along which traffic moves; they form the principal routes and arteries of the region and are also the main areas in which human activity was, and still is, concentrated.

South central Sinai has a semi-desert climate. The median low temperature in winter is 23° Fahrenheit; the median high temperature in summer is 105° Fahrenheit. Rainfall is rare and irregular. The average annual rainfall is less than 2.5 inches. However, a small amount of melt water from the snows that cover the mountain peaks in winter adds to the water supply.

Water resources also include rock aquifers (natural, subterranean reservoirs), which are sufficiently close to the surface to be rather easily tapped. Natural open pools along wadis also collect runoff rainwater. The

The Wadi Feiran oasis *provides a green refuge in the midst of the barren Sinai wilderness, of which the nearby Jebel Serbal, center, stands as a stern reminder. Early Christian monks identified this oasis as Elim, the Israelites' second encampment, "where there were twelve springs of water and seventy palm trees" (Exodus 15:27). Oases in the south central Sinai today support a Bedouin population of about 10,000, and thus could perhaps have sustained the Israelites on their Exodus journey.*

Canaanite pioneers *in the south central Sinai built more than 40 small settlements that have been discovered by the author and dated to the Early Bronze Age II period (2850-2650 B.C.). The settlements comprised five to twenty families living in a corresponding number of sunken stone houses, lower center, grouped in small, belt-like compounds spaced about 100 feet apart. These settlers raised goats and produced copper from locally mined ores and then transported the copper by caravan to Canaan. Such settlements demonstrate that south central Sinai was indeed capable of supporting a population in ancient times.*

water accumulated in these pools can be drawn on for many months of the year. In a few places, springs fed by high ground-water levels flow into the wadis. It is at these places where oases, such as the Feiran oasis in the west and Ein-Kid oasis in the east, have developed. A fairly dense growth of typically stunted, desert trees and bushes covers the streambeds and the nearby plain areas. This growth is exploited by the local Bedouin for grazing, as well as for fuel.

Today, the area has a population of approximately 10,000 Bedouin, who live in both temporary and permanent settlements. Their dwellings consist mostly of tents, wooden huts and, at the more permanent sites, a few stone structures.

In the 15 years between 1967 and 1982, when Israeli archaeologists had access to Sinai, it was clearly shown that the largest concentration of ancient settlements was in this mountainous region of south central Sinai. Except for the coastal strip, all other areas of Sinai have few economic resources and little water, as a result of which there is almost no regular or settled population. Central Sinai is called in Arabic "Badyat el-Tih," the Desert of the Wanderers. It is a flat area of limestone and sand, unsuitable for farming of any kind. Even the wild flora struggle to survive because of the lack of water.

Based on this evidence, I believe that the southern

route is the one most likely taken by the Israelites on their trek from Raamses to Kadesh-Barnea. As compared with other regions of Sinai, here in south central Sinai they would have found a reasonably adequate water supply and a relatively comfortable climate that makes it possible to maintain a daily lifestyle suitably adapted to the conditions of the desert. Moreover, the high mountains of south central Sinai are geomorphologically adapted to providing plenty of rock shelters; the high cliffs shield settlements established in their lee against the blasts of the cold winter winds.

Compared to other parts of Sinai, this region is ecologically better adapted to the sustenance of life, because it is covered by assorted vegetation consisting of acacia and palm trees and a fairly dense growth of perennial bushes, along with a seasonal cover of grasses and weeds suitable for pasturing sheep and goats.

In a pastoral economy (where ordinary argiculture is not possible) a flock of goats is essential. The Bedouin flocks even today are mostly black goats of a special dwarf breed physiologically adapted to arid conditions As experiments have shown, this breed of goat can go for as long as 14 days without water. At the end of the two-week period, the goats will have lost 40 percent of their body weight. Although deprived of water for this entire period, however, the goats show no ill effects and continue to carry out their bodily functions normally. Then, when given water, they gulp up enough in two minutes to equal 40 percent of their body weight.

This animal's ability to endure for weeks without water allows Sinai pastoralists to wander long distances with their flocks. The economic existence of the ancient population of south central Sinai was probably dependent on the domestication of the desert goat, which provided the populace not only with meat and milk, but also with hides and perhaps with wool as well.

In our excavations,* we found numerous animal bones of black, dwarf-breed goats from as early as the third millennium B.C. With flocks of such goats, the pastoralists could range across south central Sinai without having to worry about a nearby water source, such as a pool, a cistern or a well.

The concentration of Bedouin in this area today confirms our analysis of the situation in ancient times. In this respect, things haven't changed very much.

But there is another reason why I believe that this is the area most likely traversed by the Israelites on their way through Sinai. That relates to the area's geographic isolation vis-à-vis the regions that surround it. This isolation results from the region's geomorphological structure, which cuts it off from the mountain ranges to the north and from the Red Sea gulfs on the east and west.

Whether for this or for other, additional reasons, ancient Egyptian hegemony never extended into south central Sinai. As we have seen, the Egyptians did reach the western strip of southern Sinai, where they worked the turquoise mines of Serabit el-Khadem and similar

* See my article, "Fifteen Years in Sinai," BAR, July/August 1984.

Proposed Locations of Mt. Sinai
Scholar and Reference

Robinson, Edward.
Biblical Researches in Palestine, Mount Sinai and Arabia Petraea (London, 1838)

Bartlett, Samuel C.
From Egypt to Palestine Through the Wilderness and the South Country (New York, 1879)

Simons, J.
The Geographical and Topographical Texts of the Old Testament (Leiden, 1959)

Palmer, Edward H. *The Desert of the Exodus* (New York, 1972)

Burckhardt, John L.
Travels in Syria and the Holy Land (London, 1822)

Petrie, W. M. F.
Researches in Sinai (London, 1906)

Aharoni, Yohanan.
The Land of Israel in Biblical Times: A Geographical History (Jerusalem, 1962)

Ilan, Z.
(unpublished, oral communication)

Har-El, Menashe.
The Sinai Journeys (Jerusalem, 1968)

Anati, Emmanuel.
The Mountain of God (New York, 1986)

Jarvis, Claude.
Yesterday and Today in Sinai (London, 1938)

Gressman, H., J. Wellhausen, and B. Stade in H. Bar-Deroma.
Hanegev (Jerusalem, 1935)

Beke, Charles T.
Sinai in Arabia and of Midian (London, 1878)

Lucas, Alfred.
The Route of the Exodus of the Israelites from Egypt (London, 1938)

Neilsen, D.
The Site of the Biblical Mount Sinai (Copenhagen, 1928)

Cross, Frank M.
"The Epic Traditions of Early Israel," in *The Poet and the Historians,* ed. Richard Elliot Friedman (Cambridge, MA, 1983)

mines at nearby Wadi Maghara. But despite the fact that south central Sinai contains copper deposits that were highly prized in ancient times, there is no evidence to indicate that the Egyptians were active in the exploitation of these copper deposits.

Perhaps they refrained from penetrating into the south central mountain region, because they feared a conflict with the local population, which enjoyed a clear strategic advantage over any foreign invader. This is suggested by an Egyptian rock relief discovered in the Wadi Maghara. This relief, dating to about 2600 B.C., depicts the pharaoh Sekhemkhet, the third king of the third dynasty, smiting an enemy. Whether the depicted act was an actual historical event is irrelevant; the fact remains, the Egyptians perceived the need to invoke magical powers against their enemies in this region.

In any event, for whatever reason, we find no evidence of an Egyptian presence in south central Sinai at any time in the entire history of ancient Egypt.

Location	Mountain
Southern Sinai	Jebel Musa
Southern Sinai	Jebel Musa
Southern Sinai	Jebel Musa
Southern Sinai	Jebel Safsafa (Part of J. Musa)
Southern Sinai	Jebel Serbal
Southern Sinai	Jebel Serbal
Southern Sinai	
Northwest of Southern Sinai	Serabit el-Khadem
Central-Western Sinai	Jebel Sin Bishar
Negev Highlands	Har Karkom
Northern Sinai	Jebel Halal
Land of Midian, east of Gulf of Eilat	
Upper north of Midian, northeast of Aqaba	Jebel Baghir
Upper north of Midian, northeast of Aqaba	Jebel Baghir
Land of Edom, near Petra	
Land of Midian	

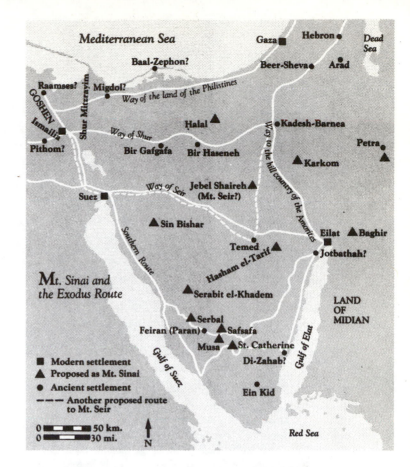

Mt. Sinai and the Exodus Route

■ Modern settlement
▲ Proposed as Mt. Sinai
● Ancient settlement
--- Another proposed route to Mt. Seir

0 — 50 km.
0 — 30 mi.

N

So south central Sinai was suitable as the wandering ground of the Israelite tribes not only from an economic-ecological viewpoint, but also from the geopolitical viewpoint. It was a region free of any Egyptian presence. Here, in short, the Israelites were safe.

Yet there is a problem. Nowhere have we found any material remains of human occupation at the time (Late Bronze Age—1550-1200 B.C.) when the Exodus is supposed to have occurred.* Perhaps it will be argued, by those who subscribe to the traditional account in the Bible, that the Israelite material culture was only of the flimsiest kind that left no trace. Presumably the Israelite dwellings and artifacts consisted only of perishable materials.

* For the earlier date, see John J. Bimson and David Livingston, "Redating the Exodus," **BAR,** September/October 1987; for the later date, see Baruch Halpern, "Radical Exodus Redating Fatally Flawed," **BAR,** November/December 1987.

But it must be pointed out that we did find substantial evidence of human occupation from even earlier periods. We discovered scores of settlements, especially from the so-called pre-pottery Neolithic period (sixth-fifth millennia B.C.) and from the Early Bronze Age II period (first half of the third millennium B.C.). In the EB II period, a Canaanite population established a series of small settlements in south central Sinai. The principal economic activity of these settlements was the production of copper from locally mined ores, which was then transported by caravan to the large population centers in Canaan.

What are we to conclude then from all this evidence? It is clear that no single, consistent picture of the Exodus emerges. But what we can say is that if a large-scale Exodus as described in the Bible, or even a small-scale Exodus, did in fact occur, it probably followed the southern route through the Sinai.

[1] Itzhaq Beit-Arieh, "A Pattern of Settlement in Southern Sinai and Southern Canaan in the Third Millennium B.C.," *Bulletin of the American Schools of Oriental Research* 243 (1981), pp. 31-54.
[2] U. Armer, "Ancient Cult Sites in the Negev and Sinai Deserts," *Tel Aviv* 11 (1984), pp. 115-131.
[3] William M. Flinders Petrie, *Researches in Sinai* (New York: Dutton, 1906); see also Beit-Arieh, "Fifteen Years in Sinai," **BAR,** July/August 1984, pp. 26-41, 46-54 [20-48]; and Beit-Arieh, "Serabit el-Khadim: New Metallurgical and Chronological Aspects," *Levant* 17 (1985), pp. 89-116.
[4] William F. Albright, *The Proto-Sinaitic Inscriptions and Their Decipherment* (Cambridge, MA: Harvard Univ. Press, 1969); Frank Moore Cross, "The Evolution of the Alphabet," *Eretz-Israel* 8 (1967), p. 12; and Joseph Naveh, *Early History of the Alphabet* (Jerusalem: Magnes Press, Hebrew Univ., 1982).

Ze'ev Herzog's article on Beer-sheba and the patriarchs drew the following comments from readers (**BAR**, March/April 1981):

> The problem of the absence of finds from the Patriarch Age at Beer-sheba does not exist if you read the Bible carefully. At the time of the patriarchs, Beer-sheba was just a watering hole in a barren region. Abraham and others just camped there occasionally.
>
> It was not on the list of cities that Joshua conquered, but Hormah, its big neighbor, was.
>
> It was first mentioned as a village when the land was distributed to the people of Israel after the conquest by Joshua was completed, and that was after the age of the Patriarchs.
>
> Ernest W. Zentgraf, Bethlehem, Pennsylvania

> Ze'ev Herzog tells us that in building his own city at Beer-sheba, King David "destroyed almost all earlier remains of the older Iron Age site" . . . . Yet despite such rapid disappearance of even later "evidence" Herzog still thinks that his failure to find typical Bronze Age remains there disproves habitation by the patriarchs in the early second millennium B.C. And even granting his Chalcolithic or Iron Age dating for all he has found, just what Bronze Age remains does he expect from the occasional nomadic visitations of the patriarchs? Once again the pedantic application of a stratification chart has replaced both common sense and the clear chronology of the Bible.
>
> Tim Hensgen, Cincinnati, Ohio

> Has the possibility been considered that Tel Masos is the site of Biblical Beer-sheba? Your article describes Tel Masos as a large and well built city. I assume that a large city must have been fortified and must have had a safe water supply.
>
> Certainly the modern name of Tel es-Saba, while it cannot be ignored, cannot be considered as decisive.
>
> Leslie Regel, Ph.D., Pittsburgh, Pennsylvania

Dr. Herzog responded (**BAR,** May/June 1981):

> I was very pleased to receive copies of readers' letters regarding my article on "Beer-sheba of the Patriarchs." It certainly provoked considerable interest and also some disagreements. I would like to comment on some of the questions and suggestions offered:
>
> To Tim Hensgen: The builders of the city of Beer-sheba at the time of the United Monarchy did remove most of earlier remains on top of the hill but not on the eastern slope where we found the Iron I settlements. It is impossible to assume a Late Bronze occupation because not a single find in the whole dig may be dated to the period between the 16th and 14th centuries B.C. Moreover, this period (the Late Bronze Age) is also unrepresented in all other sites in the Arad—Beer-sheba valleys.
>
> To Leslie Regel: Tel Masos may be identified with Biblical Beer-sheba [only] if one wants to ignore the tradi-tional name of the site (Tell es-Saba). Moreover, Tel Beer-sheba is the only possible location of the monarchical royal city which served as an administrative center in the 10th-8th century B.C. Tel Masos has no remains from this later period. Tel es-Saba (Tel Beer-sheba) is also centrally located in the Biblical Negeb and is thus more suitable as the administrative center. In any event, the earliest occupation at Tel Masos dates very closely to the early strata of Beer-sheba, thereby posing the same difficulties regarding the patriarchs.
>
> The objective of the archaeologist working in the land of the Bible is to uncover factual evidence for the material culture of ancient times. We do not intend to credit or discredit the Biblical story. However, the archaeological data should be compared with other sources of that period and a reasonable synthesis offered. As has happened many times in the past, documents and new finds from excavations permit better understanding on some points, but also raise new problems. This is the nature of scientific inquiry.

Dr. Herzog is right that it is not the archaeologist's task either to confirm or to deny the Biblical account but rather to follow the evidence where it leads. In this instance, however, has he been too quick to follow the evidence in what may be only an apparent direction? The readers quoted above raise two important questions, neither of which may have been satisfactorily addressed by the author.

Might Biblical Beer-sheba be elsewhere than Tel es-Saba? Herzog is certainly correct in arguing that, in the absence of any other candidate in the region, Tel es-Saba must have been the royal fortress city of that name during the tenth to eighth centuries B.C. But since the excavators found no settlement history at the site prior to the 12th century, is it not possible that the Iron Age builders (or David himself) simply took the name of Beer-sheba from the sacred traditions already attached to the region and appropriated it for the new royal city?

We have an analogous situation later in Biblical history with Jericho. Long after the famous ancient city of Jericho had been abandoned, King Herod adopted the name for the winter palace he built in the same general region but several miles away.

Another question posed above deserves closer scrutiny. Should we expect the Biblical patriarchs' Beer-sheba to have produced archaeological deposits? On the one hand, Herzog might have strengthened his comments by noting that even temporary seasonal nomadic encampments have left traces that are detected in a careful archaeological survey. As examples, he could have cited some of the evidence of ancient transitory campsites Beit-Arieh notes in his article "Fifteen Years in Sinai." Herzog implies this awareness when he notes that "not a single find" at Tel es-Saba or nearby gave evidence of a Late Bronze occupation, but he does not go on to make it clear why at least some pottery might be expected as witness to even a short-term tent encampment and why its absence, even in later disturbed contexts, could therefore be significant.

On the other hand, Herzog only speaks about the absence of *Late* Bronze Age artifacts, even though he opens his article by noting that scholars have tended to date the patriarchal age in the *Middle* Bronze Age, either in the 21st to 19th centuries B.C. or in the 19th to 16th centuries B.C.

Is his comment about the absence of Late Bronze artifacts therefore a sufficient rejoinder to the question? He could have extended his comment further back in regard to Tel es-Saba and pointed to the absence of evidence for any Middle Bronze or even Early Bronze occupation, but he would not have been able to make that claim for the region as a whole. East of Tel es-Saba, both Tel Masos and Tel Malhata had major fortified cities in the Middle Bronze Age, and lesser deposits have been noted elsewhere in the region.

If Abraham's Beer-sheba need not have been located exactly at Tel es-Saba, then we cannot rule out the possibility that the Genesis traditions contain some authentic memory of an Abrahamic Beer-sheba elsewhere in the nearby area during the Middle Bronze Age.

The presence of an ancient well at Tel es-Saba is, of course, irrelevant to the question of the site's identification. If Tel es-Saba was not the Beer-sheba of Abraham or Isaac, then the fact that there happens to be a well at the site makes no difference to the argument. The Biblical well might be one of the other known wells in the vicinity, or some yet-unexcavated well.

Turning to Itzhaq Beit-Arieh's articles on the Sinai and the Exodus traditions, note that the wealth of new evidence at Beit-Arieh's disposal does not lead him to a greater sense of certainty about the Exodus route. Indeed, he acknowledges that the archaeological record has been frustratingly silent on what he identifies as the most likely period and places of the Israelites' wilderness lodgings (the Late Bronze Age in the southern Sinai and at Kadesh-Barnea).

It may seem ironic that the accumulation of more archaeological information can lead to less, rather than more, historical certainty. That has often been the case in recent years, not only for Biblical archaeology but for research in other regions of the world as well. This does not diminish the importance of archaeological evidence. On the contrary, it underscores how vital a role archaeology plays. Obviously, it is satisfying to have the physical record substantiate a favored interpretation, but it is equally important to discover when the "documents" from the soil do not fit our theories so neatly.

In this case, Beit-Arieh demonstrates a responsible scholarly stance: caution. While the ecological conditions in the Sinai and the archaeological evidence for patterns of settlement lead him to look favorably on southern Sinai as a locale for the Israelites' wilderness sojourn, he acknowledges the absence of supporting archaeological evidence and therefore properly avoids drawing any dogmatic conclusions.

For Further Reading

Concerning the Patriarchal Age

William H. Stiebing, Jr., "When Was the Age of the Patriarchs?" **BAR**, June 1975

Nahum M. Sarna, "Abraham in History," **BAR**, December 1977

John Van Seters, "Dating the Patriarchal Stories," **BAR**, November/December 1978

Aharon Kempinski, "Jacob in History," **BAR**, January/February 1988

Concerning Archaeological Evidence of Nomadic Camps

Steven A. Rosen, "Finding Evidence of Ancient Nomads," **BAR**, September/October 1988

Concerning Sites in the Sinai

Suzanne F. Singer, "From These Hills . . . ," **BAR**, June 1978

Ze'ev Meshel, "Did Yahweh Have a Consort?" **BAR**, March/April 1979

Rudolph Cohen, "Did I Excavate Kadesh–Barnea?" **BAR**, May/June 1981 (*see Section F*)

Emmanuel Anati, "Has Mt. Sinai Been Found?" **BAR**, July/August 1985

Aviram Perevolotsky and Israel Finkelstein, "The Southern Sinai Exodus Route in Ecological Perspective," **BAR**, July/August 1985

Concerning the Dating of the Exodus

William H. Stiebing, Jr., "Should the Exodus and the Israelite Settlement in Canaan Be Redated?" **BAR**, July/August 1985

John J. Bimson and David Livingston, "Redating the Exodus," **BAR**, September/October 1987

Baruch Halpern, "Radical Exodus Redating Fatally Flawed," **BAR**, November/December 1987

John J. Bimson, "A Reply to Baruch Halpern," **BAR**, July/August 1988

Manfred Bietak, "Contra Bimson, Bietak Says Late Bronze Age Cannot Begin as Late as 1400 B.C.," **BAR**, July/August 1988

In the Time of the Judges—A Visit with an Early Israelite Family; Evidence for Early Biblical Cult Sites

The articles in this section cover the period from the end of the Late Bronze Age through the first two centuries of the Iron Age (12th-11th centuries B.C.) in the central hill country of Canaan, generally associated with early Israelite settlement and activity.

Scholars disagree as to how and exactly when the Israelite occupation of Canaan began. Some cite evidence for a cluster of city destructions shortly before 1200 B.C. and argue for a sweeping military "conquest" similar to the Book of Joshua. Others believe there was a gradual and largely peaceful settlement over a longer period by initially separate tribes who occasionally joined forces against the Canaanite ruler of a particular region—as suggested in some portions of the Book of Judges. (One article reprinted in Section C—David Ussishkin's "Lachish—Key to the Israelite Conquest of Canaan?"—considers a variant of the Israelite military campaign view; that is, the possibility that Israelites were responsible for destructions at major Canaanite cities but in a sequence of separate actions spread from the 13th century B.C. [e.g., Hazor] well into the 12th century [e.g., Lachish, level VI]).

Whatever the differing views concerning an Israelite "conquest," however, archaeological researches during the 1960s and 1970s provide increasingly clear evidence, starting from about 1200 B.C., for new settlements in the land of Canaan which probably can be identified as Israelite (or at least as "proto-Israelite"). The evidence comes from excavations of town sites and from regional surveys in Upper Galilee, in the central hill range stretching through the territories of Manasseh, Ephraim, Benjamin and Judah and in the northern Negev Desert.

The pattern is essentially the same through all of these regions: In areas where there was little or no occupation during the preceding Late Bronze Age, numerous small settlements spring up in the 12th-11th centuries. They tend to be unfortified and have modest architecture; they tend to be located in the thinner-soiled hilly areas away from natural water sources and to compensate for this by the cutting of cisterns into the chalky bedrock; they often exhibit evidence for both agricultural and pastoral activities—folds for flocks of sheep and goats standing next to threshing floors and grain silos; and they introduce a new type of house architecture that distinguishes them from the indigenous Canaanites.

The three archaeologists who report their discoveries in this section all were acquainted with this general pattern of evidence, and it stands in the background of their descriptions and interpretations of their own finds.

Joseph Callaway, in "A Visit with Ahilud," provides a good example of responsible reconstruction from sparse archaeological remains of an entire Iron Age I house complex. In his fleshing out of Ahilud's house, Callaway is able to draw by analogy from the "three-room" and more elaborate "four-room" houses previously reported at other Iron Age sites such as Beer-sheba and Tel Masos (see For Further Reading), and few would disagree with his reconstruction of Ahilud's house at Raddana or with his identification of it as a typical early Israelite home of the so-called three-room type.

By contrast, the remaining articles and comments show the very sharp controversies generated by two other excavators' attempts to identify cult sites within early Israelite contexts. Both their interpretations of the installations as cultic and the suggestions that they were Israelite evoked strong challenges from critics.

Adam Zertal's answer to the question, "Has Joshua's Altar Been Found on Mt. Ebal?" set off a heated debate which we follow like a hard-hitting volley of tennis through Aharon Kempinski's "Joshua's Altar—An Iron Age I Watchtower," then back to Zertal's "How Can Kempinski Be So Wrong!" and on to a further comment by Kempinski, "Zertal's Altar—19th Century Biblical Archaeology." Kempinski's final assault is reinforced by a comment in the same issue from Anson Rainey, "Zertal's Altar—A Blatant Phony." Immediately following that comment, however, Zertal receives some help from Michael Thompson's letter, "Kempinski's Outlandish Reconstruction."

At the same time Adam Zertal was uncovering what he took to be an altar on Mt. Ebal from Joshua's time, a few miles to the north Amihai Mazar was investigating what he decided must be a "high place" installation from the same period. He entertained the suggestion that this site might also have been Israelite in his article, "Bronze Bull Found in Israelite 'High Place' from the Time of the Judges."

Subsequently, both Zertal's and Mazar's claims were challenged by Michael Coogan in arguments originally published in the *Palestine Exploration Quarterly* and summarized by Hershel Shanks in "Two Early Israelite Cult Sites Now Questioned."

64

A Visit with Ahilud

A REVEALING LOOK AT VILLAGE LIFE WHEN ISRAEL FIRST SETTLED THE PROMISED LAND

By Joseph A. Callaway

I FIRST LEARNED OF AHILUD in 1969. I had been director of excavations at the ancient site of Ai, the second city taken by the Israelites when they entered Canaan, according to the book of Joshua (Joshua 7-8). I had been working at Ai since 1964, and our field work was nearly finished. We had uncovered a large fortified city of over 27 acres that had existed from about 3000 B.C. to about 2400 B.C. (the Early Bronze Age). Then the site was abandoned for about 1,200 years until about 1220 B.C. At that time, the first Israelites built a small 2.75-acre village on the site, which lasted until about 1050 B.C. (the Iron Age I period). Then the site was abandoned for good.

Actually, Ahilud did not live at Ai. His neighbors and perhaps some of his relatives did. Ahilud himself lived at Khirbet Raddana, a site about four miles west of Ai. Raddana too was an ancient site. We had been asked to do some emergency or so-called salvage excavations at Raddana before the encroachments of modern civilization destroyed or covered the ancient remains. Despite our limited resources, we jumped at the chance because even from the surface we could tell that Raddana had been an Israelite village at the same time as Ai. Comparisons would be invaluable.

It was then I learned of Ahilud. His name turned up on a storage jar handle at Raddana. Lined up vertically on the handle, reading from top to bottom, were three letters—*alef* (A), *het* (H) and *lamed* (L)—in old Hebrew script. The *dalet* (D) was missing, but when we pulled out our Bibles, we found references to "Jehosaphat, the son of Ahilud." The phrase appeared twice in 2 Samuel, 8:16 and 20:24. The Biblical references were contemporaneous with our jar handle. On this basis, we reconstructed the final *dalet* in Ahilud's name as a good possibility. The Biblical Ahilud must

Stone ruins of Israelite Ai *and an earlier Bronze Age city (center), seen from the air, stand out against the darker cultivated agricultural terraces. Farmers from the village of Deir Dibwan (top right) work these terraced fields, first constructed by the Israelite pioneers who built Ai in Iron Age I. The valley below (left) leads east to Jericho.*

have been a person of some prominence because his son Jehosaphat is among those in a list of officials at King David's court. Jehosaphat was the *mazkir* or official recorder; the New English Bible translates the term "secretary of state."

Although our Ahilud lived in the 11th century B.C., roughly contemporary with Samuel, it is unlikely that he was the Ahilud mentioned in the Bible as the father of Jehosaphat. Our Ahilud lived in extremely modest circumstances in a tiny village that had only six clusters of houses on a hilltop surrounded by terraced farmland; it is unlikely that he produced an educated advisor to the King. Probably he simply shared a name with a more prominent Ahilud.

Modest circumstances, however, do not mean that our Ahilud is of little interest; on the contrary, he represents village life at the grassroots level of ancient Israel's culture.

Ahilud is important to me because his house is the only one I excavated at Ai or Raddana that can be personalized with a family name. In a special way, he is representative for me of the villagers in scores of nameless settlements that dotted the hilltops of ancient Judea and Samaria during the period of the Judges. When the excavation ended and I was faced with the enormous task of analyzing the results, I thought often of Ahilud. Sometimes I would sit on the hilltop where he had lived. Overlooking a deep valley to the south and surrounded by agricultural terraces, Ahilud's hilltop has preserved its ancient appearance. If I could understand Ahilud, I thought, I could understand what it meant to be an Israelite peasant in the days of the Judges, shortly before Israel emerged as a monarchy under Saul, the first king.

In the summer of 1972 I was back at Raddana and Ai, searching for the remains of other "Ahiluds" who lived there some 3,000 years ago. A delegation of archaeologists from Jerusalem came out to get a first-hand report on the most recent findings at Ai. Their names are well-known to readers of **BAR:** Trude Dothan, Abraham Malamat, Nahman Avigad, Ruth Amiran, Miriam Tadmor.

We were talking while standing in the pillared home of an ancient Israelite. As we talked, Trude Dothan stood beside one of the roof-support pillars and laid her arm across the top of it. I stopped dead in my tracks. Anyone who knows Trude Dothan knows she is of average height, about five feet two inches; yet she stood with her arm on *top* of the main support for a roof beam in the home of her ancient forebears. Were these people shorter than she was?

I again examined the buildings we had excavated. In one house I found a wall still standing to a height above that of the pillars. There in the wall at the same height as the pillars was a well-made aperture for one end of a beam that had once extended across the pillar and into the wall. The underside of the beam aperture was about five feet three

Ahilud's jar handle. *The first three letters of the name Ahilud were inscribed on this storage jar handle in the 11th century B.C. Reading from top to bottom are* alef *(A),* het *(H) and* lamed *(L), in one of the earliest Hebrew scripts. The final letter,* dalet *(D), can be assumed because contemporaneous references to an Ahilud appear in the Bible, in 2 Samuel 8:16 and 20:24. This jar handle, found in a Raddana house we now call "Ahilud's house," was the only artifact uncovered at either Ai or Raddana that was inscribed with a name.*

inches from the floor. Careful examination disclosed that all of the houses had roof supports in the range of five feet three inches to five feet six inches from the floor.

When we reconstructed an Israelite house at Ai, we placed roof slats on top of the beams and then a layer of *huwwar*, a white clay, on top of the slats to seal out the sun and rain. This is the way Ahilud's roof was finished, according to the best archaeological evidence. The beam, judging by the size of the aperture in the wall, was about six to eight inches in diameter, so the underside of the slats on top of the beam was about six feet above the floor. In effect, the roof was about six feet high, interrupted by the beam, which reduced the height by six to eight inches.

The question is whether the villagers would build all of their houses with roof beams so low they would bump their heads on them, or whether, in fact, the people were shorter than their Israeli descendants. The latter seems to be more likely, although we have no skeletal remains to prove it. If I am correct, then Saul of Benjamin who was ". . . from his shoulders upward . . . taller than any of his people" (1 Samuel 9:2) would not attract a second look today because of his height.

Ahilud's house and those of his neighbors at Ai and Raddana were so simple in plan and size that they barely met the requirements for family life. The basic plan was a simple rectangle divided into two areas by a row of four roof-support pillars. In every case, the row of pillars was nearer to one long wall, creating an area about 4.5 feet wide on the narrow side, and about 10 feet wide in the "great-room." Entry was through a small door in the front of the great-room. At Raddana, the largest house excavated had an additional room across the back of the basic rectangle. Passage to this back room was from a door in one corner of the great-room. These houses were simpler than the typical Israelite four-room house,* which apparently developed elsewhere in more prosperous surroundings. Ahilud's house, therefore, was not a four-room dwelling, and was about as basic as one could imagine in meeting family needs for shelter.

When we travel today, let's say to the Holy Land, we usually take what we consider the basic necessities: a toothbrush, cosmetics or shaving articles, shirts, underwear, pajamas, socks, Kleenex, etc., and, in our hotel, we do not normally sleep dormitory-style. If we could somehow turn the calendar back 3,000 years the way we turn the clock back by crossing time zones and visit Ahilud, he would be puzzled by all these things. "You won't need them in our village," he would say.

Ahilud had no toothbrush. Possibly he had a change of underwear and, most likely, he had only one outer garment. He had no pajamas, no socks, and no Kleenex.

In Ahilud's house, there was no furniture of the kind we have. People sat cross-legged on the packed clay and stone floor; there they gathered around a small open fire. For family socializing, or when guests like us would come, they would line up shoulder to shoulder on a bench-like ledge built of stone along the base of the house wall. A few flat stones placed around the fire pit probably served as makeshift stools.

There was no kitchen in Ahilud's house. Small round "ovens" for cooking bread or boiling foods were located outside the front door or in an adjoining open courtyard that was shared by two or three households. Apparently, each family cooked its own bread by stretching a thin, round cake of dough over a pottery disc inverted over the fire. Hosea's assessment that Ephraim was "a cake not turned" (Hosea 7:8) suggests that cakes of bread were simply cooked to a crust on one side, then turned over and cooked for the same length of time on the other side.

There was no bathroom in Ahilud's house. Where did Ahilud's family take baths? They didn't, at least if we define "bath" as soaking in a bathtub, or standing in a shower. Most baths probably consisted of washing the extremities occasionally. And where was the toilet? There

*For a discussion and picture of the Israelite four-room house, see "The Israelite Occupation of Canaan" by Yohanan Aharoni, **BAR**, May/June 1982.

Trude Dothan, *Hebrew University archaeologist, rests her arm on a roof-support pillar of a house at Ai, as Hebrew University Bible historian, Abraham Malamat, looks on. If Dothan, who is five feet two inches tall, towers over this pillar, similar in height to the many other roof-support pillars unearthed at the site, then the question arises—were Ahilud and his neighbors less than five feet two inches tall? Although the author found no skeletal remains at Ai to prove an answer, he believes that the Israelites in the days of the Judges were indeed people of diminutive height.*

wasn't any. Where did people go? Outside. Anywhere.

Nor were there bedrooms. As is true even today in some villages in the Bethel-Ramallah area, everyone slept on the floor of the great-room that served at mealtimes as the dining area. Various kinds of pads constituted the beds. Outer garments provided the covers during sleep. Privacy? Sooner or later everyone knew what everyone else did at night as well as by day.

If life in Ahilud's house was less than commodious, we

AHILUD'S HOUSE

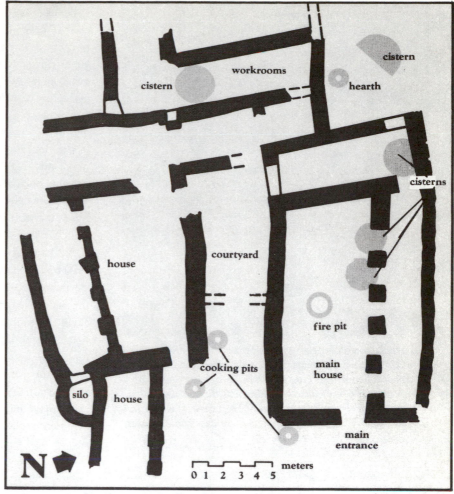

workrooms

cistern

cistern

hearth

cisterns

house

courtyard

house

silo

cooking pits

fire pit

main house

main entrance

N

0 1 2 3 4 5 meters

Joint Expedition to Ai

Although these remains of walls and roof-support pillars (left) appear to mark off only a few small rooms, in fact they once framed a cluster of three houses belonging to Ahilud and his extended family. Just behind the workman in the photo is the largest room of the main house, separated by a row of four roof-support pillars from a long narrow room, far right. To the left of the largest room is a courtyard. Sometime after this photo was taken, the areas to the left and in front of the main house and the mound of debris behind it were also excavated and a plan (above) of the entire complex was drawn.

Features of the Ahilud house complex in the plan include:

• a large fire pit in the center of the largest room of the main house.

• two cistern openings, set into the floor of the largest room of the main house.

• a long narrow room at the back of the main house, across its width, with a third cistern opening set into its floor.

• narrow workrooms behind the three-house cluster (upper left and upper center). In the far north workroom (upper right) is a hearth for metalworking. Here, metal ingots were melted in crucibles and the molten metal was poured into molds to form the daggers, spearpoints and axe heads for Ahilud's household, as well as for the other members of the community. Most of the tools and other evidence of metalworking shown on page 74 were found in these workrooms.

• silo (lower left) for storage jars filled with grain. This was Ahilud's "root cellar."

Beam hole in house wall. *The aperture at the top of the wall, above the meter stick, originally held the end of a wooden beam that crossed the room, resting on pillars. (This construction method is shown in the reconstruction drawing, opposite.) The bottom of the aperture is just five feet three inches from the floor, which gives some idea of the height of the inhabitants.*

must remember that these hill-country settlers were pioneers. During the period of the Judges, most of the Israelite villages, such as Raddana, Michmash, Rimmon, Taiyiba and Gibeah of Benjamin, were located on previously unoccupied hilltops or on the unoccupied ruins of ancient cities, such as Ai, Mizpeh and Gibeon. Generally, the new villages were small, less than five acres, and unfortified. The sites were inhospitable and marginal, the kind of places in which people live only to avoid conflict with the owners of more fertile areas.

A short passage in Joshua 17 reflects the sociological dynamics that led to hill-country settlement: "The tribe of Joseph said 'The hill country is not enough for us; yet all the Canaanites who dwell in the plains have chariots of iron, not only those in Beth Shean and its villages but also those in the Valley of Jezreel.'" (Joshua 17:16).

These early Israelites were prevented by superior military power from expanding into the fertile valleys and yet, because of population pressures, they were desperate for room to live in the hill country. These pioneers were told that "The hill country shall be yours, for though it is a forest, you shall clear it and possess it to its farthest borders"

(Joshua 17:18). Whether this passage refers to the Ai-Raddana area is not really important; the same pressures referred to in Joshua were undoubtedly felt there.

Pioneers like Ahilud, as this passage suggests, first had to clear a "forest" to provide an area for their village. We tend to think of forest as heavily wooded land, with stands of virgin timber like those encountered by pioneers in our own country two centuries ago. But this is not an accurate perception of a "forest" in ancient Judea and Samaria.

The word *ya'ar*, commonly translated "forest," really means wild, untilled land carrying permanent vegetation. It can include the cedar forests of Lebanon or open woodlands or thickets and scattered shrubs. The precise meaning must be determined by the geographical context. Were there open woodlands with stands of trees in the Ai-Raddana region, or were the hills covered with thickets and scattered shrubs? Our excavations suggest an answer.

At Ai, the houses of the Early Bronze Age city (3200-2400 B.C.) were built on bedrock; floors were leveled with clay filling in uneven areas. The temple on the acropolis of the site was also constructed on bedrock; so, too, the street along the south city wall and even the streets between houses in the Lower City. This suggests that the layer of topsoil on this hilltop site had not been very thick, probably like the thin topsoil layer on neighboring hilltops in the area today. It is unlikely, therefore, that a stand of trees like those found in open woodlands existed on this hilltop site.

When the Israelite settlers came to the site about 1200 B.C., it had been abandoned for 1,200 years, since 2400 B.C. Was the site wooded in 1200 B.C.? Apparently not, because the newcomers built their houses directly on the ruins of the early Bronze Age floors and walls. Two Israelite houses were built inside the still-standing enclosure wall of the Early Bronze Age temple. The earthen floors of these Israelite houses consisted of a few inches of soil laid down on top of the ancient, plastered floors.

The Israelite settlement was small. It covered only about 2.75 acres on the hilltop. The Early Bronze Age city with its fortified wall covered 27.5 acres. To build a small Israelite village, people like Ahilud simply cleared the ancient site of shrubs, thickets and possibly an occasional tree.

The situation was much the same on the hilltop of Raddana, although no previous city existed there. Early Bronze Age pottery dating to about 3000 B.C. was left in crevices of bedrock on the hilltop, suggesting that the surface of bedrock was exposed at that time. When Ahilud arrived about 1200 B.C., pillar houses were built on the same exposed bedrock.

These Israelite houses were abandoned about 1050 B.C. for unknown reasons. Gradually, the houses yielded to the ravages of wind, rain and sun. In one room of the ruins of Ahilud's house, we found pottery from the sixth century

Pillar house at Ai. *Here, an artist has reconstructed the best-preserved house excavated at Ai or Raddana. Ahilud lived in a house very similar to this one, basically a simple rectangle separated into two areas by a "room divider" of roof support pillars. Beams rest on the pillars; across the beams are roof slats topped by white clay. In the far corner of the one-room house, a curved wall encloses a silo for storage jars of grain. The spaces between the stone piers at left were once filled in, forming a wall with a second room behind it. This second room could be entered through the doorway at the far left.*

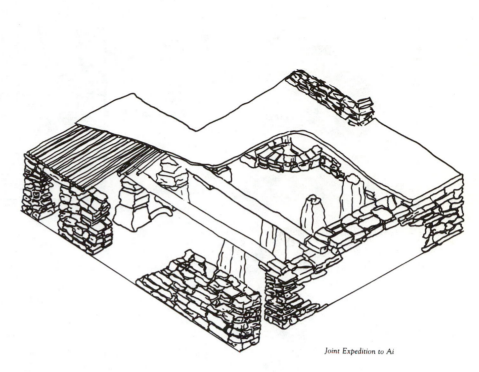

Joint Expedition to Ai

A.D., left by a shepherd.

To clear the sites of shrubs and thickets, the Israelite settlers used crude mattocks and blades. In Ahilud's house at Raddana, we found the handle socket of an iron mattock, which may have been used for this purpose.

Although most of the land was covered with low shrubs and thickets, there were undoubtedly some trees available for building purposes in the Ai-Raddana region. Cypress and pine wood was used at Gibeah of Benjamin in the 11th century B.C., and large poles were used as roof support beams at Ai and Raddana. By the time of the monarchy, however, few, if any, trees were left. As always, the newly settled population cut down trees on land that could not easily renew such timber resources.

One of the puzzles about these hilltop sites is that they are far from natural springs, which normally provided settlements with water. Ahilud's people brought with them a well-thought-out strategy for dealing with this problem. At both Ai and Raddana, we found bell-shaped cisterns cut into the rock underneath and adjacent to each new house. These rainwater reservoirs provided a water source independent of the natural springs in the valleys, springs that had held earlier villages hostage to such vulnerable locations. Because these cisterns were hewed out of the rock when the houses were constructed, we must assume that the confident new settlers understood cistern-building techniques—and quite sophisticated ones at that.

The rock on most of the hilltops in this area north of Jerusalem consists of thick layers of Senonian chalk interspersed with thinner layers of Lower Cenomanian limestone. The Israelite villagers cut the cisterns into the chalk layers, which seem to have a self-sealing quality when wet. The thin layers of hard limestone most often were at the bottoms of the cisterns.

The cisterns were bell-shaped with narrow openings at the top. One bell-shaped cistern at Ai was connected with two other cisterns located under the adjacent house. The three cisterns operated together as a filtration trap system.

We literally stumbled onto the first cistern outside the house. When we explored this cistern, we found a hole in its side that led to the second cistern. Inside the second cistern, we looked up and saw that the cap on top was in place just as it had been left 3,000 years ago when the house was abandoned. The cap was set in the great-room floor of the house. The family that had lived here had an indoor water supply that would have been exhausted only when the three interconnected cisterns had been emptied. The second cistern also had a hole in the side that led to the third cistern. The holes in the sides that connected the three cisterns were located above the cistern-bottom level, so that impurities would settle and be left behind when the water flowed from one cistern to the next.

A rock-cut channel led to the cistern that collected the rainwater outside the house. In front of the cistern's open-

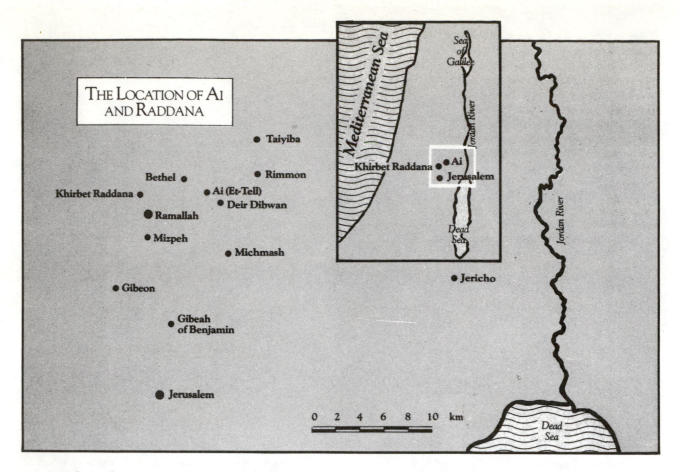

THE LOCATION OF AI
AND RADDANA

Taiyiba

Bethel

Rimmon

Khirbet Raddana

Ai (Et-Tell)

Deir Dibwan

Ramallah

Mizpeh

Michmash

Gibeon

Gibeah
of Benjamin

Jerusalem

Mediterranean Sea

Sea of Galilee

Jordan River

Khirbet Raddana

Ai

Jerusalem

Dead Sea

Jericho

Jordan River

Dead Sea

0 2 4 6 8 10 km

ing, a round trap about 12 inches deep was filled with rocks that strained out the larger impurities. The successive "settling traps" in the bottom of the first and second cisterns removed additional impurities. Similar systems were found in several houses. In an adjoining house, two cisterns functioned together as a system. The larger one received the rainwater from a channel located outside the house. This cistern served as a trap for the smaller one. When the large cistern was full, the pure water overflowed through a small, round aperture near the cistern's top.

Household cisterns were especially important, because the springs near Ai and Raddana have a very small flow and are located in deep valleys far from these villages. We studied the spring in the Wadi el-Jaya north of Ai and calculated its flow at 12.5 gallons per hour. This is not insignificant, and for people with patience and time the spring would have provided a backup water supply for the household cistern system, which depended on rainwater. We also calculated the capacities of the cistern systems in two other houses.* One was 28.3 cubic yards and the other was 23.2 cubic yards. If, as one unpublished study suggests, a person adapted to this arid environment got along quite

*This work was done by James B. Davis, a graduate student at the Southern Baptist Theological Seminary, Louisville, Kentucky.

Freshly plowed terraces *at Khirbet Raddana. Like their modern counterparts in Israel today, the Israelites who built Khirbet Raddana and nearby Ai were farmers. When they settled here in about 1200 B.C., the Israelites constructed agricultural terraces by building walls along the outer edges of the natural limestone terraces that stepped down the hillsides below their settlements.*

well on 2.6 cubic yards per year, the house cisterns we examined could have supplied the water needs of eight to ten people.

Estimates of the population of these villages may also be based on the amount of living space available (roofed floor area and adjacent courtyards). Assuming 12 square yards per person, the 20 Israelite houses at Ai would have been home to about six or seven people each. On this basis, we may estimate the population of Ai at not more than 150 persons. Raddana, with six houses, was much smaller, with a population of not more than 50 people.

If we were to visit Ahilud and his neighbors, another dimension of village life at Ai and Raddana would be immediately obvious. Sheep and goats, which provided a significant part of the local economy, were quartered in enclosures adjacent to the houses. Usually, the enclosure was located on the east so that the prevailing western winds would waft the odor of the sheepfold away from the living

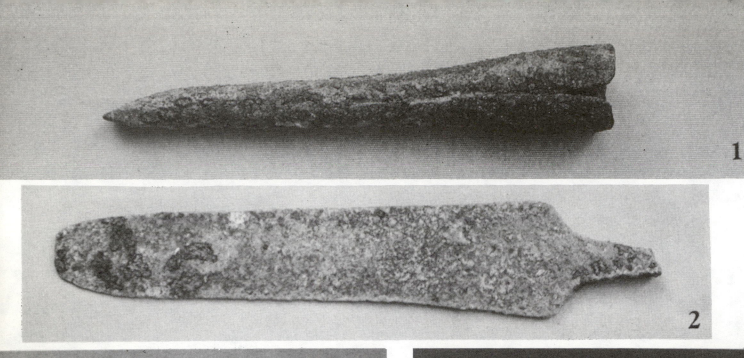

1

2

3

4

5

Artifacts from Ai and Raddana. *Life was simple in small Israelite villages during the early Iron Age, 1200 B.C. to 1050 B.C.; these remains are typical of the finds the author discovered at the Ai and Raddana excavations.*
•*A bronze dagger (1) from Ai.* •*A bronze chisel (2) from Ai, used to shape pillars for houses and to cut cisterns in the rock. These hilltop villages were far from natural springs. When each house was built, the Israelite pioneers also cut a cistern out of the rock under and next to the house to collect rainwater from the roof and from the courtyard. Apparently these settlers had brought with them an advanced knowledge of cistern building.* •*Lamp and flask (3) found in a pillar building at Ai. A characteristic Iron Age I pottery form, the flask is globular in shape and decorated with a concentric circle design.* •*A small bronze axe head (4) from Raddana, about 12 inches (30 cm) long.* •*Large grinding stone (5) found on the surface at Raddana. The smooth top of this saddle-shaped stone shows years of use. A worker would stand next to the stone and grind wheat into flour by rubbing the grains across the width of the stone with a small rock.*

quarters. Nevertheless, the odor, we would notice, was fairly constant and despite the prevailing winds penetrated the living quarters.

Perhaps we should be reminded that odors were not as offensive to people in ancient times as they are to many people in the 20th century. One implication of the meager water supply is that Ahilud and his friends did not take daily or even weekly baths. One's odor was a part of one's identity. When Esau's blind father, Isaac, said to Jacob, who was pretending to be Esau, "Come near and kiss me, my son," (Genesis 27:26), Isaac "smelled the smell of his garments" which were "the smell of a field." If Esau had taken a long shower and had washed his clothes with soap, he would have lost some of his identity!

Agriculture was the basis of the economy at Ai and Raddana. The villagers were farmers. One of the Israelite agricultural terraces at Ai was constructed on a contour of the Early Bronze Age city ruins. This agricultural terrace was first built about 1200 B.C. It was rebuilt once before the village was abandoned in about 1050 B.C. Later, the same terrace was repaired and strengthened in the Byzantine Period, and again in the Islamic Period. Most recently, it was repaired by villagers from Deir Dibwan who own and still cultivate the site. Thus, the Israelite terrace has been in continuous use from ancient to modern times. A 20th-century plow even now continues to churn up to the surface ashes and artifacts from the buried Early Bronze Age city, abandoned 4,400 years ago.

As Ahilud and his neighbors introduced cistern building to the area, so they introduced techniques of terrace building. While Israelite houses at Ai were constructed on terraces, the Early Bronze Age houses had simply followed the slope of the hillside. Agricultural terracing was simply an extension of the technique used in leveling house sites. Ahilud and his neighbors grew cereals on these terraces, as evidenced by the abundance of stone cereal-processing tools excavated at Raddana, and lying on the surface of the site. Cereal-growing on a hillside staircase of narrow terraces was an inefficient use of the land—such terraces were better suited to vine, nut and olive cultivation—but we must remember that these Israelite farmers were pioneers who probably considered mere survival a major success. Efficient use of the land would have to be developed by later generations.

A survey of settlements in Judea and Samaria during Iron Age I—the period when Ahilud lived—reveals that the hill country was literally covered by small villages like those at Ai and Raddana. Of 102 sites identified, some 90 were newly founded, indicating that Israel had its beginnings in unpretentious small villages that formed a microcosm of its society. Characteristically, the villages were unfortified and occupied by apparently peace-loving people.

Cistern with cap still in place. *Undisturbed for almost 3,000 years, this bell-shaped cistern clearly shows the strata of rock from which it was carved: thin layers of hard limestone circle the bottom of the cistern; the thick upper layers are soft Senonian chalk. This was one of three interconnected cisterns under two houses in the village of Ai. Its cap was set into the floor of one house, giving the family easy access to an almost inexhaustible water supply.*

In fact, one reason they relocated in an inhospitable environment that had not previously supported anyone was to escape conflict with the better-equipped inhabitants of the more fertile lowlands. Each village existed virtually in isolation, as an economic entity depending upon its own subsistence base rather than a market system. This seems to be reflected in the concluding statement of the Book of Judges: "In those days there was no king in Israel; every man did what was right in his own eyes" (Judges 21:25). Although there is some evidence of trading, especially in metals, which were apparently obtained in ingots and shaped into tools by the villagers, the society as a whole may be characterized as isolationist and highly individualistic. This has profound implications for our understanding of the social structure and political organization of ancient Israel.

If the village formed a microcosm within the larger hill-country settlement area, the household functioned similarly as a microcosm within the village itself. This may in part explain the conflicts that arose and that made it so difficult to establish a monarchy, as we learn from the Biblical accounts. From the beginning, Israel was self-sufficient, family-centered and characteristically independent. To preserve these qualities of life, her pioneer families settled the hilltop villages in what later came to be known as Judea and Samaria.

All photographs in this article were taken by the author.

Has Joshua's Altar Been Found on Mt. Ebal?

Adam Zertal

To appreciate fully the significance of the unique altar and cult center we are excavating on Mt. Ebal, one must first understand the archaeological context in which these discoveries were made.

We found the altar and cult center, not in the course of excavating a tell, but in the course of conducting an archaeological survey. The recent history of archaeology in Israel and in adjacent lands has seen a slow movement away from the excavation of large, well-known tells in favor of surveys of larger geographic areas. A survey not only provides a comprehensive background of an area, but it also gives the ar-

Preceding pages: *The hills and fields of Israel are dotted with stone piles (p. 76) created by farmers clearing their land. When the author explored this mound, only telltale pottery sherds scattered on the surface distinguished it from dozens of other stone-strewn mounds. But the sherds were enough to warrant archaeological investigation at the site.*

Digging beneath this particular pile of stones revealed a nine-foot-high structure dating to the early Iron Age (1220-1000 B.C.), the time archaeologists assign to the settlement of the Israelites in Canaan. In Biblical terms, this was the period when the Israelites under Joshua entered the Promised Land. According to the Bible, Joshua built an altar on Mt. Ebal, where all Israel gathered and worshipped. Could the nine-foot-high structure be Joshua's altar?

As the view of Mt. Ebal on p. 77 shows, even those people who stood not next to the altar, but on the hillside beneath it would have had a clear view of the altar and of the ritual performed on it.

chaeologist a broader understanding of individual sites discovered during the survey.

It would be difficult to find a better example to illustrate this than Mt. Ebal and the altar and cult center we found on it. To understand what we found, we must understand not only the site itself, but the mountain on which it was discovered and, indeed, how this mountain relates to the surrounding area in a particular time period.

An archaeological survey is conducted by surveyors who systematically walk over a defined area, so that trained eyes examine the surface of every square meter of land, slope after slope, ridge after ridge, field after field, searching for evidence of human occupation. All such evidence is carefully examined, recorded, mapped, and in the case of our survey, programmed into a computer. Sometimes limited excavation is undertaken at key sites. A survey is thus a slow, tedious process; paradoxically, it is at the same time exciting.

Our survey, which began in 1978, intends to cover the area allotted to the Israelite tribe of Manasseh. We expect to complete the survey by 1990.

Incidentally, the altar and cult center on Mt. Ebal have not been our only important discoveries. Another was Khirbet el Hammam, which has now been conclusively identified as ancient Narbata, where the First Jewish Revolt against Rome started in 66 A.D. And the city in the stratum just beneath Narbata has been identified as Arubboth, the third district capital of King Solomon (I Kings 4:10). But this site will be the subject of another article. Let us return to Mt. Ebal.

Our survey of Mt. Ebal itself began in February 1980, nearly two years after we began our survey of Manasseh. Ebal is a huge mountain—about six and a half square miles (18 square kilometers)—in the southern part of

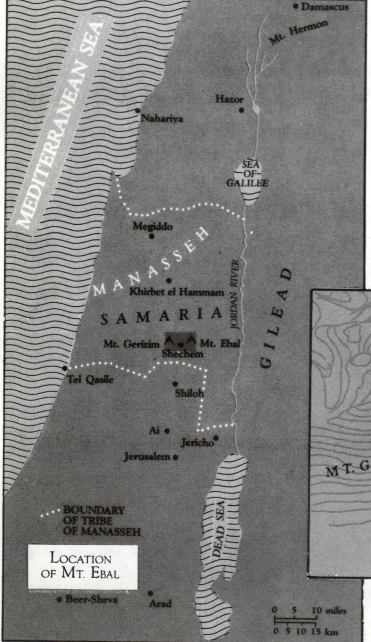

LOCATION OF MT. EBAL

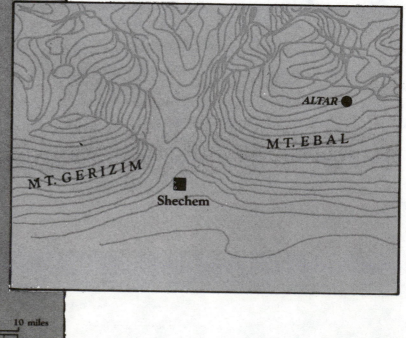

On the slope of Mt. Ebal, *the Israelite altar overlooks terraced rows of olive trees to the east. In the distance, the settlement of Elon Moreh, center, interrupts the ridge line rising toward the summit of Jebel Kebir.*

Manasseh. It is also the highest mountain in northern Samaria, rising over 3,000 feet (940 meters) above sea level. From its peak, on a clear day, we could see the snows of Mt. Hermon in the north, the mountains of Gilead across the Jordan to the east, the Mediterranean Sea to the west, and the hills surrounding Jerusalem to the south. Our survey of this mountain alone took nearly two months to complete.

Mt. Ebal, known from Deuteronomy, chapters 27 and 28, as the mountain where the curses were pronounced, is separated on the south from Mt. Gerizim, the mountain of the blessings, by the deep narrow valley of Shechem.

On a cool spring afternoon in April—April 6, 1980, to be exact—when we had nearly completed our survey of the mountain, we came upon a large heap of stones that

was not very different from the thousands of stone heaps we had already found, collected by farmers as they cleared their fields for planting. True, this stone heap was somewhat larger than the typical one, but what really distinguished it was the great quantity of pottery sherds lying around it.

We were immediately able to date these sherds to the early part of the period archaeologists call Iron Age I (1220-1000 B.C.), the period during which the Israelites entered Canaan and settled there. Iron Age I also includes the period of the Judges.

Our survey of the territory of Manasseh proved very rich in the number of sites from Iron Age I. To date, we have discovered approximately 160 sites from this period. This was hardly surprising. The Bible tells us that Israel was really born here—in the central hill country and especially near the ancient city of Shechem (Genesis 11:31, 12:6; Joshua 24).

But Mt. Ebal itself was different. Except for the heap of stones mentioned above, there was not a single site from Iron Age I on Mt. Ebal. Here, amidst evidence of dense Iron I occupation in the hill country of Manasseh, in an

79

The **rectangular altar** on Mt. Ebal was once filled with alternating layers of earth, ash and fieldstones. Here, inside the altar's exterior wall, bordering the edges of the photo, we see the excavation of the fill in progress.

When archaeologists removed that fill, they discovered an interior dividing wall, center, extending part of the way across the altar. As the archaeologists continued to excavate, they came to an ash layer (to the left of the dividing wall), which they preserved for a time. To the right of the dividing wall, they continued excavating and reached bedrock. The walls of the altar had been built directly on bedrock.

Sometime after this photo was taken, the area in front of the dividing wall was excavated, and a circular structure on bedrock was revealed (opposite).

area identified in the Bible with the new Israelite settlements, was a prominent mountain devoid of any Iron Age sites, except one—our heap of stones. We discovered more than ten other sites on Mt. Ebal, but none of these was occupied in the Iron Age.

It took us two years to raise funds to excavate the heap of stones, and to organize our expedition. But I must confess we did not rush, for we never dreamed that the site would prove to be the earliest and most complete Israelite cultic center ever discovered and the prototype of all later ones. It took us another two years and three seasons of digging to find out what we were really excavating.

The heap of stones was called *El Burnat* by the local fellahin. It means "the hat" in Arabic. It is located on the northeastern side of Mt. Ebal on a low, stony ridge, on the so-called second step of the mountain. The site is enclosed on three sides by beautiful little valleys, producing an amphitheater-like setting. Here, we began to dig with eight volunteers in September 1982.

We have completed four seasons of excavation; one in October 1982, two in 1983, and the last in the summer of 1984, and we now have a reasonably complete picture of the site.

The central feature of the site, found under the heap of stones, is a rectangular, nearly square structure. Today it stands to a height of almost nine feet. Since it is so beautifully preserved, we conclude that this is probably close to its original height. It is constructed of large, unhewn field stones. The outside measurements are 24.5 feet by 29.5 feet. Its walls are 5 feet (1.4 meters) thick. Our first season, in October 1982, concentrated on this central structure. Our initial thought was that this was a farmhouse or perhaps a watchtower. But it was different in almost every respect from the farmhouse's watchtowers we know from examples all over the country. When we reached the bottom of the structure, we immediately noticed that there was neither a floor nor an entrance. The walls were laid directly upon bedrock. Obviously, we were not dealing with a building that had been regularly lived in.

To explain the structure as a watchtower is even less satisfactory, because there is no reason for a watchtower to be here. Mt. Ebal has always been an obstacle to transportation. All transportation routes have avoided it. There is, thus, no road for a watchtower to observe. And there were no Iron Age settlements nearby.

The strangest feature of the structure was the filling, which, together with the structure, formed a kind of stage. When we excavated the fill within the structure, we found that it consisted of deliberately laid strata or layers of field stones, earth and ashes, one layer on top of the other. The earth and ashes contained pieces of pottery, all from Iron Age I, and animal bones. The ash was of different kinds of burnt wood, principally evergreen oak (*Quercus Calliprinos*).

Getting a little ahead of my story, I will tell you that the bones, which were found in such large quantities in the filling, were sent for analysis to the zoology department of the Hebrew University in Jerusalem. The bones proved to be from young male bulls, sheep, goats and fallow deer. Most of the bones had been burnt in open-flame fires of low temperature (200-600 degrees C.). Some of the bones were cut near the joints. The first chapter of Leviticus describes the animals that may be offered as sacrifices. A burnt offering must be a male without blemish (Leviticus 1:3). It may be a bull (Leviticus 1:5) or a sheep or a goat (Leviticus 1:10). The close match of the bones we found in the fill with this description in Leviticus 1 was a strong hint as to the nature of the structure we were excavating. Although fallow deer were not included in the Biblical description, they are a kosher animal that may be slaughtered and eaten, so it is possible that during the early stages of the Israelite religion, a fallow deer could also have served as an acceptable sacrifice.

But all this analysis of the bones actually occurred much later. At the end of our first season, when the winter rains began, and it turned cold on Mt. Ebal, we still had no idea what this mysterious structure was.

When we excavated under the fill, we found some curious stone-built installations. One installation consisted of a circle made of medium-sized field stones laid on bedrock and located at the exact geometric center of the structure. The outside diameter of the circle of stones was

Circular structures of small fieldstones. Constructed on bedrock at the exact center of the rectangular structure at Mt. Ebal, the circle (top) was filled with a layer of ash and animal bones. Its location and filling tell archaeologists that it was built sometime before the rectangular structure was erected and was probably used for animal sacrifice.

In the courtyards of the altar, seven other variously shaped stone installations were uncovered, such as the one (bottom) just to the man's right. Inside these installations, excavators found either complete pottery vessels, which originally probably contained offerings, or animal bones and ashes.

Behind the installation above, both the higher level and the slightly lower level ramps are visible, sloping downwards from the top left to the middle right of the photo.

81

6.5 feet. The circle of stones was filled with a thin, yellowish material that we have not yet identified. On top of this yellowish layer was a thin layer of ash and animal bones.

This installation as well as the others inside the structure were clearly used in some fire-related activity before the structure was built. It is quite obvious, now, that the installations at the bottom of the structure represent an earlier phase, and the large structure itself represents a later phase—both from the same Iron I period.

Two cross-walls divide the structure. If these cross-walls extended further, they would meet and divide the structure in two. They are too short to meet, however. One of these short walls was built over the circle installa-

The excavated altar is situated on the northeastern slope of Mt. Ebal in the Biblical territory of Manasseh. At this stage of the excavations, the structure in the center of the photo appears as a large rectangle to which a square is attached on its left. The lower horizontal "wall" of the square on the left is, in fact, a ramp leading up to the rectangular altar platform. On either side of the ramp are courtyards. These structures can be easily distinguished in the drawings on pages 86 and 87.

In this view from the southeast, a thin wall of fieldstones is barely visible to the left of the courtyards. A thicker retaining wall appears as a line separating the dark area to the right of the altar and the light-colored stone slope. Both the thin wall and the earlier, thicker wall originally looped entirely around the excavated structures to form a sacred area archaeologists call a temenos.

Although the territory of Manasseh is dotted with sites that date to Iron Age I, the period when the Israelites settled here, this structure is the only Iron Age I site on Mt. Ebal.

tion at the center of the structure.

Another curious discovery: two corners of the structure point precisely (within an error of less than one degree) to the north and the south; since the structure is rectangular, the other two corners point nearly but not exactly east and west.

Attached to the structure on the southwestern side

were two adjacent, stone-paved courtyards. In each courtyard were stone-built installations, three in one and four in the other. Some of these installations were paved with crushed chalk. They contained either ashes and animal bones, or complete pottery vessels (jars, jugs, juglets and pyxides)—one or the other, but not both.

What at first glance appears to be a wall separating the two courtyards outside the rectangular structure actually rises from the far side up to the main structure at an incline of 22 degrees. This is in fact a ramp leading up to the stage on top of the main structure. This ramp is a bit over 3 feet wide and 23 feet long. It is made of medium-sized field stones. The highest point of the ramp indicates that the main structure was one layer of stones higher than its present elevation, rising to a height of approximately 10 feet. So both the ramp and the excellent state of preservation of the structure indicate it has been preserved to nearly its full original height.

This structure, together with its ramp and courtyards and adjacent area, is surrounded by a thin elliptical wall enclosing about 37,650 square feet (3,500 square meters). We refer to this wall as the temenos wall. (*Temenos* is a Greek word meaning "an enclosed sacred place.") The temenos wall stands to a height of about one and a half feet and is made of small field stones. This wall is built on the edge of the slope. About seven feet west and down the slope from this wall is a retaining or revetment wall, which we now assume to be an earlier temenos wall, made of very large boulders. The space between the two walls is filled with field stones that support the later temenos wall.

During the last excavation season, we located the gateway through the temenos wall. It consists of two parallel walls perpendicular to the temenos wall, 23 feet apart. Three wide steps lead up the slope and through the gateway. The entrance is beautifully paved with large, flat stones, creating a very wide and precisely detailed processional entrance. No parallel to this entranceway has been found in Iron Age Israel. This beautiful entrance emphasizes the significance of Mt. Ebal as a sacred cultic center.

Within the temenos or sacred precinct but outside the main structure, we found different stone installations, in addition to those already described. They are mostly built of small flat stones and are arranged in three groups. In some we found pottery vessels but no ashes or trace of fire. Originally, the vessels probably contained some kind of offering. In other installations, we found ash and animal bones but no pottery.

A word about the pottery. In the past few years our knowledge of the pottery of this period in the area of Manasseh has increased greatly. We can now say with considerable confidence that the site on Mt. Ebal consists of two distinct levels, to which two very similar groups of pottery are related. The earlier level is from the second half of the 13th century B.C., and the later from the first

A ramp three feet wide, flanked on its left side by a slightly lower ramp, or ledge, makes a gradual ascent to the top of the Mt. Ebal altar. The ledge turns left, or north, when it meets the altar top and gradually widens on the altar's north side. In this view from the west, we see the 23-foot-long ramp and two courtyards, one on either side of the ramp.

An artist's reconstruction of the Ebal altar (opposite) shows the ramp with its ledge, the two courtyards and other features: the retaining wall around the sacred precinct and the temenos wall with its wide three-step processional entrance.

half of the 12th century B.C. Much of the later pottery is uniquely adorned on its handles with a reed-hole decoration and a "man's face" decoration. (See illustrations on p. 92). Both were discovered and studied during our survey in Manasseh, and now we consider these handles to be the clearest indication that the particular stratum in which they are found dates to the Israelite settlement period—especially in the territory of Manasseh.

About 70 percent of the pottery vessels are large collar-rim storage jars, which are known to have been the principal storage vessels of the newly settled Israelites.

Judith Dekel

About 20 percent of the pottery vessels are jugs and chalices. The balance are small vessels, mostly votive, specially made by hand for ritual use. We found only a small quantity of common domestic pottery, such as cooking pots.

In retrospect it seems strange, but the truth is that the finds I have just described did not suggest to us that the structure itself was an altar. That insight came only toward the end of the third season. Up to that time we remained in the dark as to what our mysterious structure was. We looked for parallels by which to interpret it, but could find none; it seemed our structure was unique. Then the light dawned—in a flash.

I remember it vividly. It was a Thursday, the morning of October 13, 1983. A friend of mine, a young archaeologist named David Etam visited the site, and I gave him a tour. I was explaining the site to him, especially the difficulty we were having understanding the function of the strange central structure that had been filled. David interrupted me: "Why don't you think the opposite? Why don't you think that the filling is the important part, rather than the building?"

For months we had been trying to understand the structure by thinking of the filling as secondary. We were concentrating on the outside structure. David's insight stunned me. I grabbed a Bible and opened it to Exodus 27:8, which describes the portable Tabernacle altar the Israelites were commanded to build in the wilderness: "Make it hollow, with boards. As you were shown on the mountain, so shall it be made."

Then I went to a Biblical encyclopedia and looked under "altar" and read as follows: "The Tabernacle altar is described as having four walls; it was filled with earth and stones to its full height. On this filling the fire was burned. This construction method is well-known from Assyrian altars. That is why the altar is described [in the Bible] as being ' hollow with boards ' (Biblical Encyclopedia, Vol. 4, p. 773 [Hebrew])."

Suddenly it all became clear: the filling and the structure were *together* one complete unit—an altar!

That evening, after a long day of excavating and washing pottery, I took a piece of paper and pencil and drew a rough sketch of what I thought the structure would have looked like, assuming it was an altar. I showed my sketch to one of the staff. He was dumbstruck. He ran from the room and soon returned with a Mishnah.* He opened the Mishnah to a passage in tractate *Middot* that minutely describes the Second Temple and surrounding structures. The particular edition he was using contained a drawing of the Second Temple altar as it was described in *Middot*. The drawing in the book was almost identical to the sketch I had drawn. Now it was I who was dumbstruck.

Beyond question, our site is a cultic center. The more than 50 installations containing either animal bones and ashes (the remains of sacrifices) or pottery vessels (which must have once contained offerings) seem irrefutable evidence of the cultic nature of the site. The special

(continued on p. 88)

* *Mishnah:* (from the Hebrew, to "repeat") The body of Jewish oral law, specifically, the collection of oral laws compiled by Rabbi Judah the Prince in the second century.

Mt. Ebal Altar Part of a 2,000-Year-Old Architectural Tradition

Huge stepped structures called ziggurats are well-known from the third and second millennia B.C. in Mesopotamia. One of the most famous examples is the ziggurat of Ur (below), built about 2100 B.C. Originally, this ziggurat had four stages or steps; each of the upper three was smaller than the one below. A stepped ramp

© GEORG GERSTER/PHOTO RESEARCHERS

ascended to all the stages. The first, tallest stage and its steep ramp, seen here, have been restored by the Iraqi authorities to their original size. Author Zertal suggests that the stepped ledges and ramp of the Mt. Ebal altar reflect architectural traditions of Mesopotamian ziggurats. The altars of Solomon and Ezekiel described in the Bible also resemble Mesopotamian ziggurats. However, the design of the distinctive Mesopotamian ramp was modified in the later Israelite versions. The Israelite ramps were less steep than those of the Ur ziggurat and, as described in Exodus, they did not have steps: "Neither shalt thou go up by steps unto mine altar . . . " (Exodus 20:26).

The persistence for more than 2,000 years of this architectural tradition of ledges and a ramp is suggested by a drawing (right) based on a description in tractate *Middot* of the Mishnah, a collection of oral Jewish laws compiled in the second century A.D. The drawing shows the first-century B.C. altar from the Jerusalem Temple. The similarity of this drawing to the artist's reconstruction of the Mt. Ebal altar is dramatically evident. A plan (lower right) showing an overhead view of the Mt. Ebal altar also indicates the ramp and ledges. In all three renderings, a lower ledge colored light gray surrounds three sides of the top of the altar and continues as a narrower, lower ramp along the side of the broad, main ramp. The rectangular structure and the main ramp leading up to it are colored dark gray.

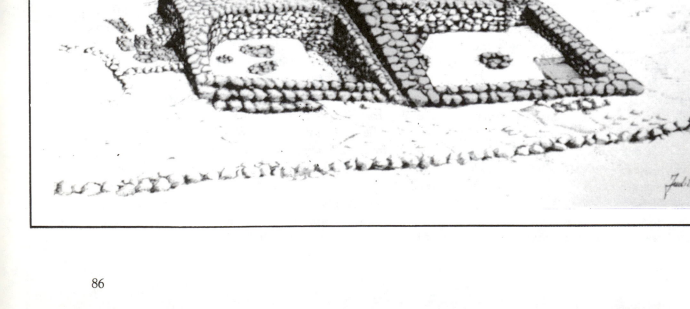

Judith Dekel

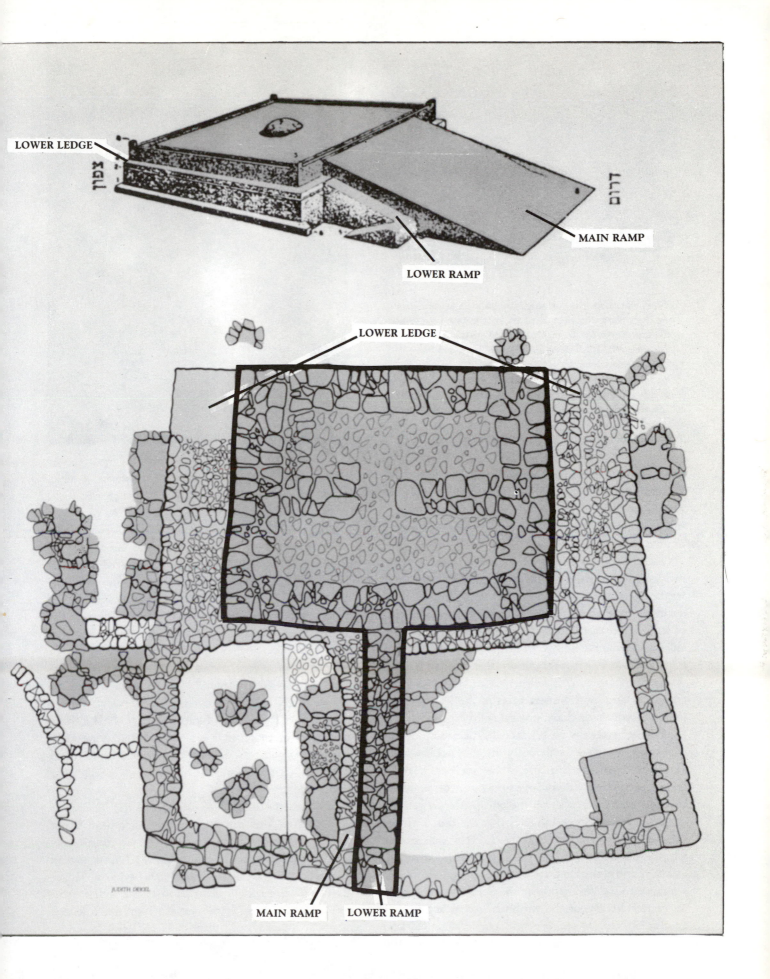

LOWER LEDGE

אבן

נבד

דרך

MAIN RAMP

LOWER RAMP

LOWER LEDGE

JUDITH DEKEL

MAIN RAMP   LOWER RAMP

Animal sacrifices were made on this Israelite altar from Beer-Sheva (above), and incense was burned on a much smaller altar from Israelite Megiddo (right). Unlike the Mt. Ebal altar, both of these altars have horns at their corners.

The Beer-Sheva altar stands three cubits high (5 1/4 feet), like the altar described in Exodus 27:1, on which the Israelites offered sacrifices when they were camped in Sinai. The Megiddo incense altar is only 27½ inches high and 16 inches square.

nature of the bones further supports this conclusion. The isolated location of the site on a prominent mountain further strengthens the case. But the most striking feature of the site is the central structure, which, it seems, must now be interpreted as an altar.

One curious feature of our structure provides well-nigh conclusive evidence that it is an altar. About three feet below the top of the altar is the top of a thin wall that encircles three sides of the altar, in effect creating a kind of ledge attached to the outer wall of the altar. As this ledge goes from the northwest side to the southwest side, it gradually widens from about two feet until it reaches a width of 7.5 feet. This ledge also curves around the corner formed by the intersection of the altar and the ramp and continues down one side of the ramp.

There is absolutely no functional explanation for this thin wall or ledge. Obviously it was not built to strengthen the main structure, whose walls are made of large stones. These walls of large stones were certainly not supported by a thin wall on the outside. Moreover, the archaeological evidence indicates that the thin wall was built at the same time as the thick inner wall against which it leans; the thin wall was not a later addition.

The puzzle of this thin wall or ledge was again solved by reference to the description of the Second Temple altar in tractate *Middot* of the Mishnah. According to this description, the square Second Temple altar had two ledges surrounding it. The base of the altar was 32 cubits wide. One cubit from the base, the altar narrowed to 30 cubits, leaving a two-cubit ledge around it, or as the Mishnah calls this ledge, a "surround." Five cubits higher, the altar again narrowed to 28 cubits, leaving another two-cubit ledge or surround. The ledge created by the second narrowing curved around and down the ramp leading up to the altar. The Mishnah calls it a "small ramp," made for the priest to ascend to the "surround."

This is exactly what we have at our site, except that there is only one ledge or step instead of two. The step or ledge of our altar even curves around and goes down the ramp, thus creating a beautiful "small ramp" attached to the main one.

Of course, the Second Temple altar was built a thousand years or more after our altar, but it now seems beyond doubt that the Second Temple altar, as described in *Middot*, preserved ancient traditions of Israelite altar construction.

Although the Biblical description of the Tabernacle altar built by the Israelites in the wilderness is not absolutely clear on this point, there is a hint that it, too, was constructed with a narrower block set upon a wider base. The Bible speaks of this altar's having a "ledge" (Exodus 27:5). Ezekiel's description of the future Temple's altar is clearer. It will have a number of ledges, creating a stepped tower (Ezekiel 43:14).

As early as 1920, the great American archaeologist William F. Albright suggested that the Israelite altar had a Mesopotamian origin, ultimately based on the well-known ziggurat, a huge multi-stepped temple that some have suggested is the model for the Tower of Babel. The Bible tells us that the Judean king Ahaz, in the latter part of the eighth century B.C., ordered a new altar to be built for the Jerusalem Temple, based on the plan of an altar he had seen in Damascus, where he had met the Assyrian king Tiglath-Pileser III (2 Kings 16:10-16). This, too, suggests Mesopotamian influence on the Israelite altar.

Sacred traditions tend to endure. The two ledges on the Second Temple altar as described in the Mishnah may well preserve a very ancient tradition. And the ledge surrounding much of our altar on Mt. Ebal may also reflect this tradition of the Mesopotamian altar built up with ledges.

Yet another detail of our altar suggests its Mesopotamian roots. The four corners of our altar point north, south, east and west. In Mesopotamia, all sacred structures were oriented so that each corner was directed to a point on the compass. By contrast, the Second Temple was oriented so that its sides, not its corners, faced the four directions of the compass. The Temple altar had this same orientation. We are not told the orientation of the First Temple—Solomon's Temple—but it, too, probably faced east. The altar associated with Solomon's Temple doubtless followed the same orientation as the Temple itself. Why this difference in orientation between our Mt. Ebal altar and the Temple altars? Perhaps altars associated with temples were oriented differently from open-air altars not associated with temples. Other explanations, however, are also possible.

At this point, it may be instructive to consider what we know about altars from the Bible and how our altar illuminates or is illuminated by these passages.

Altars are frequently mentioned in the Bible. There are two principal types: the small incense altar and the large altar for burnt offerings. Archaeologists have uncovered many incense altars. Each is square, carved from a single stone and small—never measuring more than about a foot and a half in any direction. A depression on the top held the burning incense presumably used in the temple. Some incense altars have horns at the upper corners; others do not.

The burnt offering altar was much larger and was used for animal sacrifices. Animal sacrifice was at the core of Israelite cultic activity. Comparatively few burnt offering altars have been found in archaeological excavations in Israel, however. As we shall see, our Mt. Ebal altar is one of only three Israelite burnt offering altars ever discovered, and of these ours is both the oldest and the most complete.

There seem to have been two kinds of burnt offering altars—one associated with a temple where, in the Near Eastern religious purview, God dwelled. The other might be called an independent burnt offering altar, because it was not associated with a temple.

Although the subject is not free from controversy, it appears that the independent altar is part of what the Bible describes as a *bamah* or high place, probably an open-air cultic center where sacrifices were offered. For example, in 1 Kings 3:4, we learn that King Solomon went to Gibeon to sacrifice there, for that was the great high place (*bamah*); on that altar Solomon presented a thousand burnt offerings. There God appeared to Solomon in a dream.

If this analysis is correct, our Mt. Ebal altar is an independent altar (not associated with a temple), the central structure in a *bamah*.

It might be helpful briefly to place our altar in a general context of ancient Near Eastern altars that have been found throughout the region—in ancient Mesopotamia, Syria, Egypt, Anatolia, Greece, Cyprus and the Aegean Islands. In Israel, altars have been found from the Early Bronze Age (3150-2200 B.C.) to the late Iron Age (800-586 B.C.). From the Bronze Age, altars have been found at Megiddo, Shechem, Hazor and Nahariya. From the Iron Age, a Philistine altar was found at Tel Qasile, and Israelite altars were discovered at Tel Arad and Beer-Sheva.

From this very considerable archaeological material, we get some idea of what ancient altars were like, but only a partial idea as to the form of an Israelite altar. In general, Near Eastern burnt offering altars, like our Mt. Ebal altar, are square or rectangular structures of considerable size. They are built of worked and squared ashlar blocks. Sometimes they have horns at the upper corners (as at Beer-Sheva and Kition in Cyprus), and sometimes they do not (as at Arad).

Altars were ascended by stairs—at least this is true in cases where the means of ascent have been preserved. Unfortunately, until now, no ascent to an Israelite altar has been discovered in a preserved state, but the ramp on our Mt. Ebal altar indicates a strict adherence to the law in Exodus 20:26, which requires a ramp rather than steps.

In many cases, Near Eastern altars are stepped; that is, they are built in square or rectangular layers, each one higher and smaller than the one beneath. This is especially the case in Mesopotamia, Anatolia and Syria.

Some altars, like ours, have outer stone frames and are filled on the inside with earth or pebbles. This is true of altars in Greece and Assyria, and it may also be true of the Israelite altar at Arad. We cannot be sure about the Arad

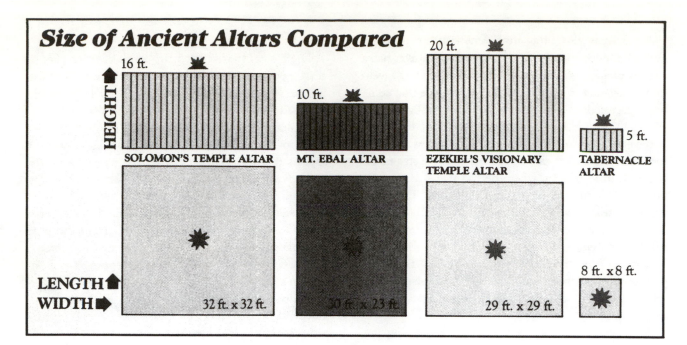

Size of Ancient Altars Compared

HEIGHT

16 ft. — SOLOMON'S TEMPLE ALTAR

10 ft. — MT. EBAL ALTAR

20 ft. — EZEKIEL'S VISIONARY TEMPLE ALTAR

5 ft. — TABERNACLE ALTAR

LENGTH / **WIDTH**

32 ft. x 32 ft. — SOLOMON'S TEMPLE ALTAR

30 ft. x 23 ft. — MT. EBAL ALTAR

29 ft. x 29 ft. — EZEKIEL'S VISIONARY TEMPLE ALTAR

8 ft. x 8 ft. — TABERNACLE ALTAR

altar because a section has never been cut through it that would reveal what lies inside the outer stone frame.

The size of ancient Near Eastern altars varies from about 3 feet on a side (Alalakh) to about 20 feet on a side (temple 2A at Shechem). It is difficult to tell their original heights because they are not usually well preserved. Before our altar was discovered, the height of the highest preserved altar was about five feet.

Our altar fits well within the pattern established by these other altars, although it is the best preserved and stands almost to its original height (ten feet). Our altar apparently did not have horns, or they were not preserved.

Every other ancient altar that has been discovered thus far, however, was connected with a temple, or as at Beer-Sheva, was in a city where we may suppose a temple existed in connection with the altar (2 Kings 23:8). With the possible exception noted below,* our altar alone seems to have been an independent altar in the country-side, not associated with a temple or a settlement. This is probably because the Mt. Ebal altar and its associated cult site were built at a very early period in the development of Israelite cult and religion; at that time, there was no temple. Moreover, the Mt. Ebal cult center lasted for only a relatively short time. It is unlikely that a temple could

---

* The possible exception is an open-air cult center also from the period of the Judges. This site was found very recently. It was investigated by Amihai Mazar, who has already written a report for **BAR** readers ("Bronze Bull Found in Israelite 'High Place' from the Time of the Judges," September/October 1983). This cult center was built on a mountain, as was our site. It was surrounded by an elliptical wall, as was our site. But if it had an altar, it was preserved only in a single stone about four feet long, three feet high and about one and three-fourths feet thick.

develop in such a short time. Even at Shiloh, which was the site of the successor to the Mt. Ebal cult center, no temple was built.

It may be interesting to compare the size of our altar to other altars mentioned in the Bible—the Tabernacle altar in the wilderness, the altar in Solomon's Temple, and the altar associated with Ezekiel's future Temple. As the table (above) shows, the Tabernacle altar was much smaller than the other two; the Mt. Ebal altar is closer to the larger ones.

While the Biblical altars are all square, ours is slightly rectangular. Many other Near Eastern altars are rectangular, and it may be that independent Israelite altars not associated with temples were rectangular rather than square.

The Bible makes it clear that there were many independent Israelite altars. During the religious reforms of King Hezekiah (eighth century B.C.) and King Josiah (seventh century B.C.), these outlying ritual centers were suppressed and destroyed, in order to centralize the cult in Jerusalem.

In terms of height, and in terms of width and length, our altar is closer to the altar in Solomon's Temple and in Ezekiel's visionary Temple than to the Tabernacle altar.

Incidentally, the Second Temple altar was much larger than all these altars. Although slightly different figures are given for the Second Temple altar in the various sources—the Mishnah, Josephus, and the newly published Temple Scroll from the Dead Sea caves—all agree that it was much larger than the altars described in the Bible.

After discussing all these technical data, important as they are, and proving that we are dealing here with a burnt offering altar in an Israelite cult center, we come now to the most intriguing question: Is this altar related to the Biblical traditions which describe Joshua's building of an altar on Mt. Ebal?

The building of an altar on Mt. Ebal is described in two places in the Bible, once in Deuteronomy, when the Israelites are commanded to build the altar after they pass into the Promised Land, and again in the book of Joshua, when the altar is actually built.

In Deuteronomy 27:1-10, Moses, in some of the most dramatic and awe-inspiring words in the Bible, commands the people to build the altar:

Now Moses and the elders of Israel commanded the people, saying, "Keep all the commandments which I command you this day. And on the day you pass over the Jordan to the land which the Lord your God gives you, you shall set up large stones, and plaster them with plaster; and you shall write upon them all the words of this law, when you pass over to enter the land which the Lord your God gives you, a land flowing with milk and honey, as the Lord, the God of your fathers, has promised you. And when you have passed over the Jordan, you shall set up these stones, concerning which I command you this day, on Mount Ebal, and you shall plaster them with plaster. And there you shall build an altar to the Lord your God, an altar of stones; you shall lift up no iron tool upon them. You shall build an altar to the Lord your God of unhewn stones; and you shall offer burnt offerings on it to the Lord your God; and you shall sacrifice peace offerings, and shall eat there; and you shall rejoice before the Lord your God. And you shall write upon the stones all the words of this law very plainly." And Moses and the Levitical priests said to all Israel, "Keep silence and hear, O Israel: this day you have become the nation of the Lord your God. You shall therefore obey the voice of the Lord your God, keeping his commandments and his statutes, which I command you this day."

With this commandment, Israel has become the people of the Lord.

The ceremony on Mt. Ebal is described in Joshua 8:30-35:

Then Joshua built an altar in Mount Ebal to the Lord, the God of Israel, as Moses the servant of the Lord had commanded the people of Israel, as it is written in the book of the law of Moses, "an altar of unhewn stones, upon which no man has lifted an iron tool"; and they offered on it burnt offerings to the Lord, and sacrificed peace offerings. And there, in the presence of the people of Israel, he wrote upon the stones a copy of the law of Moses, which he had written. And all Israel, sojourner as well as homeborn, with their elders and officers and their judges, stood on opposite sides of the ark before the Levitical priests who carried the ark of the covenant of the Lord, half of them in front of Mount Gerizim and half of them in front of Mount Ebal, as Moses the servant of the Lord had commanded at the first, that they should bless the people of Israel. And afterward he read all the words of the law, the blessing and the curse, according to all that is written in the book of the law. There was not a word of all that Moses commanded which Joshua did not read before all the assembly of Israel, and the women, and the little ones, and the sojourners who lived among them.

In Deuteronomy 27:11-13, we are told that half the tribes are to stand on Mt. Gerizim for the blessing of the people, and half on Mt. Ebal for the curses. The curses are recited in Deuteronomy 27:14-26; then in Deuteronomy 28:1-14 come the blessings, followed by additional curses in Deuteronomy 28:15-68.

If the people follow the Lord's commandments, they will be blessed; if not, they will be cursed. As foretold in Deuteronomy 11:22-29:

If you diligently keep all these commandments that I now charge you to observe, by loving the Lord your God, by conforming to his ways and by holding fast to him, the Lord will drive out all these nations before you and you shall occupy the territory of nations greater and more powerful than you. Every place where you set the soles of your feet shall be yours. Your borders shall run from the wilderness to the Lebanon and from the River, the river Euphrates, to the western sea. No man will be able to withstand you; the Lord your God will put the fear and dread of you upon the whole land on which you set foot, as he promised you. Understand that this day I offer you the choice of a blessing and a curse. The blessing will come if you listen to the commandments of the Lord your God which I give you this day, and the curse if you do not listen to the commandments of the Lord your God but turn aside from the way that I command you this day and follow other gods whom you do not know. When the Lord your God brings you into the land which you are entering to occupy, there on Mount Gerizim you shall pronounce the blessing and on Mount Ebal the curse.

After these references to Mt. Ebal, the name Ebal is never mentioned again in the entire Bible.

A question may arise concerning the identification of our Mt. Ebal altar with the one described in the Bible because our altar is not on the very peak of Mt. Ebal. Mt. Ebal descends in what may be described as four very wide terraces or steps. Our altar is on the second step from the

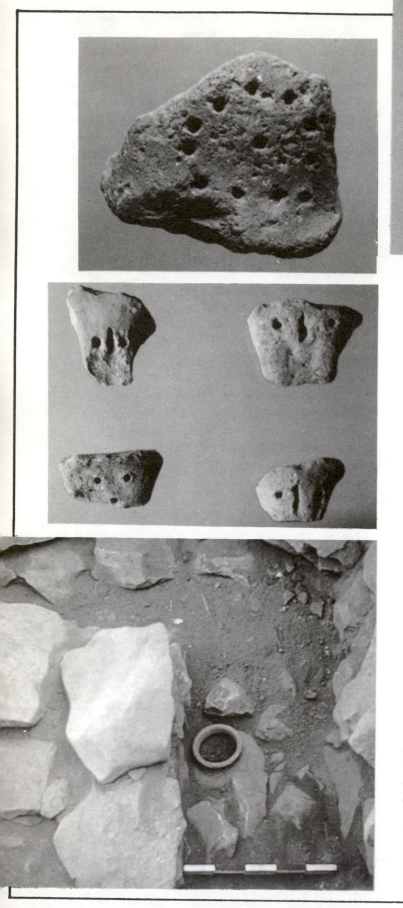

Evidence for Dating the Mt. Ebal Altar

In the fill of the Mt. Ebal altar, along with bones and pottery sherds, we found an Egyptian-style scarab (above). Within an oval frame, the scarab displays a geometrical pattern consisting of a four-petal rosette and, between the petals, four branches. From each branch comes a uraeus (an Egyptian cobra).

This scarab is very rare; only five known parallels exist—one from Egypt, three from Israel and one from Cyprus. All these parallels date this special find to the period between the reigns of Ramses II (19th dynasty; 13th century B.C.) and Ramses III (20th dynasty; beginning of 12th century B.C.).

This scarab fixes the earliest date for the construction of the Mt. Ebal altar; it could not have been built before the 13th century B.C. Moreover, because this scarab comes from a stratigraphically sealed locus, together with a well-dated pottery sequence, it has even greater chronological significance—it gives us an approximate date for the original erection of the altar and cultic center.

Other distinctive pottery forms buttress the argument for a 13th-12th century B.C. date for the Ebal altar. Collar-rim jars were commonly used storage vessels during the settlement period and are dated by archaeologists to the 13th through the 11th centuries B.C.

Excavators discovered a collar-rim jar (bottom left) in a circular stone installation in the altar's courtyard. Since they found no ashes in the vessel, they assume that it once contained a non-burnt offering.

Pottery handles decorated with designs of reed-holes (top left) and a "man's face" (center left) were discovered during the survey of the territory of Manasseh. The clearly recognizable handles are now used as indicators that the strata in which they appear date from the Israelite settlement period.—A.Z.

top. Moreover, Mt. Gerizim cannot be seen from our site.

On the other hand, the Bible itself hints that Joshua's altar was not built at the top of the mountain. In Joshua 8:30, we read that Joshua built the altar *b*-Mt. Ebal. The Hebrew letter *beth* (pronounced "b") usually means "in" rather than "on top of." This might suggest that the altar was not built on the top of Mt. Ebal. In Deuteronomy 27:4, where the instructions are given to build the Mt. Ebal altar, we find the same verbal construction, with a *beth*.

By contrast, in Deuteronomy 11:29, where the instructions for pronouncing the curses are given, we are told that they are to be pronounced *al* Mt. Ebal, that is, *on* Mt. Ebal.

For a Biblical archaeologist, a comparison between the Bible and archaeological finds is always inspiring, but like a mine field as well. Is the cultic center altar unearthed by us on Mt. Ebal the one mentioned in the Bible? How can one judge such a fundamental issue? What criteria should we use for such a judgment?

The main problem, I suppose, is that archaeology has not always corroborated the Biblical stories of Joshua's time. At Jericho, Ai, Arad, and other sites, archaeology does not corroborate what the Bible tells us. No evidence from the period of Joshua has been found at these sites.

With respect to the Mt. Ebal altar, however, all the scientific evidence fits very well with the Biblical descrip-tion. The three main factors that correlate precisely are the period, the nature of the site, and the location. True, no inscriptions have been found as yet. But apart from that one point, it may be said with all scientific restraint that there must be a connection between the strong, important and authentic Biblical tradition that identifies Mt. Ebal as a central Israelite cultic center and the gathering place of the Israelite tribes, on the one hand, and the site unearthed by us, on the other. There are still debates about most of the issues: Who was Joshua? When did the Israelite tribes enter the Land? Did they enter from the east, as the Bible states?

But this rare case, where Biblical tradition and concrete archaeological evidence coincide, cannot be ignored. We have on Mt. Ebal not only the complete prototype of an Israelite altar, but moreover, a site that might prove to be directly related to the Biblical traditions concerning Joshua's building of an altar on Mt. Ebal.

We have a few more seasons of work at least before any further conclusions can be drawn. Certainty as yet eludes us; all the evidence has still not been analyzed. For the moment, we leave the reader to reach his or her own conclusion. As scientists, we must say that the case has not yet been proven.

Unless otherwise noted, all photographs in this article were taken by M. Weinberg.

AHARON KEMPINSKI

Joshua's Altar— An Iron Age I Watchtower

I vividly remember a hot day in late October 1982—October 27, to be exact—when, with two other archaeologists, I first visited Adam Zertal's excavation on Mt. Ebal. Even then, during the first season of excavation, rumors had spread that Zertal had found "Joshua's altar." It seems that from the beginning Zertal really thought he had discovered "Joshua's altar." By the time we visited the site, notices had already appeared in the Israeli daily press that the altar that Joshua had built on Mt. Ebal, according to Joshua 8:30-35, was being excavated.

Text continues on p. 96

Excavated remains on Mt. Ebal from the air. It's simply an old farm house— not an altar—says archaeologist Aharon Kempinski of this stone structure near the summit of Mt. Ebal, in the Biblical territory of Manasseh. The excavator of the Iron Age I structure, Adam Zertal, contends that this is an altar, perhaps the altar built by Joshua, where all of Israel assembled to hear the words of the law (Joshua 8:30-35).

One element in Zertal's identification is the ramp (arrow) leading up to the top of the structure. Kempinski explains the ramp as an

94

internal house wall that deteriorated most toward its outer end and least toward its inner end, thereby appearing as a slope. Kempinski observes that the dull gray color of the lowest end of the wall, on the left, is the result of the long exposure that led to its deterioration. The higher end of the wall, where it was buried and protected from weathering and loss of stones, retains its bright hue.

For a detailed description of the square structure, according to both Kempinski and Zertal, turn to pages 98-99.

ADAM ZERTAL

How Can Kempinski Be So Wrong!

Although Dr. Kempinski's article begins with archaeology, it is quite obvious that his ideological attitude preceded his purely archaeological examination. His ideas about the dating of Deuteronomy and Joshua, together with his "new" ideas concerning how the Pentateuch was "corrected" by the Jews to refer to Mt. Ebal rather than, as the Samaritans originally had it, to Mt. Gerizim—all point to a very clear preconception of what *ought* to be found on Mt. Gerizim and on Mt. Ebal. Despite all this, I shall deal first with Kempinski's archaeological arguments:

Text continues on p. 101

Joshua's Altar—An Iron Age I Watchtower

Continued from p. 94

As we* climbed to the isolated excavation area on the ridge of a terrace far from any road or track, Zertal explained to us how he had come to the site: He was conducting an archaeological survey for his Ph.D. dissertation under the direction of Professor Moshe Kochavi of Tel Aviv University. In the course of the survey, Zertal had found a square structure, about 25 feet by 25 feet. Zertal described the wall surrounding the square structure as a *temenos*** wall, thus implying the cultic nature of the site. Some Iron Age I (1200-1000 B.C.) pottery sherds suggested that the square structure dated to the period of the Israelite settlement in Canaan.†

When we arrived at the site and walked around it, it appeared to us to be the remains of a small settlement enclosed by a wall. In the center of the village was the major structure—a building or the base of a tower. Zertal had already identified this structure as an "altar." Only half of it had been excavated at the time. A large collar-rim pithos, or storage jar, typical of the Israelite settlement period, appeared sunk into the floor *inside* the structure. This pithos was resting against a small, thin wall (see plan, p. 98).

After visiting a newly excavated site, I usually write for my own files a short report with some sketches of what I saw, since it often takes years before anything is published. This habit sometimes proves very useful, and it certainly did in this case, for I drew the pithos *in situ*. In the report published in **BAR**, nothing is mentioned about this pithos *inside* the structure.†† One would hardly expect to find a whole storage jar inside an altar—if it were an altar!

When we looked at a vertical section inside the half-excavated structure—that is, at a vertical wall of unexcavated strata that preserved the history of the fill inside the structure—we did *not* see what Zertal would later describe in **BAR** as "deliberately laid strata . . . of stones, earth and ashes." As a matter of fact, the "fill" inside the structure looked more like the normal debris or remains usually found after a building has been destroyed.

My impression, looking at the structure, was that it had two rooms, with storage installations in each room at opposite corners.

Now having read Zertal's account in **BAR**, and after re-reading my notes, I am more than ever convinced that what Zertal found on Mt. Ebal is simply a three-phase village from Iron Age I, the so-called Israelite settlement period. These three-phase villages are not at all rare during Iron Age I; on the contrary, they are quite common between about 1230 and 1000 B.C.

To describe the three phases of this settlement, I have simply taken apart the drawing that appears on page 87 of Zertal's **BAR** article, dividing it into the three phases. These three phases are shown in the drawings on page 98.

In the first phase of the settlement, seminomadic peasants occupied the site. They lived in tents or huts. Few architectural remains from these structures have survived. The principal occupational remains are pits, bins and small installations.

In the second phase, more stable habitation units were built. At this time, a two-room or perhaps a three-room house was built in the center of the settlement (the part shown in blue on Zertal's plan). The settlement was also enclosed with a wall at this time. (A similar wall enclosed a similar ancient settlement recently excavated by Amihai Mazar at Giloh, two miles south of Jerusalem; see page 100.)

The third phase of the settlement followed the destruction of phase 2, perhaps by the Canaanites from nearby Shechem or possibly by the Philistines who invaded the area in about 1070 B.C. Or was this phase destroyed in an Israelite intertribal clash? In any event, the phase 2 settlement was destroyed, thus demonstrating the need to improve security with a watchtower. In phase 3, a watchtower was built; debris was probably added to the inside of the phase 2 building to create a podium for the watchtower—a common feature of Iron Age watchtowers as, for example, at Giloh.* The remains of the phase 2 building were also used for the courtyard of the watchtower.

This phase 3 structure is what Zertal identified as an altar!

Phases (or strata) similar to phase 1 and 2 at Mt. Ebal are very well attested at most of the tribal settlements from this period. This pattern was recently found at the Israelite settlement of Izbet Sartah (strata 3 and 2, de-

---

* Benjamin Mazar and Amihai Mazar. The views expressed here are mine alone, however.

** A *temenos* is an enclosure wall of a temple or holy area.

† "Has Joshua's Altar Been Found on Mt. Ebal?" Adam Zertal, **BAR**, January/February 1985 [p. 76].

†† I wonder if this pithos is the one pictured at the bottom of page 92 of Zertal's article and reprinted here on p. 97.

---

* I would like to thank Amihai Mazar for allowing me to publish this evidence here. A report on the Iron Age I Giloh tower will be published soon.

A storage jar, called a pithos, found inside the square structure on Mt. Ebal. Kempinski argues that this jar's presence demonstrates that the square structure was a typical Israelite house—with storage in the corners. An altar, he says, would not contain a storage jar.

scribed several years ago in **BAR**.*) The same pattern has also been found at other excavations, such as Hazor (strata XII and XI), Tell Beit Mirsim (strata B3 and B2), and Tell Masos (strata IIIB and IIIA-II), an excavation I directed in the Negev.**

Zertal relies on the fact that his Mt. Ebal site is the "only settlement on Mt. Ebal of that period" when he suggests that he has found a cult site with a huge central altar. But there is nothing unusual about the existence of a single settlement on Mt. Ebal. Zertal found ten settlements from other periods on Mt. Ebal spread over many centuries. Since he does not specify to which periods these other settlements belong, his comparison (ten against one) is useless. Are there other periods when there was only one settlement on Mt. Ebal? Or two? Even today, most of Mt. Ebal serves as an agricultural or herding area for Arab peasants. A single settlement in such an area should not be surprising.

As for the tower in phase 3, we have an almost identical example at Giloh. After the Giloh settlement was enclosed with a protective wall and houses were built adjacent to the wall, a tower was built on a filled rampart. Still later, during Iron Age II, another tower was built nearby.

Once we understand this general settlement pattern, it becomes easy to explain most of the so-called cultic features Zertal claims to have found. In fact, they can be explained in very simple, secular terms. I will discuss here only the most outstanding cultic features.

Zertal sees a ramp leading up to the "altar." In this perception, he relies on a Mishnaic interpretation of Exodus 20:23 (20:26 in Hebrew). In the Biblical verse God

instructs Moses to tell the Israelites, "Do not ascend My altar by steps (ma'alot), that your nakedness may not be exposed upon it." Whether or not ma'alot means steps is unclear from the Biblical text alone. More than a thousand years later, during the time when the Mishnah† was written (c. 200 A.D.), this verse was interpreted to require a ramp instead of steps. But, in fact, during the First Temple period, steps led up to temple altars.†† For example, steps lead up to the altar at Tel Dan* and extend along the altar's entire width.

But Zertal's architectural evidence does not qualify as either steps or a ramp. His "ramp" is slightly over three feet wide. This would be a dangerous passageway whether a ramp or steps. Imagine climbing up to the altar by so narrow a passage, especially if one was taking a sheep, goat or cow up with him.

In fact, Zertal's ramp is nothing more than a wall of a room or courtyard that slopes down the hill. The remains of this wall slope down from the tower wall because the maximum height was preserved nearest the tower wall; the closer the wall was to the tower wall, the more it was protected by the debris from the destroyed tower. This is a common phenomenon in archaeological excavations. Indeed, in the picture on page 82 of Zertal's **BAR** article, one can see that the part of the wall (Zertal's "ramp") closer to the tower wall has a yellowish color. The debris from the destroyed tower covered and preserved this part of the wall to nearly its original height and preserved its color as well. The part of the wall (Zertal's "ramp") further from the tower wall is mostly whitish because it was exposed even before the excavation began and therefore had been eroding over the centuries, creating, for Zertal, the appearance of a ramp. Because the wall originally was built down a slope, it eroded more as it extended down the slope. This wall is most assuredly *not* a three-foot-wide ramp.

Next let us look at Zertal's "cultic installations." According to Zertal, there were round cultic installations under his "altar." I am ready to suppose there was cultic activity here before the building and the tower were constructed. Such cultic activity would hardly be surprising. Evidence of cultic activities in Iron Age I was found in the cult room at Ai and at the so-called bull site

---

* "An Israelite Village from the Days of the Judges," Moshe Kochavi and Aaron Demsky, **BAR**, September/October 1978.

** "Israelite Conquest or Settlement? New Light from Tell Masos," Aharon Kempinski, **BAR**, September 1976.

† The Mishnah (from the Hebrew, to "repeat") is the body of Jewish oral law, specifically, the body of oral laws compiled by Rabbi Judah the Prince in the second century.

†† See M. Haran in *Encyclopedia Biblica*, s.v. "Altar" (in Hebrew); and D. Conrad *Studien zum Altargesetz* (Marburg, 1968), pp. 123-139.

* John C. H. Laughlin, "The Remarkable Discoveries at Tel Dan," **BAR**, September/October 1981.

Text continues on p. 100

Kempinski Takes the "Altar" Apart

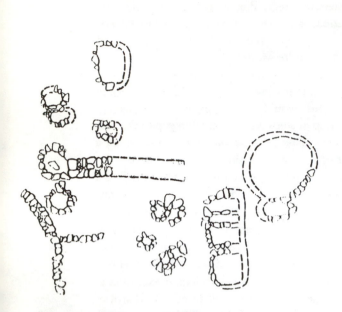

Phase 1—Pits and Silos

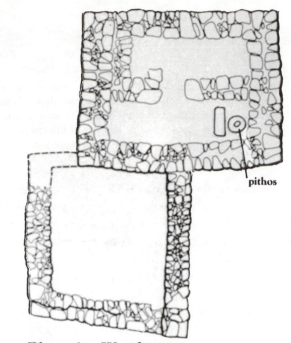

pithos

Phase 3—Watchtower

Israeli archaeologist Aharon Kempinski contends that the square structure and its installations that Adam Zertal identified as an altar (plan, opposite, bottom) actually reflect three separate and successive Iron Age I settlement phases: first, pits and silos; second, a two- or three-room farm house; and finally, a watchtower.

The phase 2 house was destroyed in the 11th century B.C., says Kempinski—perhaps by Canaanites or perhaps in an attack by another Israelite tribe. Phase 3 settlers, Kempinski suggests, then created a defensive watchtower (above) by filling in the destroyed house to use it as a base for the watchtower. The pithos that Kempinski saw within the structure is located in his phase 3 plan.

But the excavator of the square structure, Adam Zertal, says that the cultic nature of the Mt. Ebal site cannot be denied. The dark gray walls (opposite), according to Zertal, are part of an altar platform for burning sacrifices and a three-foot-wide ramp leading up to it. He maintains that the light gray structures, built at the same time as the dark gray, are two courtyards and a lower ramp that runs alongside the higher ramp and then turns into a ledge surrounding the altar platform (artist's reconstruction, opposite, top).

Although Zertal disagrees with Kempinski's contention that the circular installations (above left and around the outside and in the open areas at bottom, opposite) are non-cultic pits and silos, Zertal does attribute these installations to an earlier phase than that of the altar.

Zertal denies that any destruction occurred at Mt. Ebal in phase 2 or at any other time; he says that there was never a need for a watchtower at this cult site.

Phase 2—Farm House

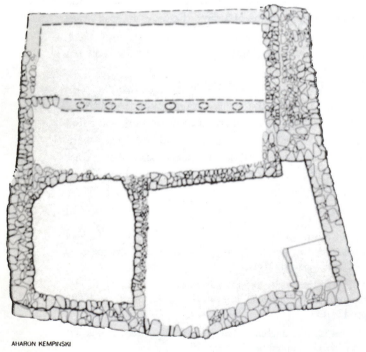

AHARON KEMPINSKI

Zertal's Altar Reconstruction

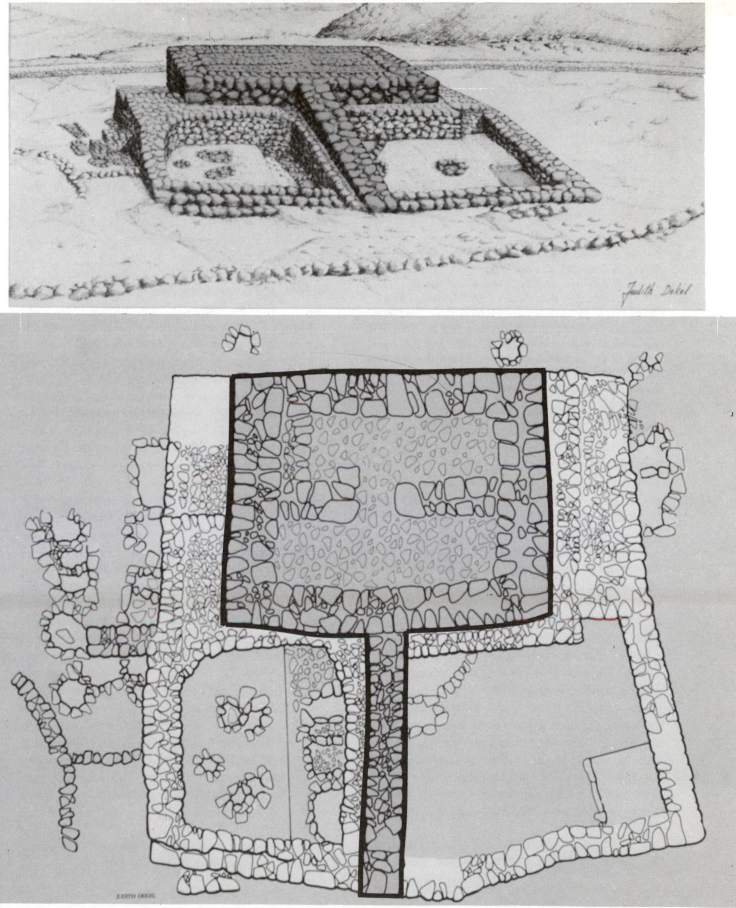

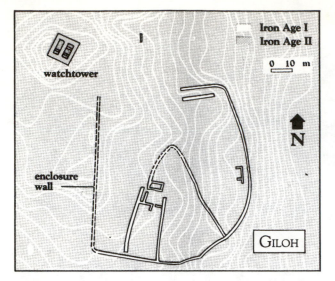

Giloh. *According to Aharon Kempinski, this plan of Giloh, an Iron Age site near Jerusalem, shows a square structure, top, left, similar in shape and details to the Mt. Ebal structure that Adam Zertal identifies as an altar. The plan has been drawn by Amihai Mazar, the excavator of Giloh. Mazar identifies this building as a watchtower, built in Iron Age II (1000-586 B.C.) and reused in the Middle Ages. Mazar's plan shows a wall built around the Iron Age settlement that, according to Kempinski, closely resembles Zertal's temenos wall at Mt. Ebal.*

recently excavated by Amihai Mazar.* In our excavation at Tell Masos, we also found buildings where cultic activities had occurred. Almost every Iron Age I settlement has one or more cultic installations. But the discovery of pits in which cultic activities took place—such as on Mt. Ebal—is not proof that Joshua's altar was built on top of the pits.

What about the fill in the structure Zertal interprets as an altar? As I already mentioned, this fill appeared to me to be simply destruction debris from the destroyed watchtower. Or it could have been fill deliberately laid to create a surface or podium on which to build the tower in a later period.

Finally, there are problems with the osteological evidence—the bones that Zertal found and that he claims support his interpretation. These bones came from bulls, sheep, goats and fallow deer—all kosher animals and, except for the deer, animals mentioned in the Bible as appropriate for burnt offerings (Leviticus 1:5,10). If Zertal were to excavate modern rubbish pits from nearby Nablus, he would find the same osteological material. Pigs—an unkosher animal—would not be expected either in Nablus or in the central mountain ridge of Canaan during

* Amihai Mazar, "Bronze Bull Found in Israelite 'High Place' from the Time of the Judges," **BAR**, September/October 1983.

the settlement period. The fallow deer bones Zertal found show that the excavated bones simply reflect the faunal conditions in the area and the diet of the people involved. How did this osteological material get inside the tower's base? It was either part of the destruction debris when the tower was destroyed, or it may have been placed there as part of the fill for a later construction phase.

In short, there is no basis whatever for interpreting this structure as an altar.

No doubt Zertal was led to his mistaken identification by an uncritical reading of the Bible. He accepted literally the passages in Deuteronomy 27 and Joshua 8 that supposedly describe an altar on Mt. Ebal. Actually, the earliest version of the text probably placed the altar on nearby Mt. Gerizim, which is where the Samaritan version of the Pentateuch places it.

On March 31, 1984, Israeli television aired Zertal's story, in a presentation very similar to his **BAR** article. But the program also included an interview with Mr. Binyamin Zedakah, one of the leaders of the Samaritan community. This interview was unfairly edited on television. So the next day, Mr. Zedakah wrote his complete argument for the newspaper *Ha-Aretz*, which published it on April 4, 1984. Zedakah reminded us that Zertal's site was first discovered by Victor Guérin in the 1860s. Even at that early date, Guérin identified it as Joshua's altar. In arguing that Joshua's altar was built on Mt. Gerizim, however, the Samaritan's holy mountain, Zedakah asks us this question: If Joshua's altar was built on Mt. Ebal, why was such an important cult place totally forgotten in the later Iron Age? Why is there no archaeological or historical tradition at Mt. Ebal from the period of the Israelite monarchy for the existence of such a site?

I would phrase the question somewhat differently: According to our best understanding, the Deuteronomic school was active during the eighth and seventh centuries B.C. and the earliest edition of the Book of Joshua was written in the seventh century B.C. For the purposes of my argument, however, it does not matter if these dates are off by 100 or 150 years. If the original texts of Deuteronomy 27 and Joshua 8 had references to Mt. Ebal rather than Mt. Gerizim, surely there would be some remains on Mt. Ebal from the period when these texts were written. Yet we have Zertal's word for it that there is not a single sherd from the period of the Israelite monarchy, that is, after the 11th century B.C.

It is tempting to agree with Zedakah that the earlier version of Deuteronomy 27, as well as Joshua 8, referred to Mt. Gerizim and not Mt. Ebal. On Mt. Gerizim, the Samaritans still preserve and celebrate what they believe to be the traditional site of Joshua's altar.

In the early Israelite text, as presented in the Jewish Masoretic version, why was Mt. Gerizim changed to Mt. Ebal? To answer this question, we must look into the highly complicated political and theological disputes between Jews and Samaritans in the late Persian and early Hellenistic periods (late fourth to early third centuries B.C.). It was then that the final schism occurred between what were two branches of early Second Temple Judaism. It was then that the foundation of the Samaritan Temple was laid on Mt. Gerizim, emphasizing the final separation of the Samaritans from Jerusalemite Judaism. The rivalry between Gerizim and Jerusalem resulted in "correcting" the Biblical passages in Deuteronomy 27 and Joshua 8, so that they referred to Ebal instead of Gerizim, which had become (and remains) the center of Samaritan worship. This textual change most probably occurred between 350 and 300 B.C.

Biblical archaeology is not simply field archaeology using the Bible as a guidebook. Biblical archaeology must also be based on a sound grounding in the scholarship of Biblical studies. Without this basic knowledge of the development of the Scriptures, Biblical archaeology can easily be transformed from a science to a theology. In short, without realizing it, Adam Zertal is strangely playing a role in a longstanding theological drama that was set up by the Samaritans and the Jews, a drama that was first played at the beginning of the Hellenistic age in the Jewish center of Jerusalem and the Samaritan center of Shechem. ◾

How Can Kempinski Be So Wrong!

Continued from p. 95

1. His one-hour visit to our Mt. Ebal dig on October 27, 1982, was during our first season of excavation. Since then, we have conducted four additional seasons, which have provided us with very rich and new archaeological material.* Kempinski has not the slightest idea of what has been found in those four seasons, since he never asked, nor came again to the site. His criticisms are based solely on a single, early visit, and on my popular, nontechnical article in **BAR**. Consequently, I take pleasure in bringing to the layperson and the scholarly world—including Kempinski—some of our rich new data.

2. The survey of the hill country of Manasseh, begun

---

* 1982—one season; 1983—two seasons; 1984—one season; 1985—one season.

in 1978 and continuing ever since, is one of the largest surveys ever to be conducted in Israel. It covers a huge area of 540 square miles (1,500 sq. km; one-third of the territory of the central hill country). We have discovered more than 600 sites, 500 of them unknown before. In the course of our work, we developed many new techniques concerning surveying, registration and data-compilation. Among other innovations, our survey was the first to introduce the full-scale use of a computer in site analysis.

3. In 1982, when Kempinski visited our excavation on Mt. Ebal, no one would or could have used the term "altar," because at that time we had no idea what the nature of the site was. The decision to dig was made because of the need to explore a site from the Israelite settlement period in the territory of Manasseh. Such sites in Manasseh were important to Biblical history and none had yet been explored archaeologically. I clearly expressed in my **BAR** article (p. 80) that we initially thought we were exploring an ordinary settlement. Consequently, at that time we did not use any terminology ascribing a sacred nature to the site. True, many indications pointed from the very beginning to the site's special character; among these were the absence of any remnants of exposed architecture; the special style of the enclosure wall, encircling a vast empty area; the strange location of the site, across the middle of a ridge, etc. None of these factors apply to the Iron Age I villages in the hill-country, so we assumed that we were not dealing with a settlement or a regular village.

4. The first announcement concerning our discovery of an altar site was published in the Israeli newspaper *Ha-aretz* on Sunday, November 3, 1983. This was exactly a year *after* the time that Kempinski indicates that the news was already in the Israeli daily press, during his visit in 1982.

5. Kempinski indicates that he saw a collar-rim jar sunk into the floor inside the altar. On pages 80-81 of my **BAR** article, I emphasized quite clearly that "It is quite obvious, now, that the installations at the bottom of the structure represent an earlier phase, and the large structure itself represents a later phase—both from the same Iron I period." The collar-rim jar together with other finds—all unknown to Kempinski—belong to Level II, the earlier phase of the altar site. It is hard to understand what he means when he says this find contradicts our conclusion that the later altar buried the earlier cultic structure—including the jar!

6. If Kempinski would just read Victor Guérin, he could easily learn that Guérin never claimed that he discovered the location of this altar. Guérin wrote:

"In order to find this precious monument [i.e., Joshua's altar] I have thoroughly explored the southern pla-

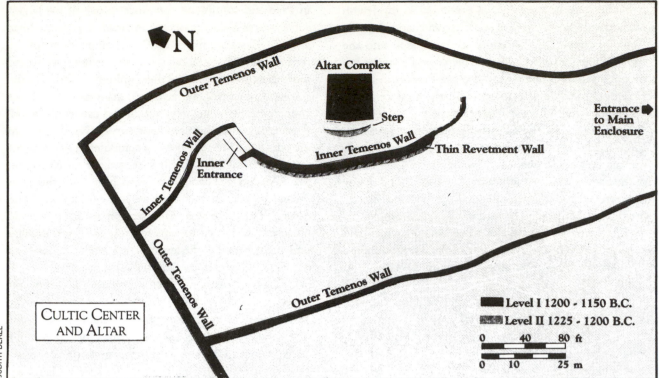

CULTIC CENTER AND ALTAR

Level I 1200 - 1150 B.C.

Level II 1225 - 1200 B.C.

| 0 | 40 | 80 ft |
| 0 | 10 | 25 m |

teau [of Mt. Ebal] with the northern as well; but all my explorations were in vain." (*Description Géographique, historique et archéologique de la Palestine*, Tome IV *Samarie* [Amsterdam, 1969, reprint] p. 451.)*

7. The "three-phase" settlement model applied to our site by Kempinski is a purely hypothetical invention, not related to Mt. Ebal at all. In fact, our stratigraphy may be described as follows:

A. The site has two levels, or strata, not three.

B. No seminomadic or nomadic settlement left any trace of remains.

C. No pits or bins have been found at the Mt. Ebal site.

D. No defense wall surrounded the site in any stratum. In Level II (the earlier stratum), a revetment wall of big boulders was laid upon the western slope only; in Level I, a *temenos* wall surrounded the whole area, thus creating a sacred precinct. This later wall is low, with a poor foundation, and is constructed of small stones (see plan, above).

E. No evidence of destruction of any kind was found at Mt. Ebal in either Level I or Level II. So Kempinski's entire "destruction thesis" is out of the question. On the contrary, the transition from Level II to

* The original French reads as follows:
"*Pour retrouver ce monument précieux, j'ai parcouru avec soin tout le plateau méridional de la montagne, de même que j'en avais exploré le plateau septentrional; mais toutes mes recherches ont été vaines.*"

Since Adam Zertal *wrote "How Can Kempinski Be So Wrong!" his ongoing excavations have shed still more light on the building phases, or levels, at the Mt. Ebal site. This plan incorporates the new information. According to Zertal, the earliest (Level II) construction (mottled) on the site was paved courtyards and a revetment wall of large boulders laid against the steep slope to support the courtyards. Zertal also uncovered a raised step behind the courtyards, which he assigns to Level II. Animal bones from Level II have been found in the area of the courtyards; these bones are not burnt and thus are probably the remains of meals, not sacrifices. Cultic installations in the area of the later altar are also attributable to this early phase.*

In Level I (the later phase), many new structures were added (black). The Israelites constructed a thin stone wall parallel to the old revetment wall. They filled in the space between the Level II revetment wall and the Level I wall with medium-size stones to make a sturdy temenos wall that supported the courtyards. At the same time, says Zertal, they built the altar. Surrounding the inner temenos, the altar and the courtyards, an outer temenos wall was constructed. Entrance to this larger walled area was from an opening on the southeast. A three-stepped entrance from the west in the inner temenos wall gave access to the altar area.

Level I was peaceful; it left no signs of violent change. We prefer to ascribe the transformation from Level II to Level I to a decision to build a large and newly designed ritual center.

F. It is archaeologically impossible for Kempinski's

supposed "watchtower podium" to have been filled with debris from a Level II destruction, because there was no such destruction. Moreover, our efforts to restore some vessels from the fill layers inside the altar were in vain; this proves that the fill was collected from a wide area before the erection of the altar. In our stratigraphic section in the southern courtyard of the altar (locus 81), we found, beneath the floor, primitive hearths with much ash and burned bones. Some broken vessels were found near this installation. The whole character of the area had a highly cultic appearance. Therefore, it is impossible that these were the remains of "phase 2 building," as Kempinski would have it.

G. Kempinski's "watchtower" theory was discussed in the **BAR** article (p. 81) and was found to be untenable because "there [was] no reason for a watchtower to be here." If there was no destruction, then no watchtower was needed, even according to Kempinski's argument!

8. The fact that no other settlement dating to the Iron Age was found on Mt. Ebal was not used by me to argue for the cultic character of the site. It is just an interesting additional and unexplained phenomenon. The other sites on Mt. Ebal are: one prehistoric, one Middle Bronze IIB, two from the beginning of the Persian period and eight from the Roman-Byzantine period. It is typical of Kempinski's argument that he uses such out-of-context points to argue his case.

9. Now, what about the ramp? Is it a ramp or isn't it? It is true that many of the Biblical and Mishnaic terms are not clearly understandable today. The main reason for this is the lack of good archaeological evidence showing the exact meaning of the terms. This is particularly true regarding cultic terms, since very little, if any, Israelite cultic architecture has been unearthed (see p. 89 of my **BAR** article). But I claim that the discovery of a full-scale, untouched and very early Israelite cultic center enables us to study afresh the whole issue. In this context, it is clear that a ramp to climb up an altar was used since the 12th century B.C. in Israelite religious architecture, and that the Mishnaic description of the Second Temple altar is validly based on much earlier prototypes. Moreover, it is now beyond doubt that Israelite altars maintained an old tradition and remained relatively unchanged for 1,200 years. This phenomenon of the persistence of architectural details is well known in cultic and religious architecture.

If Kempinski had looked at the plan (p. 87) and the reconstruction (p. 86), he would have seen that the ramp cannot under any circumstances be a wall. The steps that provided access into the courtyards show that there could

never have been a freestanding wall where the ramp is because there were no walls on the western (outside) line of the courtyards.

10. Now to the fill inside the altar: It took us more than two weeks to excavate this fill. We found it to be deliberately laid strata. It is beyond my understanding how a supposed scientist can rely on his one-hour visit to the site three years ago, not yet knowing the whole problem, to analyze this fill. A clear indication that the fill consists of deliberately laid strata is the fact that from the hundreds of sherds found in the fill, not one complete vessel could be restored. A destruction level of a house should contain many complete, although broken, jars and bowls. This is well known to every beginner. Moreover, since no destruction occurred during the history of the Mt. Ebal site, from where would the inhabitants have taken the ashes in order to fill their new (and unnecessary) watchtower?

11. With respect to the bones, instead of replying to Kempinski's argument, I will quote here a part of the report (to be published soon with my complete preliminary report of the five seasons) relating to the bones found on Mt. Ebal. This report, entitled "Faunal Remains from the Early Israelite Site of Mt. Ebal," was written by Liora Kolska-Horwitz of the Department of Zoology, The Hebrew University of Jerusalem. Under the heading "Conclusions" Miss Kolska-Horwitz writes:*

"When compared to other Iron Age habitation sites, some interesting differences are apparent between Ebal and the others. The first is the difference in emphasis in species present. *Equids* [the genus that includes horses, donkeys, etc.], pigs, carnivores and gazelle (both wild and domesticated) are absent at Ebal, but present at the Iron Age sites of Lachish, Tel Qasile, Tel Miqneh, Tel Dan, Hazorea, Tel Michal, Shiloh, Beer-Sheva, Tel Masos and Izbet Sartah. The species represented and their frequency suggest that only edible animals are present at Ebal, while at other sites animals possibly used for various purposes (such as *equids*) are present. The specific absence of gazelle and pig remains is of interest considering their presence in the immediate vicinity of the site, both in antiquity and today. This is further emphasized by the high frequency of fallow deer, which shares a similar environment to wild pig, though the latter does not appear to have been hunted at Ebal.

"An aspect which further highlights the difference between Ebal and habitation sites is the number and distribution of burnt or scorched bones from Ebal (28 bones forming 9% of the diagnostic bone sample)

---

* The following quotation omits citations and references to tables in the text.

When Ramesses II reigned (*about 1290-1224 B.C.*) *this carnelian scarab was issued to honor Thutmosis III (1479-1425 B.C.). Found recently just north of the Mt. Ebal altar, the rare artifact pinpoints the date of the altar to this period in the 13th century B.C.*

What looks like a capital letter "B" in the center of the scarab is a double bow held by a kneeling archer, far left. The cartouche of the great conqueror Thutmosis III appears at the far right. At the top is a crawling salamander, an Egyptian symbol of abundance.

HEBREW UNIVERSITY OF JERUSALEM

compared with 8 bones (0.8%) from the Iron Age levels at the City of David (from a bone sample of approximately 1,000 bones). Wapnish has reported that 15% of the *equid* material (total of 65 bones) from Tel Jemmeh had cut marks and burning. Though the exact period distribution of this 15% is not specified, this and the City of David data indicate that the burnt material from Ebal is slightly, but not significantly higher in proportion to the total bone sample. However, the most salient feature of the Ebal burnt material is the concentration of the bone in the altar area (17 of the 28 bones or 61% of the total burnt bone samples from the site). This further suggests some difference in activities between the areas at the site.

"Ebal differs from other Iron Age sites in the absence of certain species such as *equids*, pigs, gazelle and carnivores and in the presence of a high frequency of fallow deer. In addition, the comparative data on burnt bones suggests a frequency at Ebal, slightly higher than that expected from a bone sample of this size.

"All of these features indicate a different pattern of animal utilization at Ebal to that found at Iron Age habitation sites.

"It is suggested that the Ebal faunal assemblage represents a narrow range of activities either in func-

tion or time. The absence of animals prohibited for consumption but frequent at other Iron Age sites, suggests conformity with Biblical tenets.

12. Let us turn now to *other cultic features* found at Mt. Ebal. Somehow, Kempinski does not mention all these other features, for which no interpretation other than cultic can be given.

    A. The absence of any architectural connection between the courtyard and the altar, apart from the ramp.

    B. The secondary ramp and the surround, issues not even discussed by Kempinski. As explained in my article, a possible explanation for this very special construction is to be found in the special construction required in an Israelite altar (p. 88).

    C. The installations containing clay vessels, not found in any other Iron I settlements or at other sites at all.

    D. The installations containing ashes and bones.

    E. The complete absence of features common in Iron Age I villages: no buildings with columns or monoliths; no bins or pits; no buildings built on the so-called three- or four-room plan; the unique nature of the altar plan with its absence of entrance and floor, etc.

In the last part of his paper, Kempinski deals with ideology rather than science. What is the proof that "the earliest edition of the Book of Joshua is in the seventh century B.C."? When the Book of Joshua was written is one of the most intriguing issues in Biblical studies; the *Encyclopedia Biblica* (in Hebrew) devotes three pages to the different opinions regarding this date (Volume 3, pp. 543-548). Is it possible to argue that, since no sherds from the seventh century were found on Mt. Ebal, therefore no altar can be found there?

Consider the opinions of only two leading Biblical scholars, among the many who have expressed their opinions about the credibility of the description of Joshua's altar in Deuteronomy 27. In 1934 Albrecht Alt wrote:*

"But if an entire category of Israelite law fits into the scene described in Deuteronomy 27, this provides strong support for the view that the account is not simply the product of the writer's imagination, bearing no relation to reality, but preserves at least the recollection of a sacral action that actually took place at one time in Israel. The recently established view that this same sanctuary of Yahweh at Shechem was visited and used in common by the whole federation of Israelite tribes, and may perhaps have been their only sanctuary in Palestine, brings the scene in

* A. Alt, *Essays on Old Testament History and Religion* (Oxford, 1966), pp. 125-126.

Deuteronomy 27 quite within the bounds of historical possibility."

On the same issue, Benjamin Mazar writes:[*]

"According to Joshua 8:30-35, the first deed of the leader after the conquest of Jericho and the Ai was to fulfill Moses' command (Deuteronomy 27) to build an altar to Yahweh on Mt. Ebal....This Deuteronomistic source is based undoubtedly upon historical event, well attested in the people's memory."

I do not mention Martin Noth, Yehezkel Kaufmann and many, many other scholars. Even scholars who look upon the Samaritan material as having historical significance have never tried to argue that it is the original version. Even their attitude is based simply on the later date of the Samaritan Pentateuch. We know that the schism between Judaism and Samaritanism took place in the Late Persian-Early Hellenistic period. So it would seem that the Samaritans changed the existing Pentateuch, since the Jewish text was well known by this time. What is the proof for the idea expressed by Kempinski that the Samaritan version of the Pentateuch is the original? On what historical material can he substantiate his thesis?

To sum up the archaeological evidence: In the last quarter of the 13th century B.C., as shown by the two unique Egyptian scarabs unearthed at the site,[**] a local cultic center was founded on the third ridge of Mt. Ebal, looking northeast toward Wadi Far'ah. Although we do not yet possess all the information, it is clear that on the highest point of this ridge there was a building serving fire-related activities in some kind of cultic function.[†] To the west a revetment wall was built on the steep rocky slope, supporting a whole series of what now seems to be paved courtyards. Around the central building many other fire-related activities took place.

In Level I (the later level), around 1200 B.C., the site underwent a complete change. A large burnt-offering altar was erected upon the earlier cultic area, burying it under the debris of the earlier cultic activities and leaving the central feature of the earlier stage or platform in the exact center of the new one. The altar complex included

Ritual chalice, *or possibly an incense burner, from the 13th century B.C., the period when the altar was built. Made of very light volcanic basalt, the 4.75-inch-high artifact was found at the bottom of the altar.*

DOUGLAS SPRINGER

courtyards, installations, a surround on the altar and ramps leading to it—all typical of the Israelite-altar model found in the Book of Ezekiel and the Second Temple altar described in Mishnaic sources.

At the same time that the altar was built (in Level I) an inner *temenos* wall was added, surrounding the site and enlarging the earlier cultic area four times. There were no structures besides the altar within the inner *temenos* wall. A wide gateway in the inner *temenos* wall was constructed. Also, a second and much larger enclosure wall (the outer *temenos* wall) was constructed, thus creating one enclosure inside the other.

No doubt, this ritual center was intended mainly for the gathering of a relatively large number of people. The evidence for this lies in the special location of the enclosure, in a way that the viewer could see the ceremonies on the altar from outside the enclosure wall.

How long did this cultic center exist? Archaeologically speaking, not very long. The evidence of the pottery cannot be stretched beyond the middle of the 12th century B.C.[*] I would estimate this center's existence to be not more than 50 years. The site was never destroyed, however. Rather, it was deserted while in a complete and finished state. Why? We do not yet know. Its desertion, just as its erection, seems somehow to have been the result of a deliberate decision, and not of a natural development. There was no reason for such an abandonment based on environmental conditions. But such desertions are well known at Iron Age I sites; Mt. Ebal is no exception.

The desertion of the site resulted in the fact that we now have a complete and untouched Israelite cultic center from the time when monotheism began—to be studied by archaeologists, Biblical scholars and other concerned scientists, both Jewish and Christian, from all over the world. ◾

[*] B. Mazar, "The Place of Shechem—A Sacred Land for the Children of Israel," in *Canaan and Israel—Historical Researches* (Jerusalem, 1974), p. 149 (in Hebrew).

[**] These scarabs are unique in Israelite settlement sites. The second scarab was found in the fifth season; it is securely dated to Ramesses II's reign. Therefore, two scarabs date the possible founding of the site to the third quarter of the 13th century B.C.

[†] In this we find a great similarity to house 314 at Masos, locus 1735 from stratum VI A from Megiddo, and other parallels from Ai, Hazor, Hazorea, etc.

[*] The most recent analysis of Level I pottery has necessitated raising the date of the end of this level about 50 years.

ZERTAL'S ALTAR—19TH CENTURY BIBLICAL ARCHAEOLOGY

To the Editor:

Adam Zertal's defense of his altar theory ("How Can Kempinski Be So Wrong!" January/February 1986) is a beautiful example of 19th-century Biblical archaeology scholarship.

Zertal criticizes me for forming opinions after only a one-hour visit to the site. One hour is more than enough, however, to examine a structure eight by nine meters. And seeing it during the process of excavation is more important than visiting it afterwards when most of the evidence is no longer *in situ*.

Moreover, when I visited the excavation in October 1982, Zertal had already adopted his "Joshua's altar" theory. He had mentioned the possiblity that this structure was Joshua's altar even before the excavation. Several archaeologists will testify to this. This closes the matter of objective research, which Zertal so emphatically stresses in his rejoinder to my article ("Joshua's Altar—An Iron Age I Watchtower," January/February 1986).

Now to the merits of Zertal's argument:

1. Modern archaeology works mainly by analogy. We know that a building is a storehouse because we have modern examples or other analogies for the structure. We know that a horned altar from the Iron Age II period (1000-587 B.C.) is in fact an altar because we can trace its development until the Hellenistic period when inscriptions also testify to its function. The best analogies for the structure excavated by Zertal are the hundreds of watchtowers of all periods spread all over the hills and mountainous areas of Palestine. Their size, proportions and other technical features are almost identical with the structure Zertal excavated on Mt. Ebal.

Zertal argues that there is no reason for a watchtower to be located on the northeastern slope of Mt. Ebal, but ancient man's reasons are not always clear to our modern way of thinking. Zertal's argument is irrelevant in explaining the structure.

Moreover, there is no reason for an altar to be there, if we did not have the Biblical text that Zertal leans on for support.

From a purely archaeological viewpoint and on the basis of analogy, the structure is a tower; any other interpretation has to use really convincing arguments before it will be accepted by professional archaeologists.

2. Altars were holy objects. They were purified and cleaned. The ashes and remains of the offerings were removed from them. Altars from the Canaanite and Israelite periods have been found, but not a single one was used as a *favissa*.* Zertal claims that the inside of his "altar," on which the animals were sacrificed, was used as a burial place for their ashes and the bone remains. There is absolutely no analogy for this. I cannot understand how Zertal imagines the ritual: Were the animals slaughtered on the side walls of the structure and later their remains deposited layer after layer inside the "altar"? Or was the top of the "altar" surface reopened each time in order to deposit the bones?

3. And speaking of bones, how many are there inside "Joshua's altar" after all? I read with interest what Ms. Kolska-Horwitz wrote about the bone remains as quoted by Zertal; and this simply convinced me that they are typical of what we would expect in a peasant community of that period. Professor E. Tchernov and Dr. I. Drori have written a very fine report about a similar bone assemblage that was published in our final report on Tell Masos.** We paid no attention to the percentage of burnt bones, but as far as I recall they exceeded the nine percent recorded by Zertal on Mt. Ebal. So there is no unusual percentage of burnt bones. We would ordinarily expect at least nine percent of the bones (only 17 bones or bone fragments were found burnt at Mt. Ebal!) to be burnt; this is simply a normal percentage. If this were a special place for sacrificial offerings, we would expect a much larger percentage of burnt bones.

4. As to Zertal's "ramp" and "secondary ramp," he must be so bound to his altar theory that he cannot see that these are the remains of earlier walls that belonged to structures that existed before the watchtower was built. In my proposed plan (January/February 1986, p. 46 [98]), I suggested that the "ramps" are earlier walls of a building that existed before the watchtower was built. In a later phase some of these early walls were incorporated into the room attached to the tower (phase 3). Field archaeology tries to explain architectural remains. Zertal's contention that the "ramp" was a free-standing wall is only one of many other explanations that must be synchronized with the whole architectural system excavated. As I have already explained in my **BAR** article, Zertal's narrow "ramp" could never be used as such; it would endanger the priests who would wish to climb up to the "altar."

I have tried in vain to understand Zertal's Biblical arguments as set forth in his rejoinder. The earliest extant manuscripts of Deuteronomy 7 came from the Dead Sea caves at Qumran. They date to the second/first centuries B.C. No one can be sure what the text was in the fourth/third-century B.C. *vorlage*, especially when the question concerns a place name (Mt. Ebal) that could have been changed in any edition before the Qumran copies.[1]

The remains of buildings in the area around the altar (left of the arrow on p. 42 [94], January/February 1986), what Zertal calls the "Inner Entrance," provide an excellent indication of the character of the settlement. The similarity to the Giloh settlement (which I cited) is astonishing. Both sites, one in Judea and the other in the hills of Samaria, provide a beautiful archaeological example of the earliest stage of the settlement of the Israelite tribes in the hill country. But there is no altar here.

On May 8, 1867, Victor Guerin climbed the slopes of Mt. Ebal looking for what he called a "precious monument"—the Altar of Joshua. For a mid-19th-century scholar, such an investigation was the most natural way to practice his profession. This was years before modern Biblical criticism had been developed, and almost a century before the "Qumran revolution" changed Biblical studies. Guerin mentions how empty the Ebal area was. He surveyed the few ruins he found. At noon he arrived at Khirbet Kalise (or Kanisse, the church), which faced the southern slope of Mt. Ebal. Since this was an ideal place for Joshua's altar, according to the Biblical account, he started looking for it among the ruins. A square enclosure attracted his attention and he suggested that this might have been where Joshua's altar once stood.*

It took some 140 years until Adam Zertal, walking in the footsteps of a 19th-century scholar found this "precious monument"— Joshua's altar—not on the top of the mountain but on the northeastern slope. The circle of 19th-century scholarship has been closed.

Aharon Kempinski
Tel Aviv University
Tel Aviv, Israel

---

* A *favissa* is a reservoir or underground storage chamber for a temple. [**Ed.**]

** Volkmar Fritz and Aaron Kempinski, *Ergebnisse der Ausgrabungen auf der Hirbet el-Msas* [Tel Masos], Vol. 1 (Weisbaden, 1983), pp. 213-222.

* V. Guerin, *Description de la palestine—2nd part —Samarie* (Paris, 1974), Chap. 26, s.v. Hirbet Kalise.

ZERTAL'S ALTAR—A BLATANT PHONY

To the Editor:

With reference to the so-called altar on Mt. Ebal published by Adam Zertal ("Has Joshua's Altar Been Found on Mt. Ebal?"January/February 1985), I wish to add my voice to that of Aharon Kempinski ("Joshua's Altar—An Iron Age I Watchtower," January/February 1986) in rejecting the interpretation of this site as an altar. The entire interpretation by Zertal is a fabrication of wishful thinking and partial evidence. It is obvious to me and to other scholars that it is not an altar.The following points are decisive: (1) An altar would not be filled with animal bones; (2) The building had more than one phase, as seen by Kempinski; it was an early dwelling, later converted into a typical watchtower; (3) The supposed similarity to the picture of an altar taken from a popular edition of the Mishnah is pure fiction; (4) At a lecture he gave on February 9, 1986, at the Midwest SBL meeting in Berrien Springs, Michigan, Zertal let it slip that there are bones from *nondomesticated* animals in the fill along with sheep and goats! As for any relation to the altar ascribed to Joshua at Mt. Ebal (Joshua 8), the site touted by Zertal does not have eye contact with Mt. Gerizim. The ceremony depicted in the Bible clearly refers to a site where Gerizim is on one side and Mt. Ebal on the other. Only the very gullible will continue to support Zertal's theory. All the facts are against it. The question must be raised about **BAR**'s editorial policy. Don't the professionals on your advisory board ever get consulted? Is it your intention to pander to the sensational at the expense of scientific honesty? I speak for several professionals who agree about Zertal's site but who probably won't take the trouble to write. But I speak especially for myself. The Zertal altar on Ebal is a blatant phony.

Anson F. Rainey
Institute of Archaeology
Tel Aviv University
Tel Aviv, Israel

KEMPINSKI'S OUTLANDISH RECONSTRUCTION

To the Editor:

Talk about letting your theological presuppositions color your archaeological opinion! Aharon Kempinski takes the cake. His article in the January/February 1986 issue begins with the assumption that Adam Zertal can't interpret his own dig, even after five seasons of work there, while of course, Kempinski can do better with the benefit of one hour of examination and a single nontechnical article.

His outlandish reconstruction of who changed what mountain's name in Deuteronomy is by far the most amusing though. Ignoring the fact that the Samaritans were the ones with the axe to grind and almost all serious Biblical scholars consider their version of the Pentateuch the later "corrected" edition, he then assumes the truth of his fantastic claim that the Jews changed the text out of jealousy; and then builds a complicated and unlikely scheme of redaction on this unfounded assumption. Remember, Kempinski, "Without this basic knowledge of the development of the Scriptures, Biblical archaeology can easily be transformed from a science into a theology." In short, Kempinski is strangely playing into the hands of the Samaritans who set up this little drama out of jealousy for the Jews lo, these many years ago.

Michael P. Thompson
Golden, Colorado

[1] Zertal's reference to Benjamin Mazar's paper is very strange. Mazar refers to a hypothetical enclosure at the foot of Mt. Ebal, not on it, just outside the city walls of Tell Balata (ancient Shechem). Anyone who reads Mazar's paper would certainly not get the impression that he believes that an altar was built on Mt. Ebal. Being very cautious, Mazar speaks about "old traditions" of a cult place in Shechem.

Albrecht Alt's view of the sanctuary of Yahweh in Shechem (which Zertal mentions) is a similar case where Zertal reads what is not in the text. I leave it to the many disciples of Alt to explain to Zertal Alt's concept of the development of Israelite religion.

Bronze Bull Found In Israelite "High Place" From the Time of the Judges

By Amihai Mazar

When he found it, Ofer Broshi was on army duty. Army life can be exhausting or boring—or sometimes both. At that moment, Broshi, a rugged young kibbutznik, was more bored than tired. He was resting on the summit of a hill in northern Samaria, above the ancient road connecting the Biblical towns of Dothan and Tirzah.

He looked aimlessly at the ground. Then suddenly he saw something staring back at him from beneath the soil. It was obviously not alive. He reached to see what it was, brushing away the dirt that partially covered it. He was startled to discover that the eyes he had seen belonged to a beautiful bronze figurine of a young bull, which he soon held in his hand, turning it every which way in disbelief.

Broshi brought the figurine back with him to his kibbutz. Almost every kibbutz has at least one amateur archaeologist and Kibbutz Shamir of which Broshi is a member was no exception. There kibbutznik and amateur archaeologist Moshe Kagan arranged to have the bull displayed in the kibbutz antiquities collection.

It was there that I first saw it. I immediately recognized its importance and promptly notified the Department of Antiquities. Negotiations between the kibbutz and the Department resulted in the transfer of the bull to the Israel Museum in Jerusalem for study. It is now displayed there in a special showcase. (In exchange, the Department of Antiquities donated various other artifacts of less importance to the kibbutz collection of antiquities.)

But it was equally important to study the context in which the bull had been uncovered. Thanks to Ofer Broshi's precise information and to the cooperation of the Department of Antiquities, I was able to locate the site and explore it.

I vividly recall my first visit to the site. It is located on the summit of a high ridge. In the distance I could see the most important ridges in northern Palestine. There to the north were Mount Tabor and Mount Meiron; to the west was Mount Carmel; to the northeast was Mount Gilboa; and to the south was Jebel Tamun.

We commenced a detailed archaeological survey of the ridge but found no remains of an ancient settlement. What

Ridge in northern Samaria *where an Israelite cult site was uncovered. No evidence of a permanent occupation was found here, but the site proved to be at the center of a number of tiny Iron Age I (1200 B.C.) settlements. The open-air cult site atop this ridge probably served the people of these small settlements, who were very likely Israelites of the tribe of Manasseh.*

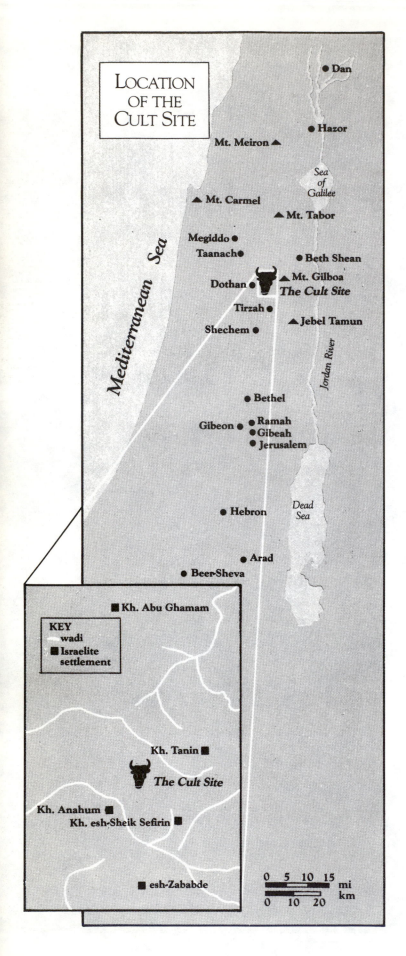

we did find on the hill was rather startling—the remains of an ancient cult site!

In a few days of excavation, we were able to expose whatever was left of this cult site, which, although badly damaged by erosion, proved to have important significance for our knowledge of Biblical "high places."

In the excavation we found a handful of potsherds, the indestructible pieces of pottery which mean so much to archaeologists. We found the rims of some cooking pots, some pieces of rounded bowls, the neck of a flask, some disk bases of shallow bowls. By studying these fragments we were able to date the occupation of the site to the period archaeologists call Iron Age IA—about 1200 B.C.—a time when the Israelite tribes started their permanent settlement of the Land of Israel. Our dating task was made somewhat easier because this was a one-period site. It had been used for only a short time and was then abandoned. Thus, we concluded, the bronze figurine of the young bull was probably used in some religious ritual in the days of the Judges in the land assigned to the tribe of Manasseh.

More exciting than the pottery were the structural remains on the top of the ridge. The structure had been built on bedrock. Most of it had unfortunately eroded away. But enough was left to identify a wall built of large field stones that had once enclosed an elliptical area about 70 feet in diameter.

At the eastern part of the enclosure we found a large stone over four feet long, three feet high, and about one and three-quarters feet thick. It had been worked, but only slightly. The sides were left rough and uneven. Nevertheless, it was easy to distinguish this large stone slab from the other largely unworked stones used to build the enclosure wall.

The uneven bedrock in front of the three-foot-high stone had been leveled with a paving of rough flat stones.

The site appears to have been an open-air cult center comprising a massive stone enclosure wall with a large rectangular stone slab set on a special pavement. The stone slab—although wider than it is high—may be identified in Biblical terms as a kind of "standing stone" or *massebah* (compare Genesis 35:14). Or perhaps it was a kind of altar which stood in front of the pavement of flat stones.

In front of this *massebah* or altar and on the pavement next to it were other finds. One was a fragment of a bronze object we cannot identify. The fragment includes a folded piece of a flat bronze sheet and part of a handle. It may have been a bronze mirror of the Egyptian type. But the major significance of the piece is that its excellent state of preservation indicates that a bronze object would not corrode in the *terra rosa* soil of the site. Our bronze fragment thus served to authenticate the finding of the bronze bull figurine at this site.

Altar or massebah. *Four feet long and three feet high, this* massebah *or stone altar was the center of an Israelite cultic site after the Exodus. Near this "standing stone," the bull figurine was found. In the same area, archaeologists uncovered a folded bronze sheet that may have been an Egyptian-style mirror and a squared pottery fragment that may have been the corner of an incense burner.*

Among the stones of the pavement, near the *massebah* or altar, we found a fragment of a pottery object, which originally was part of a square incense burner or similar cult object like those found at Taanach, Megiddo and Beth Shean, or it might possibly have been a model of a cult-shrine such as was found at Tirzah (Tell el-Farah [North]). In either case, this pottery fragment confirms the cultic nature of the site.

Also consistent with this activity are a few remains of some animal bones, possibly from sacrificial animals.

We may assume that at other places in the enclosure, now completely eroded, there were other installations for cultic functions. Perhaps a sacred tree, often mentioned in the Bible in connection with cult places on top of hills and mountains, grew in the center of the enclosure where our excavations uncovered no finds at all (see Ezekiel 6:13).

The bull figurine itself is unique. It is not only the largest bull figurine ever found in Israel—indeed, in the entire Levant—it also combines naturalistic and stylized elements in an unusual way (see following page).

The bull is seven inches long and five inches high. It can stand on its feet without support or tang. It was made by the so-called "lost wax" technique. The animal was first created in wax. Then the wax was covered with clay. Several holes were made in the clay cover. Hot molten bronze was then poured into the clay cover through one of these holes. The molten metal naturally melted the wax, which poured out through other holes. What is perhaps the remains of the hole into which the molten bronze was poured can still be seen at the top of the animal's neck.

The treatment of the legs is clear evidence that the bull was first modeled in wax. Each pair of legs was molded as a separate long strip which was bent above the body of the animal, thus creating a ridge on its body and back, continuing the line of the legs.

The rounded eyes of the animal consist of protruding ridges around depressions which must have once contained inlays of glass or semi-precious stone, thus giving the animal an intense and vivid expression.

Some of the bull's other features are quite naturalistic. In addition to the eyes, look at the ears and horns. The legs too are quite lifelike. The male organs were sculpted in detail, an indication of power and fertility.

On the other hand, other characteristics are stylized and schematic. The body is rectangular. The breast is a heavy triangle. The neck is flat. The head is triangular from the front, and long and narrow from the side. The mouth is a straight slot at the flat bottom of the head. All these features give the animal a simplistic look.

The small hump on the back of the animal, above its forelegs, enables us to identify the bull as a "Zebu Bull" (*Bos indicus*), a type which originated in India and reached the Near East as early as the fourth millennium B.C. It is known in various artistic representations from the ancient

Bull figurine. *Standing firmly on four hooves, this young bull differs from similar artifacts, such as that from Hazor (far right), which were found with extensions from the hooves to attach the figures to cult vessels. An artist's drawings of three views of the bull (right) show well-defined genitalia demonstrating potency and power and deep eye sockets which may once have held semi-precious stones. Perhaps the bull was a votive offering symbolizing the strength and virility of a pagan god, or perhaps the bull was worshipped as a deity itself. Either or both aspects may help us understand the cult of the golden calf in the Bible.*

Near East, and actual bones of such bulls were excavated, for example, at Deir Alla in the Jordan Valley. Our figurine was probably the product of a local, non-professional artisan lacking a defined artistic heritage.

The bull motif itself, however, is extremely common—and therefore extremely important—in Near Eastern iconography. It is a symbol both of power and fertility. Sometimes the bull appears as a cult object itself, for example, as a young striding god to be worshipped as the symbol of the deity. Other times it appears as a depiction of an attribute of the West Semitic storm god Hadad who is known in the Bible as Baal.

There are some examples from the second millennium

B.C. of representations showing the worship of a bull as a symbol of a deity. In a famous Hittite relief, a royal couple stands in prayer before a bull on an altar. In another group of artistic depictions, however, the bull appears as the attribute of the storm god Hadad (or Baal). He is sometimes shown holding the bull with reins. In this aspect the bull symbolizes Baal's strength and power. In other examples we find the storm god standing on top of a bull, the bull serving as a pedestal for the god.

This double aspect of the bull—both as a symbol of a deity itself and as an attribute of the storm god—is important in any attempt to understand the cult of the golden calf in the Bible. Scholars disagree as to the meaning of this cult. Some claim the calf was simply the pedestal of Yahweh, like the cherubim over the Ark of the Covenant in the Jerusalem Temple. If this is true, our bull figurine may have been considered only a pedestal for the god—seen or unseen—worshipped at our site. Others believe the golden calf had a much deeper meaning as a symbol of the god of Israel or even of a foreign deity. Both interpretations are supportable on the basis of the iconographic material.

Was our bull figurine a real cult object in itself, or was it just a votive offering object, symbolizing the strength of the god? Its relatively large size, the great care taken in its

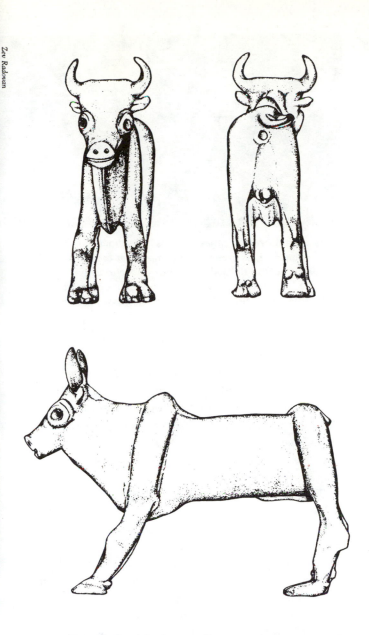

Hazor bull. *Strikingly similar in design to the bull recently studied by the author, this three-inch-long figure is made of bronze and has a large hump at its shoulders, a triangular head and a stylized straight-line mouth. Extensions from the hooves originally secured the figure to another object, perhaps a cult pedestal or stand. Found in the area H temple at Hazor, the bull dates to the late Bronze Age (1550 B.C. to 1200 B.C.), shortly before the period of the bull figurine recently found at the cultic site in northern Samaria.*

manufacture, the inlaid eyes, all suggest that it was a cult object of great importance. Yet we cannot be sure of its exact significance.

From finds at other sites, we know that the Israelites continued Canaanite metallurgical technology and metallurgical traditions during Iron Age I. And, indeed, Israelite metal artisans are referred to in Judges 17:4-5. So our bull figurine may be the product of a local Israelite craftsman inspired by Canaanite traditions, or it may have been obtained by the Israelites through trade with Canaanites in the villages of northern Israel.

What is the basis of the site's identification as an *Israelite* cult place? The first thing to note is that the site is not near any major ancient Canaanite city. The closest mounds are between four and six miles away. However, a series of small Iron Age I sites has been discovered in the vicinity during archaeological surveys of the region. Our site is located in

the middle of a cluster of such small sites. These small sites can probably be related to the settlement process by the Israelite tribes in this area. These sites flourished as small agricultural villages and our cultic enclosure probably served as a central ritual place for a group of these settlements. We can thus conclude that Israelites, probably from the tribe of Manasseh, were the builders of this cult site.

Open cult places were a permanent feature of the Israelite cult from patriarchal times until the religious reform of Josiah in the late seventh century B.C. In the patriarchal narratives we find altars (*mizbeah*) erected by the Patriarchs in the open—close to major cities like Shechem, Bethel, Jerusalem, Hebron and Beer-Sheva. Some of them were erected near a sacred tree (Genesis 12:6-7, Genesis 13:18), and in at least one case, the installation included a sacred stone (*massebah*) (Genesis 35:14). Such altars were probably simple installations, providing a place for sacrifice or the placing of offerings in a well-defined enclosure. Our cult place is no doubt an illustration of such an ancient "altar" built in the open, outside a group of small settlements. The large stone defined by us as a *massebah* was part of the cult place, just as the *masseboth* in the patriarchal narratives. Our example is the earliest known open cult place which may be attributed to Israelites (later ones are known from Arad and Hazor), and it is the only one situated outside a settlement on top of a remote ridge.

The Biblical term *bamah* (1 Kings 14:23, 2 Kings 17:9-11, 23:13-14), usually translated as "High Place," should also be mentioned in relation to our site. Although the exact meaning of the term is still open to debate, all agree that the *bamah* was an open cult place of some sort. It appears in the Israelite cult as early as the time of Samuel and continues throughout the monarchic period until the reform of Josiah. Sometimes the *bamah* is an open cult place on hills or mountains (1 Kings 14:23; 2 Kings 17:9-11; 23:13-14; 18:20, 29). Sometimes a *bamah* is mentioned without definite location or is located inside towns. The *bamot* at Ramah, Gibeah and Gibeon mentioned in con-

Dave Davis

This folded bronze object *tells us little about its original shape. However, its presence confirmed that bronze would not deteriorate in the soil at this site. This conclusion reassured archaeologists that the bronze bull reported to have been found here also could have survived for over three millennia.*

nection with Samuel and Solomon show how important these cult installations were at the time. Etymologically the word *bamah* derives from "body" and, metaphorically, from "mountain ridge," so the Israelite *bamah* probably originated in open cult places on tops of mountains of the kind represented by our site. Thus the "altars" of the patriarchal narratives may be related to the later *bamot*. And our site may exemplify both.

But who was worshipped here? Perhaps Baal. Or perhaps Yahweh. The relation between Yahweh and the bull among the northern Israelite tribes is reflected in the Biblical traditions concerning the golden calf. As you will recall, the northern king Jeroboam set up golden calves at Bethel and Dan after the kingdom divided following Solomon's death (1 Kings 12:28). Scholars consider the golden calves erected by Jeroboam as a revival of an old practice known among the northern tribes of Israel from their early history. Others suggest that Jeroboam introduced a new cultic practice and that the story of the golden calf at the foot of Mount Sinai in Exodus 32 is anachronistic (written long after the episode it describes) and was intended to legitimize and reinforce the *opposition* to Jeroboam's deed. The question of the nature of Israelite religion during this period is a complex one. At least one source in the book of Judges (6:25, where Gideon's father worshipped Baal at Ophrah) hints at the existence of a Baal cult among the Israelites during the period of the Judges. Thus the identification of the specific cult at our site must remain, for the time being, an open question. 🐏

(For further details, see "Cult Site from the Time of the Judges in the Mountains of Samaria," by Amihai Mazar, in *Eretz Israel*, Vol. 16, Jerusalem, 1982 [in Hebrew], and a forthcoming article in the *Bulletin of the American Schools of Oriental Research*.)

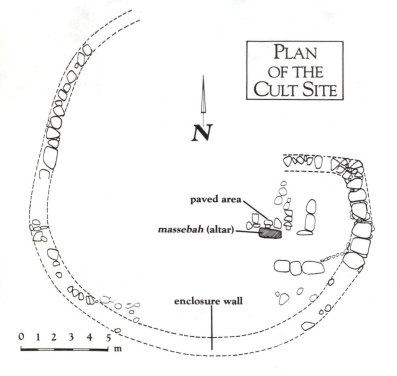

PLAN
OF THE
CULT SITE

N

paved area

massebah (altar)

enclosure wall

0 1 2 3 4 5
m

Plan of the cult enclosure. *A simple structure on the top of a high ridge, this open-air religious site is basically a wall of unworked stones defining an elliptical area about 70 feet across. In its southeastern quarter, a partially worked stone four feet long and three feet high stands in front of a special stone pavement covering the bedrock. This standing stone was very likely a* **massebah** *or altar. A pottery fragment that may have been part of an incense burner and bones found among the pavement stones also attest to the ritual function of this enclosure.*

Two Early Israelite Cult Sites Now Questioned

HERSHEL SHANKS

IN RECENT YEARS, two early Israelite cult sites have been discovered. The first is referred to as the "Bull Site" because archaeologists were led to it by the accidental discovery there of a cultic bronze statuette of a bull.[*] The second early Israelite cult site encloses the massive altar discovered in the course of an archaeological survey on Mt. Ebal.[**]

Both sites date to approximately the early 12th century B.C., the early part of Iron Age I in archaeological terms; in Biblical terms, this is the period of the Judges, when the Israelites first emerged in the Promised Land. About this dating, there is no dispute.

But a bitter dispute has arisen about the Mt. Ebal site. Is it really a cult site or is it nothing more than an old farmhouse?[†]

Now a highly regarded American scholar has entered the lists. He has not only considered the question of whether the Mt. Ebal site is cultic, but wonders about the Bull Site as well, and even questions whether these sites are Israelite sites.

In the January/June 1987 issue of the *Palestine Exploration Quarterly* (a venerable scholarly journal that appears only twice a year, despite its name), Michael Coogan, formerly at Harvard and now at Stonehill College, develops four criteria for identifying a cultic site (in the absence of written evidence):

1. *Isolation.* "In most cultures," Coogan notes, "there is a conscious separation between the holy and the profane. Architecturally this finds expression in a temenos wall which separates a holy place from its immediate context, whether natural or settled." So the first question we must ask is whether an allegedly cultic site is isolated in this way.

2. *Exotic materials.* "The special function of cultic sites will normally result in the presence of material not typical of other contexts," writes Coogan. So we are likely to find unusual artifacts such as miniature vessels, figurines or expensive objects. However, cautions Coogan, "If the cultic site was served by personnel on a regular basis, elements of normal repertoires, especially such domestic material as cooking pots, will also occur." Nevertheless, the proportion of exotic artifacts to usual ones such as domestic cooking pots will probably vary as between a cultic site and a non-cultic site.

3. *Continuity.* In multi-period sites, the cultic function of the site is likely to be retained from period to period. The outstanding example of this is the Temple Mount in Jerusalem, which has retained its cultic character for nearly 3,000 years.

4. *Parallels.* Questionable cultic sites are likely to have parallels, if they are truly cultic, at other unquestionably cultic sites. Thus, Coogan tells us, "building plans, altars, pedestals, and the like should show resemblance to cultic installations known from written or non-written sources."

Using these criteria, Coogan concludes that the Bull Site, whose cultic character has not been previously questioned, is not a cultic site, at least not a public one; he further concludes that the Mt. Ebal site, the subject of considerable controversy, probably is a cultic site.

But he questions whether either of the sites can be identified as Israelite.

---

[*] See Amihai Mazar, "Bronze Bull Found in Israelite 'High Place' from the time of the Judges," **BAR,** September/October 1983 [p. 108].

[**] See Adam Zertal, "Has Joshua's Altar Been Found on Mt. Ebal?" **BAR,** January/February 1985 [p. 76].

[†] See Aharon Kempinski, "Joshua's Altar—An Iron Age I Watchtower," and Adam Zertal, "How Can Kempinski Be So Wrong!" both in **BAR,** January/February 1986 [p. 94].

The Bull and the Site

The accidental discovery of this bronze bull figurine (right), on the summit of a high ridge in northern Samaria, alerted archaeologist Amihai Mazar to the possible existence of an important site. Standing firmly on four hooves without any other support, the 5-inch-high, 7-inch-long bull is the largest such figurine ever found in the Levant. Its empty eye-sockets probably once held inlays of glass or of semiprecious stones. The small hump on its back, above the forelegs, identifies this as a "Zebu bull" (*Bos indicus*), a species that originated in India, but which was present in the Near East as early as the fourth millennium B.C.

The bull motif is quite common in Near Eastern iconography as a symbol of power and fertility; a similar bronze bull figurine was previously found in a temple at Hazor. The Bull Site figurine may have been a votive offering, or it may have been worshipped as a deity itself, but its size, its inlaid eyes and its careful manufacture suggest the latter possibility, in Mazar's opinion.

Inspired by the discovery of this figurine, Mazar conducted an

archaeological survey of the ridge, which revealed a wall of large fieldstones enclosing an elliptical area about 70 feet in diameter. According to Mazar, these are the remains of an open-air cult site. Overlooking the ancient road between the Biblical towns of Dothan and Tirzah, the site stands at the center of a cluster of small settlements, probably located in the territory of the Israelite tribe of Manasseh, dating to Iron Age I (1200-1000 B.C.). Although no settlement remains were discovered at the Bull Site, potsherds found there have been dated to Iron I A (about 1200 B.C.)

Within the enclosure, Mazar found a 4-foot-long, 3-foot-high, slightly worked boulder (left, center) standing beside a pavement of flat stones. He regards this as a *massebah* (standing stone) or altar. Michael Coogan, as the accompanying article observes, questions this conclusion. The discovery nearby of a folded, flat sheet of bronze helped to authenticate the bronze bull by showing that bronze could resist corrosion in the site's *terra rosa* soil. Other finds at the site included a piece from an object that Mazar believes may have been an incense burner or similar cult object and some animal bones, which Mazar suggests could be the remains of sacrificial animals.

ZEV RADOVAN

DAVE DAVIS

117

The Mt. Ebal Site

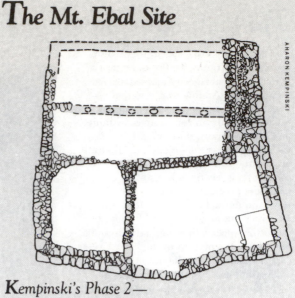

**Kempinski's Phase 2—
Farm House**

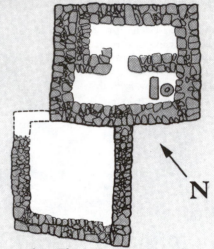

**Kempinski's Phase 3—
Watchtower**

N

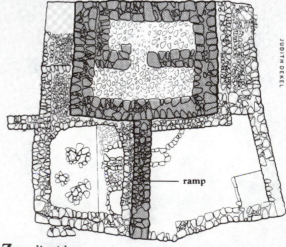

Zertal's Altar

The Bull Site, located on the summit of a high ridge in northern Samaria, consists of a dilapidated wall of large fieldstones that had originally enclosed an elliptical area about 70 feet in diameter. Found within the enclosure were a slightly worked stone, 4 feet long and 3 feet high, which may have served as an altar, and a paving of rough, flat stones that is adjacent to this worked stone.

Is the site cultic?

As Coogan points out, "There are five other small unexcavated sites with Iron Age pottery within a 5 km. radius" of the Bull Site. So it cannot be said to be isolated. It did have a circular enclosure wall, but this need not have any cultic significance in this context. This enclosure wall could well be a corral for livestock with a dwelling for the shepherd.

The scanty pottery found at the site "represents a typical domestic repertoire," argues Coogan. A fragment of the base of a ceramic object belonged, according to the excavator, Hebrew University's Amihai Mazar, to a large cult-object, either a model shrine or an incense burner. But, according to Coogan, "since the pottery base is only a small fragment Mazar's conclusion is not compelling." In addition, a number of flints were found (used in animal sacrifices?) that Coogan describes as "a typical domestic flint assemblage." The large, partially worked stone that Mazar interprets as a standing stone (a *massebah*) or, lying flat, an altar, could as easily be, according to Coogan, a table top or a pillar of a house. Such pillars were commonly used in houses of the period. Thus, for Coogan, "the only significant piece of evidence which cannot easily be interpreted as domestic is the bull figurine."

Since the Bull Site is a one-period site, the criterion of continuity is irrelevant. As to parallels, Mazar has not cited any close ones.

Coogan therefore concludes that the Bull Site is not a cultic site. "The pottery and lithics are unexceptional, and fit best into a domestic context." As for the bull figurine, Coogan concedes this "probably had a ritual function." But "it could just as easily have been used in some sort of private, domestic ritual."

The Mt. Ebal site, however, fares better in Coogan's judgment. Located on a rocky northeastern ridge of the highest mountain in northern Samaria, the site's principal feature is a nearly square, stone structure that stands almost nine feet high. According to the excavator, Haifa University's Adam Zertal, a ramp once led to the top of the structure, which he has interpreted as an altar. A thin, elliptical wall, possibly a temenos

M. WEINBERG

of Ramesses II (1290-1224 B.C.) to honor Thutmosis III (1479-1425 B.C.), helps to pinpoint the date of the founding of the site. What looks like a capital "B" in the scarab's center is really a double bow held by a kneeling archer, far left. The cartouche of Thutmosis III appears at the far right, and a crawling salamander, an Egyptian symbol of abundance, adorns the top. A second scarab dated to Ramesses II's reign was also found at the site.

Kempinski contends that the site comprises three phases of settlement. In the first phase, nomads or seminomads left behind pits (which Zertal believes were cultic installations); then a farmhouse arose in the second phase; and finally, after a period of destruction, a watchtower and defensive wall were built. (Kempinski's second and third phases are shown in the upper two drawings at left.) But according to Zertal, there are no remains of a nomadic or seminomadic settlement, very little domestic pottery, no evidence of a destruction and no need for a watchtower because no ancient road passed near the site.

As explained in the accompanying article, Michael Coogan concludes, based on the criteria he has developed for identifying cult sites, that the Mt. Ebal site is indeed a cult site.

Mt. Ebal, the highest mountain (over 3,000 feet) in northern Samaria, the mountain where the curses were pronounced (Deuteronomy 27-28) and the mountain where Joshua raised his altar (Joshua 8:30-35), now figures in a bitter dispute. Long hidden under a stone heap on a northeastern ridge of Mt. Ebal, a controversial stone structure (above) may be the remains of an independent altar—the principal structure of a *bamah*, or "high place"— or of a farmhouse/watchtower, according to differing interpretations of the evidence. Discovered by Haifa University's Adam Zertal during a 1980 archaeological survey of the mountain, the site has many potsherds dating from the early part of Iron Age I (1200-1000 B.C.), the period generally accepted as the date of Israel's settlement of Canaan.

Large, unhewn fieldstones compose walls 5 feet thick and 9 feet high, forming a nearly square (24.5 feet by 29.5 feet) structure, at center right in the photo and dark gray in the upper half of the drawing at bottom left. Laid directly on bedrock, with neither a floor nor an entrance, and originally filled with layers of stones, earth and ashes, these walls are the walls of the altar's platform in Zertal's opinion. Zertal also believes they were surrounded by a slightly lower ledge, light gray in the same drawing. Mixed with the earthen fill were Iron Age I potsherds and animal bones that closely

match the description of animal sacrifice in Leviticus 1. Two corners of this structure point exactly (with less than one degree of error) to the north and the south, an alignment that suggests to Zertal a cultic function.

Archaeologist Aharon Kempinski views the structure differently. He believes that a house was filled in to form the base for a watchtower.

The 23-foot-long wall, or ramp, marked by the arrow in the photo and dark gray in the lower half of the drawing at bottom left, also provokes two interpretations. In Zertal's view, its 22-degree incline from left to right (as seen in the above photo) gives it the appearance of a ramp (as required by Exodus 20:26), but Kempinski argues that its width of slightly more than 3 feet is too narrow for a ramp. Kempinski regards the "ramp" as a wall and explains the incline as being the result of a common pattern of structural collapse, whereby the inner part of the wall was protected by debris from the watchtower while the outer, unprotected portion fell apart; he cites the variation in color from yellowish (protected) to whitish (exposed) as evidence for his explanation. The other walls adjoining the "ramp" are seen by Zertal as courtyard walls, light gray in the lower half of the drawing at bottom left, and are viewed by Kempinski as house walls (see drawing at top left).

A recently discovered carnelian scarab (right), issued during the reign

HEBREW UNIVERSITY OF JERUSALEM

119

wall, surrounds the supposed altar and the land that is adjacent to it.

Turning again to the criteria for determining whether this is a cultic site, Coogan notes that "there are no other Iron Age sites on the mountain; this site is therefore isolated."

As for the pottery, 70 percent of the vessels were collar-rim storage jars; 20 percent were jugs and chalices. It is significant that a number of miniature vessels were uncovered, but "very few cooking pots were found," observes Coogan.

Although the site is a one-period site, it did have two phases. In the early phase, stone installations were found in association with ashy debris, which might represent a continuity of cultic functions. In addition, the excavator cites a number of archaeological and literary parallels to other cultic sites.

As to the Mt. Ebal site, Coogan concludes:

"In view of the absence of significant numbers of elements of the ordinary domestic ceramic repertoire and the presence of miniature vessels, the isolation of the site from contemporary settlements, and some of the parallels adduced by Zertal, I tentatively concur with his interpretation of the function of the site as cultic."

But Coogan questions whether either site is Israelite. In identifying the sites as Israelite, the excavators relied on geography and chronology. Both sites are in areas assigned to the tribe of Manasseh in the Bible, and they flourished during a period (Iron Age I) when the Israelite tribal confederation is said to have occupied the land. To this Coogan responds:

"The problem of identification is, however, not so simple. The division of the land as described in Joshua is an ideal picture, as the early chapters of Judges make clear; this ideal is in many cases a retroversion of later geopolitical realities."

Just because a site is within these ideal boundaries does not mean it is necessarily Israelite. As Coogan points out:

"What distinguished the Israelites from their non-Israelite contemporaries was metaphysical, not physical . . . acceptance of Yahweh, the god of Israel, and concomitant allegiance to fellow Yahwists."

Coogan goes on to say:

"The biblical record makes it clear that as Israel developed in Canaan it grew in part by the conversion of individuals and groups who had not been part of the original nucleus . . . . Just as Israelites could commit apostasy by 'yoking themselves' to such deities as Baal Peor (Numbers 25:3; Psalms 106:28), so non-Yahwists could commit themselves to Yahweh and his adherents and join Israel. Notable examples include Rahab and her family (Joshua 2, 6:25) [and] the Gibeonites (Joshua 9, 18:25)."

Coogan argues that the houses and pottery of Yahwistic Israelites and their non-Yahwistic Canaanite neighbors are indistinguishable. He also notes that certain features such as collar-rim jars and the so-called four-room house,* which were previously thought to identify the early Israelites, have "now [been] prove[n] to have a much wider distribution." Both the collar-rim jar and the four-room house, says Coogan, "must now be seen as characteristic of the period throughout the larger region rather than isolated to one specific [ethnic] group."

In questioning whether these sites are Israelite, Coogan also relies on the similarities and continuities between Canaanite material culture of the Late Bronze Age and Israelite material culture in the succeeding Iron I period in the same geographical area.

Coogan concludes:

"Given the demonstrable continuities between the Late Bronze Age and the Iron Age and the complicated biblical picture of the origins of Israel, it is methodologically questionable to label specific exemplars by a designation which is religious and political. Only toward the end of the Iron I period do distinct national cultures emerge; until then it would be wise to avoid labels such as Israelite or Canaanite unless there is conclusive evidence for using them.

"Neither the enclosure where the bull figurine was found, nor the cultic installation on Mount Ebal, were necessarily Israelite, and it is misleading and ultimately unhelpful for the larger historical task of biblical archaeologists . . . to presume that these sites were Israelite."

In conclusion, Coogan raises the possibility that the Mt. Ebal site may have been "a local Canaanite shrine which was also (or later) used by Israelites, or at least that it was 'Israelitized.' "

---

* For an example of a four-room house, see Yohanan Aharoni, "The Israelite Occupation of Canaan," **BAR**, May/June 1982, p. 23.

Archaeological materials often present the interpreter with something of a three-dimensional Rorschach blot. That is, one may be tempted to find what one expects to find. The temptation can be doubly strong when dealing with artifacts or installations in the Biblical world. Not only does the interpreter have the extensive ancient library of the Biblical texts to suggest in advance what might be found in a given place and time, one also cannot help but have some personal inclination either toward finding materials that "fit" the Biblical accounts or toward being automatically suspicious of such findings when others claim to have made them. Where purported cultic objects or sites are concerned, there have been enough past instances of flamboyant claims that it would not be surprising that some scholars might tend to treat any new claim with scorn.

If Adam Zertal's installation was not on Mt. Ebal, would it have seemed as plausible to interpret the same physical evidence as either an altar or Israelite? On the other hand, might Aharon Kempinski have been inclined to overstate his counter-arguments in part because of some scholarly desire to distance himself from an interpretation he instinctively considers to be academically naive and romantic?

The Rorschach-blot syndrome not only can affect the interpretation of archaeological discoveries; it also can result in a too-hasty reading of the Biblical text. *Both* Zertal and some of his critics have assumed that the altar described in Deuteronomy 27 and Joshua 8 must be located at the place of cursing in the "blessing and curse" ceremony also described in those chapters. This assumption was made by Zertal in his initial article. Among his critics it was perhaps best expressed in a letter by Benyamin Tsedaka, director of the Institute of Samaritan Studies (**BAR** March/April 1987):

> The main witness against identifying the site as Joshua ben-Nun's altar is its location. The site discovered by Zertal is remote and inaccessible, on the northeastern slope of Mt. Ebal. From the site, it is not possible to view Mt. Gerizim, the mountain situated opposite Mt. Ebal, and certainly not Shechem. These facts irreconcilably contradict the Biblical description linking the erection of an altar with the "blessing and curse" ceremony performed on Mt. Gerizim and Mt. Ebal on sites opposite each other and overlooking Shechem (Joshua 8). The description in Joshua 8 notes the location of the ceremony as the valley between the two mountains.

On an initial reading it would be natural to infer that the altar of Deuteronomy 27:1-8 and Joshua 8:30-32 was associated with the ceremony described immediately thereafter in Deuteronomy 27:11ff. and Joshua 8:33-34. On closer reading, however, it must be acknowledged

that no specific reference is made to the ceremony in the descriptions of the altar-building and no reference is made to the altar in the descriptions of the ceremony. The Biblical editors may have brought together in these chapters two independent cultic traditions connected with Mt. Ebal.

Even if both traditions are historical and accurate as recorded, there is no inherent necessity for the ceremony to have made use of the altar. One could as easily find reasons why the altar and the ceremony might not have been at the same place. If Joshua built an altar on Mt. Ebal, as asserted by Joshua 8, at the outset of the conquest and before mention of any Israelite settlement at Shechem or elsewhere in the central hills, it is quite possible that the altar might have been placed at a "remote and [relatively] inaccessible" place on the mountain, well away from the Canaanites still occupying Shechem. Later, however, after Israelites had established themselves at Shechem (cf. Joshua 24), it would make sense for them to institute cultic ceremonies at locations nearer to the city on the facing slopes of the two nearby mountains.

Such a two-stage historical reconstruction would be thoroughly in harmony with the conquest account in Joshua. Zertal could even have proposed such a sequence of events to explain the abandonment of his proposed altar site in mid-12th century B.C. If Joshua had, indeed, built the installation Zertal discovered, it might well have been abandoned within the following century in favor of an as-of-yet undiscovered site on Mt. Ebal's southern slope nearer to Shechem.

For Further Reading

Concerning Early Israelite Three- and Four-Room House Architecture

Aharon Kempinski, "Israelite Conquest or Settlement? New Light from Tell Masos," **BAR**, September 1976

"**BAR** Readers to Restore Israelite Village from the Days of the Judges," **BAR**, January/February 1979

Yohanan Aharoni, "The Israelite Occupation of Canaan," **BAR**, May/June 1982

Concerning Israelite Cult Sites and Objects

"Horned Altar for Animal Sacrifice Unearthed at Beer-Sheva," **BAR**, March 1975

Hershel Shanks, "Yigael Yadin Finds a Bama at Beer-Sheva," **BAR**, March 1977

John C. H. Laughlin, "The Remarkable Discoveries at Tel Dan," **BAR**, September/October 1981

"Tom Crotser Has Found the Ark of the Covenant—Or Has He?" **BAR**, May/June 1983

"Is the Cultic Installation at Dan Really an Olive Press?" **BAR**, November/December 1984

Ze'ev Herzog, Miriam Aharoni and Anson F. Rainey, "Arad—An Ancient Israelite Fortress with a Temple to Yahweh," **BAR**, March/April 1987 (*see Section D*)

Concerning the Israelite Conquest and Settlement

Aharon Kempinski, "Israelite Conquest or Settlement? New Light from Tell Masos," **BAR**, September 1976

Yigael Yadin, "Is the Biblical Account of the Israelite Conquest of Canaan Historically Reliable?" **BAR**, March/April 1982

Yohanan Aharoni, "The Israelite Occupation of Canaan," **BAR**, May/June 1982

David Ussishkin, "Lachish—Key to the Israelite Conquest of Canaan?" **BAR**, January/February 1987 (*see Section C*)

Israel Finkelstein, "Searching for Israelite Origins," **BAR**, September/October 1988

The Citadel of Lachish Bears the Scars of Biblical Wars

Among the many smaller towns and villages that dotted ancient Canaan, a handful of major-sized cities emerged in the Bronze Age and continued to dominate the landscape through the rise and fall of the Israelite kingdoms in the Iron Age. Citadels such as Hazor and Megiddo in the north and Gezer on the southern coastal plain, along with a few other cities, were positioned where they could control rich agricultural areas and guard the main military and commercial corridors through the land.

These prominent sites mirrored in a special way the fortunes of those who ruled the land. During times of strong and aggressive leadership, they were the regional centers of political, commercial and cultic life. Here we find the most sophisticated fortification systems, more elaborate temples and shrines, concentrations of wealth and, occasionally, even palatial architecture. When political fortunes shifted, these cities tended like lightning rods to attract enemy assault, their periodic destructions leaving permanent scars as witness to those major moments of military crisis in Biblical history.

This section focuses on one of these sites in depth—the 18-acre mound of Tell ed-Duweir, about 25 miles southwest of Jerusalem in the foothills where it could guard the approaches to Judah from the south along the coastal plain. Extensive excavations by a British team in the 1930s and, since 1973, by the Israeli archaeologist David Ussishkin have provided a particularly rich spectrum of finds from a major Judean royal city at this site.

The findings are of special significance because the mound has been identified almost certainly as Biblical Lachish. As such, we can expect the site to bear grim testimony to the two great invasions that ultimately led to the fall of the Israelite state of Judah, the campaigns of the Assyrian king Sennacherib in 701 B.C. and of the Babylonians under Nebuchadnezzar in 587/586 B.C.

A major siege of Lachish during the earlier of these campaigns is not only mentioned in the Biblical histories (2 Kings 18:13-14,17; 2 Chronicles 32:1,9) and in Assyrian annals, it is also dramatically depicted on reliefs from the walls of Sennacherib's palace at Nineveh, uncovered by Austen Henry Layard in the 1840s. If the Lachish stratum associated with that siege could be determined with certainty, we would have a secure chronological anchor point for establishing Judean pottery typology at the end of the eighth century B.C. This, in turn, could lead to better dating of materials elsewhere in the Late Iron Age.

In the first article of this section, David Ussishkin summarizes the results of the British excavations and his own early seasons of excavation at Lachish and explains how he was led to redate the famous destruction of level III to 701 B.C.—the date of the Assyrian invasion.

Reflecting several further seasons of excavation, the second and third articles bring together the results of Ussishkin's investigations of siege and counter-siege works built in connection with Sennacherib's attack on Lachish. These are correlated with dramatic pictures from the ancient Nineveh reliefs portraying Sennacherib's siege of Lachish.

In the fourth article, we enjoy the results of a successful dialogue between the archaeological evidence and ancient pictorial evidence as Yigael Yadin interprets the meaning of an enigmatic length of chain uncovered by Ussishkin in the siege debris.

Digging deeper and reaching further back in time, Ussishkin's more recent excavation seasons have focused on the Late Bronze Canaanite layers at Lachish and on the two destructions the city experienced at the end of that period, one in the 13th century and a final one in the later 12th century B.C. Here again, the archaeological record has special importance in relation to the Biblical account. Joshua 10:31-32 claims that

> Joshua passed on from Libnah, and all Israel with him, to Lachish, and laid siege to it, and assaulted it; and the Lord gave Lachish into the hand of Israel, and he took it on the second day, and smote it with the edge of the sword, and every person in it, as he had done to Libnah.

In the final article, we see how Ussishkin interprets the evidence from Lachish as it relates to the Biblical conquest account. This is followed by two readers' alternative interpretations of the evidence, with Ussishkin's response.

Sennacherib's destruction of Lachish
identified; dispute over a century's difference
in Israelite pottery dating resolved by new
excavations; stamp impressions of Judean
kings finally dated.

Answers at Lachish

By David Ussishkin

LACHISH was one of the most important cities
of the Biblical era in the Holy Land. The impressive mound, named Tel Lachish in Hebrew or
Tell ed-Duweir in Arabic, is situated about 25 miles
southwest of Jerusalem in the Judean hills. Once a
thriving, fortified city, the almost 18 acre tel* today
stands silent and unoccupied (see p. 129).

* Readers may be confused by the use of the two spellings of
"tel" and "tell" to refer to an ancient mound. "Tell" is the
transliteration of the Arabic word and is used with an Arabic
site name; "tel" is the transliteration of the Hebrew word and
modifies a Hebrew site name. When speaking of *specific*
mounds we use the appropriate spellings; but when speaking in
general we use "tell."

Assyrian archers *march in formation in Sennacherib's palace at Nineveh on one of the reliefs commemorating a military victory.*

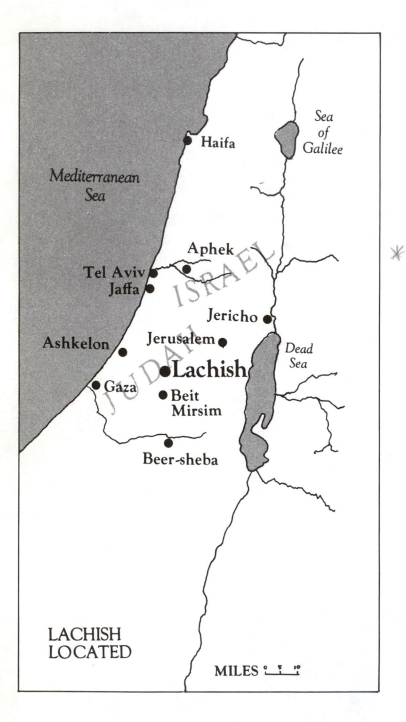

LACHISH
LOCATED

MILES 0 5 10

Settlement began here in the Chalcolithic period, toward the end of the fourth millennium B.C. By the third millennium Lachish was already a large city. In the Middle Bronze Age (first half of the second millennium B.C.), Lachish was heavily fortified by a glacis* which gave the mound its present prominent shape. In the Late Bronze Age (16th-13th centuries B.C.), Lachish was a large Canaanite city-state. A few letters from Lachish were found in the 14th century royal Egyptian archives at Tell el-Amarna. They were sent from the Canaanite king of the city to the Egyptian pharaoh.

Lachish played a major role in the story of the Israelite conquest of Canaan as related in Joshua 10. Japhia, king of Lachish, joined an alliance of five kings whom Joshua defeated on the day the sun stood still. After defeating these armies and killing their royal leaders, Joshua proceeded to attack their cities. Lachish was able to defend itself against Joshua's forces only for a single day. On the second day of the attack, Joshua took Lachish. He destroyed the city and killed its inhabitants. Excavations have confirmed a major destruction level at about this time (12th century B.C.). The archaeological record has also revealed that for about the next 200 years, until the 10th century B.C., Lachish was mostly abandoned.

Following the division of the United Kingdom into Judah and Israel at Solomon's death, Lachish was rebuilt and heavily fortified by one of the kings of Judah, who turned it into a garrison city and royal stronghold. Undoubtedly the most important Judean city after Jerusalem, the city was defended by two massive city walls, the outer one built half way down the slope and the inner one extending along the edge

* A glacis is an artificial ramp built against a slope in order to fortify it. This was the typical fortification used in the country during the Middle Bronze Age.

of the mound. A large gate complex on the southwest side protected the city at its entrance. A huge palace-fort crowned the center of the city. Lachish played a major role in Judah until its destruction at the hands of Nebuchadnezzar's Babylonian army in 588/6 B.C. The city was rebuilt again in the Persian-Hellenistic period (sixth-fourth centuries B.C.), when it served as a district capital. Then it was abandoned forever.

A British expedition headed by James L. Starkey conducted large scale excavations at Tel Lachish between 1932 and 1938. This was one of the largest and most methodical excavations carried out in Palestine before the Second World War. Starkey systematically planned the work many years ahead. He spent the first years principally in preparatory work, away from the mound itself. He dug ancient graveyards in the vicinity of the tel, cleared areas on the slopes, and built a convenient expedition camp. Some, but relatively little, work was done on the mound proper. The excavations, however, came to an abrupt halt in 1938. While travelling from Lachish to Jerusalem, to attend the opening ceremony of the Palestine Archaeological Musuem, Starkey was forced by Arab bandits to stop near Hebron. Without warning the bandits shot him dead. After Starkey's murder, the excavation was wound down, while his assistant Olga Tufnell worked for twenty years on the data and finds, in the end producing a meticulous excavation report.

The mound remained untouched until the present excavations, except for a small dig carried out by Professor Yohanan Aharoni of Tel Aviv University on the eastern part of the mound.

One of the main areas excavated on the mound proper by the British expedition was the city gate complex and the roadway which led to it from outside the city. The city gate is situated near the southwest corner of the mound, and, in fact, the topographical

James L. Starkey *headed a British expedition which conducted large scale excavations at Tel Lachish between 1932 and 1938. Rarely photographed, he is shown here in the expedition camp. His excavation was one of the largest and most methodical carried out in Palestine before World War II. It came to an abrupt halt in 1938, when Starkey was murdered while en route to the opening ceremony of the Palestine Archaeological Museum (known today as the Rockefeller Museum in east Jerusalem).*

The inner gateway. *The Lachish ostraca were found in a room in the outer gate of the double gate complex. In the upper right corner three people stand at the entrance leading through the gateway. The inner gateway was originally composed of four piers forming three rooms. Before the Assyrians destroyed Level IV-III in 701 B.C., an identical set of piers and rooms stood opposite. This is the largest city gate known from the Israelite period, measuring about 100 feet long by 75 feet wide.*

An inscribed ostracon *records the death throes of Lachish, just before the Babylonians razed the city in 588/6 B.C. Twenty-one ostraca, written in clear Biblical Hebrew, were buried under the debris of the Level II outer gate guard room. Lachish Letter IV poignantly portrays the last days of Lachish in a letter from a soldier (Hoshaiah) at a settlement some distance from Lachish to his commander at Lachish (one Yaosh): "And let (my Lord) know that we are watching for the beacons of Lachish . . . we cannot see [the beacons from] Azekah." Hoshaiah assumes that, since the beacons of Azekah no longer burn, it has already fallen. Azekah is just 11 miles northeast of Lachish. Jeremiah (34:7) records that Azekah and Lachish were the last Judean strongholds to be taken by the Babylonians.*

lines had revealed its existence even before work began. As often happens in ancient Biblical cities, a number of city gates were found superimposed on one another, each associated with a different occupation level, each having been used during a different period in the city's history.

The first city gate uncovered by Starkey was naturally the uppermost and the latest one. It dated to the Persian period, and was in use until the final abandonment of the site. This gate and the related level, forming the uppermost archaeological stratum, was labelled Level I by the British. On penetrating further, the excavators found that the Level I gate and roadway were constructed above an earlier gate complex, which was accordingly labelled Level II. This earlier gate had been destroyed in an enemy attack, as evidenced by a thick layer of destruction debris over the remains of the Level II gate.

At that point Starkey made his most famous discovery: a small room, later called the guard room, was found within the Level II gate-complex. The floor of the guard room was covered by the ashes of the destruction. Beneath the ashes were sealed hundreds of storage jar fragments blackened by the intense fire which accompanied the destruction. Eighteen of these pottery fragments contained ancient Hebrew inscriptions written in ink. These ostraca, that is, inscribed pot sherds, are known today as the Lachish Letters. They were sent to a military commander at Lachish during the last days of the kingdom of Judah, when Nebuchadnezzar, king of Babylon, had already begun to conquer Judah.

That Lachish was attacked and almost certainly destroyed by Nebuchadnezzar at that time (588/6 B.C.), is proven by the striking words of the prophet Jeremiah (34:7): "And the king of Babylon's army attacked Jerusalem and the remaining cities of Judah, namely Lachish and Azekah; for these were the only

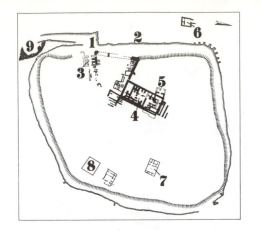

Tel Lachish: *1. Bastion, 2. Outer Wall, 3. Level IV-III Inner Gate, 4. Judean Palace-Fort, 5. Late Bronze Age Temple, 6. Fosse Temple, 7. Solar Shrine, 8. Shaft, 9. Siege Ramp.*

Tel Lachish *viewed from the northeast. The Judean Palace-Fort appears as a raised rectangular area on the far side of the top of the mound.*

Judean soldiers *defend the main city gate of Lachish;
below, an exodus of women enter captivity. To the right of
the gate, Assyrian footmen with battering rams attack the
weakened city walls. At the bottom of the wooden tracks,
three hapless defenders are impaled. For more details, see
the overleaf, "The Siege of Lachish."*

fortified cities left in Judah." The discovery of the
'Lachish Letters' in the city gate together with late Judean pottery indicate that the destruction of the
Level II city-gate—and the associated city—must be
assigned, in accordance with the testimony of
Jeremiah, to the Babylonian conquest. From the
archaeological point of view, this means that Level II
was destroyed and sealed under destruction debris in
588/6 B.C.

As the excavations in the gate area continued,
Starkey soon discovered that the Level II city-gate
complex was built above an even earlier gate-complex, which he accordingly labelled Level III. This
gate-complex was much larger and more massive, and
only small parts of it were uncovered by the time the
excavations ended in 1938. It was nevertheless clear
that the Level III gate had been razed in an intense
conflagration. Remains of this terrible destruction
were also found wherever the excavator's spade
reached contemporaneous remains in the city. Shops
and houses built along the road which led from the
gate into the city, the huge fortified palace (probably
the seat of the Judean governor), and houses built
beside the palace—all had been destroyed and were
covered with a fiery debris. It was clear that Level III
had been a fortified and densely populated Judean
city which was completely destroyed in a fierce enemy
attack. The question was: When and by whom was
the Level III city destroyed.

By 1937 Starkey's views had already crystallized.
Greatly influenced by William F. Albright's dating of
the Judean levels at Tell Beit Mirsim (situated a short
distance to the southeast of Lachish), Starkey suggested in a London lecture that Level III at Lachish
was destroyed in the Babylonian campaign of 597
B.C. In that year Nebuchadnezzar beseiged and occupied Jerusalem, deposed King Jehoiachin, put
Zedekiah on the throne of Judah, and deported a large
segment of the population (2 Kings 24:15 ff). Starkey
believed that the close resemblance between the pottery of Level III and Level II indicated that a
relatively short period must have elapsed between the
destruction of the two levels. The dating of Level II to

588 B.C. seemed certain, so this observation concerning the similar pottery fit well with Starkey's conclusion that Level III must have been destroyed in 597
B.C., only about a decade before the destruction of
the superimposed Level II.

When Olga Tufnell worked on the material after
Starkey's murder, she reached different conclusions.
In her opinion there was a clear typological difference
between the pottery of Level III and Level II. Tufnell
relied especially upon material from Level II which
had been uncovered in the windup of the excavation
after Starkey's death. Tufnell also discerned two
phases in the Level II gate, each of which had been
destroyed by fire. If there were two phases within
Level II, this made it even more unlikely that only a
decade separated Level II and Level III. Tufnell thus
concluded that a much longer period must have
elapsed between the two levels, and that Level III
must have been destroyed much earlier than 597 B.C.
She assigned its destruction to the Assyrian conquest
of 701 B.C., a famous and well-documented historical
event which will be discussed later in this article.

The dispute over the dating of Level III reflected
one of the most serious and central dating problems in
Palestinian archaeology. So long as it remained
unresolved, scholars would disagree by more than 100
years about the dating of Level III pottery. This pottery repertoire had been found not only at Lachish
but at a host of other sites as well.

The effort to resolve this dating problem focused
primarily on Lachish. In scholarly shorthand the
problem was put at countless scholarly meetings and
conversations. What was the destruction date of
Lachish Level III? The reason the spotlight was
directed at Lachish Level III rather than at contemporaneous levels at other sites was because of the clear
and unambiguous stratigraphy at Lachish, the rich assemblages of pottery and other finds, and the historical connections of the site. All this turned Lachish
into a key site and the question of the date of the
destruction of Level III became a problem of sustained scholarly attention. Many famous scholars expressed their opinion on the matter. The 597 B.C.
date was supported by W.F. Albright, B.W.
Buchanan, G. Ernest Wright, Paul W. Lapp, Frank
M. Cross, Jr., H. Darrell Lance, J. S. Holladay, Jr.
and Dame Kathleen Kenyon. Dame Kathleen based
her opinion on the results of excavations at Samaria,
located in the northern part of the country. Samaria,
the capital of the kingdom of Israel, was conquered in

The relief of the Siege of Lachish *from Sennacherib's palace at Nineveh commemorates one of the Assyrian king's greatest victories. The storming of the city gate, shown here, illustrates the powerful Assyrian war machine described in Sennacherib's annals. Preserved in several cuneiform accounts, these annals boast that Sennacherib "laid seige to 46 . . . strong cities . . . by means of well-stamped (earth) ramps, and battering rams brought (thus) near (to the walls) (combined with) the attack by foot soldiers, (using) mines, breaches as well as siege engines."*

On the far left, the relief depicts soldiers from Lachish standing on the city's crenelated walls; the wall is reinforced with a series of round shields (top). Below the walls (on the far left), we see the Judean hilly terrain depicted as rows of scallops. On the bottom from the far left can be seen Assyrian archers scaling the first of seven wooden log tracks leading to the city gate. These tracks were laid on beaten earth siege ramps and were used to roll battering rams toward the walls. These battering rams, which are being pushed up each set of log tracks, are encased in a four-wheeled siege engine which not only

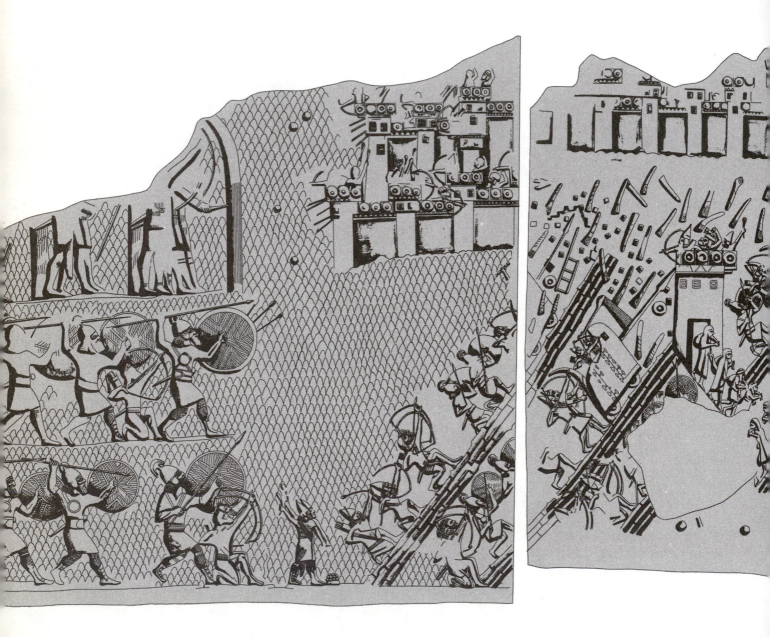

protects the soldiers pushing inside but provides a platform for Assyrian warriors as well. Judean soldiers fighting from the walls above the Assyrian siege ramp hurl torches, slingstones, and arrows at their attackers.

Note the battering ram along the diagonal of the second track from the left. As a safety measure against the flaming torches which the Lachishites fling toward them, an Assyrian soldier pours water over the battering ram facade with a large ladle. Directly in front of this battering ram is the main city gate of Lachish. Through it a line of Judean women leave the city. Above the heads of the Lachish

soldiers on the gate are the walls of what may be the Palace-Fort (see p. 136). To the right of the city gate five battering rams breach the city walls; below them (bottom center) three Judean defenders impaled on posts are displayed by Assyrian soldiers.

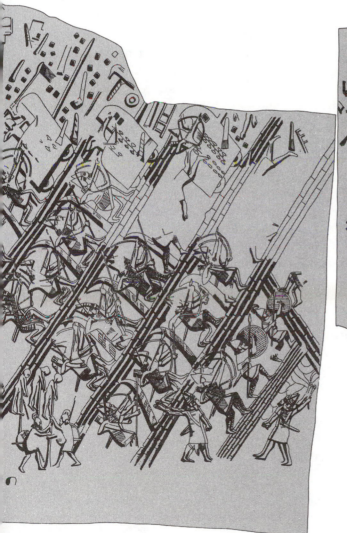
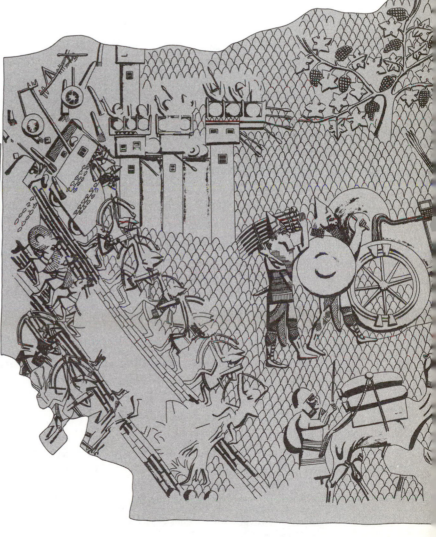

Tel Lachish *(in an artist's rendering) with its double fortification wall, impressive double gateway complex, residences crowding the mound, and the large Palace-Fort crowning the center of the city.*

720 B.C. by Sargon, king of Assyria. Dame Kathleen assigned the destruction of Period VI to this event. The pottery of Period VI could thus be securely dated to that time. The Samaria Period VI pottery (c. 720 B.C.) differed sharply from the Lachish Level III pottery, so Dame Kathleen concluded that a long span of time must have passed between Period VI at Samaria and Level III at Lachish. To her, in light of the Samaria Period VI pottery, 701 B.C. was too early for Lachish Level III; therefore the destruction level must be assigned to 597 B.C. In this reasoning, she assumed that pottery styles changed along similar lines in the northern and southern parts of the country—an assumption now known to be of very doubtful validity for many periods.

The 701 B.C. date for Lachish Level III was supported, on the other hand, by Ruth Amiran, Benjamin Mazar, R.D. Barnett, Anson F. Rainey, and especially by Yohanan Aharoni. For more than a decade Aharoni excavated in Judah, studying its history and material culture, and in 1966 and 1968 he carried out excavations on the eastern part of Tel Lachish, in the "Solar Shrine" area. This work added vast quantitites of material relevant to the subject. Aharoni believed that sharp differences exist between the Level III and II pottery assemblages, differences which could be easily recognized in contemporary assemblages all over Judah. It thus seemed impossible to him that only a decade separated the two levels.

In 1973 Tel Aviv University's Institute of Archaeology and the Israel Exploration Society began renewed excavations at Lachish under my direction.*

* These excavations are sponsored by a number of public bodies, primarily by the Samuel H. Kress Foundation in New York, as well as The Northwest Christian College in Eugene, Oregon; Central College in Pella, Iowa; Florida College in Florida, and the University of South Africa in Pretoria.

Six excavation seasons were conducted between 1973 and 1978. The next season is planned for the summer of 1980.

The new excavations have concentrated on three main excavation areas or fields, to use the jargon of the trade: (1) the Judean palace-fort and the Canaanite buildings underneath (under the supervision of Christa Clamer); (2) the Judean city gate and its environs (under the supervision of Y. Eshel); and (3) another area at the western part of the mound (under the supervision of Gabriel Barkay). The palace-fort and the city gate areas had already been partially dug by Starkey; here we are continuing his work. In the new area on the western part of the mound, we have dug a relatively narrow trench cutting through the edge of the mound which will eventually extend to the lower slope. Here we hope to penetrate the lower levels of the mound, and get a sectional view of the various levels down to bed rock, following the pattern set by Dame Kathleen Kenyon in her excavations at Jericho. Last year we also started an archaeological survey of the Lachish area (under the supervision of Y. Dagan).*

After a few years of systematic digging in these areas the stratigraphic picture of Lachish in the Israelite period including Level III, has now been completely clarified. All the areas uncovered by Starkey at the western part of the mound have been stratigraphically connected to our new excavation areas. All our excavation areas have now been linked to one another through monumental structures: The Judean palace-fort has been connected to the massive wall labelled "the enclosure wall." The latter, cross-

* In addition to those mentioned above, the archaeological core-staff of the expedition includes A. Urweider from Switzerland, architect, and Orna Zimhoni, recorder. Song Nai Rhee from Oregon is the U.S. expedition's coordinator.

ing our "section area," has been physically connected to the inner city-wall built along the upper periphery of the mound, which in turn has been linked to the massive city-gate. All these monumental structures may be looked upon as forming the skeleton of the mound. In turn, we established the relationship of each monumental structure to its adjacent habitation levels and accumulated debris, the latter representing the flesh of the mound and providing the relevent stratified data for the related monumental structures. At a number of points the stratigraphy of the mound was checked down to the Late Bronze Age (that is, to the latest Canaanite city level), confirming Starkey's allocation of six strata between the Late Bronze Age and the Persian-Hellenistic period. In addition, an independent—but similar—stratigraphical picture was observed by Aharoni in his trench at the eastern part of the mound. The following picture clearly emerges:

Level VI represents the final Late Bronze Age (that is, Canaanite) city. At that time Canaanite Lachish reached its prime, a prosperous and flourishing city with a rich material culture. The city came to a sudden end and was destroyed by fire in the 12th century B.C. We believe that this destruction should be attributed to the invading Israelites, as recorded in the book of Joshua 10:31-32.

Level V: Following the complete destruction of the Canaanite city, the site was abandoned until the tenth century, the period of the United Kingdom of Israel. At that time, settlement was renewed, and is represented by Level V. Many small houses were then built all over the site, but no defense wall along the edge of the mound protected the city. This settlement was also destroyed by fire. A monumental structure known as Palace A dates from this period and became the first stage of the Judean palace-fort. It is not clear whether Palace A was contemporaneous with the rest of the Level V houses, or whether it was built after

THE STRATIGRAPHY OF TEL LACHISH
(as interpreted by the current expedition)

Present to 1000 A.D.	Medieval graves; remains of Israel's 1948 War of Independence
Post-exilic period (Babylonian, Persian, Hellenistic) 1st century B.C. to 6th century B.C.	LEVEL I: fortified city in main phase; city wall and gate; Residency; Solar Shrine; houses and pits
588/6 B.C.	Destruction: Babylonian conquest LEVEL II: sparsely populated Judean city; city wall and gate; the Lachish letters
	Intermediate stage in deserted gate area
701 B.C.	Destruction: Assyrian conquest LEVEL III: densely populated city; same fortifications and rebuilt palace-fort (Palace C)
	LEVEL IV: royal Judean fortified city; two city walls and gate; palace-fort (Palace B)
Late 10th century B.C.	LEVEL V, Late Phase: Palace A—Rehoboam's fort(?)
c. 925 B.C.(?)	Destruction: Shishak's campaign(?) LEVEL V, Earlier Phase: unfortified(?) settlement; cultroom; houses
	gap in habitation—site deserted
12th century B.C. Late Bronze Age III	Destruction: Israelite conquest(?) LEVEL VI: prosperous, densely populated and unfortified Canaanite city under Egyptian control; Fosse Temple III
14th century B.C. Late Bronze Age II	Destruction LEVEL VII: city of el-Amarna period; Fosse Temple II
Late Bronze Age I	mound sparsely populated; Fosse Temple I
16th century B.C. Middle Bronze Age III	Destruction LEVEL VIII: fortified city; glacis and fosse; palace
Middle Bronze Age I-II	Mound levels not excavated
Intermediate EB-MB Period	Cemetery 2000; settlement outside mount
Early Bronze Age 3rd millennium B.C.	Mound levels not excavated; tombs; caverns; Khirbet Kerak ware
Chalcolithic Period (Ghassulian) 4th millennium B.C.	First settlement on mound
Prehistoric periods	Remains in general area of Lachish

A massive foundation wall *of the Judean Palace-Fort. Initially uncovered during the Starkey excavations in the 1930s, this wall supported one of the largest, most impressive buildings from the Iron Age (see p. 129). Presently crowning the central part of the mound, the palace extends over half an acre. The foundation walls, at one point preserved to a height of more than 35 feet, were filled with soil to provide a gigantic substructure for the palace.*

their destruction. In either case, we are inclined to assign the construction of Palace A to Rehoboam, since in 2 Chronicles 11:5-12, 23 Lachish is mentioned among the cities fortified by him.

Level IV represents a royal Judean fortified city constructed by one of the kings of Judah who reigned after Rehoboam. We are not sure which one. This city was built according to a unified architectural concept, and—in comparison with other provincial Judean cities—on a grandiose scale. The summit was crowned by the huge palace-fort (Palace B). Auxiliary buildings which served as stables or storehouses flanked Palace B. The city was defended by two rings of fortification walls connected to a massive gate-complex. Many open spaces suggest that at the beginning of Level IV Lachish was probably a garrison city rather than a settlement of the usual type. The city of Level IV probably served as a royal garrison city for a relatively long period of time. Level IV came to a sudden end, but it seems clear that this was not caused by fire. In any case, the data points to the continuation of life without a break at the end of Level IV: The Level IV fortifications continued to function in Level III, and other structures of Level IV were rebuilt in Level III.

The Level III city continued to function as a royal Judean fortified city. The fortifications and the palace-fort (Palace C) continued to be used with some modifications. The main change which took place was construction of a large number of houses which were uncovered in the area between the city-gate and the palace-fort. The houses are small and densely built, and are quite different from the neighboring monumental structures. These houses, which contained an enormous amount of pottery and other domestic utensils, clearly reflect a substantial increase in the population. An intense fire destroyed all the buildings of Level III, monumental and domestic.

An intermediate stage between Level III and Level II consists of a poor habitation level lying on the ruins of the destroyed city gate of Levels IV-III; no fortifications existed at this time.

In Level II the city was partly rebuilt. A new city wall and city gate were constructed. The palace-fort, however, apparently remained in ruins. Houses were built sporadically all around. Level II was totally destroyed by fire, almost certainly in the Babylonian conquest of 588/6 B.C.

Level I represents the post-exilic remains, including the Persian city-walls, city gate, and small palace (the Residency).

Needless to say, from the beginning of our work, the paramount question in our minds was the date of destruction of Level III. It seemed to us that a satisfactory and conclusive solution to this problem could be found only by means of direct stratigraphical evidence recovered from the mound. After a few years of digging and deliberations, and after the stratigraphy of the mound has been clarified as summarized above, we think the problem has been solved. Before presenting the suggested solution, however, I should first set before the reader the events of 701 B.C., which have considerable bearing on the problem.

During the last part of the eighth century B.C. the Assyrian empire was at its prime. Centered in northern Mesopotamia, the area of the upper Tigris River, it politically dominated the entire Near East. In 720 B.C. the Assyrians conquered the kingdom of Israel; the Israelites were deported (and became the ten lost tribes) and the country became an Assyrian province. The kingdom of Judah, however, remained independent for a few more years. In 705 B.C. Sennacherib ascended the Assyrian throne. One of his first tasks was to deal with an alliance against Assyria which included Egypt, some Philistine city-states along the Mediterranean Sea, and King Hezekiah of Judah, who

reigned in Jerusalem. In 701 B.C. Sennacherib took on the coalition. The events of Sennacherib's military campaign are recounted in detail both in the Bible and in contemporary Assyrian records (the different sources are, however, somewhat inconsistent). Sennacherib's army first marched south from Phoenicia along the sea coast. Here Sennacherib successfully repelled the Egyptian army and subjugated the Philistine cities. The Assyrian monarch next turned on Judah. He conquered most of the country except for Jerusalem, where Hezekiah somehow managed to withstand the siege (see 2 Chronicles 32; 2 Kings 18-19). Sennacherib tells us in his royal annals inscribed in cuneiform that he "laid siege to 46 . . . strong cities, walled forts and to countless small villages (of Judah) in their vicinity, and conquered (them) by means of well-stamped (earth-) ramps, and battering-rams brought (thus) near (to the walls) (combined with) the attack by foot soldiers, (using) mines, breaches as well as siege engines." As to the inhabitants, he "drove out (of them) 200,150 people, young and old, male and female, horses, mules, donkeys, camels, big and small cattle beyond counting, and considered (them) booty." Other Assyrian inscriptions tell in brief that the Assyrian king "laid waste the large district of Judah." The Bible corroborates the Assyrian sources: "In the fourteenth year of King Hezekiah did Sennacherib king of Assyria come up against all the fortified cities of Judah, and took them" (2 Kings 18:13; Isaiah 36:1; also 2 Chronicles 32:1).

The city of Lachish was one of the conquered Judean strongholds, as we are informed by two different sources. First, the Bible states that Sennacherib camped at Lachish and established his headquarters there, at least during part of his sojourn in Judah (2 Kings 18:14,17; 19:8; Isaiah 36:2; 37:8; 2 Chronicles 32:9). Second, the famous Lachish reliefs at Sen-

The Assyrian and Babylonian *attacks on Lachish took place at the southwest corner of the mound (pictured here). This is the most vulnerable point of the stronghold. The British expedition removed a large vertical section from the mound. This section appears as a light, pebbly triangle on the far right side of the tell. The outer rim of the tell and the "path" (to the left center) mark the limits of this vertical section. The current excavations have proved that this exposed section and the slope above the large boulders (center left) are part of a siege ramp built by the Assyrians. The ramp was about 55 meters (180 feet) wide at its base and 16 meters (52 feet) high—terminating at the base of Lachish's outer city wall. Depicted in the Lachish reliefs (see pp. 132-133), the ramp was mounted by Assyrian battering rams and archers during the siege of Lachish in 701 B.C.*

Testimony to the ferocity *of the battles at Lachish against the Babylonians in 588/6 and the Assyrians in 701 B.C. are these sling stones and arrowheads which the British excavated in the 1930's.*

138

nacherib's palace in Nineveh record the attack and conquest of Lachish. (See pp. 124, 130, 132.)

When Sennacherib transferred the Assyrian capital to Nineveh (modern Kuyunjik), he devoted great effort to beautifying the city, especially by the construction of his royal palace. This extravagant edifice is described in detail in Sennacherib's inscriptions; he proudly called it the "Palace without rival"! Called the South-West Palace by Sir Henry Layard who excavated it on behalf of the British Museum in the middle of the nineteenth century, the building lends considerable support to Sennacherib's description. Unfortunately, the science of archaeology was in its infancy in the nineteenth century and Layard's methods as well as the records he left behind are far below modern standards. Layard did, however, prepare a partial plan of the building and uncovered a large number of stone reliefs adorning the walls.

A special room, centrally positioned in a large ceremonial suite of the palace contained the Lachish reliefs depicting Sennacherib's conquest of Lachish. The walls of this room were completely covered with reliefs in this series. The length of the entire series was nearly 90 feet. The preserved part—now exhibited in the British Museum in London—is nearly 60 feet long. The slabs at the left-hand side have been lost, but according to Layard they portrayed "large bodies of horsemen and charioteers" kept in reserve behind the attacking army. Further along, in consecutive order from left to right, are shown the attacking infantry, the storming of Lachish, the transfer of booty, captives and families going to exile, ——————— Sennacherib sitting on his throne, ——————— the royal tent and chariots and, finally, the Assyrian camp—almost certainly the camp mentioned in the Bible. One of the two accompanying inscriptions identifies the city as Lachish. The actual storming of Lachish is depicted in the center of the series, opposite the entrance to the room, so everyone approaching the room would see it.

We believe the detailed relief gives an accurate and realistic picture of the city and the siege. The relief conveys to the viewer an impression of the strength of Lachish's fortifications, as well as the ferocity of the attack. The city is built on a hill, and is surrounded by two high walls shown at the two sides of the relief. In the center of the relief is the city gate, depicted as a free-standing structure. Judean refugees are shown leaving it. An isolated structure above the gate seems to be the huge palace-fort whose remains were uncovered in the excavations. The main Assyrian siege ramp is shown to the right of the gate; here five battering rams, supported by infantry, attack the city wall. A second siege ramp is shown to the left of the gate, and here two more battering rams attack the gate and the wall. The defenders, standing on the walls, are equipped with bows and slings; they hurl stones and burning torches on the attacking Assyrians. Those Lachishites defending the city wall at the point of the siege ramp are throwing burning chariots down on the Assyrians below—probably a last, desperate attempt to stop the Assyrian onslaught. The fact that seven battering rams are involved in the attack—as compared to one or two battering rams which are usually depicted in Assyrian siege scenes—is a good indication of the unusual importance and scale of this battle.

The central architectural position of the 'Lachish room' in Sennacherib's palace, the unusual length of the relief series, the detailed portrayals, the scale of the attack—all this leads to clear-cut conclusions. First, the conquest of Lachish was of singular importance; it may even have been Sennacherib's greatest military achievement prior to the construction of the royal palace. At any rate, no other campaign of Sennacherib was recorded in a similar fashion. Thus, in

Two Judean city walls *and a Canaanite building are shown at different stages of excavation on the western edge of the mound of Lachish. In the upper picture the two walls are superimposed. The later wall (Level II), destroyed by the Babylonian army in 588/6 B.C., is seen as a row of stones on the top and flank of the sloping left side of the mound; the earlier wall (Levels IV-III), destroyed by the Assyrians in 701 BC., can be seen preserved to a considerable height, with a ladder leaning against it. Two years later, when the lower picture was taken, the Judean city wall has been removed. The earlier wall consisted of a stone foundation (or socle) and a mud brick superstructure. Here most of the mud bricks of the lower, earlier wall have been completely removed, but a section of mud brick is still visible in top center. The square flat area is the stone foundation of the earlier wall. The remains of a still earlier Canaanite building (Level VI) are visible under the lower wall, on the upper left. This Canaanite building was destroyed by fire, probably during the Israelite conquest.*

701 B.C. Lachish was a strongly fortified city, probably the strongest in Judah after Jerusalem. Second, we can conclude that Lachish was conquered, burnt and razed to the ground by the Assyrian army in that year. Although the burning and destruction of Lachish are not specifically recorded in Sennacherib's annals, and in fact are not shown on the surviving parts of the relief (the upper section of the relief which has not been preserved, however, may well have depicted tongues of fire coming out of the burning city), it nevertheless seems likely, considering the importance Sennacherib attached to Lachish, that the city was razed after its conquest.

In light of the evidence summarized above—historical as well as stratigraphic—the crucial question of the destruction date of Lachish Level III can be resolved. In 701 B.C. Lachish was a strongly fortified city which was conquered and destroyed. Thus there must be a conspicuous burnt level representing this destroyed city. Level VI, as we have seen, is a Canaanite city that was destroyed in the 12th century B.C. and Level II represents the latest Judean city, destroyed by the Babylonian army in 588/6 B.C. This leaves us with three possible "candidates" for the city destroyed by Sennacherib: Levels V, IV and III. The settlement of Level V, possibly unfortified, which is characterized by 10th century pottery, can hardly represent a large, fortified city, and cannot be dated to the end of the 8th century B.C. Level IV apparently came to a sudden end, but it seems clear that this was not caused by fire. Morever, the city walls and city gate of Level IV continued to function in Level III, and some Level IV structures were rebuilt in Level III. These facts point toward the continuation of life without a break. Considering that the fortifications remained intact, we can hardly identify this level with the city which was stormed and completely destroyed in the fierce Assyrian attack of 701 B.C. Level III thus remains the sole suitable "candidate," and we have no alternative but to conclude that this is the level destroyed by Sennacherib in 701 B.C.

The finds from this level correspond well with the accounts of the Assyrian attack describing the tragic fate of Lachish. The strong fortified city of this level was completely destroyed by fire. The palace-fort and the city gate were burnt down to their foundations, the city wall was razed to the ground, and houses were burnt and buried under the debris. Signs of conflagration are visible everywhere; in some places the accumulated destruction debris—including mud-bricks baked hard by the intense fire—reached a height of nearly 6 feet. The British expedition had the impression that some walls were even pulled down after the collapse of the superstructure. The large number of iron arrowheads found in this level are additional evidence for a raging battle. Pottery and other utensils were found crushed under the debris of the houses. There is no evidence that the inhabitants later tried to retrieve their belongings or reconstruct their homes.

A destruction date of 701 B.C. for Level III also accords better with the findings in the city gate area than a date of 597 B.C. We uncovered much pottery in this area, both in Level III and in Level II. Special mention should be made of two storerooms, one destroyed at the end of Level III and the other at the end of Level II. Both storerooms contained large assemblages of pottery vessels typical of storerooms which had been crushed and buried at the time of their destruction (see p. 145). The pottery repertoire from the later storeroom clearly differs from that found in the earlier one; obviously, it would have taken longer than a decade for these typological changes to have occurred. Also, we found a modest reoccupation on the ruins of the old, Level III gate, before the construction of the new, Level II gate. This reoccupation makes it all the more difficult to suggest that Level II followed Level III within a decade or so. There are simply too many changes for all of them to have occurred in so short a time.

In summary, the following picture emerges. The densely populated and prosperous city of Level III was attacked and conquered by Sennacherib in 701 B.C. Following the battle, the city most likely was sacked, burnt and razed to the ground by the Assyrian army, and then left in ruins. Most of the survivors, if not all, were forced to leave the city. Many were probably killed by the Assyrian soldiers, either in battle, or after having been taken into captivity. The British expedition found evidence for wholesale slaughter in one large tomb which contained a mass burial of about 1500 people. The Lachish reliefs also depict Judean prisoners being impaled and stabbed. Many of the remaining Lachishites were probably exiled and may be numbered among the 200,150 Judean deportees mentioned in the Assyrian inscriptions. The deportation scenes in the Lachish reliefs show large families as they are being driven out of the city, their belongings in their hands, or loaded on ox-carts or camels.

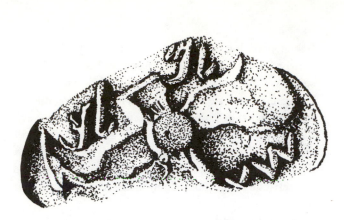

Sennacherib tells in his inscription that the towns which he had plundered were given to the Philistine cities along the Mediterranean coast. That is, to Ashdod, Ekron and Gaza. The desolate city of Lachish was probably one of those towns. It is reasonable to assume that the city was left in ruins and deserted during a large part of the seventh century B.C., even though a few people might have continued to live in the destroyed city, as we found in the city-gate area. Similar remains may still be buried in unexcavated areas of the site.

At present we possess no archaeological data indicating when the city of Level II was built, but we may assume that it was only when Lachish was once again part of the kingdom of Judah. Tentatively, we may assign the construction and fortification of the Level II city to King Josiah, who was responsible for so many reforms in the latter part of the seventh century B.C. The Level II city was constructed along different lines from Level III and was apparently much less densely populated.

Securely dating the destruction of Level III enables us to solve many significant historical and archaeological problems. One good example involves so-called royal Judean storage jars.

Since the 19th century A.D., storage jar handles with royal Judean seal impressions have been discovered in various sites in Judah. By now more than a thousand such stamped handles are known. These seal impressions include a brief Hebrew inscription and an emblem. The inscription always includes the word *lmlk*, (the handles are often called *l'melekh* handles) which means "belonging to the king." They also include the name of one of four towns, Hebron, Sochoh, Ziph, or *mmst* (The name *mmst* is not known from any other source, and its exact pronunciation is unclear). The emblem on these royal handles is either a four-winged scarab or a two-winged symbol, which

should probably be identified as a winged sun-disc. Some scholars also distinguish between emblems portrayed in a naturalistic style and those portrayed schematically.

The inscription *lmlk* indicates the direct connection of the jars to the government of Judah, but the nature and meaning of the connection remains obscure. Some say that the *lmlk* stamp indicates that the jars were produced in royal potteries: others say this indicates that the jars were associated with royal Judean garrisons; still others suggest that the *lmlk* stamp means that the produce kept in them belonged to the government. Perhaps the most popular view is that the *lmlk* stamp constituted a government-certified guarantee of the accurate capacity of the jar or of its contents.

Another uncertainty relates to the four cities which appear on the seal impressions. These cities are relatively unimportant ones, and one of them, *mmst*, as mentioned above, is not known from any other source. These cities could each represent a government administrative district in Judah, or they could be the sites of the royal potteries, or centers for the production of wine (if that was the commodity kept in these jars).

The distribution of the seal impressions among the various Judean sites where they have been found shows no consistent pattern with respect to the four cities. The seals are not concentrated in the areas of these particular cities, and seal-impressions bearing the names of the different cities are usually found together.

Another problem concerning these storage jars relates to their function. What were they meant to hold? Wine? Oil?

Still another unanswered question concerns the interpretation and meaning of the emblems.

A final and fundamental problem concerns the dating of these royal storage jars. During whose reign or reigns were these jars produced? Lacking stratigraphic evidence, the royal jars were usually dated on the basis of historical and epigraphical considerations. Many scholars believed that the royal seal impressions with a four-winged emblem date to the eighth century, and that those with the two-winged emblem date to the seventh century. Other scholars, notably Frank M. Cross and H. Darrell Lance, argued that the stamps of all types were contemporaneously used during the reign of Josiah (seventh century B.C.) and that their use ceased after his reign. Recently, A. Lemaire, who considered the epigraphical evidence, and N. Na'aman, who considered the historical evidence, reached the conclusion that the royal stamps of all types should be dated to the eighth century B.C.

The British excavation had already made clear that Lachish was a key site for solving the dating problems of the royal storage jars. Over 300 of these handles were recovered in the British excavation. In addition, the British archaeologists found 48 handles from similar jars but bearing a "private" stamp (that is, a stamp with a private name). Furthermore, they even restored one jar bearing stamps with the four-winged emblem, one jar with a "private" stamp, and a few jars of that type which were unstamped. The royal storage jars had been very popular in Level III and were limited to that level. As stated by Miss Tufnell, "Nearly all the rooms attributed to city Level III contained at least one example of this vessel, and they were virtually confined to it."

Here, then, was the first clear example of the royal storage jars which were found in a good stratigraphical context, sealed under the destruction debris of Level III. Nevertheless, the royal storage jars could not be securely dated for two reasons. First, the date of the destruction of Level III was a controversial issue. (Indeed the assumed date of the royal Judean jars based on historical and epigraphic considerations, was often used to argue for one date or another for the destruction of Level III). Second, the majority of the royal stamps recovered at Lachish had a four-winged emblem. Only a small number bore the two-winged scarab, and it remained unclear whether they were stratigraphically associated with Level III or not. The reason for this unusual distribution was not known. Some suggested that the small number of two-winged emblems may have been intrusions from a later date. Thus it was an open question as to whether jars containing the two-winged stamps were used concurrently with jars bearing the four-winged stamps. If the jars bearing stamps with a two-winged emblem were later in date (having been adopted after the destruction of Level III), this would explain why so few of them were found at Lachish.

Tufnell's report was ambiguous on the question. Lance argued that the data presented in Tufnell's excavation report indicated that the handles with the two-winged symbol originated in Level III contexts. Aharoni introduced a note of caution by emphasizing that the scholars at that time were basing their arguments not on whole vessels which could form reliable ceramic evidence, but rather with mere handles which could easily be strays out of stratigraphic context.

Our recent excavations added new data which now solves the problem conclusively. In our excavation we emphasize whole pottery restoration wherever possible. The fragments of every vessel which are lying on the ground undisturbed are methodically collected and later restored to the extent that this can be done. In this way, we were able to recover seven whole storage jars containing royal seal impressions as well as a few unsealed jars of a similar type. All these jars (like the jars uncovered and restored by Starkey) were recovered in clear loci of Level III and all of

This private seal, *found on a four-handled royal jar at the city gate, reads Meshulam [son of] Ahimelech. Two handles bore the stamp shown here. The other two handles on the jar bore seal impressions with a two-winged royal emblem, and the name of the city Sochoh. Over 50 handles with private stamps were found in Lachish as well as over 350 handles with royal winged emblems.*

them were crushed under and sealed by the destruction debris of that level. Of special interest are two jars which bear seal impressions with a two-winged symbol. One two-winged storage jar was discovered in a storeroom situated behind the gatehouse, together with storage jars which bear royal stamps with a four-winged emblem. The other two-winged storage jar, whose lower part could not be restored, was discovered in one of the gate chambers. Two of its four handles bore seal impressions with a two-winged emblem and the name of the city Sochoh. The other two handles carried a "private" stamp with the name "Meshulam (son of) Ahimelech," who probably was a government official associated with the "business" of the royal storage jars, whatever that was.

Thus we know that royal storage jars of all types—those without stamps as well as those bearing stamps with a four-winged and a two-winged symbol—were used concurrently in Level III prior to its destruction. This event, as shown above, occurred in 701 B.C., so we must conclude that royal storage jars of all types were used concurrently in Judah during the reign of King Hezekiah. It is difficult to decide whether the royal storage jars of all kinds were produced exclusively during Hezekiah's reign or not. It is possible that one or more kinds of these storage jars were produced prior to Hezekiah's ascent to the throne. Moreover, because Lachish was for the most part abandoned after 701 B.C., we do not know whether the royal storage jars were produced and used after that date, that is, during the later part of Hezekiah's reign, and during the period following his death. In any case, by the time that Level II was destroyed in 588/6 B.C. by the Babylonian army, these vessels were not in use any more in Lachish, and probably not in the rest of Judah.

In addition to the royal Judean storage jars, we can now securely date an enormous amount of pottery

Large storage jars *lie crushed on the storeroom floor behind the gatehouse where they were buried by Level III debris at the time the Assyrians destroyed Lachish in 701 B.C. Especially important among the storage jars were those containing royal Judean stamps, so-called l'melekh handles. These royal stamped handles always include the word l'melekh ("belonging to the king") and the name of one of four towns (Hebron, Sochoh, Ziph, or mmst). At Lachish over 300 l'melekh handles were found. Seven whole storage jars could be restored and some of these were found to contain l'melekh handles (see p. 142). By reconstructing whole pots from clearly datable strata, the excavators determined that royal storage jars of all known types—those bearing stamped handles with four-winged seals, with two-winged seals as well as with private seals—were used concurrently in Judah.*

found in the burnt houses of Level III, crushed and sealed under the destruction debris. These vessels were in use in these houses on the day of Lachish's destruction, so they all must date to the last decade of the eighth century B.C. Thus, we now have a large corpus of well dated Judean pottery which can serve as a bench mark for understanding pottery typology, pottery development and pottery chronology in the entire country during the period of the First Temple. Indeed, the dating of the "Lachish III pottery" (as it is now called) to the eighth century rather than to the beginning of the sixth century (as would have been the case if Level III had been destroyed in 597 B.C.), has resulted in many changes in our understanding of the development of Iron Age pottery in the land of Israel.

Finally, it should be noted that the scholarly debate concerning the destruction date of Level III continues. Our argument in support of 701 B.C., as proposed by Olga Tufnell and Yohanan Aharoni, is based on internal evidence and we strongly believe that this kind of evidence is the most convincing kind. Other scholars, however, believe that the weight of the external evidence is so great that it definitely indicates that Level III was destroyed in 597 B.C. and not before. According to this view, the evidence from Lachish itself presented above must be adapted to fit the external evidence. First and foremost among these scholars is Dame Kathleen Kenyon.　　　　She visited our excavation in the summer of 1977. During her visit we had an opportunity to analyze with her the entire question, including its various implications. In 1978 she studied the problem afresh in connection with her work on a revised edition of her *Archaeology in the Holy Land*. While she accepted the newly uncovered archaeological data as interpreted by us, she nevertheless concluded that the pottery evidence from Samaria is more important. As she wrote me on June 23, 1978, shortly before her untimely death: "I have, of course, been considering the new Lachish evidence very carefully . . . I still find it very difficult to accept the Lachish III remains as belonging to the Assyrian destruction of c. 700 B.C., both on the grounds given in *Samaria-Sebaste 3* (the report on the excavations at Samaria), and because it leaves the seventh century B.C. a complete blank for progress as indicated by pottery forms . . . I do not have a closed mind on the subject . . . but I do think that there are problems to be accommodated . . ."

Two other distinguished scholars, A.D. Tushingham of the Royal Ontario Museum in Toronto and J.S. Holladay, Jr. of the University of Toronto also believe—on the basis of the evidence external to Lachish—that Level III was destroyed in 597 B.C. In January 1979 we arranged a seminar on the question at the University of Toronto. Chaired by Dr. T. Cuyler Young, the seminar had the opportunity of hearing Tushingham, Holladay and myself present our different views. The seminar aroused much interest, and I hope Tushingham and Holladay will publish their arguments in detail so they can be judged by the scholarly world at large. Although I continue to listen with great respect, I must nevertheless restate my firm belief that the internal evidence from Lachish itself definitely carries greater weight and must prevail over the external evidence: Level III at Lachish was destroyed in 701 B.C.

The Lachish excavations will continue for many years to come. Indeed, we are following a detailed, long-term plan. We hope to uncover much more significant data in the future. The next excavation season will take place during the summer of 1980, for eight weeks, (June 15-August 8). We also plan to excavate during the summers of 1981—1982. We need volunteers to work with us; **BAR** readers who are interested in excavating at Lachish should get in touch with the project's U.S. coordinator, Dr. Song Nai Rhee, Northwest Christian College, 11th and Alder Streets, Eugene, Oregon 97401. You will be most welcome. We guarantee an exciting time discovering the past.

146

An ivory stopper (top right) in the form of a male ibex was found in a Judean house in Level IV. The stopper is perforated and liquids, probably perfumes, were poured from a vessel through the mouth of the ibex. It is only seven centimeters tall.

Reconstructed from pottery sherds found on a storeroom house floor (see p. 145), the four-handled royal Judean jar (top left), bears a l'melekh stamp on one of its handles, and a stopper in its neck. Below the jar is a close-up of the stamp with a detailed drawing of it to its left: the four-winged l'melekh stamp bears the name Hebron.

All of these pottery sherds and stamped handles were found amid the crumbled walls in Tel Lachish's Level III.

DESTRUCTION OF JUDEAN FORTRESS PORTRAYED IN DRAMATIC EIGHTH-CENTURY B.C. PICTURES

IN THE LATE EIGHTH CENTURY B.C., Lachish was the second most important city in the kingdom of Judah. Only Jerusalem surpassed it.

At that time, Assyria had risen to unprecedented power, dominating the known world. On the eve of Sennacherib's accession to the Assyrian throne in 705 B.C., the Assyrian empire extended from Elam and Babylonia on the south, to Anatolia on the north, and to the Medi-

Book Review

terranean Sea and the border of Egypt on the west.

Each year the Assyrians expanded their kingdom by a military expedition, often commanded by the king himself. Toward the end of the eighth century, the Assyrians began deporting subjugated peoples in order to blur their national identities.

Assyrian domination of the Land of Israel—then composed of the kingdom of Israel in the north and the kingdom of Judah in the south—proceeded step by step. By 732 B.C., Assyria had annexed the northern part of the kingdom of Israel. In 721/720 B.C., Assyria conquered the city of Samaria, the capital of the northern kingdom, and annexed the rest of the kingdom of Israel, bringing a permanent end to its existence. The kingdom of Judah in the south would in all probability be the next target.

Soon after Sennacherib ascended the throne in 705 B.C., an anti-Assyrian alliance was formed by Egypt, the Philistine cities of the coastal plain and Judah, hoping to take advantage of the temporary weakness attendant on a change of monarchs. Judah at that time was ruled by one of the most prominent kings of the House of David, King Hezekiah.

By the time Sennacherib was ready for his third annual campaign—in 701 B.C.—he was able to direct his attention to the defiance of these three powers.

Many details of Sennacherib's third campaign remain unclear, but two things are certain: although he laid siege to Jerusalem, for some reason or other, he was unable to conquer it; as a result, Judah remained a nation-state for more than a century afterward—until the Babylonians, who had destroyed the Assyrian empire, conquered Jerusalem in 587 B.C. Second, in his third campaign of 701 B.C., Sennacherib devastated much of Judah and utterly destroyed its second most important city, Lachish. As a result, King Hezekiah paid enormous tribute to Sennacherib, and Judah became to a large extent an Assyrian vassal state.

The destruction of Lachish is important not only historically, but also because it is uniquely documented. For no other ancient event of comparable significance is so much, and so many different kinds of, source material available. The events surrounding the conquest of Lachish, the destruction of the city and the deportation of its inhabitants are documented (or evidenced) in at least four independent contemporary sources: (1) in the Bible; (2) in Assyrian cuneiform accounts of the same events; (3) in archaeological excavations at the site of Lachish; and (4) remarkably, in monumental pictorial reliefs uncovered at Sennacherib's palace at Nineveh.

In a stunning new book by David Ussishkin, director of the most recent (and continuing) excavations at the mound of Lachish, material from these four sources is brought together to illuminate, as the title proclaims, *The*

Stunning New Book Assembles Evidence of the Conquest of Lachish

Conquest of Lachish by Sennacherib. *

The text is not only lucid (it is written for the layperson as well as the scholar), it is also vivid and even dramatic. The book is superbly designed—it won first prize for design at the 1983 Jerusalem Book Fair—in a large format that permits the photographs and drawings to be displayed so that the viewer can see even small details without squinting. A special bonus is that the royal Assyrian reliefs depicting the battle of Lachish and the deportation of the Judean refugees have been rephotographed (by Avraham Hay) and redrawn (by Judith Dekel) from the originals in the British Museum. Dekel and another artist, Gert le Grange, have also reconstructed Sennacherib's palace at Nineveh as well as views of Lachish** and the

*Tel Aviv: Tel Aviv University Publications of The Institute of Archaeology No. 6, 1982, 135 pp., 13x13 inches, $72.

**One or two scholars still question the identity of Lachish. See, most recently, G. W. Ahlström, "Tell ed-Duweir: Lachish or Libnah?" *Palestine Exploration Quarterly* (July-December 1983). Ussishkin finds the identification for the site of Lachish "weighty."

The annals of Sennacherib, *preserved in a dense pattern of Assyrian cuneiform characters on this 15-inch-high prism, include the king's arrogant account of his destruction of Judah. "Forty-six of [Hezekiah's] strong walled towns and innumerable smaller villages . . . I besieged and conquered. . . . I made to come out from them 200,150 people, young and old, male and female, . . . and counted them as the spoils of war. . . . As for Hezekiah, the awful splendor of my lordship overwhelmed him, . . . and all kinds of valuable treasures, as well as his daughters, concubines, male and female musicians he sent me later to Nineveh, my lordly city. He sent a personal messenger to deliver the tribute and make a slavish obeisance."*

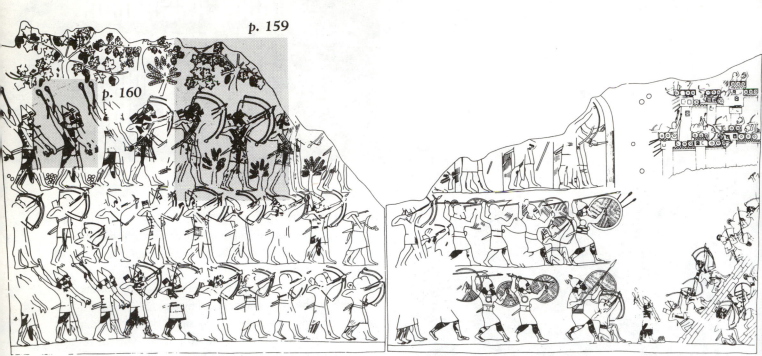

p. 159

p. 160

Slab 1

Slab 2

"I besieged and conquered," *Sennacherib tells us in his annals. Drawn here and continued on pp. 152-153 are exquisitely detailed wall reliefs from the Assyrian king's palace at Nineveh that bring those words powerfully to life. The drawings are copied from 12 slabs that covered three of the four walls of a ceremonial room in the palace, commemorating Sennacherib's conquest of the Judean city of Lachish.*

The scenario progresses from left to right, with great momentum and vitality, and with what appears to be a "cast of thousands." The figures to the far left and those to the far right, on p. 153, are disproportionately larger than those directly involved in the attack, creating the visual illusion of a panorama: In movie terms, we would say that the "camera" starts with a close-up, dollies back, then zooms in again as it continually pans across all the action.

(Page numbers in the tinted rectangles indicate the locations of details of scenes illustrated in this issue.)

Slabs 1 and 2 show infantry attacking the city with arrows, spears and slingstones. The city defenders retaliate in kind, shooting arrows and sending down a hail of stones on their attackers.

In slab 3, the Assyrians attack Lachish's central sector with battering rams under a hail of stones, arrows and torches. Corpses are stripped naked and impaled on stakes, as survivors begin an exile into slavery. In slabs 4 and 5, soldiers carrying off booty from Lachish guard rows of deportees.

battle waged against it in drawings based on all the available evidence.

From the Bible, we learn that during most of King Hezekiah's reign (which began in 727 B.C.), Judah enjoyed a period of great prosperity, despite the fact that the kingdom of Israel to the north fell to the Assyrians (see 2 Chronicles 32:27-28). Hezekiah is also known for his important religious reforms. He strengthened Jerusalem and centralized worship in the Jerusalem Temple, abolishing all shrines and sanctuaries outside Jerusalem. Recent excavations in Jerusalem have shown that the city expanded greatly during his reign.[1]

The Bible also describes Sennacherib's campaign in Judah, which ended with his unsuccessful siege of Jerusalem. To bring water into Jerusalem during the Assyrian siege, Hezekiah dug the famous tunnel that still bears his name. This tunnel may well have saved the city. According to the Bible, however, the siege was broken when the Lord killed 185,000 Assyrian soldiers in a single night, thus wiping out the bulk of Sennacherib's army (2 Kings 19:35).

But before he foundered at Jerusalem, Sennacherib had been successful elsewhere. From the Bible we learn that he attacked "all the walled cities of Judah" (2 Kings 18:13; Isaiah 36:1). Three cities are mentioned by name

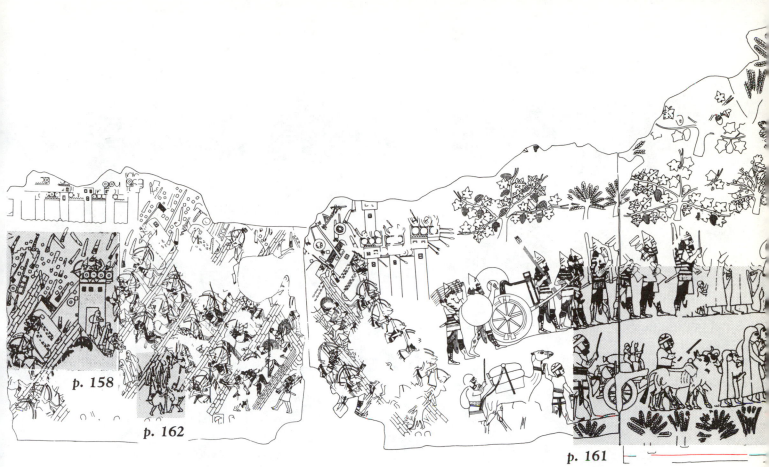

p. 158

p. 162

p. 161

Slab 3

Slab 4

Slab 5

in connection with this campaign—one of them is Lachish. In 2 Chronicles 32:9, we are told specifically that Sennacherib laid siege to Lachish. The conquest of Lachish obviously emboldened Sennacherib to try to overcome Jerusalem.

An Assyrian version of these events from Sennacherib's own annals is contained on a 15-inch-high baked clay prism of six sides covered with Akkadian cuneiform. Three complete prisms with this text have been found. One, at the Israel Museum, is illustrated in this volume. The others are at the University of Chicago's Oriental Institute and the British Museum. None was recovered in a controlled excavation.

In these annals, Sennacherib claims to have besieged and conquered 46 walled cities of Judah. Although he does not mention it by name, Lachish was surely one. Sennacherib describes his military strategy as follows: "I besieged and conquered by stamping down earthramps and then by bringing up battering rams, by the assault of foot soldiers, by breaches, tunneling and sapper operations." Much of this strategy has been confirmed by excavations at Lachish and by the reliefs at Nineveh. Sennacherib claims that over 200,000 refugees came out of these cities, "Young and old, male and female . . . the spoils of war."

Sennacherib also recounts how "Hezekiah the Jew . . . [was] shut up like a caged bird within Jerusalem, his royal city." Pointedly enough, Sennacherib does not claim to have conquered or destroyed Jerusalem.

The first major excavations at Lachish were conducted between 1932 and 1938. The expedition came to an abrupt end, however, when its director, J. L. Starkey, was murdered by Arab marauders after his car was ambushed on the way from Lachish to Jerusalem. Starkey had been on his way to the opening ceremonies of the Palestine Archaeological Museum (now the Rockefeller Museum).

For many years after this excavation ended, the archaeological community did not agree on which level at Lachish represented Sennacherib's destruction. Except for a small excavation in the 1960s, the mound remained untouched until 1973, when Ussishkin's continuing excavations, sponsored by Tel Aviv University and the Israel Exploration Society, began. These excavations have now settled, to the satisfaction of almost all scholars, that Level III at Lachish represents the city destroyed by Sennacherib (see "Answers at Lachish," **BAR**, November/December 1979 [p. 124]).

From the archaeological evidence, it is clear that during Hezekiah's reign Lachish was a large garrison city, a formidable royal citadel that boasted a huge palace-fort as

151

Slab 6   Slab 7   Slab 8

p. 164

Detailed drawings of the reliefs *of Sennacherib (continued from p. 151). Slabs 6 and 7 depict grim scenes of captives either being tortured or begging for mercy from the enthroned Sennacherib (slab 8).*

Slabs 8 through 10 show the royal tent with Sennacherib's ceremonial chariot below, and horses and attendants. In slabs 10 through 12, we see the king's battle chariot and his camp.

well as residences. The city was surrounded by a massive wall with towers and battlements.* A great gate complex consisting of an outer gate and an inner gate controlled access to the city. The inner gatehouse, as uncovered by the archaeologists, is a massive structure, the largest of its kind ever found in Israel. It is approximately 75 feet square and consists of four piers on either side. In the ashy debris left from Sennacherib's destruction—near the out-

---

*From the reliefs and the excavations, it has been assumed that two walls surrounded Lachish. Ussishkin believes only one wall protected the city. The supposed outer wall was, in his view, a strong revetment retaining the bottom of a glacis, which in turn supported the base of the city wall itself. What appears in the reliefs to be the outer wall, Ussishkin suggests, are battlements and parapets erected on the revetment wall to provide additional positions for soldiers manning the first line of defense.

ermost pier—the excavators collected numerous pieces of bronze that had once been part of the bronze fittings on the large wooden doors of the gatehouse. Chunks of carbonized wood were all that could be found of the doors themselves.

Several long narrow buildings in the city can be interpreted either as storehouses or as stables for government cavalry. The scholarly world is still divided as to the correct interpretation of these buildings (see "Megiddo Stables or Storehouses," **BAR**, September 1976). Ussishkin himself takes no position on this subject.

The Assyrians mounted their siege of the city from the southwest. Topographically this makes sense: The mound is most vulnerable at a "saddle" at its southwest corner where the city gate was located. (See News from the Field: "Defensive Judean Counter-Ramp Found at Lachish in 1983 Season," by excavator Ussishkin, p. 66 [166]).

The Assyrians made their camp on a hillock opposite the gate, near enough for Sennacherib himself to direct the battle but far enough away to be out of range of the defenders' missiles. The southwest corner of the mound of Lachish has revealed ample evidence of a ferocious battle, although the stratigraphy is not clear enough to allow the archaeologists to attribute all this evidence to Sennacherib's attack.

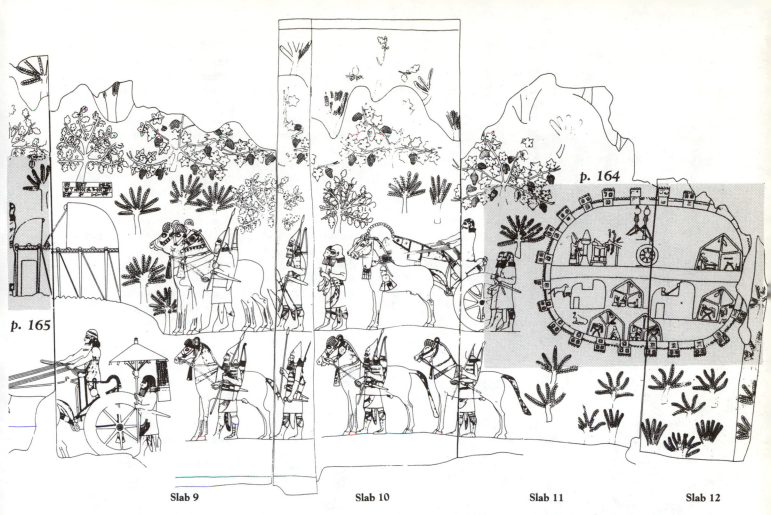

p. 164

p. 165

| Slab 9 | Slab 10 | Slab 11 | Slab 12 |

To clear the ancient roadway leading up to the gate, the expedition in the 1930s removed immense quantities of stone—"many thousands of tons," according to Starkey. In 1973, Yigael Yadin visited the site and suggested that these heaps of stones might be the remains of the Assyrian siege ramp. Ussishkin checked the possibility by further excavation and, in 1977, concluded that "the only convincing and logical interpretation of these stones is that they were used to build a siege ramp." The siege ramp was relatively wide, fanning out at the base and narrowing at the top where it reached the city wall. The stones in the upper layer of the siege ramp were cemented together with mortar. Although such siege ramps were no doubt common in antiquity, this is the only Assyrian siege ramp to have been identified in an archaeological excavation. Indeed, it is the oldest siege ramp found anywhere in the Near East.

The city of Level III at Lachish was burned to the ground by the conquering Assyrians. Ussishkin believes that the Assyrians first looted the city and forced all the inhabitants to leave. Excavators found the floors of the burned buildings strewn with smashed pottery vessels, but there were no valuables or human skeletons. The people must have left before the Assyrians put the city to the torch. In that conflagration, the buildings' sun-dried mud-

bricks were baked by the fire and turned red. In some places, the piles of burned bricks were six feet high and were covered by ashes from the roofs. We can easily imagine Assyrian soldiers brandishing their torches and lighting whatever would burn—a wooden roof beam, a straw mat, a storage jar full of oil.

Hundreds of arrowheads were found in the excavation (see p. 159), especially where the battle raged, although not all can be said to have come from Level III. Some of the

Scale armor. *Excavators discovered more than 20 pieces of scale armor at Tel Lachish. The small perforations enabled them to be attached to adjoining scales.*

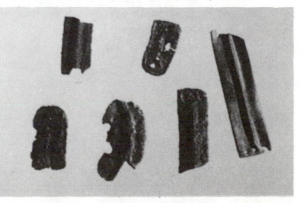

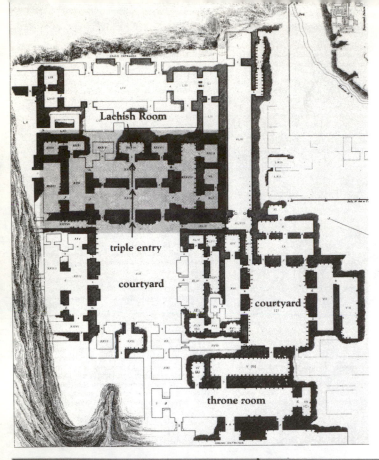

Sennacherib's "Palace Without a Rival," at Nineveh. *Sennacherib could already count several palaces among the grand structures of his capital city, and he boasted of innumerable military victories. Yet, apparently, he considered the conquest of Lachish his finest hour, because shortly after this singular victory in 701 B.C., he built a new, monumental palace whose interior architectural focus was a huge room covered with reliefs depicting every stage of his victory over the Judean city.*

"The architectural setting of the Lachish reliefs," says author Ussishkin, "was ingeniously designed to impress the beholder and instill in him awe, respect and admiration for the deeds and triumphs of the great monarch who had inspired them." The viewer entered this room of reliefs through a magnificent triple entry flanked by enormous winged bulls with human faces. Artist Judith Dekel's reconstruction of the triple entry (right) evokes its dramatic visual impact. The second and third portals and pairs of colossi were progressively smaller. Thus, anyone standing at the outer portal perceived the Lachish Room at the rear as farther away than it actually was.

The room containing the Lachish reliefs was part of a ceremonial suite, shaded in the plan at left. Its side rooms were also decorated with reliefs, but the focal point of this vast suite was the reliefs covering the back wall of the Lachish Room—reliefs that showed the storming of Lachish, the deportees, and the spoils of war.

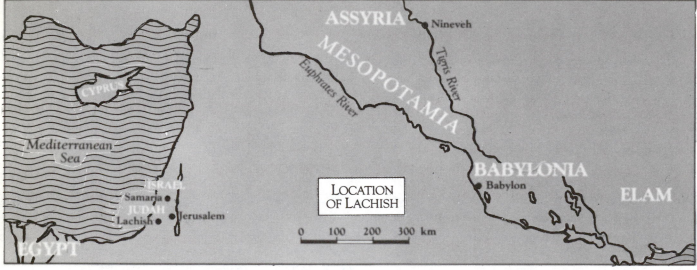

arrows shot by the Assyrians stuck in the superstructure of the inner gate; the arrowheads were found still stuck in place amid the destruction debris.

Slingstones, another type of ammunition, were also found in large quantities (see p. 161). The slingstones are mostly round balls of flint about 2.4 inches (6 cm) in diameter.

More than 20 pieces of scale armor, mostly bronze but some iron, were also uncovered. Among Starkey's unique finds was a bronze crest mount from an Assyrian helmet (see p. 163). Attached to the crest were remnants of cloth and leather fastenings and the rivets that held the mount

in place. Ussishkin allows himself to ruminate: "Is it possible we have here the helmet of an Assyrian spearman who was killed while attempting to ascend the walls?" He allows also for the possibility, suggested by fellow archaeologist Gabriel Barkay, that the crest might have been part of the finery of a chariot horse.

Finally, we come to the evidence from the Assyrian reliefs. Here we have the battle of Lachish depicted in what must be the closest thing to an ancient movie—scene after scene carved into stone—from the phalanxes prepared for battle to the deportation of the conquered Judeans.

Tel Lachish, *viewed from the southwest. Cultivated fields of an Israeli moshav, or cooperative village, frame the rectangular mound, 30 acres at its base and 18 acres on its flat summit. One of the most prominent of all the Biblical tels in Israel, Lachish commands an uninterrupted view from the Judean hills in the east to the coastal plain in the west.*

At the end of the eighth century B.C., Tel Lachish was one of the most formidable citadels in Judah, as artist Judith Dekel's reconstruction, opposite, illustrates. Its fortified gate, outer city wall with sloping glacis against it, and palace-fort protected a large and populous city. The drawing is based on the reconstruction of H. H. McWilliams prepared in 1933, integrated with data from the recent excavation.

The reliefs were found in the ancient city of Nineveh, located on a tell that rises nearly 50 feet above its surroundings on a plain opposite Mosul, Iraq. Nineveh is described in the book of Jonah as "that great city with more than 120,000 people who cannot discern between their right hand and their left hand; and also much cattle" (Jonah 4:11).

Although it had been settled since the fifth millennium B.C., Nineveh became the capital of the Assyrian empire only after Sennacherib's accession to the throne. In Sennacherib's day, the massive walls that encircled the city extended for nearly eight miles (13 km) and contained 15 magnificent gateways. Inside, Sennacherib built a variety of wide avenues lined with stelae, large public squares, streets, public buildings and palaces. A remarkable canal

48 miles (80 km) long with a 1,000-foot aqueduct (which is still standing) supported on five pointed arches carried water from the Gomel River to maintain the city's luxuriant gardens of rare and exotic plants.

Shortly after his conquest of Lachish, Sennacherib decided to build himself a new palace. He completed the project in 694 B.C. As we learn from Sennacherib's annals, the palace was built with forced labor gangs composed of foreign captives and deportees, those from Judah—very possibly including people from Lachish—among them. In his annals, Sennacherib calls his new palace the "Palace Without a Rival." Its construction was undoubtedly a major architectural enterprise.

Unfortunately, the palace was partially burned and destroyed in the internal disorders that followed Sennacherib's death in 681 B.C. (The conqueror of Lachish was murdered by his own sons; see 2 Kings 19:37, Isaiah 37:38, 2 Chronicles 32:21.) The empire then began a slow decline, which soon developed into a rapid disintegration. Finally, in 612 B.C. Nineveh was conquered and destroyed by the Babylonians and the Medes, and Sennacherib's palace was again burned. In 609 B.C. the Assyrian empire, once the ruler of the world, collapsed.

With the decline of Assyria, Lachish once again became part of the Land of Israel and was rebuilt, probably by King Josiah (639-609 B.C.). Nineveh, by contrast, remained an abandoned ruin forever, as prophesied by Nahum and Zephaniah (2:13): "He will make Nineveh a desolation and dry like a wilderness."

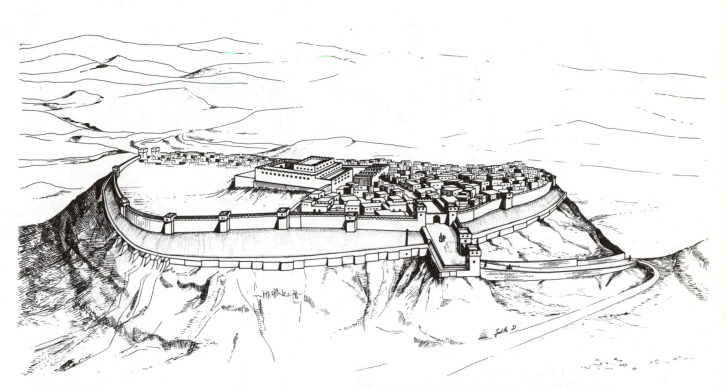

"Is this the gay city
That dwelt secure,
That thought in her heart
'I am, and there is none but me'?
Alas, she is become a waste,
A lair of wild beasts!
Everyone who passes by her
Hisses and gestures with his hand."
(Zephaniah 2:15, NJPS translation)

Thus Nineveh.

Nineveh was first excavated by the famous 19th-century English archaeologist Austen Henry Layard in 1846 and 1847. A few days after he began his second season, Layard came upon a room in the "Palace Without a Rival" that was lined with reliefs. Within a month, he discovered nine such rooms. By 1849, the extensive cuneiform inscriptions in the palace had been sufficiently deciphered to identify the name of Sennacherib. In that same year, Layard returned to the mound. Excavating the palace was a gigantic task that Layard accomplished by digging tunnels along those walls decorated with reliefs. Although this method would be unforgivable today, it was effective for its time. Layard continued excavating at Nineveh until 1851 and succeeded in unearthing large sections of the palace.

Layard himself described the work:

"In this magnificent edifice, I had opened no less than seventy-one halls, chambers and passages, whose walls, almost without exception, had been panelled with slabs of sculptured alabaster recording the wars, the triumphs, and the great deeds of the Assyrian king."

In 1853 most of the reliefs were removed from Nineveh and sent to the British Museum in London, where they are now displayed.

The "Palace Without a Rival" was of course the most important building in Nineveh. Its most magnificent feature was a large ceremonial suite whose focal point was a single room approached through three monumental portals built on a straight axis. Colossal statues of winged bulls stood at each portal, but the statues were successively smaller, thus conveying the impression to someone standing at the outer entrance that the focal room was much further away than it actually was.

The reliefs that lined the wall of this focal room commemorated the conquest of Judah and Sennacherib's victory at Lachish. We may properly call it the Lachish Room. The section of the reliefs portraying the storming of Lachish was placed on the wall opposite the entrance, making this section the focal point of the entire work and giving some idea of the importance Sennacherib attached to his conquest of this great Judean stronghold. It was apparently the crowning military achievement of his entire career.

In Ussishkin's book the reliefs are magnificently presented in long pullout pages, in photographs and in drawings, *in extenso* and in detail. Without doubt, they can be more easily and more understandably studied here than

Victory and defeat *appear side by side in this scene from the conquest of Lachish. The relief artist has used the city gate as the visual pivot of the narrative. At the left, the full pitch of battle rages, and the gatehouse is stormed. At right, defeated Lachishites leave through the gate for exile after the surrender—the result, a dramatic and evocative pictorial narrative of the historic events.*

A battering ram (lower left) climbing the siege ramp is protected by an Assyrian soldier in the body of the ram, who pours water over the ram itself so that it won't catch fire from the barrage of torches being thrown down by the defenders.

Infantrymen advance, *two abreast. With expressions as assured as the grips on their bows, archers take aim at Judean defenders manning the walls of Lachish. The attackers are well equipped with composite bows (whose ends curl back in the shape of ducks' heads) and full quivers fastened to their shoulders by wide straps.*

Archaeologists have uncovered hundreds of arrowheads at Lachish (below). Most are made of iron, but a few, like the one far right, are carved from bone.

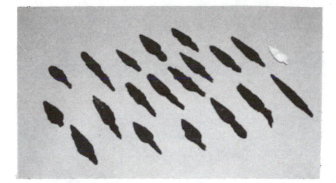

from the originals in the British Museum.

The uniform background of the reliefs is a pattern of overlapping wedges resembling scale armor or fishscales. Ussishkin interprets it as representing the stony landscape of the Lachish region. Against this backdrop, the battle unfolds in a magnificent panorama that moves through space and time.

Beginning on the left, three lines of Assyrian soldiers march two abreast, approaching the city of Lachish. In front are the archers with their composite bows. At the rear are pairs of slingers, whirling their slings around their heads. Heaps of slingstones lie at the feet of the slingers in the upper row. Each contingent of soldiers is dressed distinctly. Some have beards and long hair held in place by headbands or scarves. Sometimes a fringed edge hangs down and covers the cheek. Some soldiers wear short

skirts and wide belts. These distinctions in dress probably identify different ethnic divisions of the Assyrian army.

Further to the right (on the second slab) we see the Assyrian spearmen, each with a round shield in his left hand. The spearmen have long curly hair, long beards and wear pointed helmets with earflaps. Each has a sword thrust through his wide belt. Arrows from the city's defenders are stuck in the shield of the foremost spearman in the upper row. The battle for Lachish has begun.

The portrayal of the besieged city extends over three slabs, beginning with the right side of the second slab. In this scene the city walls are depicted at a higher level than the advancing troops. The besieged city is approached by a steep incline emphasizing the city's elevation.

The focal point of the third slab is the city gate, which is being stormed. From the archaeological excavation of

Text continues on p. 163

Barefooted deportees *leave their homes (above). With their salvaged belongings strapped to a cart pulled by emaciated oxen, a Judean family trudges through a stony landscape dotted with olive trees.*

We can distinguish the deportees from the Assyrians in the reliefs by their appearance and dress. The women and girls wear long simple garments and long shawls that cover their heads and reach the bottoms of their dresses. The heads of the men and boys are wound with fringed scarves. The men have short beards and wear sleeveless shirts with tassels attached that hang between their legs.

Slingstones *uncovered in the general area of the city gate. The round balls of flint are about 2.4 inches in diameter [6 cm], the size of tennis balls, and weigh about .55 pounds [250 grams]. In the mélange of weaponry used in the battle of Lachish, these slingstones were just one type of deadly missile. To understand how the stones were slung, see the relief opposite.*

Assyrian slingers *(left) whirling their slings around their heads. The slings are double strips of leather wrapped around the stones. Each man holds another stone in his left hand. They all have long beards and wear conical helmets with earflaps and coats of mail over fringed garments.*

161

the Assyrian siege ramp, we would not know it, but from the reliefs at Nineveh we see quite clearly that the ramp is covered with log tracks. Several such tracks are pictured leading up to the walls of Lachish. On some are formidable Assyrian battering rams or siege machines, in effect mobile assault towers. The most clearly depicted battering ram appears on the third slab. The ram approaches the city gate on spoked wheels that are partly covered by the body of the machine. The machine was apparently constructed of prefabricated parts assembled on the site with securing pins. The body of the siege machine has a turret with a window. The ram itself, resembling a large spear, extends from the front of the machine. The shaft of the ram must have hung from ropes inside the machine. Men on the floor of the machine would push the ram forward in great strokes, waiting for it to swing back before repeating the action. Thus the ram would pound systematically against a carefully selected weak point in the wall until eventually the ram broke through.

The Judean defenders of Lachish—on the walls of the city—can be seen attempting to set fire to the entire machine, which was probably made of flammable leather and wood, by showering it with firebrands. As a countermeasure, an Assyrian soldier standing in the back of the machine, partly exposed and partly protected by the turret, pours water over the machine and the shaft of the ram using what looks like an enormous ladle.

At least seven battering rams attack Lachish, the largest number of battering rams shown in any Assyrian relief of an attack on a single city.

In what must have been intended as a later scene, we see a line of Judean refugees coming out of the city gate after the surrender of Lachish. In this and the following scenes, we have the only surviving pictures of eighth-century B.C. Judeans—men, women and children.

Closest to the city gate are two Judean women wearing long dresses. Shawls cover their heads. A bag with belongings hangs over the shoulder of each woman. They may hold jugs of water in their right hands. Ahead of them are two Judean men clad in short tunics with belts. They wear headscarves that hang down.

At the bottom of the siege ramp in front of the gate, three Judean prisoners, stripped naked, have been impaled on stakes. The heads of the men sag forward, indicating they are already dead. Two Assyrian spearmen wearing

Crest of a helmet? *The modern reconstruction (top) is based on the large bronze crest (bottom) uncovered by British archaeologist James L. Starkey in his excavations at Lachish during the 1930s. Remnants of cloth, leather fastenings and rivets still adhered to the crest when it was uncovered between the city gate and the southwest corner of the mound.*

Ussishkin suggests that this crest was originally mounted on the helmet of a fallen Assyrian soldier. Another theory is that it was part of the elaborate trappings of a chariot horse. To weigh the merits of these two theories for yourself, see the soldiers and chariots in the reliefs pictured on pp. 152-153 and 162.

helmets with crests—like the one Starkey found in the Lachish excavations—secure the stake on which the slain Judean defender at the right has been impaled.

Beginning on the fourth slab are two columns of people to the right of the city. In the upper row, Assyrian soldiers carrying booty walk behind some Judean deportees. The

© 1982 Erich Lessing/Culture and Fine Arts Archive

With his two sons, *a Judean father walks to exile. On his shoulders he carries the few family belongings he has been allowed to take with him. One of his small sons, no doubt frightened and bewildered, clutches his father's shirt, as a child will do when he needs comfort.*

spoil of war carried by the first Assyrian soldier in the back group is a scepter or mace pointing, probably deliberately, downward—a symbol of authority conquered. The fourth soldier in the group carries a chair with rounded top and armrests. This must have been the seat of state of the governor of Lachish. Behind this, several Assyrian soldiers pull what must have been the official chariot of the royal governor of Lachish. This is the only documented depiction of a Judean chariot. It closely resembles

Sennacherib on a throne *(right) inlaid with figures of ivory. Approaching the king is a senior commander of his army, maybe the commander-in-chief, followed by lower-ranked commanders. A cuneiform inscription in a rectangular frame in front of Sennacherib identifies the conquered city as Lachish.*

Two eunuchs, identifiable by their beardless faces and gross facial features, stand behind the king's throne fanning him. The king's face is mutilated, a deliberate act probably done in the riots that followed Sennacherib's murder in 681 B.C.

Assyrian chariots of the period.

Further forward in this row and in the bottom row are touching scenes of Judean deportees—men, women and children. In one family in the upper row, we see the father leading a cart drawn by two oxen. The ribs of the oxen are emphasized, perhaps to indicate their malnutrition. The cart is laden with household goods. On top sit two women and two children, one in arms. Both men and women are barefoot. Other small children, both behind and in front of this scene, are walking to exile, one child's hand held in that of a parent walking alongside.

Beneath this scene, in the bottom row, as well as in front of this scene in the top row is a group of guarded Judean prisoners who have been identified by the prominent British scholar, Richard D. Barnett, as "Hezekiah's men," the king's soldiers who may have led the resistance at Lachish. Hence, they are treated more harshly. They have curly hair and short, curly beards. They walk, also barefooted, with their hands upraised in a plea for mercy.

Assyrian fortified camp *marks the end of the series of relief slabs at the right-hand side (see p. 153). The relief artist has presented a bird's-eye view of the fortifications and a frontal view of the elements inside the camp: people, animals and tents. A wide thoroughfare bisects the camp horizontally.*

Some kneel and crouch as they approach Sennacherib on his battle throne. Others are being tortured. Two Judeans in the bottom row are portrayed lying on the ground, stripped naked with outflung arms, while Assyrian archers hold their ankles. Apparently the Judean prisoners have just been flayed alive. In the upper row an Assyrian soldier holds a Judean captive by his hair and stabs him in the shoulder with a dagger or short sword.

The two lines of Assyrian soldiers and Judean captives lead to the seated figure of Sennacherib himself. The monarch sits on his battle throne in front of his personal tent, facing the now-conquered city. A cuneiform inscription just in front of and above the king reads: "Sennacherib, king of all, king of Assyria, sitting on his *nimedu*-throne while the spoil from the city of Lachish passed before him." (The king's face has been deliberately mutilated by those who came after him, presumably his murderers.)

Further to the right, the Assyrian camp is depicted as an oval. Today an Israeli moshav, or cooperative village, is situated where the Assyrian camp once stood. Ussishkin believes it was from this vantage point that the Assyrian artist who created the reliefs watched the battle that destroyed Lachish in 701 B.C. —**H.S.**

Unless otherwise noted, all photographs in this article are by Avraham Hay. All drawings are by Judith Dekel.

[1]Nahman Avigad, *Discovering Jerusalem* (Thomas Nelson: Nashville, 1983), pp. 54-60.

DEFENSIVE JUDEAN COUNTER-RAMP FOUND AT LACHISH IN 1983 SEASON

By David Ussishkin

OUR EXPEDITION TO LACHISH is described in detail in the review/article on p. 148. In this brief note I would like to describe for **BAR** readers the exciting results of our 1983 season, in which, for the first time, we extensively excavated the Assyrian siege ramp outside the city wall. We also extended inside the city wall the longitudinal trench cut through the Assyrian siege ramp. Once inside

News From the Field

the city, we discovered, opposite the Assyrian siege ramp, an unsuspected Judean counter-ramp intended to bolster the city's defenses against the Assyrian onslaught. With the discovery of this defensive Judean counter-ramp, the battle of Lachish in 701 B.C. came alive in a startling new way.

The British excavations at Lachish led by J. L. Starkey in the 1930s had discovered and partially excavated the Assyrian siege ramp outside the city wall. In 1977 our own expedition to Lachish cut a small trench into the ramp to determine how it had been built. At that time, we also surveyed the area around the ramp, inside as well as outside the wall.

This effort to understand the Assyrian siege ramp and the implications to be drawn from it directed us to the location of the Assyrian siege camp. Even more important, this preliminary study focused our attention on a raised area inside the city wall, opposite the siege ramp. It was clear that extensive excavations were called for, both

into the siege ramp itself and inside the city wall opposite the siege ramp.

We were finally able to undertake these excavations in the summer of 1983. Many of the volunteers in the 1983 season were **BAR** readers, and they all did excellent work. As in previous years, the excavations were conducted under the auspices of the Institute of Archaeology of Tel Aviv University and the Israel Exploration Society. (The area supervisor was Yehudah Dagan.)

Earlier excavations had already made it clear that the battle for Lachish had been most fiercely fought in the southwest corner of the city. This area, where the Assyrian siege ramp had been built, had borne the brunt of the Assyrian attack. Sennacherib had devised his battle plan wisely: Lachish is surrounded by deep valleys on all sides but one (see the aerial photo, p. 156). The exception is the southwest corner, where an earth saddle connects the mound to the neighboring knoll on which the modern Israeli village Moshav Lachish is built. The saddle made this sector of the site the most vulnerable point for attack. Sennacherib knew this, but so did the Judeans. They therefore reinforced their defensive fortifications at the southwest corner.

The outer revetment wall. *Built to support the base of a sloping earth glacis, which itself leaned against the city wall, the revetment is seen here as the area above and to the left of the person standing in the foreground. At the time of the Assyrian siege, a ramp was built to allow battering rams and soldiers to attack the city wall at its vulnerable southwest corner. The first stage of the ramp was built up to the revetment wall; a second, later stage covered the revetment wall and continued almost to the foot of the main city wall. Remains of these two stages are seen here as small stones massed above and below the revetment wall.*

Evidence Mounts For Fierce Resistance Before Lachish Fell to Assyrian Hordes

LACHISH AND ITS SIEGE RAMPS

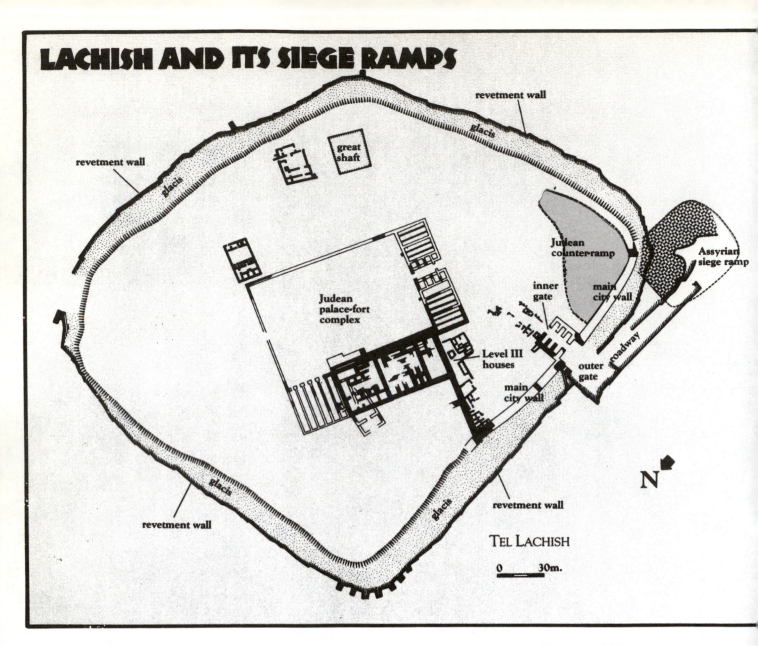

great shaft

revetment wall

glacis

revetment wall

glacis

Judean counter-ramp

Assyrian siege ramp

inner gate

main city wall

Judean palace-fort complex

Level III houses

outer gate

roadway

main city wall

revetment wall

glacis

revetment wall

glacis

N

TEL LACHISH

0   30m.

Our 1977 probe of the Assyrian siege ramp led us to the certain conclusion that Sennacherib's camp (see p. 164) was located in the area of Moshav Lachish, opposite the main point of the Assyrian attack at the southwest corner of the city. Lachish is portrayed in Sennacherib's reliefs (see pp. 150-153) as seen from a particular point in the area of the Moshav where the Assyrian camp must have been located. That is where Sennacherib, the supreme commander of the Assyrian army, must have sat on his throne as shown in the relief on page 165, watching the battle and deciding on strategy. The reliefs pictured the besieged city as seen by the monarch during the battle from his command post.

In 1983, we wanted to understand the siege ramp better and also to confirm its date. It had been assumed that the ramp dated to 701 B.C., but this had never been proven. It is important to remember that after Sennacherib's de-struction, the Judeans rebuilt Lachish (the Level II city); this rebuilt city was then destroyed in 588/6 B.C. by the Babylonians. (For the background of the Babylonian de-struction, see p. 314).

Moreover, the 1977 probe focused our attention on what seemed to be a large raised area inside the city wall opposite the Assyrian siege ramp. The southwest corner of Tel Lachish has apparently always been one of the higher parts of the mound, and even before the excava-tions by the British in the 1930s, this area had risen to such a height that it was regarded as the acropolis of the mound. The British excavators suspected that "the extra height at this point was achieved by the use of dumped soil." As it turned out, this was an understatement.

In 1983, we excavated eight squares inside the city wall, as part of a major trench cutting longitudinally through the Assyrian siege ramp and extending inside the

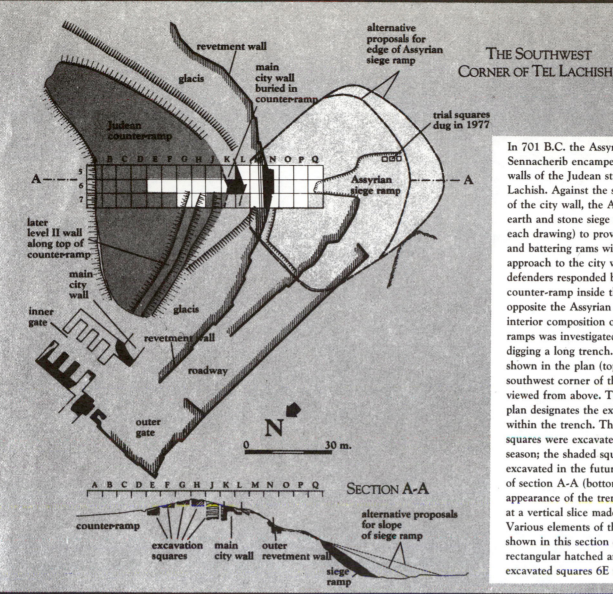

THE SOUTHWEST CORNER OF TEL LACHISH

SECTION A-A

In 701 B.C. the Assyrian army led by Sennacherib encamped outside the walls of the Judean stronghold of Lachish. Against the southwest corner of the city wall, the Assyrians built an earth and stone siege ramp (at right in each drawing) to provide their soldiers and battering rams with a high approach to the city wall. The Judean defenders responded by building a counter-ramp inside the city wall, opposite the Assyrian ramp. The interior composition of each of these ramps was investigated in 1983 by digging a long trench. The trench is shown in the plan (top) of the southwest corner of the tel, as though viewed from above. The grid on the plan designates the excavation squares within the trench. The 24 white squares were excavated in the 1983 season; the shaded squares may be excavated in the future. The drawing of section A-A (bottom) depicts the appearance of the trench as if looking at a vertical slice made along line A-A. Various elements of the ramp are shown in this section drawing. The rectangular hatched areas show excavated squares 6E through 6K.

city. From these squares inside the city, we learned that the substantial height in this area was the result of enormous amounts of soil having been dumped here in ancient times.

This fill was composed of thick layers of soil that contained debris from earlier strata of the mound—including large amounts of pottery of various periods ranging from the Chalcolithic period (fourth millennium B.C.) to the Late Bronze Age (1550 B.C.-1200 B.C.). Significantly, pottery from Level III (which was destroyed in 701 B.C.) is almost entirely absent. And there was no later pottery in this fill. The layers of soil fill were dumped in an orderly manner from certain points and therefore have a diagonal slant (see p. 170). As can be clearly seen in the sections cut parallel to the city wall, the soil fill was dumped against the face of the city wall.

On top of the soil fill was a thick layer of limestone

chips without any pottery at all. As indicated by the contours of the layers, the upper part of the city wall and the soil at the top of the adjoining counter-ramp are now entirely missing; apparently they were removed before the later Judean city wall (Level II) was built along the summit of the counter-ramp.

The soil fill was laid on pavements and flimsy structures contemporaneous with the city walls of Level III. The pottery associated with these pavements and structures was all Level III pottery, typical of the pottery found in the city on the eve of the siege. Under the soil fill, we even found a jar handle stamped with a royal seal impression (a so-called l'melekh handle).* Neither this royal seal impression nor the pottery under the soil fill had been

*For an explanation of l'melekh handles, see "Answers at Lachish" by David Ussishkin, **BAR**, November/December 1979.

Yoram Weinberg

The counter-ramp *inside the city wall of Lachish. A high area at the southwest corner of the mound has long puzzled archaeologists. Excavations in 1983—seen here as rectangular areas above and slightly to the right of the shed at left— revealed that this slope was thrown up by the defenders of Lachish against the inner face of the city wall opposite the threatening ramp of the Assyrians. The counter-ramp extends in a crescent 360 feet along the city wall. Its center is located approximately at the point of the rectangular excavation squares; its northern end reaches the city gate, seen here as the area just above the open structure at right.*

Diagonally laid layers of soil fill *make up the counter-ramp. Dumped in an orderly pattern, the fill contains pottery from earlier periods in Lachish's history, ranging from the fourth millennium B.C. (Chalcolithic period) to the end of the 13th century B.C. (Late Bronze Age). Almost no pottery from the time of the Assyrian siege in 701 B.C. and none from later periods was found in these soil layers—evidence that this ramp was constructed at the time of Sennacherib's assault on the city.*

destroyed by fire—a clear indication that the soil fill was laid in 701 B.C. but prior to Sennacherib's destruction of the city.

Undoubtedly, what we have here is a "counter-ramp" dumped against the inner city wall in 701 B.C. When the defenders of the city saw that the main thrust of the Assyrian attack was going to be directed against the southwest corner of the city and that a siege ramp was being laid there, they apparently decided to dump large amounts of soil against the inner face of the city wall in order to support it against the imminent attack.

Strengthening of city walls from inside at the point of attack is known elsewhere, but all such cases are much later. At Masada, the Sicarii used wooden beams and soil to construct an additional wall to support the inner face of the citadel wall at the point opposite the Roman siege ramp and battering rams.[1] In Dura-Europos in Upper Mesopotamia, in about 256 A.D., the Romans prepared for a Sassanian attack by dumping large amounts of soil inside and outside the city wall where the attack was expected. This strengthened the western wall of Dura-Europos and made tunneling underneath it much more difficult, if not impossible.*

Our 1983 trench revealed the composition of the Judean counter-ramp at Lachish. The general layout of the counter-ramp was determined by a surface survey. The counter-ramp is shaped like a crescent. The center is roughly in line with the central axis of the Assyrian siege ramp outside the city, a clear indication that the Judean counter-ramp was laid as a countermeasure to the Assyr-

*The ramp inside Dura-Europos buried the walls of the synagogue, thus protecting its magnificent wall paintings.

ian siege ramp. The counter-ramp extends along the inner city wall for about 360 feet, reaching the city gate at the northern end of the counter-ramp.

The excavation of this counter-ramp firmly established its date and its relation to the Assyrian siege ramp outside the city wall. It also helped to establish that the siege ramp outside the city wall was indeed the siege ramp of Sennacherib built in 701 B.C.

As noted above, our 1983 season also included for the first time extensive excavation of the Assyrian siege ramp itself. In addition, we surveyed the adjacent area, including the roadway leading to the city gate. We have now determined quite precisely the sides of the Assyrian ramp and have reconstructed its shape, despite the fact that large parts of it were removed in the British excavation of the 1930s. Originally the lower end of the ramp must have covered the ancient roadway leading up to the city. (It must have even partly filled the Middle Bronze Age fosse or dry moat near the roadway.) Unfortunately, the lower end of the siege ramp was entirely removed in the excavation of the 1930s. Thus we cannot determine with certainty the line of its lower edge. The main guiding line for reconstructing its lower edge is the angle of the lower extremity of the part still existing, using the central axis of this line. We can assume that the ramp continued at a less steep gradient below this point or at the same gradient. A less steep gradient would of course produce a longer ramp. Our plan and section drawings are drawn with two alternatives, representing the minimum and maximum dimensions. The Assyrian siege ramp appears to have been between 210 and 225 feet wide at the bottom and between 150 and 180 feet long (along the central axis up to the outer revetment wall). We have not yet

The Assyrian siege ramp. *Before their final onslaught against the Judean defenders of Lachish, the Assyrians built this ramp against the southwest corner of the fortified city. The ramp's slope extends from upper left to lower right. The triangular light-colored area between the outer surface of the slope and the darker area to the left of center is a cut into the ramp made by the British excavation in the 1930s. The cut exposes an inner section of the siege ramp showing the dense accumulation of small boulders used to construct it. Originally the fan-shaped ramp was 150 to 180 feet long on its central axis and 210 to 225 feet wide at its broad base.*

attempted to estimate the amount of boulders used in the siege ramp, but it must have been thousands and thousands of tons.

As noted, the length of the siege ramp given above is to the point where it reaches the outer revetment wall. This was in fact only its first phase! Its second phase extended from the revetment wall to the city wall. These two phases of construction of the Assyrian siege ramp corresponded to two phases of the battle for Lachish.

Before describing the two phases of the battle, corresponding to the two phases of construction of the Assyrian siege ramp, let me explain the relationship between the revetment wall and the city wall at this point on the mound.

In drawings and reconstructions of ancient Lachish, we often see the city surrounded by two concentric city walls. These reconstructions are based on two rings of fortifica-

tions found in the excavations and on what appear to be two concentric city walls in the Lachish reliefs at Sennacherib's palace at Nineveh. However, our excavations have convinced us that this outer wall was not a conventional city wall. What appears to be an outer city wall was in fact a revetment wall designed to support the bottom of a glacis sloping down from the city wall to the revetment wall. This glacis supported the base of the city wall, which surrounded the entire city on the upper periphery of the mound. Halfway down the slope, the people of Lachish built the revetment wall to support this glacis.

In the southwest corner of the mound, however, where the fortifications of the city were wisely reinforced, the revetment wall comes as close as about 15 feet to the city wall, rather than being built further down the slope. In addition, because the revetment wall at this point was so close to the city wall, the stone-faced glacis between the two walls is not very steep. It appears likely—and we hope to check this possibility in coming seasons—that at this corner of the mound, the two walls (the city wall and the revetment wall) merged to form a single structure about 45 feet wide, thus creating a platform in front of the city wall from which the defenders could fight along the outer line of fortifications. Elsewhere the revetment wall served as an independent fortification line supporting the glacis, which in turn supported the city wall.

Initially, the Assyrians built the siege ramp at the southwest corner of the mound up to the revetment wall. This was the Judeans' first line of defense. The first phase of the siege ramp's construction consisted of boulders piled on top of each other. The topmost layer consisted of stones cemented with strong mortar to create a compact surface. As the ramp approached the revetment wall, it seems that either bricks or horizontal layers of clay were incorported between the stone layers. We hope to investigate this phenomenon further in the future. But it seems likely that the Assyrians wanted to stabilize the siege ramp as it approached the outer revetment wall so that the siege machines and soldiers could be assured of firmer ground.

The battle was fierce as the Assyrian siege machines and soldiers fought their way up the ramp to the outer revetment wall. The revetment was built with a stone base, on top of which were mudbricks. In the heat of battle, the brickwork of the superstructure burned and collapsed on top of the siege ramp. As we excavated in front of the revetment wall, the remains of the first phase of the battle of Lachish were exposed. Some of the burned brick debris from the upper part of the revetment wall still contained remnants of white plaster. We also found chunks of carbonized wood, ashes, and pottery of a Level III date.

We also found 27 arrowheads in front of the revetment wall. The arrows were apparently fired toward the top of the walls where the defenders stood. One arrowhead was found embedded in the revetment wall itself. Many of the arrowheads were bent—an indication that they were shot at the wall from close range with powerful bows. Only two slingstones, both carved of flint and resembling tennis balls, were uncovered in front of the revetment wall. The ratio between slingstones and arrowheads indicates that the onslaught on the walls was supported mainly by archers rather than slingers. This accords well with the Lachish reliefs in which fewer slingers are portrayed than archers.

Included in the military equipment, we also found some scales of Assyrian armor. Finally, a rather unusual find was an iron chain about 37 cm long composed of four long, narrow links, each about 10 cm long. The chain was found lying in the burned brick debris in front of the revetment wall. This chain must have served some function in the battle, but we do not know what it was.

In the second stage of its construction, after the Assyrians had reached the revetment wall, the siege ramp was extended, covering the revetment wall and reaching nearly to the foot of the main city wall, where the second phase of the attack took place. The second—or higher—part of the siege ramp was between 66 and 75 feet wide (we cannot establish the exact width because we have not yet excavated the edges). The remains of the second stage of the siege ramp were severely damaged by the British expedition of the 1930s. But it appears that the higher

end of the second stage of the siege ramp did not abut the face of the city wall itself but stopped just short of it. Apparently the Assyrian battering rams were long enough to bridge this gap. It was along this narrow section of the fortifications that the Assyrian army concentrated its efforts, eventually breaching the walls of the city. The reliefs in the palace of Sennacherib portray five siege machines standing one beside the other on top of the siege ramp attacking the city wall, and 75 feet or so would have been sufficient for five battering rams to be arrayed for battle, one beside the other. At this point the city wall, running southwards from the gate, made a sharp turn to the east. Professor Israel Eph'al of Tel Aviv University is preparing a detailed study of the military aspects of the battle, and he has already observed that the Assyrians had a distinct advantage attacking this particular point in the city's defenses because the angle of fire used by the defenders stationed on the city walls to the right and left of the corner under attack was relatively ineffective.

At the foot of the city wall, we found more remains of the battle equipment of the Assyrian army. We unearthed 157(!) arrowheads in two excavation squares in front of the city wall. All the arrowheads but one are iron. One is carved of bone; apparently the Assyrians occasionally used bone arrowheads. The arrowheads are not uniform in size or shape, and several different types are represented. This variety might indicate the participation of different ethnic units in the attack, as can be seen from the Lachish reliefs.

The main city wall was about 17½ feet thick at this point and was built of bricks on stone foundations. On its inner side, it still stands to a height of about 14 feet. But somehow the Assyrians managed to breach it and destroy the city.

The Assyrian siege ramp and the remains of the battle, the fortifications, consisting of the revetment wall and the city wall, and the counter-ramp all combine to provide a unique picture of a fierce attack on a large Biblical city. The archaeological remains are entirely consistent with the picture we get from the other sources. All the data indicate the importance and strength of Lachish, the resolute defense of the Judeans and the exceptional military effort the Assyrians mounted to overcome it. The Assyrian siege ramp and the Judean counter-ramp are the earliest battle ramps thus far identified in the ancient Near East, and the only ones known from the Assyrian period.

The excavations in the southwest corner of Tell Lachish are far from completed. We will be back in the field during the summer of 1985. **BAR** readers are invited to join us and take part in these exciting excavations.

[1]Flavius Josephus, *The Jewish War*, VII, 311-314.

Notes

The Mystery of the Unexplained Chain

A Chain Reaction at Lachish

Yigael Yadin

IN THE MARCH/APRIL **BAR**, David Ussishkin reported on the Assyrian siege ramp and the Judean counter-ramp that he excavated at Lachish. His report, together with the review of his book on the Assyrian siege of Lachish, extensively illustrated with reliefs from Sennacherib's palace and photos of excavated finds, provides an unusual account of siege warfare in ancient times.

The elements of this warfare were all displayed with dramatic intensity: the arrows and the helmets, and the scale armor to counter the arrows' thrusts, the battering ram and the firebrands thrown from the walls by the defenders to burn the ram, and, to counter this, the water the attackers poured on the ram, and the Assyrian siege

Four links of iron chain, *each 10 cm long, lay in debris from the eighth-century B.C. battle at Lachish. Found by excavator David Ussishkin at the base of the burned outer revetment wall, the chain was an unexplained piece of evidence from the battle in which the Assyrian king Sennacherib defeated the Judean defenders. Now archaeologist Yigael Yadin has proposed an explanation for the chain's presence by referring to a relief (see photo and drawing on pp. 176 and 177) on the palace wall of another Assyrian king, Ashurnasirpal II (883-859 B.C.).*

MICHAL ROCHE BEN-AMI

ramp countered by a Judean ramp. There was one find, however, that Ussishkin could not explain—four links of a metal chain uncovered amid the destruction debris in front of the city wall where the Assyrian attack had been most intense.

This is how Ussishkin described the discovery:

"A rather unusual find was an iron chain about 37 cm long, composed of four long, narrow links, each about 10 cm long. The chain was found lying in the burned debris in front of the revetment wall. This chain must have served some function in the battle, but we do not know what it was."

What was this mysterious chain used for in the heat of battle? I believe I have found the answer.

The key to the answer lies in what I called in my book, *The Art of Warfare in Biblical Lands* (1963), a "chain reaction." This appears to be a particularly apt concept to explain the function of this mysterious chain.

The chain reaction I refer to in my book is the continuous interaction of offensive weapons and defensive devices, each trying to top the other in a never-ending chain reaction. We have seen several examples of this in Ussishkin's **BAR** article and in the review of his book on Lachish, as I mentioned above. The chain, I believe, is another example.

The chain was part of a defensive device to counter the most horrifying weapon known in ancient siege warfare—the battering ram. The body of the battering ram was made of prefabricated wood and leather segments transported from Assyria and then assembled at Lachish. The formidable siege machine was rolled up a ramp into place close to a vulnerable spot in the city wall. Within the ram, a heavy shaft was suspended on ropes from the ceiling of the turret. Two soldiers pushed the shaft backward and forward like a pendulum, each swing thrusting the shaft against the city wall until it broke through. As the shaft of the battering ram swung close to a wall, the defenders would lower a long chain outside the wall. The ends of the chain would be held by defending soldiers, each standing at some distance from the other on the wall. The middle of the chain would be lowered below the point of the thrust of the shaft. When the ram reached the wall, despite defensive efforts to prevent this, the desperate defenders on the wall would lift the chain, catching the shaft and raising it, thereby deflecting its direct attack on the wall.

I believe the chain found at Lachish is dramatic evidence of such a desperate counter-reaction to the attack of the Assyrian battering rams.

Unfortunately, the defensive chain also produced a re-action. The attackers would pull the chain down, away from the shaft, with grappling hooks. This is probably what happened at Lachish, making the chain or some of its links fall to the base of what Ussishkin refers to as the revetment wall.*

*Ussishkin explains why he believes the outer, lower wall at Lachish was only a revetment or supporting wall for the glacis, rather than an outer city wall. This subject is discussed in even greater detail in his book (*The Conquest of Lachish by Sennacherib* [Tel Aviv University Publications of The Institute of Archaeology No. 6, 1982]). I believe that characterizing this as a revetment wall is very inappropriate from the military tactical viewpoint (in contrast to the structural viewpoint). From the many Assyrian reliefs, we know that many fortified cities (particularly those built atop a high tell) each had a lower, forward wall. Its main function was to prevent attackers (and their battering rams) from reaching the main city wall. This is exactly what was found at Lachish. This lower wall served, *also*, as a revetment. But this lower wall, like the city wall higher up, was no doubt crowned with crenelations and battlements. Thus, for the attackers it mattered not that this lower wall also served a structural function—to support the glacis. The reconstruction published in **BAR** does not tally with the Assyrian reliefs. Indeed, from other sources we know that the tactical use of a fore-wall continued up to the medieval period. The reconstruction drawings of the battle of Lachish made by Gert le Grange and published in Ussishkin's book (Figs. 94-95) are definitely more accurate in this respect than the reconstruction published on page 29 of Ussishkin's book and republished on page 157 in this volume.

Ashurnasirpal's relief *depicts the Assyrian attack on an unidentified city. Two kneeling archers in front of an Assyrian battering ram (right) take aim at the city's defenders. Two other archers stand within the turret of the siege machine. The ramming shaft itself extends from the left of the machine toward the city wall. A chain held by a defender on the wall encircles the shaft; pulling up the chain deflects the ram's blow away from the city wall. Countering the chain's upward motion are two Assyrian soldiers below it pulling down the chain with grappling hooks, attempting to release the shaft from the chain.*

Two other Assyrian attack techniques are seen in the relief: far left, breaking down the wall by means of spikes held by two armor-clad soldiers, and center, tunneling beneath the wall.

Engraved by W. Holl

The use of a chain to counter the battering ram and the use of grappling hooks to counter the chain is pictured in astonishing detail in a relief of the Assyrian king Ashurnasirpal II (883-859 B.C.) uncovered at his palace at Nineveh by Austin Henry Layard in the 19th century. The relief is now in the British Museum and was carved only about 150 years before the Assyrian siege of Lachish.

In my book on ancient warfare, I described this relief as follows:

"This is the most detailed and comprehensive siege scene in the Assyrian reliefs until the period of Sennacherib. The relief shows five methods of assault being carried out simultaneously. From right to left: (1) Archers, protected by shields and coats of mail, firing volleys of arrows; (2) Battering ram and mobile tower in action; (3) Tunneling operatons—shown in X-ray style on the extreme left and extreme right of the city; (4) The low wall being demolished by armored sappers, using pikes and spears; (5) Storming parties mounting scaling ladders. A permanent feature of the art of warfare is the continuous interaction of offensive weapons and defensive devices, each trying to top the other in a never-ending chain reacton. The entire scene is, of course, an expression of it. But within the overall picture there are subsidiary actions which highlight the principle. At the right, in the battering ram detail, the defenders seek to deflect the battering pole with the aid of chains. To counter this, two Assyrian soldiers are seen trying to pull the chains away from the pole by gripping them with hooks and using the weight of their bodies for power."

Here is a rare case of ancient reliefs and archaeological discoveries complementing each other, thus explaining the chain found at Lachish.

We wish to thank Professor Ussishkin for permission to publish the chain links from Lachish. In his letter sending us the pictures, he asked us to state that he "made a similar suggestion independently in a lecture in [the] Institute of Archaeology in Tel Aviv on 14th November 1983, but did not put it in writing because none of Sennacherib's reliefs—portraying the conquest of Lachish as well as other cities—shows the use of chains in fighting siege machines. Thus this interpretation for the use of the chain remains unsubstantiated, and [he] preferred not to use it in writing."—Ed.

177

Lachish

Key to the
Israelite
Conquest
of Canaan?

DAVID USSISHKIN

IT IS NOW MORE THAN SEVEN YEARS since my first report to **BAR** readers on the excavation at Biblical Lachish. At that time (November/December 1979), I primarily discussed Iron Age Lachish, the Lachish of the Judean monarchy. Judean Lachish was twice conquered and destroyed. Lachish Level III was conquered and destroyed in 701 B.C. by the Assyrian ruler Sennacherib. Lachish was rebuilt (Level II) and then conquered again and destroyed again in 588/6 B.C. by Nebuchadnezzar the

Did a dapper Lachishite *pose for this anthropomorphic jar discovered by excavators in an open area outside the tel? Incised lines and red and black paint highlight the gentleman's features— an incongruous mix of tiny, bushy-browed eyes and an elegant, pencil-thin mustache. The unlikely Lothario stands 10.6 inches high.*

Babylonian, as is known from the Bible (see Jeremiah 34:7) as well as from the excavations and from the famous Lachish letters found in the city gate.*

Now we have dug deeper. We have reached the levels of the Canaanite city and of Joshua's time and earlier.

My previous article was titled "Answers at Lachish" and I was tempted to call this article "Answers at Lachish II," because we have found many answers in our excavations of Late Bronze Age Lachish. But the fact is that this time some of our answers, especially our historical reconstructions, are less sure. Many questions remain. We are in a period where history is less certain and scholars themselves are often in disagreement about major points. But it is also a period when archaeological evidence is especially important and abundant, providing new evidence, almost daily, about this shadowy period of Israel's origins.

achish is one of the key sites in the Bible's account of the Israelite conquest of Canaan. Today it is one of the largest (30 acres) and most significant mounds of the Biblical period in the entire land of Israel. Ample water supply from deep wells, sufficient land for cultivation and a location in the low hill country along the main route from the coastal plain to the Hebron hills all contributed to the prosperity and special importance of the city.

According to the Biblical account, Joshua conquered and destroyed first Jericho and Ai, and then made a treaty with Gibeon by which the Gibeonites agreed to serve Israel. In response, five Canaanite kings, including Japhia, the king of Lachish, formed an anti-Israelite alliance. This alliance of five Canaanite kings met the armies of Joshua on the field of battle in the Valley of Aijalon. With God's help, Joshua roundly defeated the five kings. It was then that "the sun stood still" to allow Israel time to finish the attack. In the presence of his people, Joshua addressed the Lord:

" . . . Thus the sun halted in midheaven, and did not press on to set, for a whole day; for the Lord fought for Israel. Neither before nor since has there ever been such a day, when the Lord acted on words spoken by a man" (Joshua 10:12-14).

Following swiftly on this victory, Joshua proceeded to attack Makkedah, then Libnah, and then Lachish:

"From Libnah, Joshua proceeded with all Israel to Lachish; he encamped against it and attacked it. The Lord delivered Lachish into the hands of Israel. They captured it on the second day and put it and all the people in it to the sword, just as they had done to Libnah" (Joshua 10:31-32).

Lachish thus played a significant role in the Biblical story of the Israelite conquest; and it is clear that it was one of the most prominent cities in Canaan at the time. For the archaeological excavations at Lachish, three principal questions present themselves: First, what

* "Lachish and Azekah Were the Only Fortified Cities of Judah that Remained," Rodney Wright, **BAR**, November/December 1982.

was the character and appearance of the Canaanite city that stood here at the time of the Israelite occupation? Second, can the archaeological data uncovered in the excavations shed any light on the Biblical story of the conquest and destruction of Lachish by the Israelite tribes? And third, does the archaeological evidence help us to understand the wider problems associated with the complex history of Canaan at that time, especially regarding the interrelationship between the Canaanites, the Philistines and the Israelites.

We believe that our excavations, and the excavations that preceded ours, provide significant, if sometimes tentative, answers to these questions.

Tel Lachish—which is almost certainly the site of ancient Lachish—was partially excavated long before we entered the field in 1973. Between 1932 and 1938, James L. Starkey led a large-scale British expedition that ended abruptly when Starkey was murdered by Arab bandits while traveling from Lachish to Jerusalem for the dedication of the Palestine Archaeological Museum.**

Starkey was a meticulous planner and had formulated a program of excavation that was to have extended over many years. Due to his tragic death, this program was brought to a sudden end and was never completed, although his distinguished assistant Olga Tufnell worked for 20 years on the data and finds, in the end producing an exemplary report covering the excavations that Starkey had completed.

Significantly, most of Starkey's excavations were not on the tel itself. In the years he dug, Starkey concentrated his principal efforts elsewhere. He excavated many of the graveyards in the vicinity of the tel and he cleared a slope on the northwest corner of the tel to serve as a dump for excavations planned on the mound itself. While doing this work, he hit upon the massive fortifications built in the 17th century B.C., during the later part of the Middle Bronze Age (20th to 16th centuries B.C.). These massive fortifications extended down the entire slope of the tel ending, at the bottom, in an artificial fosse or dry moat. Here Starkey made one of his most important discoveries. In this moat or fosse, Starkey uncovered a Canaanite temple—known as the Fosse Temple—constructed at the beginning of the Late Bronze Age (16th century B.C.), built when the earlier fortifications apparently went out of use.

In addition, Starkey did limited work on the tel itself. He cleared some important remains down to the Persian period (sixth to fourth centuries B.C.) and Judean period (tenth to sixth centuries B.C.). He also cut a sectional trench in the northeast corner of the mound down to earlier levels, finally reaching bedrock. From all these excavations, he was able to identify six occupational levels or strata, from I to VI, beginning at the top. We have been able to confirm his strata and have continued using the same numbering system

** Also, some excavations, limited in scope and scale, were carried out in 1966 and 1968 by Yohanan Aharoni of Tel Aviv University.

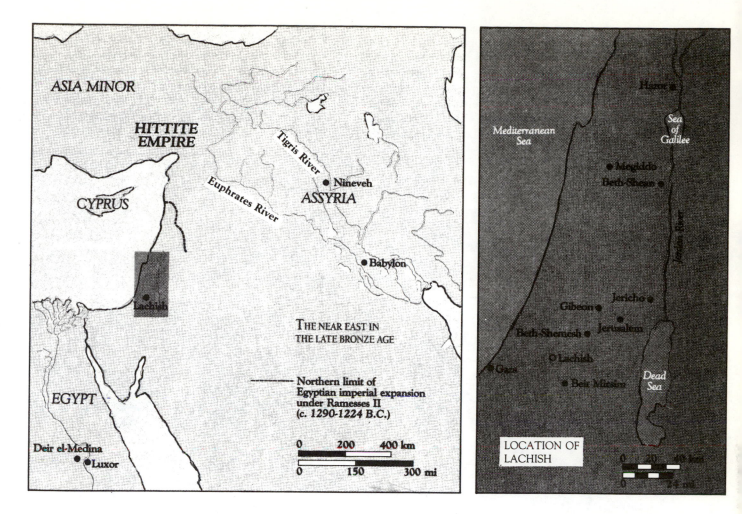

THE NEAR EAST IN
THE LATE BRONZE AGE

——— Northern limit of
Egyptian imperial expansion
under Ramesses II
(c. 1290-1224 B.C.)

LOCATION OF
LACHISH

to identify these levels.

The sixth stratum (Level VI), he correctly identified as the last Canaanite city. It was destroyed by a violent fire. Our excavations, however, have uncovered an earlier Canaanite city—Level VII—that Starkey never clearly identified. This newly discovered Canaanite city requires some drastic revisions in Starkey's archaeological conclusions.

Our excavations, sponsored by Tel Aviv University and the Israel Exploration Society, reached Late Bronze Age levels in three principal excavation areas: in a large sectional trench in our Area S; on the acropolis of the mound; and, surprisingly, in the area of the Judean entry gate complex.

Our main excavation area (Area S) is a large, narrow sectional trench at the western part of the tel. The use of such a trench was pioneered by Dame Kathleen Kenyon in her famous sectional trench at the tell of Biblical Jericho. By digging one ancient level after another in such a trench, the archaeologist obtains a sectional or vertical view of all the levels accumulated on the mound, right down to bedrock. This is what we did at Lachish. The work on this trench was supervised by Gabriel Barkay, who is familiar to **BAR** readers ("The Garden Tomb—Was Jesus Buried Here?" **BAR**, March/April 1986).

In excavating this trench we first dug through a layer of Hellenistic and Persian remains, then the layer of the city destroyed by Nebuchadnezzar in 588/6 B.C. (Level II), then the layer destroyed by Sennacherib in 701 B.C. (Level III), then through several other layers of earlier Israelite occupation, preceded by a period when the site was abandoned. Finally, we got down to Level VI, the Canaanite city destroyed by a terrible fire.

Between 1981 and 1983, we removed the remains of Level VI. Penetrating still deeper we uncovered another, earlier Canaanite level that had also been destroyed by fire. We designated this earlier Canaanite city Level VII.[1] During 1984 we carefully studied and analyzed the pottery recovered from these two Canaanite cities. One of the most significant results of this study was that we were forced to conclude that Starkey (and his assistant Tufnell) had attributed the last phase of the famous Fosse Temple, which I mentioned earlier, to the wrong city.

The reader will recall that Starkey found a Late Bronze Age Canaanite temple at the base of the mound built inside the fosse or dry moat which had been part of Lachish's massive defense system built in the 17th century B.C., during the Middle Bronze Age. This Fosse Temple actually consisted of three superimposed, successive temples, known as Fosse Temple I, II and III.

These temples were in use throughout the Late Bronze Age. The latest one, Fosse Temple III, was destroyed in a violent fire. Starkey assumed that Fosse Temple III was contemporaneous with the last Canaanite city (Level VI) since both the temple and the Level VI remains he uncovered on the tel had been destroyed by fire and no Canaanite remains were uncovered above either the destruction debris of Level VI or above the

last Fosse Temple that had also been destroyed by fire. When we compared the pottery from Level VII to the pottery from the Fosse Temple destroyed by fire, it became apparent that the latest Fosse Temple, i.e., Fosse Temple III, was contemporaneous with the Level VII Canaanite city, not Level VI.[2] We have to stress the archaeological and historical importance of this observation. Since its discovery 50 years ago, the rich

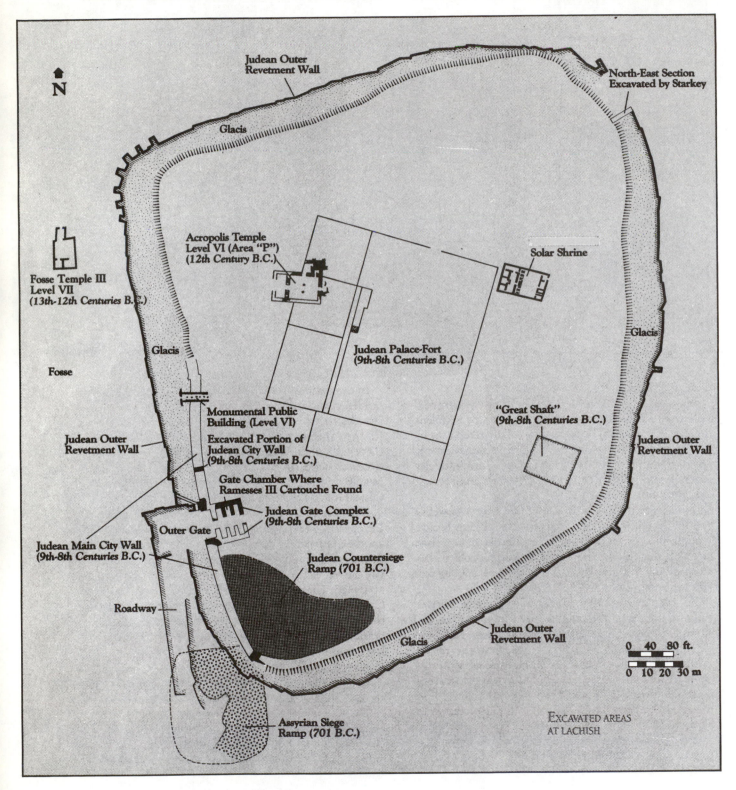

N

Judean Outer Revetment Wall

Glacis

North-East Section Excavated by Starkey

Acropolis Temple Level VI (Area "P") (12th Century B.C.)

Solar Shrine

Fosse Temple III Level VII (13th-12th Centuries B.C.)

Glacis

Fosse

Judean Palace-Fort (9th-8th Centuries B.C.)

Glacis

Judean Outer Revetment Wall

Monumental Public Building (Level VI)

Excavated Portion of Judean City Wall (9th-8th Centuries B.C.)

Gate Chamber Where Ramesses III Cartouche Found

Judean Gate Complex (9th-8th Centuries B.C.)

"Great Shaft" (9th-8th Centuries B.C.)

Judean Outer Revetment Wall

Outer Gate

Judean Main City Wall (9th-8th Centuries B.C.)

Judean Countersiege Ramp (701 B.C.)

Roadway

Judean Outer Revetment Wall

Glacis

0 40 80 ft.
0 10 20 30 m

Assyrian Siege Ramp (701 B.C.)

EXCAVATED AREAS AT LACHISH

182

Fosse Temple has become a key site for understanding Canaanite Lachish and the Late Bronze Age in Palestine in general. Thus, a change in the stratigraphical position of Fosse Temple III has widespread repercussions. Thus, if the Israelite armies destroyed the last Canaanite city (Level VI)—a subject we shall return to—they did not destroy the Fosse Temple, for that had already been destroyed at the end of the earlier Canaanite city, the city of Level VII.

Now that we have distinguished in well-stratified contexts between the two distinct Canaanite cities that existed one after another at Lachish, we have an excellent starting point for the detailed study of Late Bronze Age Lachish.

In our long, narrow sectional trench, we uncovered in Level III part of a large domestic building. Because the trench is quite narrow (27 feet wide), only part of the building was uncovered; it extends beyond the excavation area both to the north and to the south. The walls were built of mudbricks on a stone foundation. An open court was apparently paved with stones. The recovery of a large number of pottery vessels sealed beneath the destruction debris proved extremely important for dating purposes.

The latest Fosse Temple (Fosse Temple III) was contemporaneous with this domestic building. The temple, which also reflects Canaanite life in the Level VII city, was extremely well preserved because of its location at the bottom of the tel. It was protected over the millennia by a thick layer of debris eroded from the slope above. The ground plan of the last Fosse Temple was similar to that of the two Fosse Temples below it. The building consisted of a main hall, an antechamber in front of it and two smaller rooms at the back. The main hall was about 30 feet square. Four columns in the center supported the roof. Benches for priests or supplicants lined the walls.

The building was entered from the north. On the southern wall of the main hall was a raised platform and altar. Behind and above the platform a large niche was cut into the back wall of the hall forming the *cella** of the temple.

This Fosse Temple yielded a variety of rich finds, sealed by the debris. Additional artifacts were found in pits outside the temple. The finds in this area included not only a large number of pottery vessels, mainly small bowls in which tributes or offerings were presented, but also scarabs, cylinder seals, beads, faience vessels and a large number of ivory objects.

After the fiery destruction of Level VII (probably at the end of the 13th century B.C.), the city was soon rebuilt (Level VI). But the Fosse Temple remained in ruins, never again to be raised. Apparently, it was replaced during the Level VI period, as we shall see, by a new temple on the acropolis of the mound.

The similarity of the pottery in Level VII and Level VI, as well as other cultural affinities, indicates that only

* A *cella* is the central cultic place, the "holy of holies" of the temple.

a short period of time elapsed between the destruction of the earlier Canaanite city and the building of the last Canaanite city. Nevertheless, the layout of the city changed markedly, as did individual buildings. For example, the domestic building of Level VII partially uncovered in our sectional trench was replaced by a monumental public building. As I have already noted, the site of the Fosse Temple was abandoned and another temple was constructed on the acropolis of the city. The newly built temple probably replaced the earlier Fosse Temple as the central sanctuary of Lachish.

Strangely, it appears that neither of the two Canaanite cities (Level VII or Level VI) from Late Bronze Age Lachish was protected by a city wall or other fortifications such as existed in the Middle Bronze Age. The Fosse Temple was constructed in the fosse itself which had formed an integral part of the city fortifications during the Middle Bronze Age. This is a clear indication that these fortifications were no longer in use during the Late Bronze Age. Moreover, the buildings from Levels VII and VI we found in our sectional trench and the building from Level VI uncovered by Starkey in his sectional trench were all located on the periphery of the top of the tel, just where we would expect a city wall, if there had been one. There was no city wall around the edge of the city. It is quite possible that the buildings located around the periphery of the city were joined to one another, thus forming a closed ring of houses surrounding the city and protecting it from attack, but that is all. I shall later suggest why such minimal defensive measures apparently sufficed at Lachish during the Late Bronze Age.

Like the domestic building from Level VII that we uncovered in our sectional trench, the public building that replaced it in Level VI was only partially excavated by us because it too extended beyond the limits of our trench. For that reason, we have not been able to determine the complete ground plan of the building, but it included an open courtyard on the eastern side and two central halls between 45 and 55 feet long and 12 feet wide. One of these halls, which we call the pillared hall, had a row of five or six column bases extending along the central axis of the room. These column bases were embedded in the floor and consist of large flattish stones on which wooden columns probably stood. Like the earlier building, the walls were built of mudbricks on stone foundations, but these foundations are very thick, an indication that the edifice rose to a considerable height and may well have had a second story.

We were able to detect three different phases in the building's history. While it originally must have served some public function in the Canaanite city, in its final phase it was used, like its predecessor in Level VII, solely for domestic purposes. Probably, at the end, refugees

Story continues on page 188

183

Artifacts
from the
Fosse Temple

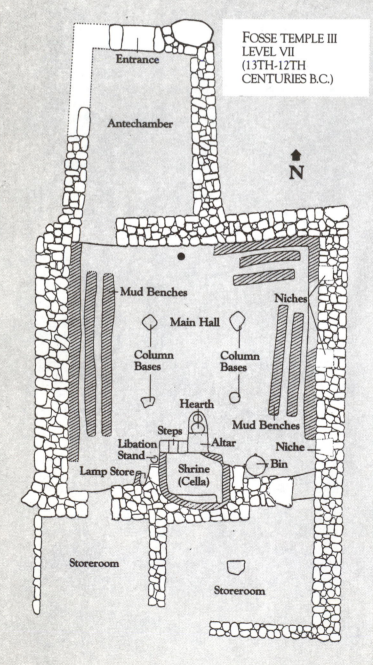

FOSSE TEMPLE III
LEVEL VII
(13TH-12TH
CENTURIES B.C.)

Entrance

Antechamber

N

Mud Benches

Niches

Main Hall

Column
Bases

Column
Bases

Hearth

Steps

Altar

Mud Benches

Libation
Stand

Niche

Lamp Store

Bin

Shrine
(Cella)

Storeroom

Storeroom

The Canaanites built three successive temples on the western side of Lachish, all constructed on the same site in the city's defensive moat, or fosse. The last of these, Fosse Temple III, had a plan (far left) very similar to the temples beneath it.

Oriented on a north/south axis, Fosse Temple III consisted of four rooms: an entrance antechamber on the northern side, a main hall and two southern store rooms. Four pillars supported the roof of the main hall, and mud benches lining its walls provided a place for offerings and seating for priests and worshippers.

A raised platform and altar adjoining the south wall of the main hall formed the *cella*, the central cultic place of the temple. Two bowl-like depressions formed a hearth in front of the altar. A libation stand, used for liquid offerings, stood to the right of the altar; on the left a large pottery bin held solid offerings.

A British expedition led by J. L. Starkey made the exciting discovery of the Fosse Temple in the 1930s. Photographed after they had cleared much of the temple, Arab workmen (below) dig near the two southern store rooms, far right. A lone Arab workman, left, stands in the main hall of the temple; to his right is the entrance to the antechamber, and behind him the mud benches lining the northern wall. The dot on the plan marks the position of the lone workman in the Fosse Temple.

Preserved by layers of protective silt at the bottom of the fosse, Fosse Temple III yielded a treasure trove of finds to excavators. Although the temple was damaged by a great fire at the end of the 13th century B.C., remains of pottery, glass, faience and scarabs were unearthed here (see photos, pp. 186-187).

A pitcher (near left) found broken in a pit outside the temple electrified the excavators. Nicknamed the "Lachish ewer," the pitcher's shoulder bears a proto-Canaanite inscription: "Mattan. An offering to my Lady 'Elat." The ewer and its now-missing contents were a tribute offered to the temple and to the deity 'Elat by a man named Mattan. Proto-Canaanite is the earliest-known form of alphabetic script—a forerunner of the alphabetic script we use today.

Perfume for a lady of rare and expensive tastes probably flowed from this ten-inch-high ivory flask (right), carved in the shape of a woman. A hole pierced through the head allowed the perfume to pour into a spoon shaped like a human hand.

Lachish, like much of Canaan, was probably a part of Egypt's New Kingdom (c. 1550-1070 B.C.) empire. As a result, artifacts found in Fosse Temple III reflect two very different artistic traditions: Egyptian and Canaanite.

Scarabs and cylinder seals (right) found in the Fosse Temple were probably offerings or tribute. The large scarab more than three inches in height, lauds Pharaoh Amenhotep III (14th century B.C.) and mentions 102 lions hunted by him in the first ten years of his reign. Used to mark possessions, the hieroglyphic writing on scarabs and cylinder seals appears in reverse. When pressed into wet clay the seals leave a correctly oriented image.

Faience beads and pendants (far right) in an Egyptian style were probably a prized part of a Canaanite woman's jewelry collection. They were discovered unstrung; the arrangement follows the restorer's sense of design. Faience may

have been the result of man's first conscious effort to produce a synthetic material. Manufacturing details are uncertain now, but it is known that faience consists of a core of quartz grains covered with a vitreous glaze. Considered especially fine in antiquity, Egyptian faience jewelry and vessels have been found throughout the Mediterranean. Egyptian manufacture of faience began in the fourth millennium B.C.

Almost untouched in the fire that destroyed the last Fosse Temple in the 13th century B.C., these ivories (left) retain much of their beauty and luster. Carved in a Canaanite style, they

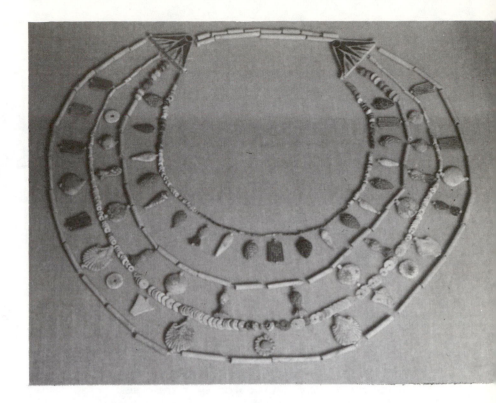

represent various animals and a human head.

Egyptian-style faience vessels and stoneware (below), still look as serviceable as on the day they were manufactured, more than 3,000 years ago.

took shelter here and left their domestic pottery as evidence of their occupation. The finds in the building were all sealed by the destruction debris. Some of the more elegant finds must belong to the earlier phases of the building. These earlier artifacts reflect great prosperity and strong Egyptian influence. They include a unique scarab portraying a Pharoah hunting, a piece of gold jewelry, an object covered with gold foil and two carved ivories. The domestic pottery, on the other hand, probably belonged to the people who settled in the building during its final phase, just before its fiery destruction.

Before discussing who might have been responsible for this destruction, let us look at the temple on the top of the mound.* This is the temple that may have replaced the Fosse Temple destroyed at the end of Level VII and not rebuilt. The Level VI temple built on the acropolis was located right in the center of the mound. We uncovered it beneath the foundations of the later edifice known as the Judean palace-fort. This temple was probably part of the palace complex of the Canaanite kings of Lachish, just as the temple built hundreds of years later on Jerusalem's Temple Mount was part of the palace complex of King Solomon.

The Lachish temple on the acropolis of the mound must have been one of the finest and most luxurious buildings of Canaanite Lachish, but unfortunately it has been badly preserved. Robbed and then destroyed during the final destruction of the Level VI city, this Canaanite temple suffered further damage during the period of the Judean kingdom. At that time, stones from the Canaanite temple and the debris covering it were removed and used in the construction of the later Judean palace-fort. Nonetheless, enough remained to enable us, in a painstaking dig that lasted a number of years, to reconstruct this magnificent shrine and to obtain a reasonable idea of its character.

We also dug farther down, beneath the temple, to see whether it replaced an earlier temple from Level VII; in other words, we wanted to know whether there were two or more superimposed temples here, as was the case with the Fosse Temple. Unfortunately, the issue remains undecided. The walls of the Level VI temple did follow the lines of an earlier structure, but we found no clear evidence that the earlier structure was also a temple.

The Level VI temple was oriented from west to east, and consisted principally of three parts, an antechamber, a main hall and a *cella*. An annex of several rooms was attached to the north side of the main hall; a similar annex may have existed on the south side but this is now covered by the later Judean palace-fort, so it is difficult to tell. The walls of the Canaanite temple were built of mudbricks on stone foundations. The entrance was from the west. A stone staircase must have led from the antechamber to the main hall because the floor of the main hall is about four feet

* The excavation of this temple was under the supervision of Christa Clamer.

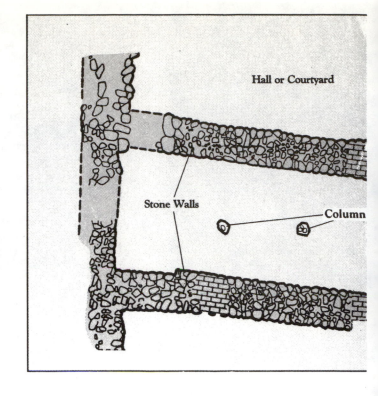

higher than the antechamber floor.

The main hall is nearly rectangular and measures about 49 feet by 40 feet—quite large, especially in ancient times. The floor is made of well-laid mudbricks. Two large, round limestone column bases, standing in the center of the hall, supported columns that in turn supported the roof. The column bases still exist but the columns themselves are gone. However, they were probably stone columns in the Egyptian style, crowned by flower-styled capitals. The roof was spanned by long wooden beams laid parallel to one another across the main hall and supported by the central columns. The charred remains of these roof beams were found lying on the floor. We analyzed them and they turned out to be cedar of Lebanon, the famous and expensive wood imported from the hills of Lebanon that was also used in Solomon's Temple much later. In the eastern part of the main hall, we found numerous fragments of painted plaster that once decorated the walls of the Canaanite temple and were perhaps used on the wooden ceiling as well. Many of these fragments were found adhered to each other. Separating and preserving them proved to be difficult. The fragments are in many colors—black, white, red, yellow and, especially, a beautiful light blue. Some fragments show traces of pattern, but not enough to describe.

The entrance from the main hall of the temple to the northern annex was lavishly decorated with beams of cedar of Lebanon. Two round wooden posts, each about five inches in diameter, flanked the doorway. At the northeastern corner of the main hall was a small storeroom that contained many pottery vessels. A plastered installation about four feet high in the

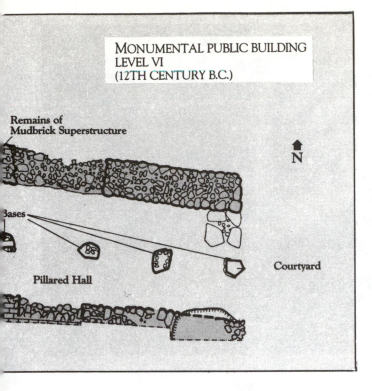

MONUMENTAL PUBLIC BUILDING LEVEL VI (12TH CENTURY B.C.)

Remains of Mudbrick Superstructure

Bases

Pillared Hall

N

Courtyard

Disinterred after centuries, *a monumental public building (below) destroyed in the catastrophe that overwhelmed the final Canaanite city in the 12th century B.C. emerges into the light of day.*

Only partially excavated, the remains of a pillared hall are clearly visible in the foreground. Another hall, or perhaps a courtyard, lies directly above the pillared hall at the top of the picture. The Judean city wall towers over the excavations. The plan (left) shows the building's layout.

The public building was built of mudbrick on a stone foundation. The thickness of the foundation indicates that this building may have had a second story.

southeast corner of the main hall was probably used to hold water.

Three round chalk* column bases were arrayed along the eastern wall of the main hall. Each of the three bases was attached to the wall by a plastered brick pilaster or pier. These column bases originally carried tapering octagonal columns, also hewn of chalk; they were removed and broken when the temple was robbed, but we found some remains in the course of the excavation. Each column was crowned by a square capital. Each side

* Chalk is a soft form of limestone.

YORAM WEINBERG

Artifacts from the Monumental Building

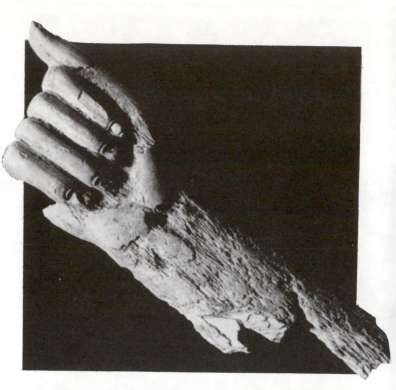

Silent witnesses to the destruction of the Late Bronze Age city of Lachish, these objects give proof of the city's prosperity and close ties with Egypt before its fall in the 12th century B.C.

An ivory hand (above, right) still seeks to clasp a now-missing object. Originally part of a human figure, the hand is approximately 5.3 inches long. A hole drilled behind the fingers allows it to grasp another object.

The unadorned beauty of a Canaanite goddess (bottom, right) shines forth from this clay plaque. Her hair, cut in an elegant Egyptian style, gives evidence of the powerful cultural and social sway Egypt exercised over its Canaanite subjects in the 13th-12th centuries B.C.

A Pharaoh (below) takes aim with bow and arrow at a lion standing in a thicket. In this unique scarab, only 0.7 inches wide, the Pharaoh's name is omitted, indicating that the scarab was not meant to commemorate a particular event in his reign.

of the capital was a continuation of one of the column shaft's eight facets; this form of the eight facets of the column continued into the capital. Each column, including its base and capital, was only about five and a half feet high. A three-inch hole was drilled into the top of each capital in order to secure it at the top. The purpose of these columns is a puzzle. Obviously, they did not serve a constructional purpose; they are too short. One attractive suggestion is that the three columns—as well as the column bases—were connected with brick pilasters to the eastern wall of the main hall of the temple, thereby forming two niches along the wall between the three columns. Here sacred statues or stelae might have been placed, facing the hall.

A monumental staircase of well-hewn chalk stone slabs, built against the eastern wall of the main hall, led up to the raised *cella*. The bottom slab of the staircase was more a threshold than a step, since it was wider and lower than the others; indeed it is nearly flush with the level of the brick floor. A circle 22 inches in diameter is engraved on the right side of this threshold-step, probably to mark the position of a stand or the like. Unfortunately, some of the slabs in the staircase were pulled out and carried away after the temple was destroyed. The four lowest steps were found complete, but the fifth and sixth steps were partly removed. The seventh step is missing altogether. The four lower steps were flanked on each side by a low parapet, made of two well-hewn stone slabs. The upper end of the parapet rested on a round column base, next to the wooden column that originally stood on the column base. These columns must have supported a small roof or canopy covering the staircase.

The *cella* of the temple unfortunately was badly preserved. It is difficult even to reconstruct its plan. The staircase just described led onto a plastered landing at the entrance to the *cella*, but that is almost all we know.

The rich temple furnishings were probably vandalized before the temple was set on fire. Relatively few finds were recovered. However, we discovered *in situ* six broken pottery stands placed in a row along the back wall of the storeroom. Other significant finds strewn about the floors included fragments of alabaster and faience vessels, fragments of ivory plaques or small bowls, painted fragments of ostrich shells, beads and pendants, pieces of oxidized iron (a rare and expensive commodity at the time) and many pottery offering bowls.

Our prize find, however, was what we call the "Lady Godiva" plaque. It is a thin gold sheet that we found crumpled and torn into five pieces. It has been straightened and put back together, and is now on tour in the United States (See **BAR**'s review of the exhibit, November/December 1986). Measuring about 7 1/2 by 4 1/2 inches, it was probably originally attached to a wooden plaque or sewn to a piece of leather or textile. The scene depicted on it is shown in high relief, achieved by pressure applied to the reverse side of the

gold sheet and accentuated by grooving. A few details were shown with the aid of insets on the front, probably colored stones that are now missing. The plaque portrays a naked goddess standing on a horse. Her headgear is composed of vertical leaves resembling a flower, with two horns at the bottom. In each hand, she holds two lotus flowers with long stems.

Finally, in a room on the side of the main hall we found a number of well-dressed stone slabs inscribed with graffiti. The most significant graffito portrays a standing god, brandishing a lance with both his hands.

Christa Clamer, of Israel's Department of Antiquities, has made a meticulous study of this god as well as of the naked goddess on the gold plaque; she has concluded that the god and goddess are both associated with the cult of the Egyptian-Canaanite divinities Qudshu, Asherah-Astarte and Resheph. This may, of course, be taken as an indication that the cultic rites of these deities were performed in the temple.

To summarize, the temple consisted of three elements located one behind the other—the antechamber, the main hall and the *cella*. The entrance to each element was located along a single, straight axis oriented from west to east; each element of the temple stood on successively higher ground: A staircase led up to the main hall and another staircase led up to the *cella*. Two massive columns in the center of the main hall supported the roof.

These same distinguishing features have been found, in part, in other temples as well, especially at the contemporaneous Canaanite temple in Beth-Shean. As I hinted earlier, these same architectural principles—except the orientation and the two central columns—were also used in Solomon's Temple in Jerusalem. Thus, it seems that our Canaanite temple at Lachish was built according to a plan that later served as a prototype for Solomon's architects. The two central columns in the main hall—which also were found in the temple of Beth-Shean—serve to illustrate the Biblical account of the Philistine temple of Dagon in Gaza, which Samson pulled down by the two central columns (Judges 16:23-30).

The plan of this Canaanite temple at Lachish seems to have originated in Egypt. Similar temples have been uncovered at Deir el-Medina near Luxor, and also at Tell el-Amarna. Deir el-Medina was the village of the ancient Egyptian workmen who cut the tombs of the Pharaohs in the Valley of the Kings. At Deir el-Medina, Chapel G, among others, consists of an antechamber, main hall with two central columns and a *cella*; the entrances and their staircases are aligned along a central axis. Various other characteristic features in our Canaanite temple at Lachish were adopted from the Egyptians— the octagonal columns, the shapes of the column bases and capitals, the staircase and its parapet, the brick-paved floor and the painted plaster. In short, our Canaanite temple at Lachish (as well as the

Story continues on page 194

Acropolis Temple

An archaeologist (photo right) is dwarfed by the main hall of the 12th-century B.C. acropolis temple. This temple, which possibly replaced the earlier Fosse Temple III, consists of three main parts oriented on an east-west axis (see plan, below): an antechamber preceding the main hall on the west, the main hall, and a tiny, raised *cella*, or sacred enclosure. (Note that the doorway between the antechamber and the main hall, seen on the plan, had not yet been excavated when the photo was taken. What appears on the photo as a solid wall between the two rooms is actually the unexcavated balk.) An entrance on the north side of the temple leads to an annex. In the photo, remains of the Judean palace-fort loom behind.

Some structural and ornamental elements survived the temple's destruction. In the main hall near the entrance

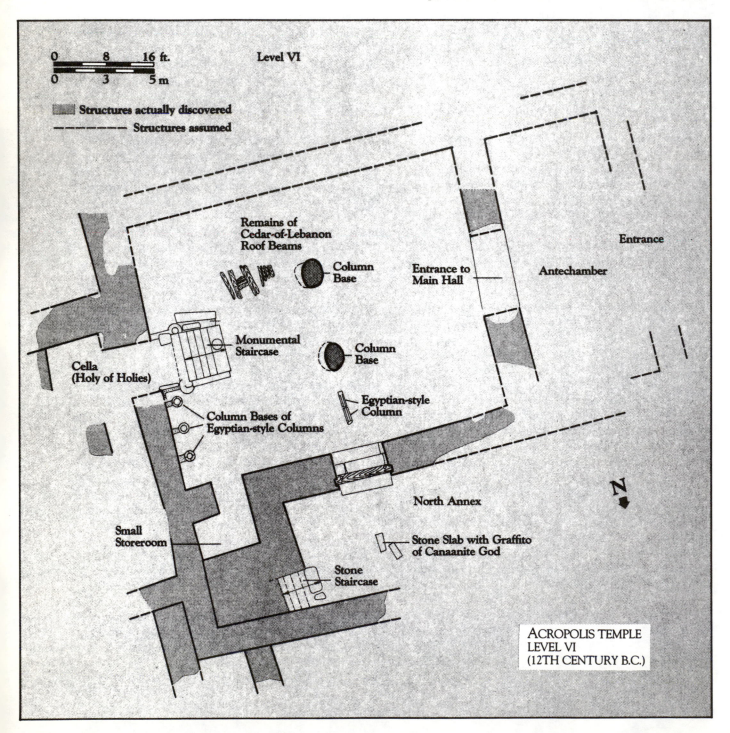

Level VI

0   8   16 ft.
0   3   5 m

Structures actually discovered
- - - - - - Structures assumed

Remains of Cedar-of-Lebanon Roof Beams

Column Base

Entrance to Main Hall

Entrance

Antechamber

Monumental Staircase

Column Base

Cella (Holy of Holies)

Column Bases of Egyptian-style Columns

Egyptian-style Column

North Annex

Small Storeroom

Stone Slab with Graffito of Canaanite God

Stone Staircase

N

ACROPOLIS TEMPLE
LEVEL VI
(12TH CENTURY B.C.)

to the north annex, an Egyptian-style octagonal column crowned with a square capital (below, far right) lies where it was found by excavators. Too small to be a structural element, this column and two similar ones, now mostly missing or broken, originally abutted the east wall of the main hall. The engaged columns formed niches in which sacred statues or stelae may have been placed, facing the hall.

A monumental stairway (below, left) leads from the main hall into the *cella*. Made of well-hewn chalk slabs, only the four lower steps are complete, though parts of the fifth and sixth steps still remain. The seventh, and crowning, step is missing altogether.

Brightly colored plaster *fragments from the walls of the main hall in the 12th-century B.C. temple retain their brilliant hues after more than 3,000 years. Such finds indicate that the walls were predominantly decorated in patterns colored in black, white, red, yellow and light blue.*

contemporaneous Canaanite temple at Beth-Shean) displays strong Egyptian influence.

Before considering what this Egyptian influence indicates, let us examine our third excavation area, where we found Late Bronze Age remains which turned out, in a way, to be the key to the entire excavation of the Late Bronze Age levels. This excavation area* was the gate complex to the Judean city which was destroyed by Sennacherib in 701 B.C. We had no thought that this area would have any significance for our study of the Late Bronze Age city. Our sole interest here was in investigating the Judean remains. We decided to open a narrow trench in one of the chambers of the Judean gate in order to examine the area below floor level to study the foundations of the gate. We reached the bottom of the foundations only after digging more than ten feet below the floor level. There we discovered that the foundations of the gate were laid on a plastered floor dating to the tenth century B.C. (Level V). We decided to make a further probe beneath this floor in order to check the date and its stratigraphic position before discontinuing work in this trench altogether.

Once we penetrated beneath the material that made up the plastered floor, we unexpectedly encountered destruction debris and pottery from Level VI, the last Canaanite city. And here—in the most unexpected place and to our utter surprise—we found a cache of

* Under the supervision of Yitzhak Eshel.

bronze objects lying buried and sealed beneath the destruction debris of Level VI (see p. 197).

This cache included a peculiar assortment of broken or defective tools—a pair of tongs, a knife blade, an axe or adze, two borers or awls. Because they were all broken or defective and all made of bronze, perhaps the collection can be explained as a scrap-metal collection destined for remelting and recasting.

One of the tools had an unusual shape; indeed, its original shape, size and function are still obscure. It was an oblong plaque with a handle welded into its back. Now broken, the plaque is six and a half inches long. When the object was cleaned in the laboratory, we found that it contained a cartouche on it. A cartouche is a royal ring surrounding hieroglyphics that spell the name of Egyptian royalty. In this case, the cartouche contained the name of a powerful Pharaoh of the 20th Dynasty, Ramesses III.

Since the object bearing his name was sealed beneath the destruction debris of Level VI, this destruction could not have occurred prior to the accession of Ramesses III to the Egyptian throne. Most Egyptologists now date Ramesses III's long reign to 1182-1151 B.C. Some time must have passed after his accession in 1182 B.C. to enable our object to have been cast in bronze, possibly imported to Lachish, and to have been used, then broken and finally discarded and set aside in this cache of defective or broken bronze objects. This cartouche is evidence that Level VI, the last Canaanite city at Lachish, was destroyed sometime around 1150 B.C. or even later.

The discovery of the cartouche of Ramesses III forced us to reexamine many long-held ideas and concepts. Until now the final destruction of Canaanite Lachish

194

was considered to have occurred in the 13th century B.C. The great William F. Albright thought that the destruction of Canaanite Lachish could be pinpointed to "about the year 1231-30, or a very little later." This date was accepted by many other authorities. Now we have to reduce this date by 80 years—to about 1150 B.C.—or even more. What are the implications of this drastic change?

Lachish Level VI was a large and prosperous Canaanite city, with characteristic Canaanite pottery, art and culture. It is also clear that this city maintained important connections with Egypt. We have already described the lavishly decorated and equipped temple which reflects so much Egyptian influence, despite the fact that nothing in the building indicated it was dedicated to an Egyptian deity. In addition to the temple, various other finds, such as scarabs and the cartouche of Ramesses III, demonstrate strong Egyptian influence.

In this respect I should mention one significant find that was uncovered by Starkey in a tomb contemporaneous with Level VI at the foot of the mound. The tomb contained two anthropoid clay coffins of the type known from a number of places in Palestine and Egypt during this period, notably Beth-Shean and Deir el-Balah south of Gaza. These coffins, cylindrically shaped, with the lid featuring a human face, represent an Egyptian funerary custom, and their use at Lachish fits the Egyptianized character of the Level VI city. One of the coffins bears a crudely executed painted depiction of two Egyptian deities, as well as a pseudo-hieroglyphic inscription written by an unskilled local scribe who was trying to copy the ancient Egyptian formulae. The clay of one of the coffins was analyzed by neutron activation in order to establish its place of manufacture, and it apparently originated in the region of Lachish.

Nothing at Lachish is more indicative of Egyptian presence, however, than four bowl fragments inscribed in Egyptian hieratic script, found out of context by Starkey in the foundation fill of the later Judean palace-fort. These inscriptions have recently been studied afresh by Orly Goldwasser, an Egyptologist at Hebrew University, in conjunction with similar hieratic bowls from Tel Sera' in southern Israel. The Lachish bowls (and the Tel Sera' bowls) document the *smw*, the harvest tax, paid to an unidentified Egyptian religious "institution." This Egyptian religious institution was probably associated with a local temple, such as our Level VI temple. According to Goldwasser—and she seems to be correct—the recording of the payment of the harvest tax on votive bowls in the temple reflects the economic exploitation of southern Canaan by the Egyptian authorities via the religious establishment. This may very well mean that Canaanite Lachish was under Egyptian suzerainty at the time, as was much of southern Canaan.

The strong ties between the Egyptian administration and the Level VI Canaanite city may well explain the city's great prosperity. The Egyptian presence may also explain why the Level VI city (and the earlier Canaanite

city of Level VII as well) did not require any fortifications to defend it: It was "protected" by Egypt. The data from Lachish and from many other sites in Canaan are consistent, providing additional support for one another and allowing us to conclude that Canaanite cities continued to prosper during this period despite the fact that the area was still part of the Egyptian empire, not only during the reign of Ramesses III, but even later, during the brief reigns of his successors, Ramesses IV (1151-1145 B.C.), Ramesses V (1145-1141 B.C.) and Ramesses VI (1141-1134/3 B.C.). During this period, Egypt apparently still had effective political, economic and military control over most of the country. The strongholds of Megiddo and Beth-Shean in northern Canaan perhaps marked the northern edge of Egyptian-held territory at the time. Egyptian hegemony was badly weakened during the third quarter of the 12th century B.C. The sudden destruction of Lachish Level VI was probably the result of the Egyptians' loss of control over southern Canaan. Without Egyptian protection, unfortified Lachish became easy prey to the enemy.

But who was the enemy?

Lachish Level VI was razed in a violent destruction accompanied by fire. Traces of the conflagration could be seen everywhere that Level VI remains were uncovered. The destruction was apparently complete, and the population liquidated or driven out. Following the catastrophe, the site was abandoned and remained desolate until the tenth century B.C.

The circumstances of the city's destruction were vividly illustrated in the ruins of the large public building in our large sectional trench (Area S). In the end the building was apparently turned into living quarters, perhaps for refugees from outside the city who fled their homes in the face of the disaster that eventually destroyed Lachish. On the floors, sealed beneath the building debris, we found human osteological remains—bones of an adult female aged 40-50 years and an eight-year-old child, as well as two skeletons: one of a two- or three-year-old child and the other of an infant of six to eight months old. Professor Patricia Smith, an anthropologist at Hadassah Hospital in Jerusalem, who is studying these remains, has concluded on the basis of the position of the skeletons on the floor, that "the child had either been thrown down on its face, or possibly died while crawling along the ground . . . the infant was thrown or fell onto the ground." Apparently, these young children were trapped and then crushed under falling debris while trying to crawl out. According to Professor Smith, the excellent state of preservation of the skeletons suggests that they were covered by debris shortly after death.

All the evidence points toward the destruction of Level VI by a powerful and resolute enemy. But again we must ask who? Unfortunately, archaeological data do not provide any affirmative clues as to the identity of that enemy or to the immediate circumstances surrounding the city's downfall.

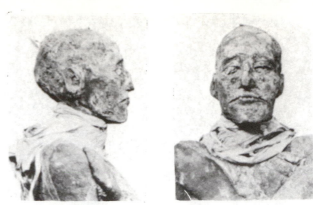

This deep section-trench *into the foundations of the Judean city-gate revealed a totally unexpected find: a cache of bronze objects, including one inscribed with the name of Pharaoh Ramesses III, whose reign has been dated to c. 1182-1151 B.C. This discovery, sealed beneath the destruction debris of the last Canaanite city at Lachish, now dates the fall of this city to no earlier than the reign of Ramesses III in the 12th century B.C. Before the discovery of this inscription, the fall of Canaanite Lachish was thought to have occurred in the 13th century B.C.*

The trench, originally dug to examine Judean remains, extends more than 12 feet beneath the floor of the Judean city-gate, marked by sandbags.

At this point, we come back to the question raised at the beginning of this article: according to the archaeological data, how likely is it that the destruction of the last Canaanite city of Lachish (Level VI) can be attributed to the Israelite armies as related in the Book of Joshua?

First, we must consider the possibility—contrary to the Biblical traditions—that Canaanite Lachish was not destroyed by the Israelite tribes, but, was instead, as sug-

gested by Olga Tufnell when she studied the remains of Level VI, destroyed during a punitive raid by an Egyptian Pharaoh. This theory may now be rejected, because the new data we have uncovered indicate Lachish's dependency on and alliance with Egypt, rather than a state of enmity between the two. It would be difficult to construct a believable scenario in which a Pharaoh of the 20th Dynasty would attack and utterly destroy Lachish Level VI.

What about the Philistines? Could they be the enemy that destroyed Canaanite Lachish?

A *priori*, the Philistines are one possibility. But a careful consideration of this possibility requires some background.

About 1200 B.C. or slightly later the Sea Peoples, who probably came from the Aegean world, swept across the Near East. In a famous battle depicted on the walls of Ramesses III's mortuary temple at Medinet Habu near Luxor, the Sea Peoples fought against the armies and navy of Ramesses III in an effort to invade Egypt. But they were repulsed and defeated.

Eventually, one of the Sea Peoples' tribes known as the Philistines settled along the coast of southern Canaan, as related in the Bible; other tribes of Sea Peoples settled farther north on the Canaanite coast. Material remains of the Philistines have been uncovered in many places; their culture is distinguished primarily by the beautifully decorated Philistine pottery. An excellent summary of the Philistines and their material culture has recently been presented to **BAR** readers by one of the world's leading authorities on Philistine culture, Trude Dothan.[3]

Significantly, no Philistine painted pottery has been found at Lachish either by Starkey or by us, with the exception of a few Philistine sherds discovered in a cave on the slope of the tel, near the northeast corner of the mound. This cave was used during the Late Bronze Age, but Iron Age pottery was also found in it, indicating that the cave must have continued in use after the destruction of the Canaanite city of Level VI. Thus, although the Philistine sherds *could* have belonged to Level VI, it is more likely that they were

His majesty unimpaired by the centuries, the mummy of Pharaoh Ramesses III (c. 1182-1151 B.C.) (left) stares blindly out from across the millennia.

Was Lachish part of the far-reaching Egyptian empire in the 12th century B.C.? Finds at Lachish seem to indicate that it was. A cache of broken and defective bronze objects (right) found in debris beneath the Judean city-gate includes (from top to bottom) a broken object bearing a cartouche of Ramesses III; a knife blade, two borers or awls, an adze or an axe; and a pair of tongs.

Ramesses is chiefly remembered because he successfully repelled an invasion by marauding Sea Peoples. It was not a victory without cost; the effort probably weakened Egypt's hold on its Canaanite possessions. Lachish's final destruction may have come at the hands of the Sea Peoples, or of Joshua and the invading Israelites, as Egyptian strength waned during the troubled 12th century B.C.

a later intrusion, perhaps left in the cave (which is located not far from the city's water supply) by someone wandering around the abandoned tel and taking shelter there. The crucial fact is that, for all practical purposes, Philistine pottery is completely absent from Lachish.

This fact has far-reaching implications. Lachish is quite close to the coastal plain, where the Philistines first settled. Lachish was thus close to the very distribution center of Philistine pottery. Two major Philistine cities, Tel Zafit (Biblical Gath) and Tel Miqne (Biblical Ekron) are but a short distance north of Lachish. Philistine painted pottery has been found at sites even farther inland than Lachish—for example, at Tel Beth-Shemesh, at Tel Eton and at Tell Beit Mirsim. Considering the geographical position, the size and the prosperity of the Level VI Canaanite city at Lachish, it is difficult to imagine that nearby Philistine pottery, which was being diffused inland from the coastal plain, would not be found in appreciable quantities at Lachish as well. Yet, apart from the few Philistine sherds found in the cave nothing was found. The only logical conclusion is that the absence of this distinctive pottery in Level VI demonstrates that Lachish simply was not settled at the time that painted Philistine pottery was being produced. Therefore, the Philistine pottery must have appeared in this region only *after* the destruction of Lachish Level VI, which we have dated to c. 1150 B.C. or slightly later. To put the matter differently, the destruction of Lachish Level VI marks the earliest date for the appearance of Philistine pottery in this region.

The evidence from Lachish is admittedly negative—it is based on the absence of Philistine pottery—but it is so absolutely negative that it provides a sound basis for concluding that it was not until after about 1150 B.C., and probably slightly later, that Philistine painted pottery appeared anywhere in the country. Similar conclusions have recently been reached by other scholars such as Amihai Mazar and Eliezer Oren based on their own excavations and studies. It thus follows—if the introduction and use of Philistine painted pottery is considered the primary criterion—that the settlement of the Philistines in southern Canaan occurred only

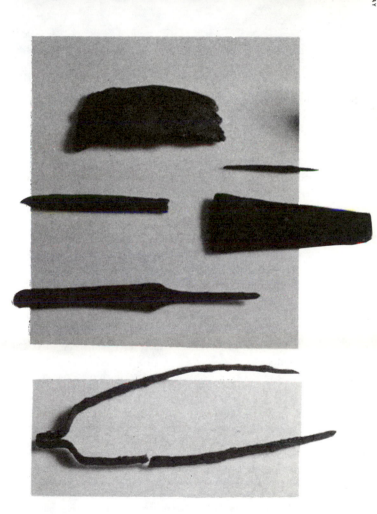

after Egyptian control began to disintegrate following the death of Ramesses III in 1151 B.C.; or even two decades later, following the complete disintegration of Egyptian control.[4] This conclusion obviously requires a revision in Trude Dothan's judgment that the Philistines settled in Canaan about 1200 B.C.

197

The idea that Level VI might have been destroyed by the Sea Peoples was considered by Tufnell and found very attractive. Ugarit and Alalakh, the two large Canaanite centers in northern Syria, were razed and abandoned at the end of the Late Bronze Age; these destructions are generally attributed to the invading Sea Peoples, and it is tempting to compare these destructions with that of Lachish Level VI. The contention that Canaanite Lachish met its end by the hand of the Sea Peoples is based on a wider historical reconstruction— that the invasion of the Sea Peoples was a prime factor in the collapse of Egyptian authority and military control over southern Canaan, which left unfortified cities such as Lachish completely vulnerable. This remains a *possibility*, even though the Philistines had not yet introduced their distinctive pottery into this region.

But let us now consider an alternative scenario—that

Mute testimony *to an ancient tragedy. A volunteer uncovers the skeletal remains of a six- to eight-month-old baby found in the destruction debris of the monumental public building from Level VI. Study of the bones revealed that the infant died after falling or being thrown on the ground. The author conjectures that this building may have become the last refuge for Lachishites from the surrounding countryside during the final days of Canaanite Lachish.*

The Bible records that "The Lord delivered Lachish into the hands of Israel . . . on the second day and put it and all the people in it to the sword" (Joshua 10:31-32). We lack conclusive evidence of the identity of the enemy who destroyed Late Bronze Age Lachish, but this and other skeletal remains, hinting at the ferocity and suddenness of the catastrophe that destroyed the city, are consistent with Biblical accounts.

A bowl inscribed *in Egyptian hieratic script was found at Lachish. The inscription mentions the "year four," probably referring to the fourth year of the reign of Ramesses III (c. 1182-1151 B.C.). The remainder of the inscription deals with a harvest tax paid to an Egyptian religious institution— more evidence that Egypt ruled much of southern Canaan in the 12th century B.C.*

Hieratic script is a form of ancient Egyptian writing consisting of abridged forms of hieroglyphics. The script was used by Egyptian priests in their records.

Canaanite Lachish was destroyed by the Israelite tribes, as strongly advocated by Albright. The archaeological data indeed fit the Biblical description: a large Canaanite city destroyed by fire, the absence of fortifications enabling the conquest of the city on the second day of the attack, complete desertion of the razed city, explained by the annihilation of the populace. On the other hand, the motive for the destruction remains obscure, since the Israelites apparently had no interest in occupying the site, which remained unsettled after this destruction until about the tenth century B.C. Indeed, Israelites did not settle anywhere in the region, as shown by the lack of early Israelite sites in the systematic archaeological surveys recently carried out by Yehudah Dagan in the surrounding Shephelah.

Consequently, whether we adopt or reject the suggestion that the Israelites destroyed Lachish depends largely on whether or not we accept the Biblical source, Joshua 10:31-32, as having a sound historical basis, a subject that is beyond the scope of this study. In any case, the conquest of Lachish stands out as a unique event in the Biblical story of the Israelite conquest of Canaan and the archaeological data fit the Biblical text in every detail.

If we assume that the destruction of Canaanite Lachish is attributable to the Israelite tribes, and if we accept the account of the Israelite conquest in Joshua

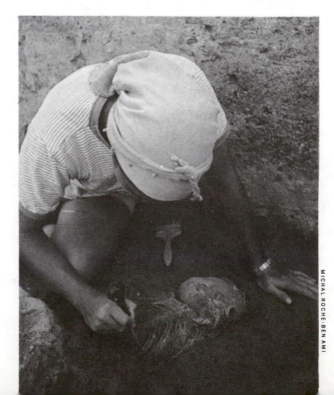

as, in the main, reliable, then two corollaries necessarily emerge. The first is that a cardinal event in the Biblical tradition of the Israelite conquest is firmly dated on archaeological grounds to about the middle of the 12th century, 1150 B.C., or even later. This is a major alteration. Scholars usually date the events of the conquest to the 13th century B.C., and the conquest of Lachish, as dated by Albright, to about 1230 B.C.—nearly one hundred years too early!

The second corollary involves the date of the destruction of Canaanite Hazor in northern Israel. All authorities agree, on the basis of internal archaeological evidence, that Canaanite Hazor was destroyed in the 13th century B.C. Yigael Yadin, the excavator, dated the destruction to the second third of the century; Kathleen Kenyon and, more recently, Pirhiya Beck and Moshe Kochavi, are inclined to date it even earlier. If we believe that the Israelite tribes also conquered Canaanite Hazor, as related in Joshua 10:10-11, then we must conclude that the Biblical concept of a swift campaign by Joshua's forces is incompatible with the archaeological evidence, because this evidence discloses that two major Canaanite cities, Lachish and Hazor, were destroyed about a century apart; the Israelite conquest must have been, therefore, a much more drawn out affair than is described in the Book of Joshua.

The results of our excavations at Tel Lachish are based on many years of painstaking work. Even so, we have uncovered a bare fraction of the potential of this unique mound. Many enthusiastic **BAR** readers have already taken part in the excavation of Lachish. 🔲

All photographs, unless otherwise credited, were taken by Avraham Hay and are reproduced courtesy of the Israel Department of Antiquities and Museums

[1] Since the beginning of the renewed excavations, we have followed Starkey's system of labeling the archaeological strata of the mound. This worked very well in the upper strata, labeled by him "Levels I-VI." However, once we penetrated into earlier levels, it became apparent that Starkey's Levels VIII-VII would have to be radically modified. Thus Level VII as uncovered and labeled by us in Area S is not identical with Starkey's Level VII. Starkey's Levels VIII-VII were still used by us in the chronological table published in **BAR**, Nov./Dec. 1979, p. 27 [135], which must therefore be used with caution.

[2] Accordingly, the position of Fosse Temple III in the chronological table published in **BAR**, Nov./Dec. 1979, p. 27 [135], has to be changed. The study of the pottery has been carried out by Orna Zimhoni and Eli Yanai of the Lachish expedition.

[3] See "What We Know About the Philistines," Trude Dothan, **BAR**, July/Aug. 1982, pp. 20-44.

[4] Another type of pottery—a local variation of monochrome Mycenaean III C:1b pottery—has to be taken into account. This pottery is derived from Aegean/Mycenaean pottery, and is typologically a forerunner of Philistine painted bichrome pottery. Its appearance in Tel Ashdod and Tel Miqne (ancient Ekron) led Trude and Moshe Dothan, the excavators of these sites, to conclude that this class of pottery represents an earlier wave of invading Sea Peoples into the country at the end of the 13th century B.C. However, the presently available data—first and foremost the fact that this pottery was used concurrently with painted Philistine pottery in these sites—makes the adoption of such a theory very difficult.

Lachish—Level by Level

Dates	Events	Major Finds
LEVEL I		
2nd century B.C.	Hellenistic kingdoms established throughout Near East.	
4th century B.C.	Alexander the Great defeats Darius III at Battle of Issos (333 B.C.). Persian Empire falls.	Solar Shrine Fortified city wall and gate
6th century B.C.	Persian Empire established (Achaemenid dynasty c. 550-331 B.C.).	Palace ("The Residency")
LEVEL II		
Early 6th century B.C.	Babylonians conquer southern kingdom of Judah (588/86 B.C.). Lachish destroyed.	Fortified city City wall and gate "Lachish letters" Palace-fort in ruins
Second half of 7th century B.C.	Assyrian Empire falls to Babylonians (612 B.C.).	
Break in habitation from second half of *7th century B.C.* to *701 B.C.*		
LEVEL III		
8th century B.C.	Lachish destroyed (701 B.C.). Assyrians conquer northern kingdom of Israel (722 B.C.).	Assyrian siege ramp Judean counter-ramp Fortified city with two walls; densely populated Judean palace-fort (C)
LEVEL IV		
9th century B.C.	Kingdoms of Israel and Judah established Rise of Assyrian Empire.	Judean palace-fort (B) Two city walls and gates
LEVEL V		
10th century B.C.	Pharoah Shishak invades Israel (c. 925 B.C.). Lachish destroyed. Solomon dies; United Monarchy ends. (930 B.C.).	Judean palace-fort (A)
Break in habitation from *11th century B.C.* to end of *12th century*.		
LEVEL VI		
12th century B.C.	Lachish destroyed by invading Israelites or "Sea Peoples" (second half of 12th century B.C.). Egyptians control Canaan, including Lachish. Reign of Pharoah Ramesses III (c. 1182-1151 B.C.)	Acropolis Temple (Fosse Temple abandoned) Monumental Public Building Unfortified city Ramesses III cartouche
LEVEL VII		
13th century B.C.	Egyptians control Canaan.	Fosse Temple III Domestic building in unfortified city

Did the Israelites Destroy Level VII at Lachish?

As usual, your January/February 1987 issue of **BAR** was excellent. David Ussishkin's well-written article "Lachish—Key to the Israelite Conquest of Canaan?" was of special interest to me, having visited Lachish on several occasions, and having spent a great deal of time studying the site in graduate school. Ussishkin's thoughtful and professional excavations may just be the most significant now taking place in Israel. In his article, however, the attribution of the destruction of Level VI to *either* the Israelites *or* the Sea Peoples left me a bit puzzled. May I make an alternate proposal to the author and to **BAR** readers?

Ussishkin reports that *Level VII*, a Late Bronze phase contemporary with Fosse Temple III, was violently destroyed by an unknown invader. Then he writes "After the fiery destruction of Level VII (probably at the end of the thirteenth century B.C.), the city was soon rebuilt" (p. 23) [183]. "The end of the thirteenth century B.C." seems to me to suggest a date near 1230 B.C., the date suggested by W. F. Albright and others for the Israelite Conquest which marked the beginning of the end of the Late Bronze Age. It also corresponds with Yigael Yadin's 1230 B.C. date for the destruction of Canaanite Hazor by the Israelites (see Joshua 11). Is it not possible that the Israelites of Joshua chapter 10 were responsible for the violent destruction and torching of Level VII and its Fosse Temple? If so, it would be another link in the chain of evidence for the generally accepted date of 1230 B.C. for the Israelite Conquest. Other sites showing a Late Bronze destruction around that time include Bethel (which was probably the real target of the Israelite attack on Ai) and, of course, Hazor.

If there was any Israelite attempt to occupy Lachish after the destruction of Level VII it would have been quickly foiled by the reestablishment of Egyptian hegemony in southern Canaan under Pharaoh Merneptah. About 1220 B.C. Merneptah's army attacked Canaan and apparently had some degree of success. In a poetic account of his campaign the Pharaoh boasted "Israel is laid waste, his seed is not." With the Israelites repulsed from the Lachish area, Egyptian-backed Canaanite occupation of the site recommenced immediately, and the Level VI city was built up, as suggested by Ussishkin, with its Temple at the acropolis. That Egypt's protective influence continued for some decades is suggested by the discovery of the Ramesses III cartouche in the Gate Area.

To whom, then, should the destruction of *Level VI* at Lachish be attributed? The Philistines, or Sea Peoples, that attacked and weakened Egypt during the reign of Ramesses III, would seem the logical answer. Finally repulsed by Ramesses, these Philistines attacked the southern coast and Shephelah of Judah in the twelfth century B.C., sacking and burning Lachish. Why is none of the distinctive Philistine pottery found on site? The Philistines simply chose not to occupy the mound. To recapitulate, then, the proposal is the destruction of Canaanite Level VII by the Israelites c. 1230 B.C., and the destruction of Canaanite Level VI by the Philistines c. 1150 B.C. The site then remained unoccupied until an Israelite presence (Level V) was established sometime in the tenth century B.C.

Jeffrey Chadwick
Ben Lomond LDS Seminary
Ogden, Utah

Although I enjoyed David Ussishkin's article on Lachish, I wonder about a major conclusion. According to Ussishkin, Lachish Level VI was destroyed by the Israelites (pp. 38-39) [198-199]. I have no quarrel with that, but from the evidence Ussishkin has presented it does not follow that Level VII could not have been destroyed by the Israelites as well. Ussishkin rejects this possibility (p. 23) [183] though he gives no alternative. Perhaps Ussishkin has read more into the Biblical evidence than there is. Joshua 10:31-32 only states that the Israelites captured the city, but it does not state that the Israelites settled there. If this was a "Blitzkrieg" without settlement then the Canaanites could have returned and rebuilt the city. It could be argued that in that case the people would have built a wall. But they did not, whoever may have been the destroyers of Level VII. As Ussishkin points out, Lachish remained within the Egyptian sphere. If my "capture without settlement" is correct (unless Ussishkin can give enough evidence to the contrary), then Ussishkin's two corollaries may not be corollaries after all.

Bert den Boggende
Hamilton, Ontario
Canada

David Ussishkin replies:
The first and most important duty of the Biblical archaeologist working in the field is to evaluate the data, and to attempt to establish the facts solely on the basis of the internal evidence recovered from the site being excavated. Once this is done, the archaeologist can then turn to evaluating the comparable archaeological material, the Biblical sources and the external historical sources.

Scrupulously following this procedure in the case of Lachish, we reached the conclusions that (a) The Level VII city was destroyed by fire; (b) The city was rebuilt in Level VI—the latter city showing a marked architectural change from Level VII, but a clear cultural continuity; (c) The Level VI city portrayed a marked Egyptian presence and influence; (d) The Level VI city was burnt and devastated c. 1150 B.C. or slightly later; (e) Following the destruction of Level VI, the city was abandoned for a long period of time. These conclusions were reached on the basis of the internal evidence and to my mind form the basis for further discussion.

Turning to the suggestions of Mr. Chadwick and Mr. den Boggende that the Israelite conquest and destruction should be ascribed to the destruction of Level VII rather than Level VI, it must be stressed that the factual data from the site cannot elucidate the matter. With the absence of inscriptions it is impossible to verify who burnt Level VII. From the purely archaeological point of view, therefore, their suggestion is possible.

Nevertheless, it seems to me difficult to consider such a suggestion on the basis of the Biblical account. If we accept Joshua 10:31-32 as an expression of a reliable historical tradition, we notice that the Israelites annihilated the Canaanite population following the conquest of the city. Thus, an Israelite conquest of Lachish which had been followed by a rebuilding and a renewed prosperity of the Canaanite city under Egyptian aegis seems unlikely and contradictory to the Biblical source. On the other hand, the destruction of the Level VI city, followed by a long period of abandonment which indicates annihilation or deportation of the populace, would fit this written account.

Tell ed-Duweir provides an interesting case study for two questions frequently asked of archaeologists: "How do you know the ancient name of a site?" and "How can you date what you find?"

In the matter of names, hardly any Biblical city has yielded clear documentary evidence of its name. Three notable exceptions come to mind because they are so rare: the name "Gibeon" was impressed on a number of royal jar handles found in James B. Pritchard's excavation of Tell el-Gib—the site that had already been suggested as Biblical Gibeon by several scholars; the name "Gezer" was found incised on boundary stones near the 30-acre mound that scholars agree must be the royal city of that name; and the name of Hazor was mentioned on a clay tablet found at that site in 1962.

The name "Lachish" does, in fact, occur on letters found at Tell ed-Duweir, but until recently the letters seemed to some to refer to Lachish as if it were somewhere else, so the letters by themselves could not resolve the question of the site's identification. In 1984, Yigael Yadin presented a new interpretation of the letters that is in harmony with a Lachish/Tell ed-Duweir identification, summarized in Section F (see p. 314). This appeared, however, only after the site's identification as Lachish seemed to be established on other grounds.

Jerusalem, of course, presents the unusual situation of a city that has never lost its identity because it has been continuously occupied from antiquity down to the present time.

In almost every other instance, the Biblical identification of a site has been determined on the basis of some combination of three elements as these have been correlated with ancient references: its location, the character of its remains and the apparent dates of its periods of occupation and abandonment.

In the case of Lachish, the Biblical references describe a city in Judah's coastal lowland (Joshua 15:33-39) that had previously been ruled by a Canaanite king (Joshua 12:11) until it was destroyed by the Israelites (Joshua 10:31-32), who would have rebuilt it at least by the time of the tenth-century monarchy of David and Solomon.

We can presume that it was destroyed in the early sixth century B.C. during Nebuchadnezzar's subjugation of Judah. Moreover, from both the Biblical account of Sennacherib's earlier campaign (2 Kings 18:13-14,17) and from Sennacherib's own palace reliefs, we would expect Lachish to be a major-sized city—one powerful enough to require a massive siege, and we would expect the city to bear the scars of destruction or at least serious damage from Sennacherib's siege.

Most scholars are satisfied that Tell ed-Duweir best fits the requirements for Biblical Lachish, although some have continued to argue against the identification. Readers can judge for themselves how well the discoveries reported from Tell ed-Duweir in the foregoing articles fit with an identification of the site as Lachish.

Tell ed-Duweir also presents an interesting illustration of the problems that can still occur in trying to date archaeological layers of the Biblical era.

In the 1890s Sir Flinders Petrie noted the changing shapes of pottery in successive layers of ancient debris, and from this he constructed a relative chronological typology of Palestinian pottery shapes. This endeavor was further developed with considerable sophistication during the first half of this century. Gradually, as situations accumulated where a particular layer or deposit could be assigned on independent grounds to an absolute date in ancient Near Eastern history, the relative chronology was refined and given certain fixed points in time. As a result, it is now possible to date most deposits that contain even a modest number of potsherds to within a century—often to within a decade or two.

For the latter portion of the Iron II period in Palestine (eighth-early sixth centuries B.C.), the most secure fixed points have been provided by destruction layers clearly attributable to Nebuchadnezzar's ravishment of the land in 587/586 B.C. and, before that, to a destruction layer at Samaria which was overlaid by a layer containing late Iron Age Assyrian imported wares. Since there is no question of identification in regard to Samaria and since we know it was destroyed by the Assyrians in 722/721 B.C., the pottery corpus from that Samaria destruction layer has been used as a typological reference point within the Iron II period.

Ussishkin's first article, however, points up the dilemmas that still remain, for example, in trying to date the destruction of Lachish level III. Should it be placed later than 701 B.C. because the pottery seems stylistically so different from that found in the Samaria 721 B.C. destruction? If level III at Lachish was destroyed after Sennacherib's destruction, who was responsible and when did it happen? Previously, Nebuchadnezzar's first invasion of Judah in 597 B.C. (2 Kings 24:10-17) had been suggested. (It had to be before the Babylonian destruction of 586 B.C., which was found in level II.)

Ussishkin opted for an earlier date for the destruction of level III, concluding it occurred in 701 B.C., because on a closer look at an enlarged corpus of level III pottery, it seemed to be more distinguishable from the 586 B.C. pottery of level II than one decade's time could explain.

Moreover, the differences between pottery from Lachish level III and the pottery from the destruction level at Samaria, which had been destroyed in 721 B.C., could be explained on the basis of recent evidence at southern sites indicating that pottery from the northern and southern kingdoms differed somewhat during the eighth century.

At the same time, Ussishkin was aware that his dating of level III at Lachish would be influenced by whether the "internal" or "external" evidence was given greater weight. The "external" evidence of the generally accepted pottery typology might argue for a later date for the level III destruction; the "internal" evidence of the absence of any earlier Iron II destruction that could be associated with Sennacherib's campaign argued for a 701 B.C. date.

But, of course, these deliberations bring us right back to the question of site identification. *If* Tell ed-Duweir is assumed to be Lachish, then the internal evidence would tend to carry more weight, to the point of being decisive—there *should be* a 701 B.C. destruction and it would appear to have to be level III. And in that case, the Tell ed-Duweir/Lachish level III destruction provides us with a new corpus of pottery which can be given an absolute date as a reference-point against which to compare materials at other southern sites.

Turning to Yigael Yadin's solution to "The Mystery of the Unexplained Chain," Yadin's suggestion received an interesting footnote in a reader's letter (**BAR** July/August 1985):

> [I] thought you might be interested in a passage from Thucydides' "The Peloponnesian War" that describes the use of a similar "anti-siege" apparatus:
>
> "At the same time as they were constructing the mound the Peloponnesians brought up siege engines against the city. One of these was brought to bear on the great barricade facing the mound, and battered down a considerable part of it, causing much alarm among the Plataeans. Others were brought up against various parts of the city wall. Some of these the Plataeans lassoed and then broke; they also suspended great beams by long iron chains fastened to the ends of two poles projecting horizontally from the top of the wall, and whenever an engine was being brought up into position they drew the beam up at an angle to the engine and let it go with the chains slack, so that it came rushing down and snapped off the nose of the battering ram."

This is a fifth-century B.C. explanation of an eighth-century B.C. artifact discovered by David Ussishkin at Lachish; although Yadin's commentary pertains to a ninth-century B.C. relief, this quote from Thucydides may be relevant, given that siege warfare did not appreciably change until gunpowder and the cannon became major factors at the end of the Middle Ages.

Susan G. Moritz, Alexandria, Virginia

For Further Reading

Concerning Lachish

"**BAR** Preservation Fund Goes to Work," **BAR**, March 1978

"Mystery Find at Lachish," **BAR**, September/October 1979

Queries & Comments: "Readers Suggest Imaginative Solutions to Mystery at Lachish," **BAR**, November/December 1979

Oded Borowski, "Yadin Presents New Interpretation of the Famous Lachish Letters," **BAR**, March/April 1984 (*see Section F*)

David Ussishkin, "Restoring the Great Gate at Lachish," **BAR**, March/April 1988

Arad—An Israelite Border Fortress

In archaeology as in other things, rich presents sometimes come in small packages. In contrast to the 18-acre citadel of Lachish, which we looked at in the previous section, the border fortress of Arad, which we explore here, measured only 60 yards across—less than two-thirds the length of a football field. Yet excavations at the site have yielded some unusually valuable new information about Israelite culture in the Iron Age.

The excavators of Arad uncovered six successive fortification building phases spanning the half-millennium from David and Solomon's tenth-century United Monarchy to the sixth-century B.C. Babylonian captivity. The site's uninterrupted documentation of changing patterns of military architecture at a border fort significantly supplements the picture obtained from larger royal cities.

The pottery from these six phases and from a modest unwalled settlement that preceded the fortress provides us with a complete sequence of ceramic forms from one southern site through the whole Iron Age, doubly valuable since several of the rebuildings can be dated with confidence in connection with important events in Judah's political and military history.

A small complex of rooms and courtyard found within the fort provides us with the first known example of an Israelite temple contemporary with the Temple of Jerusalem. As noted under the For Further Reading listings, Israelite altars have been uncovered at Beersheba and Dan, and an earlier Philistine temple has been found at Tell Qasile, but the Arad temple makes a unique addition to our knowledge of Israelite worship.

The remnants of writing found at Arad are also significant, not because the contents of any single inscription are particularly dramatic but because of the great quantity of writing fragments retrieved and because they come from stratigraphically sealed deposits spread over a 350-year period of ancient Israelite life. One cluster of inscriptions from the final days of Arad will be treated in Section F.

NOTE: *The arrow in the aerial photo on p. 209 should be 1.5 centimeters to the right, at the dark spot at the edge of the earlier Canaanite city excavation area.*

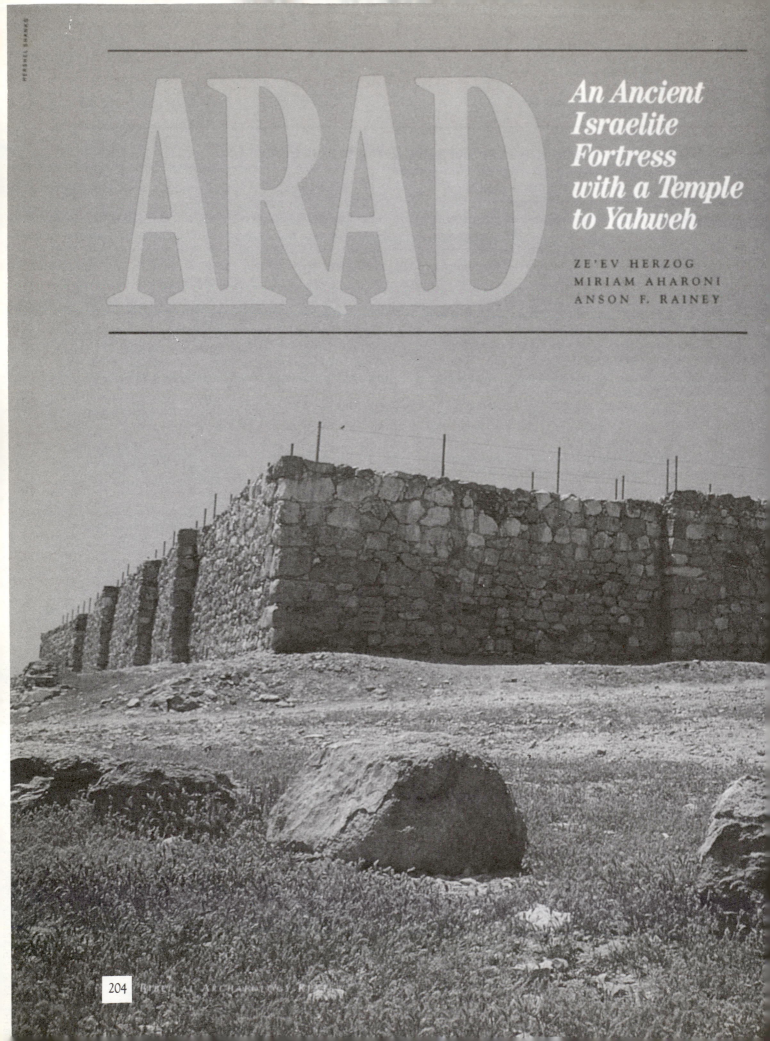

ARAD

An Ancient Israelite Fortress with a Temple to Yahweh

ZE'EV HERZOG
MIRIAM AHARONI
ANSON F. RAINEY

THE ISRAELITE FORTRESS at Arad is unique in the Land of Israel. It's the only site excavated with modern archaeological methods that contains a continuous archaeological record from the period of the Judges (c. 1200 B.C.) to the Babylonian destruction of the First Temple (586 B.C.). This distinction promises to make Arad the type-site for pottery chronology, especially in southern Israel, against which pottery from other sites can be confidently tested and dated. Not only is the pottery sequence continuous, but the time-lines between the various strata during which the Israelite fortress was built and rebuilt are for the most part clear and can often be connected with well-known historical and datable events.

Arad is also special for other reasons. The Israelite fortress there was found to contain the only Israelite temple ever discovered in an archaeological excavation.

The excavation of the fortress also yielded a unique series of inscriptions. The inscriptions, written for the most part with ink on potsherds—called ostraca (singular, ostracon)—include political, administrative and sometimes even religious documents. Other sites have yielded ostraca collections—for example, the Lachish letters and the Samaria ostraca—but each of those collections belonged to only one major stratum and time period. At Arad the inscriptions span a period of 350 years and cover six different strata. In all, more than one hundred texts and fragments were recovered. Why at Arad? The answer is twofold, relating to where and to who.

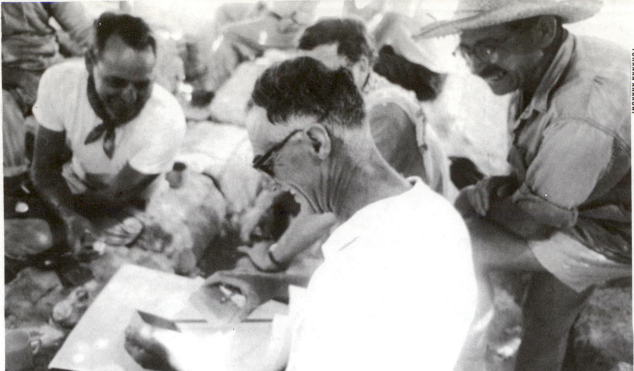

The where is the Negeb*—a place so dry, where rain falls so infrequently, that ink inscribed on potsherds and buried in the ground for 2,500 years is preserved.

The who is a man named Yohanan Aharoni, the inspired leader of Tel Aviv University's Institute of Archaeology and director of the excavation of the Israelite fortress at Arad. Aharoni died at the height of his career in 1976. He had excavated at Arad for five seasons between 1962 and 1967. At his death he had already published the inscriptions from Arad. The excavation materials were in an advanced state of preparation, but not yet completed. His colleagues, including the co-authors of this article, are completing the excavation report.

The recovery of the Arad inscriptions is largely the result of Aharoni's insistence that each pottery sherd be dipped in water and examined before being scrubbed with a brush. As a result, many traces of writing were rescued that otherwise might have been obliterated before anyone noticed them.

Still a third reason why so many inscriptions were found at Arad is that practically all of the upper tell at Arad, on which the Israelite fortress was located, was

* We use the Biblical spelling of Negeb (rather than Negev). Negeb refers to the Valley of Beer-Sheba (also the Biblical spelling; see map, opposite) where ancient Arad is located. Today the name Negev is used to designate the entire southern part of Israel.

Preceding pages: Built and rebuilt over a 500-year span (10th-6th century B.C.), the formidable Arad fortress has recently been restored to its ninth-century B.C. appearance, called fortress X by the excavators. The wall is built with a sawtooth line, creating shadows that accent height. This design of a sawtooth wall and towers flanking an eastern gate continued to be used into the seventh century B.C.

excavated. The finding of an archive was therefore not left to blind chance.

Among the inscriptions was one mentioning the "Temple of Yahweh," undoubtedly a reference to the Temple in Jerusalem. Others contain the names of known priestly families.

Arad is mentioned only three times in the Bible—and all three references are in connection with the Israelites' entry into the Promised Land. In Numbers 21:1-3a we read:

"When the Canaanite, king of Arad, who dwelt in the Negeb, learned that Israel was coming by the way of the spies, he engaged Israel in battle and took some of them captive. Then Israel made a vow to the Lord and said, 'If you deliver this people into our hand,

Dates of the Strata at Arad

These numbers for the strata at Arad were assigned by Yohanan Aharoni. The lowest number represents the highest level, which was the last to be occupied but the first to be uncovered.

Stratum		Date
I	cemetery	10th-16th centuries A.D.
II	caravanserai	7th-9th centuries A.D.
III	Roman fort	1st century A.D.
IV	Hellenistic tower and fort	3rd-2nd centuries B.C.
V	Persian	4th century B.C.
VI	Israelite	early 6th century B.C.
VII	Israelite	late 7th century B.C.
VIII	Israelite	late 8th century B.C.
IX	Israelite	early 8th century B.C.
X	Israelite	9th century B.C.
XI	Israelite	10th century B.C.
XII	Kenite	early 12th century B.C.

Yohanan Aharoni analyzes pottery on site at Arad. Aharoni directed excavation of the Arad fortress from 1962 to 1967—and published the Hebrew, Aramaic, Greek and Arabic inscriptions found there—before his death in 1976.

The very first excavation season at Arad, spring 1962, quickly yielded 30 ostraca. Aharoni decided to pay special attention to sherd treatment: he added a dunk in a pail of water for each sherd before routine scrubbing was done, so that any writing would become visible.

we will proscribe their towns.' The Lord heeded Israel's plea and delivered up the Canaanites; and they and their cities were proscribed."

Another passage in Numbers refers to "the Canaanite, king of Arad, who dwelt in the Negeb" (33:40). Finally, the king of Arad is listed in Joshua 12:14 as one of the kings Joshua defeated.

From the archaeological evidence, we know that there was a major urban center at Arad in Early Bronze Age I and II (c. 3000 to 2650 B.C.), but that Arad was destroyed and then abandoned long before the Israelite Exodus from Egypt and entry into Canaan. When Arad was resettled, about 1,500 years later, after 1200 B.C., the new inhabitants chose to build on the eastern hill,

the highest point of the site. This new site later became Israelite Arad, and the location of the fortress we shall be examining.

But these hilltop settlers who constructed an unwalled village sometime after 1200 B.C. (stratum XII) were not Israelites. Who, then, were they? Our educated guess is that they were Kenites, descendants of Moses' father-in-law (Judges 1:16). The Kenites, traditionally associated with metalworking, apparently lived in the eastern Negeb. In the Biblical Negeb, the Amalekites were the dominant ethnic element (Numbers 13:29). Their relationship with the Kenites is unclear. The Bible credits the Amalekites with preventing Israelite penetration into the Promised Land from the south (1 Samuel 15:21); they were therefore Israel's sworn enemy forever (Deuteronomy 25:17). The Kenites, however, had showed kindness to the Israelites when they left Egypt, so they were not regarded with the same animosity as the Amalekites. The settlement of the area around Arad by Kenites rather than Amalekites is reflected in the Bible's reference to the "Negeb of the Kenites" (1 Samuel 27:10; Judges 1:16).

Little was found of this "Kenite" village at Arad—

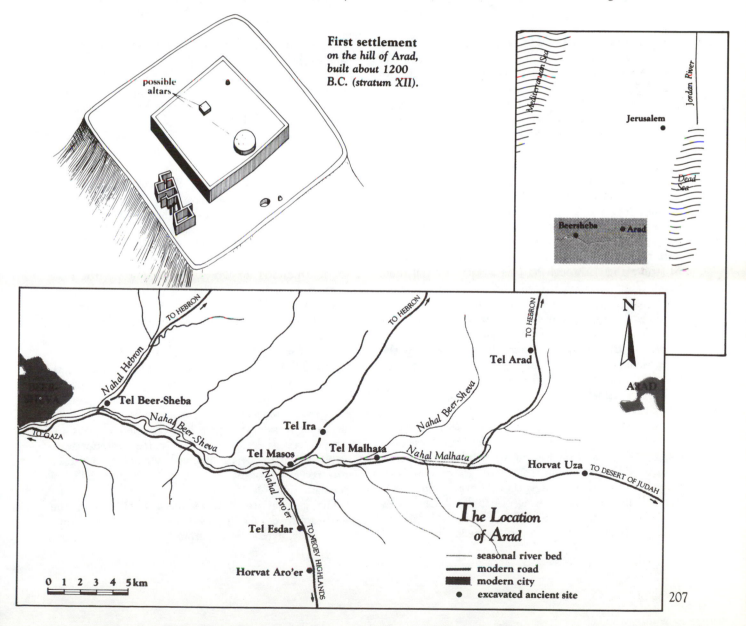

First settlement *on the hill of Arad, built about 1200 B.C. (stratum XII).*

possible altars

The Location of Arad

— seasonal river bed
---- modern road
▬ modern city
● excavated ancient site

0 1 2 3 4 5km

Last Israelite fortress *at Arad, early sixth century B.C. (stratum VI).*

a few dwellings, some silos for storage, some pottery. At one point, a low stone fence, hardly sufficient for defense, had been built around the top of the hill. Two finds are of special significance. In the center of the village was an open courtyard with a circular platform nearly 20 feet in diameter and also a rectangular platform about 7 feet long by 7 feet wide. Both platforms may have been altars. It is especially likely that the rectangular platform was an altar because here, centuries later, an Israelite altar was built, reflecting, as is so common in the ancient Near East, a continuity of cultic traditions despite an ethnic discontinuity.

Beginning in the tenth century B.C., and ending in the sixth century B.C., six successive Israelite fortresses were built or rebuilt on the hill corresponding to strata XI (the earliest) through VI (the latest). We call them Israelite fortresses even though, after Solomon's death, Israel was divided into the kingdom of Israel in the north and the kingdom of Judah in the south. After this split, Arad was part of the kingdom of Judah.

Each of the six Israelite fortresses was essentially the same shape—square, about 160 feet on each side, basically covering the hilltop.

The first Israelite fortress, the fortress of stratum XI, was probably built by King Solomon (c. 970-930 B.C.), although we can date its destruction more precisely than its construction. A fiery conflagration destroyed the first fortress (XI) toward the end of the tenth century B.C. We know that five years after King Solomon's death the Egyptian Pharaoh Sheshonq (Shishak in the Bible, 1 Kings 14:25-28; 2 Chronicles 12:2-12), led a destructive military foray into Judah and Israel, both of which had been weakened by internal dissension. In his victory inscription at the Temple of Karnak at Thebes, Shishak claims to have destroyed two places named Arad, both described as fortresses.[1] One of these was undoubtedly the Israelite fortress of stratum XI, Solomon's fortress, so we can date its destruction to 926 B.C.

Even before King Solomon, King David organized the Negeb into a unified administrative entity (2 Samuel 24:7). Under King Solomon, the commercial trade routes between the Philistine coast and the port of Elath grew in importance. The establishment of fortified centers like Arad strengthened Solomon's defenses in the south and facilitated close supervision of the roads from Philistia to Elath, thereby giving King Solomon exclusive control of them. Pharaoh Shishak's campaign in the Negeb was evidently aimed at breaking that monopoly.

To construct his fortress at Arad, Solomon first created a flat, buildable surface with fill. The fill's depth varied from 1 to 3 feet. The basic outside wall of the fortress was designed according to the casemate pattern: Two parallel walls enclosed a space in between. On the fort's eastern side, the space between the two walls was exceptionally wide, as much as 16 feet. Interior walls perpendicular to the parallel walls subdivided the space into rooms—forming a type of structure called a casemate wall.

The gateway to Israelite fortress XI was in the northeastern corner. It was a narrow passageway, only 5 feet wide, extending out from the eastern wall about

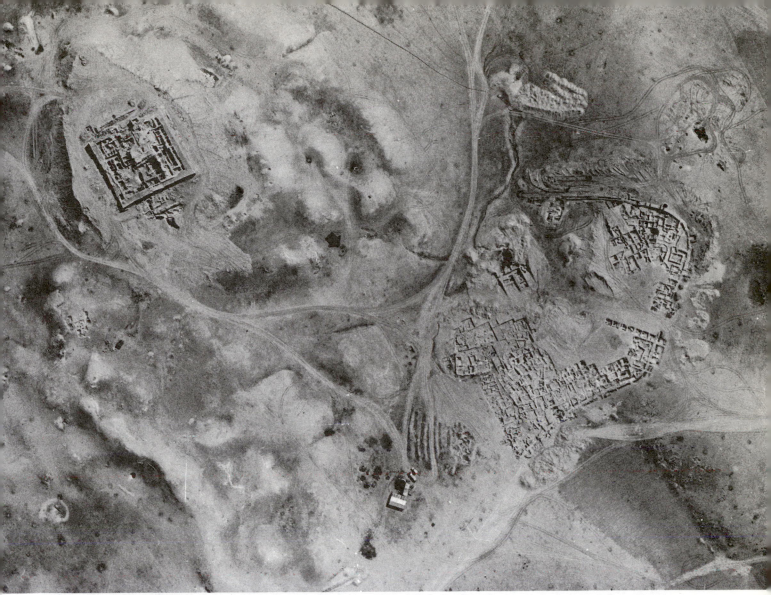

22 feet. On the north side of this passage was a tower with a room at the bottom. The entryway of the gate led to a room within the casemate wall. From there one entered the fortress itself.

Other towers protruded from the walls at the corners and on the northern and western sides of the fortress. These towers permitted flanking fire on any attacker who might get close to the wall and whom it would otherwise be difficult to hit. But in the end, this fortress was not strong enough to withstand the fire power of Pharaoh Shishak, who conquered and then burned it.

In the ninth century, the fortress Shishak had destroyed was rebuilt. A solid wall replaced the casemate system. Remains of some casemate rooms were preserved; they were filled in with earth and stones to serve as foundations for the new wall. The towers Solomon had built were not restored. Moreover, the outer face of the wall was not built in a straight line, as before, but was staggered at small angles in a sawtooth pattern. The purpose for this angling was not military, since the corners did not project sufficiently to permit enfilading fire. The motivation was evidently to gain stability by building a series of cross segments

Two Arads *On the right (west), the excavated Canaanite city (3200-2050 B.C.) sprawls across 25 acres in Israel's Negev Desert. Its enclosure wall with three towers budding outward around the curve may be seen clearly. Atop the nearby hill, left, the Israelite citadel (1200-586 B.C.) emerges from the sand.*

Between the two sites, in a depression in the hill (arrow), excavators discovered remains of the water-collecting systems the ancients had devised: a reservoir used by the Canaanites and a well dug later in the same location by the Israelites.

inside the wall, perpendicular to it. Perhaps the angles also created a series of vertical shadows, enhancing the impression of height and providing a psychological deterrent. In any case, the builders did not depend on this alone, but gave their solid wall an average thickness of over 12 feet.

The problem of defending the area at the base of the wall was probably solved by building balconies with slots in their floors, enabling the Israelites to rain a fusillade of fire on the enemy below.

209

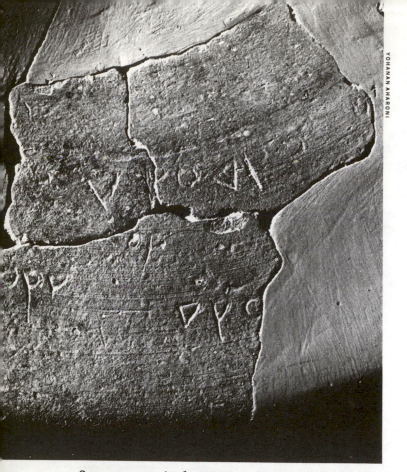

Someone practiced *writing "Arad" on this potsherd—and made a few mistakes. The surviving inscribed fragments from that exercise originally made up part of a bowl.*

The three letters of the name Arad—ayin, resh and dalet— are incised four times, twice in succession on the first line, reading right to left, followed by a single ayin, and twice on the bottom line.

However, on the bottom line, the second "Arad," left, is written from left to right. An ayin and resh (without the dalet) also written from left to right, appear between the top and bottom lines. It is possible that in writing left to right someone was practicing to write on a seal so that when the seal was pressed into wet clay the writing would appear in its correct right to left orientation.

In addition, a new gateway was built in the center of the eastern wall. This gate was defended by two massive towers, one erected on each side of the entryway. Access to the gate from inside the fortress was between two walls that took a turn at either end to attach themselves to the rear of the towers. As a result, the defenders enjoyed a direct field of fire on anyone trying to force the entrance; the gate enclosure became a deathtrap to the attacker.

Another innovation in the fortification system was the strengthening of the foundations of the fortress by the addition of a sloping earthen rampart supported at the base by a revetment wall. Portions of this stone revetment wall were found 35 feet down the slope from the western side of the fort, which gives some idea of how big the earthen rampart must have been. The

earthen rampart was added to prevent both natural erosion of the foundations and enemy attempts to undermine the fortifications. The steep slope (the glacis) created difficulty for attackers and appreciably reduced the blind area below the wall.

The fortress planners also gave their attention at this stage to improving the inhabitants' water supply so the fort could withstand siege for a longer period. A channel about one foot wide was cut in the bedrock. This channel ran under the western revetment wall, under the earthen rampart, and under the fortress wall itself, for a length of 80 feet. Inside the fortress the channel led to two well-plastered underground cisterns, quarried in the bedrock. Outside the fortress, water was collected from a well. This water was transferred to the fortress in containers of various types; it was poured into the channel and ran into the water cisterns. Thus the risky chore of hauling water around to the gate on the opposite side of the fortress was eliminated. The channel was sloped inward to permit the water to run into the cisterns. The cisterns held about 9,000 cubic feet (250 cubic meters); stain lines on the plaster inside the cisterns testified to the fact that they had been actively used.

Who built Israelite fortress X following the destruction of Israelite fortress XI by Shishak? It may have been the work of King Asa (2 Chronicles 14:4-6; 1 Kings 15:23) at the end of the tenth or the beginning of the ninth century B.C. (between 910 and 870). On the other hand, the son of Asa, Jehoshaphat (870-848 B.C.), is depicted as the initiator of extensive building projects (2 Chronicles 17:1-2, 13; 21:3). He is also described as the master of the route to Elath (1 Kings 22:47-48). To exact tribute from the Philistines and the Arabs (2 Chronicles 17:10-12), Jehoshaphat would have had to control caravan traffic. This would have required maintaining a strong military presence in the Negeb, so it may well be Jehoshaphat who constructed Israelite fortress X.

Fortress X was probably the longest-lived of all six Israelite fortresses, as evidenced by the pottery.

It is difficult to tell precisely the circumstances under which this occupation came to an end. It probably happened during the reign of Jehoram (848-841 B.C.). At that time, Edom seceded from Judah (2 Chronicles 21:8, 10), thus weakening Judah's control of the Negeb. This weakness was exploited by the Philistines and the Arabs, who invaded Judah and plundered the royal house (2 Chronicles 21:16-17). Israelite fortress X was probably destroyed in this military campaign, about 842 B.C.*

Israelite fortress IX was simply a rebuild with minor

* An alternate date would be around 813 B.C. in the reign of Jehoash (Joash), when Judah was hard hit by Hazael, king of Damascus (2 Kings 12:17ff; 2 Chronicles 24:23-26). Judah's southern enemies might have taken advantage of this situation, perhaps in consort with Hazael. But it is strange that the Bible is silent about any invasion of the south at this time. Miriam Aharoni dates the destruction of stratum X to the first quarter of the eighth century B.C.

Water channel. *Hewn from bedrock, this carefully graded, one-foot-wide conduit passes under the fortress's western wall, its glacis and the revetment wall reinforcing the glacis.*

The 80-foot-long channel received water drawn from the well outside the fortress and carried it up the hill to the channel opening outside the wall. From there the water flowed into two underground, plastered cisterns (see plan, pp. 216-217) within the fortress. The reserve thus created could be reached safely in times of siege.

changes. It represents renewed Judean control of the Negeb and the trade routes from Arabia to the Mediterranean coast during the eighth century B.C. No doubt this was accomplished by Uzziah (also known as Azariah), who not only rebuilt Elath in or after 767 B.C. (2 Kings 14:22; 2 Chronicles 26:2), but also regained the upper hand over the Philistines and the Arabs (2 Chronicles 26:7-8).

The enemies of Judah launched a counterattack about 735-732 B.C., during the reign of Ahaz. Elath was retaken by the Edomites (2 Kings 16:6), who then coordinated an attack with the Philistines against the towns of the Shephelah and the Negeb of Judah (2 Chronicles 28:17-18). This attack on the Negeb must have included the conquest and destruction of Israelite fortress IX.

In the destruction debris of Israelite fortress IX, sherds comprising about half a bowl were found. On the inside of the bowl the name Arad was incised several times (Inscription 99), thus removing any doubt that this site was indeed ancient Arad. (The name Arad also appears on a small ostracon found in Israelite fortress VIII [Inscription 48] and on a major inscription from Israelite fortress VI [Inscription 24].)

Israelite fortress VIII was a rebuild of fortress IX by King Hezekiah in the late eighth century B.C. It was, no doubt, part of Hezekiah's preparations for his rebellion against Assyria (2 Chronicles 32:27ff). He similarly fortified Beer-Sheba at the other end of the northern valley of the Negeb.

The stratum VIII fortress was destroyed in the late eighth century B.C. by the Assyrian ruler Sennacherib, or perhaps by his Edomite and Philistine allies.[*]

In the course of the destruction of Israelite fortress VIII, appreciable segments of the solid wall were severely damaged. To avoid the expense and effort of dismantling the entire wall and rebuilding it, the planners of Israelite fortress VII inserted an inner wall at a distance of six feet from the foundations of the former wall. This new wall can be traced all along the inside of the southern wall and in parts of the eastern and northern walls of the fortress. An interesting combination was

[*] Stratum VIII at Arad was destroyed at the same time as stratum III at Lachish. The Lachish destruction was commemorated in the famous Assyrian reliefs in Sennacherib's palace depicting the siege and conquest of Lachish (see Hershel Shanks, "Destruction of Judean Fortress Portrayed in Dramatic Eighth-Century B.C. Pictures," **BAR**, March/April 1984 [p. 148]).

Collapsed wall *on the western side of the fortress. In antiquity, a glacis, or sloping wall of earth, protected the fortress walls. But once the walls were uncovered, water could erode the foundations and cause extensive damage like this.*

thus created between the solid and the casemate methods of fortification. By adding the inner wall, the dwelling units on the southern side were divided in two. At the same time, the western side of the fort was strengthened by the addition of a projecting tower at the middle of the western wall.

Israelite fortress VII was not rebuilt until the latter part of the seventh century B.C. The reason was simple: At the end of the eighth century, Sennacherib, king of Assyria had devastated Judah. He had even laid siege—though unsuccessfully (2 Kings 18:13-19:36; 2 Chronicles 32:1-21; Isaiah 36:1-37:38)—to Jerusalem. By his own account, which survives in cuneiform records, he destroyed 46 Judean cities. Sennacherib took great portions of Judah's territory and gave them to the Philistines. During the entire first half of the seventh century B.C., there was no chance for Judah to rebuild her forts in the Negeb.

In 687 B.C. Manasseh came to Judah's throne, after having ruled for a decade as co-regent with his father Hezekiah. Manasseh sought to improve Judah's political and economic status by strengthening ties with her immediate neighbors, especially the Phoenicians in the north and perhaps even with the Arabs in the south. This he did by introducing his neighbors' cults and worship into the local shrines of Judah* (2 Kings 21:3;

* As Ahab king of Israel had done over a century earlier.

cf. 1 Kings 16:31). There is no sign that Judah's control over the Negeb routes was restored, however. Quite the contrary; the Assyrians took measures to assure their own control over the whole Levantine coast, with a view to a future conquest of Egypt.

The Assyrians needed the support of the Arabs for their attempted invasion of Egypt in 673 B.C. Although they failed in their first try, two years later they gained control of Lower Egypt. The assistance rendered by the Arabs in this campaign is stressed in surviving Assyrian records of Esarhaddon, the Assyrian monarch;[2] obviously no invasion of Egypt would have been at all possible without Arab support. There can be no question but that the trade routes from Arabia across the Negeb to the Philistine coast were in the hands of the Arabs, the arch-rivals of Judah (2 Chronicles 21:16; 26:7-8). This situation continued until 669 B.C., when Esarhaddon started on another campaign to Egypt; however, he died on the way.

During the reign of the next Assyrian king, Asshurbanipal, the pendulum of power began to swing away from Assyria. Psammeticus I, a former vassal of Assyria

Restoring the fortress. *Stones toppled by weathering and by ancient conquerors are placed in the reconstructed fortress wall at Arad. Just in front of the two workers in the foreground, one of the wall's insets can be seen. Originally, cross walls may have been built at these insets to strengthen the double fortress wall.*

First built as a casemate wall—a thick double wall with interior cross walls creating rooms—it was filled in as seen here in the ninth century B.C.

in the Egyptian delta, managed to unite all of Egypt by about 656 B.C. From 650 to 648 the Assyrian king and his brother, ruler of Babylon, fought a war. The Arabs and Phoenicians supported the brother and shared his defeat. Manasseh was arrested and taken to Babylon (2 Chronicles 33:11-17). At Babylon, Manasseh was given a new lease on life by Asshurbanipal (c. 648 B.C.) and was sent back to Judah. There he broke all his ties with his rebellious neighbors by cleansing Judah of its foreign cults. At Jerusalem, he built a wall to strengthen its defenses, and he restored commanders to the fortresses of Judah. It would seem that Asshurbanipal had decided to trust Manasseh and to return him to a key position *vis-à-vis* the Arabs in the south and other rebellious states that had disappointed him. Just how much Manasseh could have achieved in the last six years of his reign (until 642 B.C.) is uncertain. In 641 B.C. the

child-king Josiah ascended the throne of Judah (2 Kings 21:24-22:1; 2 Chronicles 33:25-39:1). With the Arabs in disgrace, Judah must have regained the franchise to control the Negeb trade routes. By 622 Josiah had the military and fiscal base to aspire to local regional domination (2 Chronicles 34:9), while the Assyrian Empire was on the road to dissolution.

Therefore, the rebuilding of the fortress, Israelite fortress VII, may be ascribed to the second half of the seventh century B.C., either at the end of Manasseh's reign or under Josiah, who built new fortified settlements in the Negeb, as we know from other excavations.

In 605 B.C., the Assyrians were defeated by the Babylonians at Carchemish, and Babylon then became the dominant world power. Not long after, she began to punish Judah. The final destruction came in 587 B.C. But Nebuchadnezzar had made another, earlier campaign to Jerusalem in 597 B.C. Israelite fortress VII was probably destroyed in a softening-up operation by Nebuchadnezzar in preparation for that campaign of 597 B.C. (2 Kings 24:1-2; Jeremiah 13:18-19).

It is likely that the last Judean fortress at Arad, fortress VI, was built in the fourth year of Zedekiah's reign, 594 or 593 B.C., about three years after this destruction of the previous fortress by Nebuchadnezzar. Israelite fortress VI was planned along new lines, using the solid wall only as a deep foundation. A casemate

Text continues on p. 216

213

DIGGING DOWN

Six Centuries of Fortresses, One Beneath the Other

Israelites occupied the hill of Arad for about 500 years, building, rebuilding and modifying a series of six walled fortresses. Here, and on pages 216-217, we show those fortresses in different ways: to the left—reconstructed to show the outer walls complete—the fortresses are lined up with the latest fortress on top and the earliest on the bottom, in the order they were found. Below is a plan on which the remains of the fortresses are shown as archaeologists found them, a jumble of wall fragments, many built at one time and reused at later periods. Also shown on this plan (center) is a huge, third- to second-century B.C. Hellenistic tower, about 60 feet square. This tower, built on bedrock, obliterated all earlier remains below it. On the following pages is a stratigraphic section drawing, showing architectural features as they would appear if the mound were sliced in half vertically.

Let us now look closely at each reconstructed fortress, starting with the earliest (bottom left).

The first Israelite fortress (XI), built in the tenth century B.C., was surrounded by a casemate wall, a double-walled enclosure divided into rooms. In the fortress's northwest corner stood a small temple, with a Holy of Holies as well as a sacrificial altar. Note on the plan (below) that the large gateway on the northeast corner and the protruding tower are part of the stratum XI fortress. After the destruction of fortress XI by Pharaoh Shishak, a modified fortress (X) followed in the ninth century. The casemate wall of XI

became a solid wall with sawtooth insets on its outer face; the gateway shifted south to the center of the eastern wall, and the temple was enlarged. The early eighth century B.C. saw additional modifications (IX), including dwelling quarters along the southern wall and new chambers in the temple precinct. Toward the end of the eighth century (VIII), the sacrificial altar was covered with fill, and rooms began to encroach on the temple area. At the end of the eighth century, this fortress was destroyed—either by the Assyrian Sennacherib, or by his Edomite or Philistine allies. Rebuilt again in the late seventh century, the Arad citadel (VII) seems to have lost all signs of its earlier temple; to strengthen the southern wall an additional wall was built parallel to it, on the inside, creating a series of casemate rooms. A tower was built on the west.

The last Israelite fortress at Arad (VI) stood during the early sixth century. Once again we see a full casemate construction. A major modification was made—the gate was moved to the northern wall, where it opened near the area formerly occupied by the western wall. A tower projected from the western wall; here excavators found early sixth-century B.C. vessels. In one of the rooms along the southern side of fortress VI, archaeologists discovered an impressive archive (see "The Saga of Eliashib," p. 318).

Israelite occupation of Arad finally ended in 587 B.C. when the Babylonians or their Edomite allies destroyed the fortified Israelite citadel.

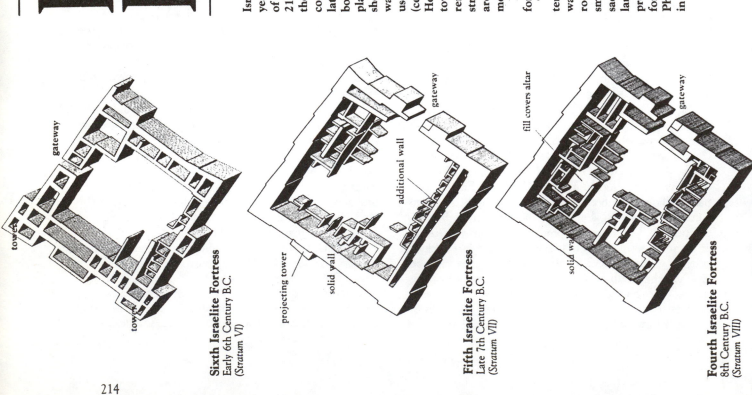

Sixth Israelite Fortress
Early 6th Century B.C.
(*Stratum VI*)

Fifth Israelite Fortress
Late 7th Century B.C.
(*Stratum VII*)

Fourth Israelite Fortress
8th Century B.C.
(*Stratum VIII*)

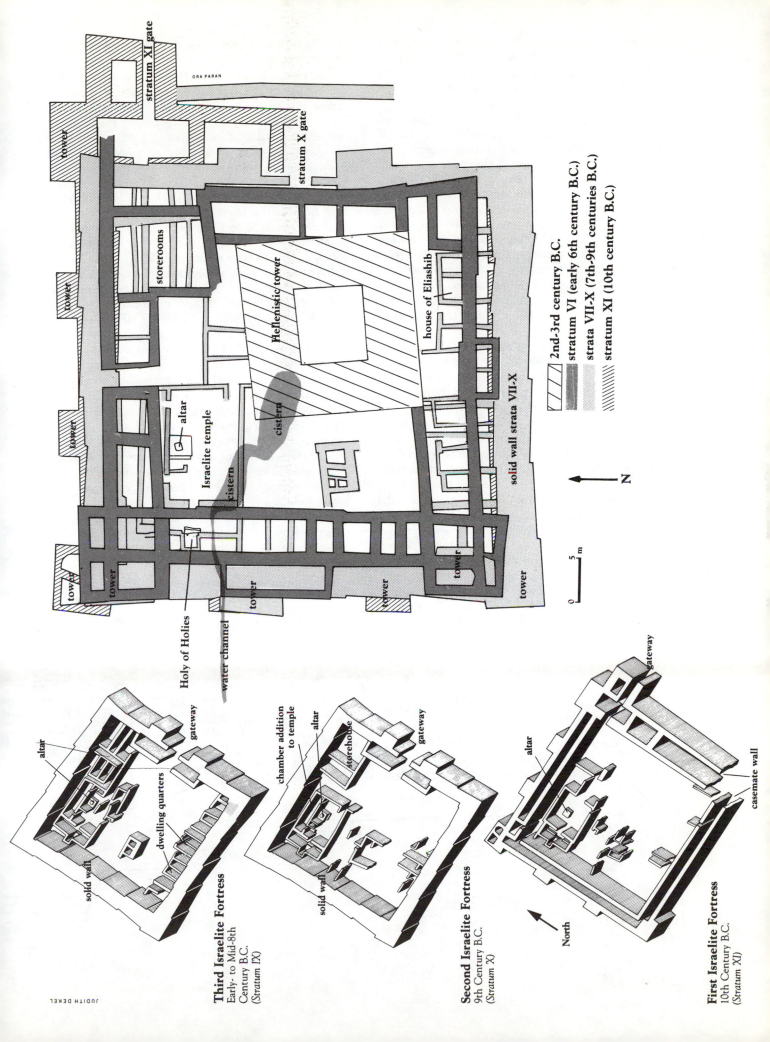

stratum XI gate

ORA PARAN

tower

stratum X gate

storerooms

tower

Hellenistic tower

altar

Israelite temple

cistern

tower

cistern

house of Eliashib

Holy of Holies

water channel

tower

tower

tower

tower

tower

solid wall strata VII-X

N

2nd-3rd century B.C.

stratum VI (early 6th century B.C.)

strata VII-X (7th-9th centuries B.C.)

stratum XI (10th century B.C.)

0 5 m

Third Israelite Fortress
Early- to Mid-8th
Century B.C.
(Stratum IX)

altar

gateway

dwelling quarters

solid wall

Second Israelite Fortress
9th Century B.C.
(Stratum X)

chamber addition
to temple

altar

storehouse

gateway

solid wall

North

First Israelite Fortress
10th Century B.C.
(Stratum XI)

altar

gateway

casemate wall

JUDITH DEKEL

system was constructed on the ruins of the previous fortresses; it consisted of two parallel walls with a space in between. On the northwestern and southwestern corners were projecting towers. Midway along the western side was a rectangular tower.

The fortified gate of the former strata was not rebuilt; instead, the entry to the fortress was moved over to the northern side. It was a simple opening, six feet wide, inserted between two of the casemates.

Fortress VI was probably destroyed in the Edomite invasion of the Negeb at the time of the Babylonian conquest of Judah (Obadiah 10-14; Psalm 137:7).

Until now, we have said nothing of the interior of these fortresses. The most fascinating interior feature was a unique Israelite temple dedicated to Yahweh—the only temple dedicated to the Hebrew God ever found in an archaeological excavation. But before discussing the temple, let us mention the reason for a large gap in our information concerning the interior of the fortresses.

In the Hellenistic period (third to second centuries B.C.) a new fort was built on the site, smaller than before, but with a massive square tower that covered nearly half of what had been the interior of the earlier Israelite fortresses. This huge Hellenistic tower measured about 60 feet on each side. It is unique at Arad in that its builders founded it on bedrock after digging out all the previous occupation deposits on their building site. That is why the plan of this tower appears on the plans of all six Israelite fortresses (see p. 214)—not to indicate the Hellenistic tower but to indicate the absence of any other remains in that area. We simply don't know what was there before the Hellenistic tower.

Fortunately, this Hellenistic tower did not destroy what must have been the most important building complex within the Israelite fortress—the temple to Yahweh. Moreover, this temple goes back to the first Israelite fortress at Arad, the time of King Solomon in the tenth century B.C..

The temple is located in the northwestern corner of the interior of the fortress, near the site of the cultic center of the Kenite settlement at the time of the Judges. The Main Hall (*Hekhal* or Holy Place) of the temple consisted of a broad-room, so called because it is oriented on the broad side. The entrance to the room is on the long wall, rather than on the short wall. Opposite the entrance is a niche that projects out from the back wall and represents the Holy of Holies (*Debir*).

In front of the Main Hall was a comparatively large courtyard, over 30 feet square, enclosed by a wall and paved with small wadi* stones. In the center of the courtyard stood a large sacrificial altar.

Everyone is naturally curious to compare the plan of the Arad temple with the plan of the nearly contemporaneous temple Solomon built in Jerusalem.

Such a comparison immediately demonstrates a fundamental difference, especially with regard to the Main Hall. At Arad this was a broad-room, while the corresponding room in the Solomonic Jerusalem Temple was clearly a long-room. Solomon sought to give his Jerusalem Temple a distinct character by borrowing the plan common in north Syria (and perhaps also in Phoenicia), based primarily on the megaron-type long-room. At Arad, however, the structure apparently utilized the broad-room, which was part of the standard "four-room house" commonly encountered in the Israelite period; "four-room houses" consisted of a broad-room with three long-rooms extending from it perpendicularly. Thus, the broad-room temple derived directly from Israelite domestic architecture. The Jerusalem Temple, on the other hand, looked to foreign cultic models.

* A wadi is a dry river bed or small river common in Israel and the surrounding regions. The American equivalent would be "arroyo."

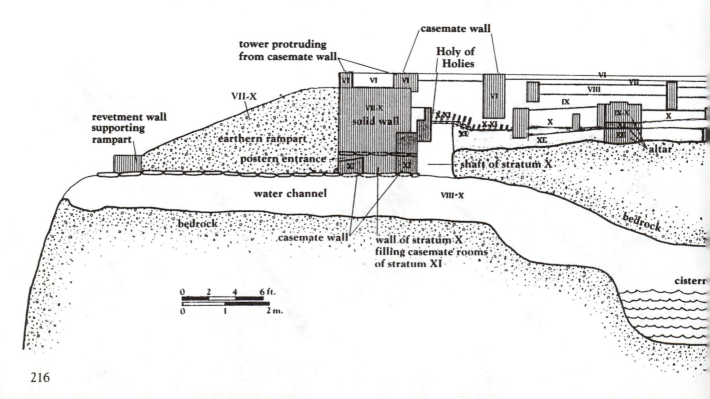

216

It is worth noting that these two variations in temple layout were suited to their respective functions: The broad-room at Arad permitted those entering the courtyard a closer relationship to the Holy of Holies; this plan suited the temple's function as a popular shrine. The long-room temple in Jerusalem kept the crowds at a distance from the symbols of the divine presence, which suited its function as a royal temple. In the Holy of Holies in the Jerusalem Temple, the Ark of the Covenant found its permanent home.

The Holy of Holies at the Arad temple was approached by two steps. At the entrance to the Holy of Holies were two small limestone incense altars. Within the Holy of Holies, on a small platform, was a smooth stele, or standing stone. What, if anything, was originally painted or inscribed on this stele we have no way of knowing. On either side of the Holy of Holies, on the wall of the Main Hall, were plaster-covered benches on which offerings could be placed.

The reader will recall that Israelite fortress XI was destroyed by Pharaoh Shishak about 925 B.C. When the fortress was rebuilt, the temple was also rebuilt, although with some alterations. The Main Hall of the temple was made even broader by adding about two feet in the north. The location of the Holy of Holies was not changed, so the northern addition made the room somewhat lopsided—the Holy of Holies was no longer in the middle of the back wall. The addition to the Main Hall on the north was also carried into the courtyard; this produced a long-room on the northern side of the courtyard, which provided storage space for ritual vessels and offerings.

The large sacrificial altar in the courtyard was rebuilt directly over the old sacrificial altar, but slightly to the north of its predecessor. The remains of the earlier altar served as a step at the foot of the new altar. This new sacrificial altar measured exactly "five cubits long and five cubits broad," the measurements of the tabernacle altar, as described in Exodus 27:1. Moreover, this new altar was made of unworked stones, as required by Exodus 20:22: "If you make for me an altar of stones, do not build it of hewn stones; for by wielding your tool upon them you have profaned them."

The unhewn stones of the Arad sacrificial altar in the temple courtyard were laid in a mud base. Whether or not there were horns at the corners of this altar, we do not know. Perhaps they were fashioned from plaster or wood and thus are not preserved. On top of the altar a large flint slab with plastered channels collected the blood and fat from the sacrifices. A metal rack probably held the coals on which the burnt offerings were laid; soot stains on some ashlar stones of a sacrificial altar at Beer-Sheba indicated that it had had such a rack. Similar evidence was not preserved at the Arad altar, however.

In a small room adjacent to the sacrificial altar on

Cutting Through the Arad Citadel

An imaginary slice through Tel Arad provides a view of the fortress's complex stratigraphy, or layers of occupation.

Many of the structures, including the altar and the outer walls, continued in use during more than one period of the fortress's history. During periods when the citadel was abandoned, loess (fine blown sand) accumulated to a thickness of up to 16 inches (40 cm) between strata.

On the far right and left the glacis slopes up to the city wall, supported at its lowest end by a revetment wall. The water channel passes below the western revetment wall, left, the glacis and the city wall before opening into a large cistern beneath the city.

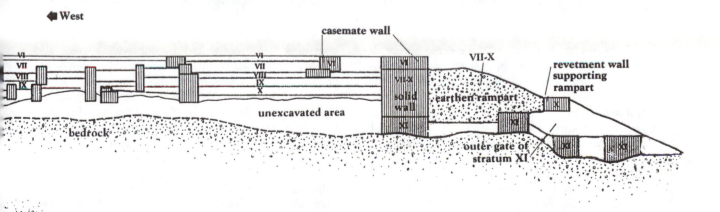

◄ West

casemate wall

VII-X

revetment wall supporting rampart

earthen rampart

solid wall

unexcavated area

bedrock

outer gate of stratum XI

stratum VI (early 6th century B.C.)
strata VII-X (7th-9th centuries B.C.)
stratum XI (10th century B.C.)
stratum XII (early 10th-11th century B.C.)

the west, excavators found a red-slip incense burner. It was made in two parts: a high, hollow base topped by leaves, and a deep small bowl, made to fit onto the stand and decorated at the base and rim with downturned leaves.

Two shallow bowls, found on the step at the foot of the sacrificial altar, bore inscriptions. The inscriptions were the same and consisted of two Hebrew letters *qop* and *kaf*. This is evidently an abbreviation for *qōdeš kôhanîm*, "set apart for [or holy to] the priests." The bowls were probably used to receive the portions of the offering designated for the officiating priest.*[3]

In Israelite fortress IX (early eighth century) the temple remained the same, but the rooms around the

* For a similar inscription see André Lemaire, "Probable Head of Priestly Scepter from Solomon's Temple Surfaces in Jerusalem," **BAR**, January/February 1984.

courtyard were reorganized by subdividing areas and creating additional rooms. As a result, the open space of the courtyard was appreciably reduced, suggesting some modifications in the nature of the ritual practiced there. During the offering of sacrifices on the altar, there was room for only a few people other than the officiating priests. Moreover, the entrance to the courtyard was shifted to the southeast corner. Opposite this new entrance was a stone installation, forming an elliptical basin on the inside. Perhaps a metal tub was originally placed within this basin to hold water; the installation stands where one would expect the laver for priestly ablutions.

In this stratum, a beautiful small bronze figurine of a resting lion was found beside the sacrificial altar.

In Israelite fortress VIII, the sacrificial altar was abolished. The courtyard of the temple was covered

Text continues on p. 222

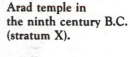

Arad temple in
the ninth century B.C.
(stratum X).

The Israelite Temple
to Yahweh

Steps flanked by limestone incense altars lead into a niche in the Holy of Holies at the Arad temple's rear wall. In this four-foot by four-foot niche, two stone pillars (*massevot*) rise against the rear wall. The pillars and the incense altars are replicas, placed in position after the original artifacts were removed for safekeeping to the Israel Museum in Jerusalem.

When the Israelites built their first fortresss (XI) at Arad in the tenth century B.C., they included a temple with a Holy of Holies. Through the centuries, as they modified their fortress, they preserved the temple. Finally, in the late seventh century B.C., the temple was abolished, during religious reforms by either King Josiah or King Hezekiah; the incense altars were reverently laid on their sides and were covered with earth.

219

מזבח הקרבנות
SACRIFICIAL ALTAR

Near the altar, archaeologists found a small bronze lion figurine (right) and an incense burner (opposite). The beautifully preserved, red-slip pottery stand was made in two parts: a deep bowl for incense and a tall, hollow base. Downturned leaves decorate both the bowl and the base that supported it.

Two views of the temple altar—from the side (opposite) and from the top (left)—show the requisite unworked stones prescribed in Exodus 20:22 and the five by five by three cubits dimension (approximately 7.5 by 7.5 by 4.5 feet) described in Exodus 27:1. In the view (left), a central flint slab is visible, and a channel to drain the sacrifice's blood and fat.

When the Israelites built this altar, they used the few remaining stones of the earlier altar (lower left, in the view, left), as a step. The altar also preserves an even earlier cultic tradition; it is built on the site of another platform that may have been a Kenite shrine in the 12th century B.C.

When the step was uncovered, archaeologists found on it two small, shallow bowls that had been used to hold offerings (photo, below). Near the rim of the bowl pictured here are inscribed two Hebrew characters, *qof* and *kaf*. This is probably an abbreviation for Qōdeš Kôhanîm, "sacred to the priests."

Vandals recently broke open the altar, discovering, as did archaeologists who repaired the damage, that the altar was filled only with dirt and clay.

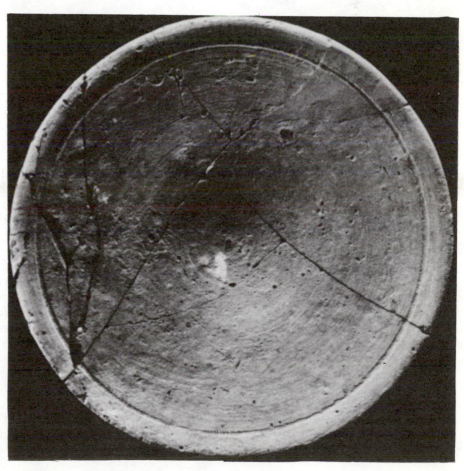

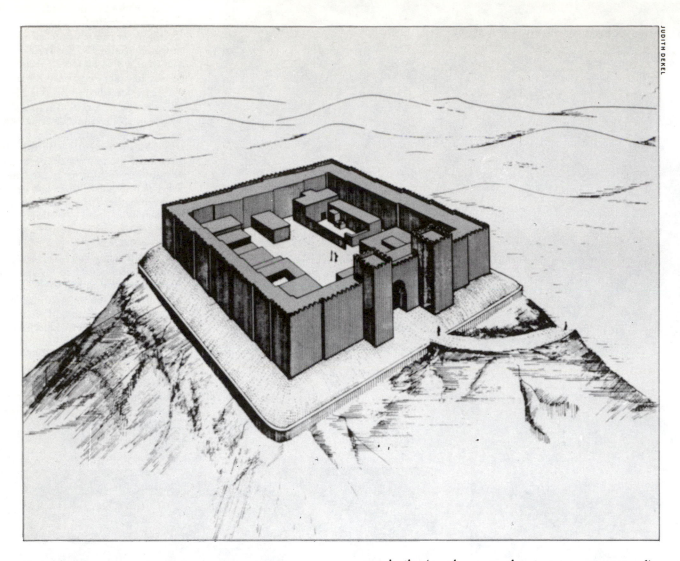

Ninth-century B.C. Israelite fortress (X). *Rebuilt following Pharaoh Shishak's destruction of the previous tenth-century fortress, this one includes features that enhance its defensibility. A solid wall averaging 12 feet in thickness surrounds the fortress. Sawtooth insets on the outer wall surface may indicate perpendicular cross walls—a strengthening device within the outer wall. A sloping earth glacis, supported at its lowermost outer edge by a low revetment wall, added additional strength to the fortress walls and made them more difficult to approach. The glacis helped prevent natural erosion of the steep hillside and enemy undermining of the walls.*

with a fill about three feet thick, which completely covered the altar. The adjacent stone basin also went out of use, and the entire courtyard became an open, level area. The altar of previous strata and the stone installation were found when we excavated *under* this fill, as were the two inscribed bowls mentioned above.

The temple itself, unlike the sacrificial altar, continued to exist in Israelite fortress VIII. Indeed, the temple wall of the hall to the north of the Holy of Holies was doubled in width. Two additional structures

were built (partly over the previous courtyard), evidently to serve as stores for the temple. In a room beside the Holy of Holies, several important ostraca were found. Several other ostraca that originated with those discovered in this room were found in the debris thrown out of the fort on the slope nearby. In all there were eight ostraca. On each ostracon was inscribed a single name, either of an individual or a family. Two of these names are known to us from the Bible as members of the priestly cadre of Judah, Meremoth and Pashhur (Ezra 8:33; 1 Chronicles 9:12). Others, such as Eshiyahu and Netanyahu are Yahwistic; that is, they contain a linguistic element (yahu) corresponding to the Hebrew God Yahweh. All this is additional evidence that this was indeed an Israelite temple dedicated to Yahweh. At least some of these ostraca apparently had to do with the casting of lots for assigning duties in the temple and may have been used in setting up the duty roster.

The base of a burnished bowl from a room on the eastern side of the temple courtyard was inscribed with administrative entries including references to payments from or allotments to groups such as "the sons of

Korah" and "the sons of Bezal(el)," also well known from the Bible as priestly families (Psalm 42:1; Exodus 31:1-11). From these strong Biblical associations, there can be no doubt that the officiants at the temple were Israelites of the recognized priestly and levitical orders, and that the temple itself was dedicated to the worship of the Israelite God Yahweh.

But why was the sacrificial altar in the courtyard of the Arad temple abolished? The abolition of this altar was no doubt associated with the religious reforms carried out by Hezekiah beginning in 715 B.C.

Hezekiah's abolition of sacrifical altars that might be thought to compete with the central altar in Jerusalem is exceedingly well documented in the Bible. In 701 B.C., when one of Sennacherib's officers was sent to urge the besieged citizens of Jerusalem to abandon Hezekiah and surrender to Sennacherib, the Assyrian officer taunted the Jerusalemites with these words:

"Hezekiah is seducing you to a death of hunger and thirst, saying 'The Lord our God will save us from the king of Assyria.' But is not Hezekiah the one who removed His shrines and His altars and commanded the people of Judah and Jerusalem saying, 'Before this one altar you shall prostrate yourselves, and upon it make your burnt offerings'?" (2 Chronicles 32:11-12)

The same speech is found in 2 Kings 18:22 in slightly different words:

"And if you tell me that you are relying on the Lord your God, He is the very one whose shrines and altars Hezekiah did away with, telling Judah and Jerusalem, 'You must worship only at this altar in Jerusalem'." (This speech is again repeated in Isaiah 36:7.)

When Hezekiah carried out his religious reforms, the northern kingdom of Israel had already fallen to the Assyrians (in 721 B.C.) and was no more. Hezekiah tried to unite the northern tribes with those of the south in their allegiance to Jerusalem as the sole religious center.

Hezekiah sent couriers throughout "all Israel and Judah" to proclaim the message.

"O you Israelites! Return to the Lord God of your fathers, Abraham, Isaac, and Israel, and He will return to the remnant of you who escaped from the hand of the kings of Assyria. Do not be like your fathers and brothers who trespassed against the Lord God of their fathers and he turned them into a horror, as you see. Now do not be stiffnecked like your fathers; submit yourselves to the Lord and come to His Sanctuary, which He consecrated forever, and serve the Lord your God so that His anger may turn back from you" (2 Chronicles 30:6-8).

The northerners, like the southerners, were invited by Hezekiah to join in the great Passover celebration to be held in Jerusalem. Hezekiah apparently sought to prove to the northern Israelites that he was giving them treatment equal to that of the residents of Judah. He therefore felt it was politic to order the abolition of separate cults in the cities and fortresses of Judah, just as he was demanding that the northerners should give

up their shrines in Samaria, Bethel and elsewhere. This then is the religious and historical background behind the archaeological evidence at Arad showing the abandonment and covering over of the sacrificial altar in the temple courtyard. Incidentally, this is also the reason for the dismantling of the sacrificial altar discovered in the excavations at Beer-Sheba.

In the next stratum (Israelite fortress VII), the temple itself was abolished—in connection with another famous religious reform, this time by King Josiah in the late seventh century. We may read at length of Josiah's religious reform in 2 Kings 23. Specifically, we learn that "he brought all the priests from the towns of Judah [to Jerusalem] and defiled the shrines where the priests had been making offerings—from Geba to Beer-Sheba" (2 Kings 23:8).

Although the temple at Arad was abolished, this was done with a certain reverence. Out of respect for their sanctity, the two incense altars that stood on the steps at the front of the Holy of Holies inside the temple were laid on their sides and covered with a layer of earth that completely concealed all traces of the former shrine. Over this fill were constructed thinner walls of what appears to have been a dwelling unit. And so the temple of Yahweh at Arad came to an end.

In the stratum of Israelite fortress VI, just before the Babylonian destruction of Jerusalem, excavators found an ostracon that contained a reference to "the house of Yahweh." This can refer only to the Temple in Jerusalem. The Arad temple had already been abolished. This mention of the Jerusalem Temple points to a connection, however, between the officialdom at Arad and the religious center in Jerusalem, somewhat reminiscent of the levitical administrative role "for all the work of Yahweh and all the service of the king . . . everything pertaining to god and the king" (1 Chronicles 26:30, 32). ▨

---

[1] In Shishak's inscription, the Egyptian scribe defines the two Arads by the term ḥqrm, "fortress enclosures." Two scholars, Martin Noth and Benjamin Mazar, long ago had seen that the Egyptian spelling represented the equivalent of later Aramaic ḥagra'. Elsewhere in the inscription, a few other places in the Negeb area are defined as p3-ḥqr, "the fortress enclosure," with the Egyptian definite article for masculine singular nouns. But the form with final -m, the typical plural suffix of Semitic languages, only appears with the two Arads. The fact that this is the only place where ḥqr is followed by two towns with identical names is proof that ḥqrm is meant for a plural. The scribe did not add the Egyptian definite article for the plural, which is n3, not p3, because of the Semitic inflection; he did not think that the article was necessary.

[2] James B. Pritchard, Ancient Near Eastern Texts (Princeton, NJ: Princeton University Press, 1969), p. 292.

[3] Frank Moore Cross, who also made reference to the supposed confusion in the stratigraphy at Arad, suggested that the second letter was not kaf but a Phoenician shin of the sixth century B.C. On one of the bowls, the central stroke is so long as to preclude any association with a Phoenician shin; therefore, we reject his paleographic argument out of hand. Furthermore, those bowls were buried beneath a fill of stratum IX which itself was sealed by floors of the later strata. The stratigraphy here is absolutely certain and in no way confused.

In their interpretation of the sequence of Arad fortresses, the excavators dated the elaborate water channel and cistern system described on page 210 to Arad stratum X, the *second* period of fortification. A reader wrote (in **BAR**, September/October 1987, p. 70) to raise a relevant question:

> I have one question concerning the water supply system. If the well outside the fortress walls was not planned as part of the water system until the time of Stratum X, how was the fortress of Stratum XI of Solomon's time able to provide itself with a reliable supply of water?
>
> Ed Nunes-Vaz, Calgary, Alberta, Canada

A reply was provided by one of the excavators, Anson Rainey. Noting that the temple of stratum XI as well as the fort would have needed an internal water supply, he wrote:

> Though it is true that the water channel seems to have been cut in the rock when the solid wall of Stratum X was built, it does not necessarily follow that the underground chambers were cut at that time. I have always believed that those chambers were carved out from natural caves that had existed in bedrock under the fortress. . . .
>
> I believe the stratum XI temple [and fortress] had an entry into the underground water cisterns via the southwest corner of the temple. Whether this entryway was from a room of the temple or from just outside of the building is hard to say.

In other words, Rainey explains that the Arad water system went through two stages of development. (1) When the Israelites constructed the stratum XI fort with its temple in the tenth century B.C., they adapted a cave cavity beneath the fort into two connected cisterns which they reached through a vertical shaft descending from inside the fort wall (see the section drawing on p. 216). Presumably the cisterns collected winter rainwater from the rooftops and other surfaces of the fort above. (2) At the time of the stratum X rebuilding, a channel was cut beneath the fortress wall to carry additional water from outside the fort into the underground cistern chambers, and a well was dug in the lower ground below the fortress hill from which water could be hauled to feed the channel. (For descriptions of other Israelite defensive water systems, see Section E.)

Arad provides a good example of the tight stratigraphic buildup of successive occupational layers characteristic of sites in Iron Age Palestine. Having read the summary of the Arad building phases as they came to be sorted out, look again at the photo on page 212 of the mound of rubble that initially confronted the excavators. When you consider that the remains of a half-millennium of history and seven building phases stood only about 20 feet high, you can appreciate the three-dimensional jigsaw puzzle archaeologists often face.

Those who have worked on an archaeological excavation anywhere will appreciate even more fully the problems of separating several such closely intertwined sequential phases of building. Much painstaking care and close scrutiny of the soil is required over a number of seasons to extract the data responsibly and interpret it intelligently.

Finally, Arad presents us with a good example of both the prospects and the problems of archaeological reconstruction. The excavators and the Israeli Department of Antiquities decided that since the complete groundplan of a reasonably compact fortress had been uncovered it would be physically feasible and academically responsible to supplement what remained of the original walls and recreate the fortress to nearer its original height. The decision to do so will be appreciated by generations of visitors who come to the site, as well as by those who view the reconstructed Arad fortress in photographs.

Consider the decisions that had to be made, however, to undertake the reconstruction. Some will question one or another of those decisions, as they do with any decision relating to archaeological reconstruction.

First, it had to be decided which of several phases of a building should be chosen for reconstruction. To rebuild one means to forfeit the opportunity to reconstruct an earlier or later period's remains *in situ*. It had to be decided that the excavators' interpretation of the chosen stratum's architecture was secure and accurate. There are always some phasing designations about which there can be disagreement, and there are almost always some dotted lines where walls or installations were partially eroded or interrupted by later activities in the area. Reconstructing the architecture one way rules out the option to reconstruct it another way.

It was decided that areas above and beneath the proposed reconstruction had been adequately investigated; the new construction will remove any remnants of later layers of material that might otherwise have remained available for examination above the walls to be reconstructed, and it will make access to any remaining soil or rubble layers below more difficult.

Reconstruction allows us all to gain added benefit from what the archaeologist has discovered. The price is that it involves the risk of limiting us to one interpreter's judgments. Most who have followed the excavators' work at Arad and have visited the site since the ninth century B.C. walls were restored would say that in this case the risk was small and the benefits great.

For Further Reading

Concerning Arad

Joan Borsten, "A Heritage in Danger," **BAR**, September 1977

"Rodman Makes Gift to Excavate Israelite Well at Arad," **BAR**, September/October 1984

Ruth Amiran, Rolf Goethert and Ornit Ilan, "The Well at Arad," **BAR**, March/April 1987

Anson F. Rainey, "The Saga of Eliashib," **BAR**, March/April 1987 (*see Section F*)

Concerning Other Southern Israelite Border Fortresses

Rudolph Cohen, "The Fortresses King Solomon Built to Protect His Southern Border," **BAR**, May/June 1985

Rudolph Cohen, "Solomon's Negev Defense Line Contained Three Fewer Fortresses," **BAR**, July/August 1986

Israel Finkelstein, "The Iron Age Sites in the Negev Highlands—Military Fortresses or Nomads Settling Down?" **BAR**, July/August 1986

Concerning Iron Age Temples, Altars and *Bamahs*

"Horned Altar for Animal Sacrifice Unearthed at Beer-Sheva," **BAR**, March 1975

"Philistine Temple Discovered Within Tel Aviv City Limits," **BAR**, June 1975 (Tell Qasile temple)

John C. H. Laughlin, "The Remarkable Discoveries at Tel Dan," **BAR**, September/October 1981

"A New Generation of Israeli Archaeologists Comes of Age," **BAR**, May/June 1984 (Tell Qasile temple)

(See also Section B)

Bringing Iron and Water from the Rock— Two Emerging Technologies in Ancient Israel

Modern archaeological investigation is concerned not only with uncovering the what and the where of ancient peoples but also with considering the how and why— that is, "How did they make this?" and "Why did they do it this way at a particular time and place?"

The articles in this section focus on two emerging technologies in Iron Age Palestine and suggest reasons why they developed when and as they did. James Muhly's study, "How Iron Technology Changed the Ancient World—And Gave the Philistines a Military Edge," deals with the development of iron metalworking during Iron Age I (twelfth-early tenth centuries B.C.), while Dan Cole's treatment of Israelite city water systems, "How Water Tunnels Worked," draws attention to developments in Israelite hydraulic engineering somewhat later in Iron Age II (tenth-eighth centuries B.C.).

In both studies, the new technologies are examined against the background of changing conditions or circumstances that may have influenced their development. The emergence of new techniques for forging tools and weapons from iron in Iron I may be seen as a response to the crisis caused by the breakdown in international trade networks in the eastern Mediterranean at the end of the Late Bronze Age. The breakdown in trade constricted access to the tin essential for bronze-casting. The ambitious Israelite city water systems cut during Iron II, for their part, were in a general way responses to the increasing threat from siege warfare tactics employed by the Israelites' neighbors, particularly the Assyrians.

How Iron Technology Ch
And Gave the Philistines a Military Edge

anged the Ancient World

By James D. Muhly

Modern historians divide the roughly 3,000-year-period beginning approximately 3200 B.C. into two major segments—the Bronze Age and the Iron Age. The Bronze Age extends from about 3200 B.C. to 1200 B.C.* Thereafter it is the Iron Age.** This is some indication of the enormous importance (as well as the date generally) of the discovery of iron technology in the eastern Mediterranean.

Archaeology and modern science are now beginning to clarify how this fundamental change occurred, and in so doing a new dimension has been added to our understanding of Biblical history in general as well as to our understanding of particular Biblical passages.

As a result, we may even be able to answer the much-mooted question: Did the Philistines have an iron monopoly that enabled them, at least for a time, to dominate the

*The Bronze Age is subdivided into Early Bronze (3200-2000 B.C.), Middle Bronze (2000-1550 B.C.) and Late Bronze (1550-1200 B.C.). Each of these is also further subdivided.

**The Iron Age is subdivided into Iron Age I (1200-1000 B.C.), Iron Age II (1000-586 B.C.), and, sometimes, Iron Age III (586-330 B.C.).

Israelites? Answering this question will involve us in a consideration of the famous passage from 1 Samuel:

"There was no smith to be found in all the land of Israel, for the Philistines had said to themselves, 'The Hebrews might make swords or spears!' So all Israel would go down to the Philistines to repair any of their plowshares, mattocks, axes or sickles. The price was a paim for plowshares and mattocks and a third of a shekel for

Overleaf: *Foundrymen on an Attic vase cast a life-size bronze statue. This foundry scene, the most detailed to survive from the ancient world, decorates an early fifth century B.C. vase known as the Berlin Foundry Cup. It shows a constuction technique, the piece casting of a life-size bronze statue, that simply would not have been possible when working with iron. On the left is the furnace in which bronze was melted; the young man peering out from behind it is probably working the bellows. The objects hanging to the right of the furnace are interpreted as votive offerings to ensure the successful outcome of the casting, but the presence of the saw has never been explained. On the far right, a foundry worker taps the mold with a hammer to release the statue from its mold. Between this worker's feet is the statue's head, ready to be joined to the bronze body.*

Copper ceremonial objects *belong to a magnificent hoard of more than 400 copper pieces found in the Judean wilderness near the Dead Sea. Hidden in a cave in Nahal Mishmar, the hoard dates to the Chalcolithic period (fourth millennium B.C.). The beauty and workmanship—unique for its time but extraordinary at any time—make this the earliest and most important collection of metal artifacts found anywhere in the world.*

The objects may have been used in cult rituals at a nearby temple. At the center is a "crown"; to the right is a standard with ibex heads; other implements include mace heads and scepters.

The Nahal Mishmar hoard demonstrates the exceptional sophistication of copper metallurgy that had developed in fourth millennium Palestine. The objects were made by what is called the "lost wax" process. Wax was carved in the shape of the artifact; a clay mold was then built around the wax model; the wax was melted away and, finally, molten copper, sometimes with an admixture of arsenic, was poured into the cavity.

picks and axes or setting an ox-goad. So at the time of the battle of Michmash neither sword nor spear was available to any of the soldiers who were with Saul and Jonathan—only Saul and Jonathan had them." (1 Samuel 13:19-22; *Anchor Bible* translation)

Until about 1200 B.C., bronze was the predominant metal in the ancient world—for a very simple reason. The melting point of copper is about 1100°C. The melting point of iron is 1530 °C. This roughly 400° difference was crucial in terms of the capabilities of ancient technology.

From at least the fifth millennium B.C. copper was worked as a molten metal.* In the fourth millennium, an arsenical alloy of copper was developed in the Middle East. This alloy usually contained from two to four percent arsenic. The best examples of this alloy come from the famous hoard of over 400 copper objects from the cave of Nahal Mishmar on the west bank of the Dead Sea.

The Bronze Age, beginning in about 3200 B.C., witnessed the introduction of an alloy known as bronze, consisting of about 90 percent copper and 10 percent tin. During the Bronze Age, an elaborate bronze casting technology was developed. Many bronze casting molds have been found throughout the Bronze Age world, often matching the surviving objects cast from them. The entire casting operation is depicted on the walls of Egyptian New Kingdom tombs, the most famous of which is that of the vizier Rekhmire (first half of the 15th century B.C.).(See p. 236). Larger objects were sometimes cast in the sand, rather than in molds, as we know from the Bible passage describing Hiram's manufacture of the bronze utensils to be used in Solomon's Temple.

"All these furnishings made by Hiram for King Solomon for the Temple of Yahweh were of burnished bronze. He made them by the process of sand casting in the Jordan area between Succoth and Zorethan." (I Kings 7:45-46, *Jerusalem Bible* translation)

A temperature of 1200°C to melt copper could be attained in an ancient furnace by the use of a bellows and tuyères** that supplied the necessary forced draft of air. But the melting point of iron, 1530°C, seems to have been beyond the capability of an ancient furnace.

This does not mean that iron was not used at all. On the contrary, iron objects are known from as early as the fifth millennium B.C. But until the coming of the Iron Age, iron was an exotic, semi-precious metal used, for example, in jewelry. We even have examples of an iron bezel in a gold ring from Late Bronze Age Greece. Iron was also used for the manufacture of ceremonial weapons. An iron battle axe from Ugarit (about 1400 B.C.) and a dagger from the tomb of Tutankhamen in Egypt (about 1350 B.C.) are examples (see p. 235).

These early iron objects were not cast, because the iron could not be heated to a molten state; instead they were wrought. The iron was forged, after smelting, while it was in a semi-solid spongy state.

Pure iron worked in this way is not very utilitarian. Indeed, plain wrought iron is decidedly inferior to tin-bronze, being both softer and less durable. The work-hardened edge on a bronze cutting instrument is far superior to anything that can be produced in plain wrought iron.

Thus for the 2,000 years of the Bronze Age (3200-1200 B.C.) bronze was the predominant metal in the ancient world. This is especially ironic, if I may be pardoned the pun, because iron was so much more widely dispersed than copper. But, from the viewpoint of Bronze Age technology, these vast iron deposits were relatively worthless.

Moreover, not only was copper less common than iron, but tin, the second component of bronze, was indeed quite scarce. In the Mediterranean world, alluvial tin, or cassiterite, is known from the Eastern Desert of Egypt. While there is geological evidence for its presence in these areas, there is no evidence of its ancient exploitation. Apart from Egypt, alluvial tin is known only from regions as far away as southern England (Cornwall) in the West and Afghanistan in the East. The Biblical reference to tin from Tarshish (Ezekiel 27:12) is not very helpful in locating ancient tin deposits because we cannot locate Tarshish.

At the end of the Late Bronze Age, there was a worldwide upheaval of destructions, invasions and migrations.

---

*Pure copper metallurgy developed to a high degree, not only in the old world from Eastern Europe to Pakistan but even in North America.

**A tuyère is an opening in a furnace through which a blast of air enters, facilitating combustion.

Zev Radovan, courtesy the Israel Museum

Iron tools and weapons *from Middle Eastern sites: a) knife found in a tomb at Tell el-Farʻah (south), b) Tell el Farʻah (south) arrowhead, c) Tell Jemmeh knife; d) Tell Jemmeh hoe, e) chisel from Al Mina in northern Syria.*

Whether the crises were related to one another is unknown. But these upheavals plunged the world into a Dark Age of poverty and isolation. This was the time when Troy was destroyed, when the Dorians moved into Greece from the northwest, when the Phrygians migrated to Anatolia, when the Sea Peoples, including the Philistines, attacked (but were repelled by) Egypt and finally settled on the Palestine coast, and when the Israelites occupied Canaan. At this time, Mycenaean sea power ended, the Hittite empire collapsed, the great city-states in Syria were destroyed, and the Arameans migrated into Mesopotamia and Syria. These destructions marked the end of the great empires of the Late Bronze Age and of the palace economies that developed around the urban centers associated with these empires.

The Late Bronze Age, until the very end, had been a time of prosperity and extensive international trade. Late Bronze Age levels of excavations, wherever they are located, characteristically uncover substantial quantities of "imported" pottery, frequently painted and decorated. But all this came to an end in the waning years of the Late Bronze Age. International trade routes were permanently disrupted and local communities withdrew into themselves. No longer could vast supplies of copper, and especially tin, be brought over long distance by land and sea. During the Bronze Age, according to the most recent scholarship, the tin used in Middle Eastern bronze came all the way from Afghanistan. Although the proof for this statement has not been fully supplied, it does suggest the kinds of production

problems that ensued following the disruption of international commerce. Copper supply dwindled and tin became almost unavailable.

In the archaeological levels from the first part of the Iron Age, precious metals are no longer found and imported materials are extremely rare. There were, of course, areas where Bronze Age culture, including metalworking, survived, but this was the exception, not the rule.

As is so often the case in human history, necessity became the mother of invention. While bronze was easily available, there was no necessity for the development of iron technology. In short, the inception of the Iron Age came about in response to a materials shortage, a crisis created by the disruption of international trade routes. When bronze became scarce, those smiths living in areas that had not been invaded and devastated were forced to fall back on local resources and to make do with what was available nearer to home. Iron metallurgy developed against this background.

Not only were iron deposits more likely than copper to be available locally, but iron was more easily extracted from the earth. Iron ore deposits, even when found in association with copper deposits, tend to be on the surface and therefore their extraction does not require any elaborate mining technology. Copper ores, on the other hand, tend to be located in veins running deep into the ground and often require a network of underground shafts and galleries in order to be mined. Archaeologists have found a number of early copper mines, some going back to the fifth millennium B.C., but no ancient iron mines, perhaps because iron was mined on the surface.

The famous Biblical description of the riches of the Promised Land reflects the fact that copper mining requires underground shafts and galleries but iron mining utilizes

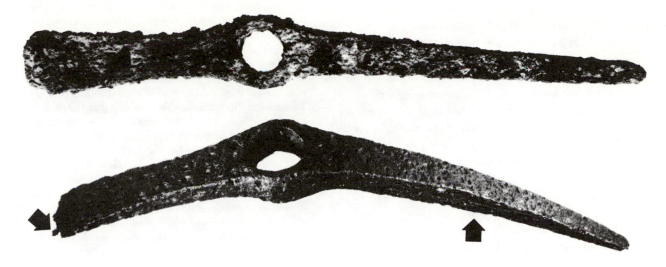

An iron pick *from Har Adir in the upper Galilee. This tool's remarkable state of preservation belies its date—from the 12th or early 13th century B.C. On the top we see it as it was excavated; on the bottom, after cleaning and preservation. This pick is especially noteworthy because it is one of only two artifacts from this period that have undergone metallurgical analysis. In the bottom photo, the arrow far left points to the tiny metal chip removed for this scientific study. The right arrow indicates where hardness readings were made. The hardness readings and the results of metallographic examination show that the pick was made of carburized iron (steel) that had been quenched and then tempered.*

surface deposits. In addition to its agricultural wealth, the land of Canaan was "a land where the stones are of iron, where the hills may be quarried for copper." (Deuteronomy 8:9, *Jerusalem Bible* translation). Actually, ancient Palestine has only limited deposits of iron ore,* but the Biblical author accurately described the conditions under which the two metals could be found.

While local accessibility and ease of extraction might be thought to have given iron the edge (again, excuse the pun), only the scarcity of bronze provided the goad for the development of iron technology.

Perhaps this is understandable because iron technology is difficult and complicated. As we have seen, in antiquity iron could not be heated to the melting point, so it had to be wrought or forged in a semi-solid spongy mass (or bloom,

---

*There are a number of minor deposits—in the Makhtesh southwest of the Dead Sea, in the Galilee and in the Wadi Arabah—but the only major ore deposit is that at Mugharat el Wardeh in the vicinity of Ajlun, about 20 miles north-northwest of Amman, a deposit that would be exploited today were it not so inaccessible.

as it is called). Moreover, this porous mass of agglomerated iron had trapped within its interstices quantities of impurities called gangue, consisting basically of silica. In order to consolidate the metal, it was necessary to hammer or forge the red-hot bloom, thus forcing out or extruding the unwanted gangue. But even when this was done, the resultant pure iron was soft compared to bronze.

The essential factor in the technological development of iron metallurgy was the introduction of up to .8 percent carbon into the red-hot iron, accomplished by a kind of osmosis through prolonged contact with glowing charcoal in the forging furnace. The introduction of this carbon transformed iron from an exotic, semi-precious metal into a metal that would give its name to the age. For carburized iron (iron to which carbon has been added) is, in fact, steel.

The technology is not simple, however. When red-hot carburized iron (or steel) is suddenly cooled off by plunging it into a vat of cold water (quenching), the result includes the formation of material called martensite. Martensite is earth's second-hardest substance. Only a diamond is harder. The problem is that martensite, though extremely hard, is also very brittle. An object of pure martensite will shatter upon impact.

When carburized iron is quenched, however, the result is not pure martensite. Usually only the outer layers of the object will be converted into martensite; the inner layers will be composed of pearlite, consisting of alternate layers (or lamellae) of ferrite (pure iron) and cementite (a compound of iron and carbon). Just how much martensite will be produced depends upon mass and temperature.

In order to relieve the brittleness of the metal, it was necessary to reduce some of the martensite through tempering; that is, reheating the iron, at temperatures above 150°C, in order to decompose some of the martensite and thus reduce the brittleness of the metal. This resulted in an elaborate trade-off of hardness versus durability that became the hallmark of advanced iron metallurgy.

The technology of working with iron thus became far more complex than anything connected with copper or bronze, and it all had to be learned empirically. No Iron Age smith was aware even of the existence of carbon, an element not identified until the end of the 18th century A.D.; he only learned empirically of its effect. But once these ancient smiths learned that iron subjected to the elaborate heat-treatment of carburization, quenching and tempering was far superior to bronze, a new age was ushered in. Iron was no longer a curosity but one of the most useful resources in the crust of the earth.

The Iron Age became the age of the blacksmith. The village blacksmith standing at his forge before an anvil, holding a lump or bar of red-hot iron in a pair of tongs, was a metalworking scene unknown to the inhabitants of the Bronze Age world. But this scene became common when iron emerged as the dominant metal, largely replacing the casting technology used for copper and bronze.

A vivid artistic representation of a smithy appears on a sixth century B.C. amphora from Athens. ——— An assistant, who is partially obscured by a furnace, holds a red-hot bar of metal with a pair of tongs while the blacksmith stands in front of the anvil, raising a sledge-hammer with a wedge-shaped head, ready to strike the bar. Two bearded men holding staffs sit and respectfully observe. Lying on the floor and hanging on the wall are a saw, tongs, a vase, a garment, a knife, a chisel, a sheathed sword and sledge-hammers with wedge-shaped heads and with double concave heads.

The first recorded reference to the profession of blacksmith comes in an archival text from the reign of the Assyrian king Ninurta-tukulti-Assur, about 1132 B.C.[1]

The work of the blacksmith is vividly described in the Bible. For example, in Isaiah 44:12, we learn about the manufacture of iron idols:

"The blacksmith works on it over the fire and beats it
    into shape with a hammer. He works on it with his
    strong arm til he is hungry and tired; drinking no water,
    he is exhausted." (Jerusalem Bible translation)

The same image is projected in Ecclesiasticus 38: 29-31, part of a section dealing with trade and crafts:

"So it is with the blacksmith sitting by his anvil;
    he considers what to do with the iron bloom,
    the breath of the fire scorches his skin,
    as he contends with the heat of the furnace;
    he batters his ear with the din of the hammer,
    his eyes are fixed on the pattern;
    he sets his heart on completing his work,
    and stays up putting the finishing touches."

A gold dagger (top) and an iron dagger, *each with its own scabbard. These exquisite weapons were found among the treasures buried with King Tutankhamen about 1350 B.C. Gold daggers are known from other contexts, going back to the Royal Cemetery of Ur (c. 2500 B.C.), but this iron dagger is unique in the Bronze Age world (and for this reason the Egyptian government allowed the gold dagger to travel about the world as part of the exhibition of The Treasures of Tutankhamen, but insisted that the iron dagger remain in Cairo). The best description of the iron dagger is that of Howard Carter, the excavator of the tomb, first published in 1922: "The haft of the dagger is of granulated gold, embellished at intervals with collars of Cloisonné work of colored rock crystal; but the astonishing and unique feature of this beautiful weapon is that the blade is of iron still bright and resembling steel!"*

It is assumed that the blade of this dagger is made of meteoritic iron, but no technical study of it has ever been made.

    (Jerusalem Bible translation, but reading "iron bloom"
    instead of "pig iron")

Indeed, the red-hot iron furnace came to be used metaphorically for Egypt, from which God delivered the Israelites. Solomon prays to Yahweh on behalf of his people: "They are your people and your heritage whom you brought out of Egypt, that iron furnace." (1 Kings 8:51; Jerusalem Bible translation). The image is repeated in Deuteronomy 4:20 and in Jeremiah 11:4.

Bronze of course continued to be used in the Iron Age, especially for purposes for which iron was unsatisfactory. The basic difference between bronze and iron technology determined, to a very great extent, the ways in which the two metals were used. With bronze it was possible to make large, elaborate and intricate castings from the molten metal in shapes impossible to duplicate by forging a bar of iron. A life-size statue was almost commonplace in bronze, but unheard of in iron. Iron came to be used for objects of rather simple shape and design, requiring great hardness and strength. This meant cutting and chopping instruments such as axes, adzes and chisels,* digging instruments such as hoes and plowshares, and, above all, weapons. Because of its hardness and its ability to take and hold a sharp cutting edge or point, iron was ideal for swords, spearheads, knives, daggers, and even arrowheads. Thus, iron soon became the metal of war, producing the iron armory described in Job 20:24. But all of this was possible only with the use of carburized iron (or steel) and the development of a technology involving quenching and tempering.

In the Bible, iron is a symbol of strength. In Job 40:18 we are told of Behemoth, the brute whose bones are "as hard

*See 13th century B.C. iron sickle, **BAR**, May/June 1982, p. 18.

Courtesy Cairo Archaeological Museum and Egyptian Department of Antiquities

as hammered iron." And in Daniel 2:40 we read the prophecy of the four kingdoms:

"There will be a fourth kingdom, hard as iron, as iron that shatters and crushes all. Like iron that breaks everything to pieces, it will crush and break all the earlier kingdoms." (*Jerusalem Bible* translation)

The sharpness of the edge of an iron dagger is assumed in these lines from a Babylonian Wisdom text known as *The Dialogue of Pessimism*[2]: "Woman is a pitfall—a pitfall, a hole, a ditch. Woman is a sharp iron dagger that cuts a man's throat."

The problem of tracing the development and spread of iron technology should be an ideal one for archaeology in combination with modern science. More than 40 years ago, R.J. Forbes, then the world's leading specialist in ancient technology, observed: "If there ever was a problem of ancient metallurgy in which the technical aspect can give us the correct solution it is that of the coming of the Iron Age."[3]

Today, archaeologists in cooperation with metallurgists, can discover a great deal of information from a small metal sample taken from an ancient iron artifact. After the archaeologist excavates an iron object, the modern metallurgist can determine hearth temperatures reached at the different stages of production such as forging or tempering.

Hirmer Verlag, Courtesy Aleppo Museum

A ceremonial battle axe *from Ugarit (c. 1400 B.C.). Atop the bronze socket of this elegant weapon, cast in a mold and inlaid with gold, is a crouching wild boar. The blade was probably wrought or hammered from a piece of meteoritic iron, as were many iron artifacts of this period. No proper metallographic analysis has been made of this blade, but based on available information, metallurgist H. G. Richardson said of the axe: "It is not a formidable weapon in any sense—size, weight, hardness or inherent soundness. In a finish fight the bronze socket would be far more dependable than the iron blade."*

235

Egyptian metal workers *melt metallic copper. This painting decorates the wall of Vizier Rekhmire's tomb from the 15th century B.C. on the west bank of the Nile near Thebes.*

Each hearth has a light blue center, representing either ashes or a floor of clay or stone. The two figures above remove a clay crucible of molten metal from the hearth. The vase above them may contain a copper/tin mixture or water to douse the hot lifting rods.

Between the two lower figures are a vase and a pile of charcoal. The men use foot bellows to direct a forced draft of air onto the hearth in order to increase the intensity of the fire. Although this technique has now been studied in some detail, the best description of it is still that of Norman de Garis Davies (The Tomb of Rekhmire at Thebes, 1943): "The hearth, when in use, was fed with air from two pairs of bellows, each of which was operated by a man who threw his weight from one bag to the other. When he stepped off a depressed bag he raised its upper side by means of a string, and while it was filling again he was deflating its fellow. The air from the bag under pressure was discharged into the heart of the fire through a pipe of reed, ending near the fire in a pottery nozzle [tuyère]. The bellows consisted of a red leather bag mounted on a white object of the same size and shape, which may be a flat stone or another bag . . . . No valve is shown, but air may have entered through a hole which the operator closed with his heel. The upper bag was tied horizontally round the middle with cord to enable it to stand the distension better."

From a study of the penetration of carbon into the iron object, the metallurgist can make rough calculations of the length of time the object was held in the charcoal fire and even at what temperature in order to achieve that particular carbon penetration. Very recently we have learned to use even corrosion product in new analytical techniques developed at the University of Pennsylvania. The problem is that permission to take the necessary samples from ancient artifacts has proven quite difficult to obtain. Some modern countries refuse to authorize such research because it involves taking a small sample of metal from the ancient artifact. The exceptions are Israel and Cyprus.

For the past five years Professors Robert Maddin and Tamara Stech and I (all colleagues at the University of Pennsylvania) have been working together on a detailed program involving the scientific study of early metal artifacts throughout the eastern Mediterranean, concentrating on objects that could be dated within the limits of the crucial transition period from 1200 to 900 B.C. (from the end of the Bronze Age to the full Iron Age). Metallurgical analyses of individual artifacts have added significantly to the largely archaeological surveys that follow. After five years of study, we can state that iron technology probably first developed in the Eastern Mediterranean, with Greece

and Cyprus playing the dominant roles, and that the introduction of iron metallurgy into Israel came about through contacts with the Aegean world and the migrations of the Philistines and other Sea Peoples.

The development of iron metallurgy occurred in areas where a surviving tradition of Bronze Age metalworking was combined with an ability to respond to the new pressures of a difficult, even hostile environment. This can clearly be seen in the Aegean, where the concentration of 12th century iron artifacts comes from just those areas where the Late Bronze Age Mycenaean heritage is most apparent, areas that somehow managed to avoid the devastations and destructions that marked the end of the Late Bronze Age throughout the eastern Mediterranean. Examples are the sites of Perati in East Attica, Mouliana in Crete, Lefkandi in Euboea and the Kamini cemetery on the island of Naxos.

With the introduction of a strong Aegean element into Cyprus, probably the result of the arrival of Greek colonists in the early 12th century B.C., comes the first use of iron on Cyprus, followed there by the rapid development of iron technology. Again, this occurs at Cypriot sites, such as Kition, that maintained strong elements of continuity with the culture of the Late Bronze Age, and at sites in the

Grim Episode from Homer's *Odyssey* Evokes Early Steel-Making Techniques

This chilling scene on the neck of a Proto-Attic amphora from the early seventh century B.C. portrays the encounter of Odysseus with the giant, Polyphemus, who was called the Cyclops because he had a single eye in the middle of his forehead. Odysseus and his men, trapped in the cave of Polyphemus, managed to escape by getting the giant drunk on wine and then, after he had fallen asleep, blinding him by thrusting a glowing olive wood pole into his eye socket. Homer describes the result in a passage of gruesome intensity (*Odyssey*, IX: 389-94):

> "The blast and scorch of the burning ball singed all his eyebrows and eyelids, and the fire made the roots of his eye crackle. As when a man who works as a blacksmith plunges into cold water a great axe or adze which hisses aloud, 'doctoring' it, since this is the way that steel is made strong, even so Cyclops's eye sizzled about the beam of the olive." (Translation after that by Richard Lattimore)

The *Odyssey*, although it incorporates older material, was first written down in the late eighth century B.C. Homer's description of Polyphemus's agony is the earliest literary description of the quenching of carburized iron, or steel. So graphic a simile could only have been created by someone who had himself watched the blacksmith at work. It is such passages that make the study of the Homeric poems so complex and yet so important for understanding the transition from bronze to iron and the beginnings of the Iron Age. Homer, in the *Iliad* and the *Odyssey*, wrote about a period (during and after the Trojan War) at the end of the Late Bronze Age, and bronze is the metal used by his heroes, both Greek and Trojan. But in vivid descriptive passages, such as this one of the Cyclops, Homer frequently draws upon material from his own daily world, the world of the eighth century B.C. In such passages iron suddenly appears as the metal in common use.

The Polyphemus passage is also important for what it

tells us about the development of iron technology. The fact that it was possible to harden a material by plunging it into water was obviously a puzzle to Homer. The Greek word that describes this peculiar property of carburized iron (and only carburized iron, because quenching would not change the properties of wrought iron) is translated here as "doctoring" but is etymologically related to English words such as pharmacy. Homer and the inhabitants of Dark Age Greece must have seen the transformation of carburized iron through quenching as something bordering on the magical. They did not understand the exact nature of the physical change created by the act, but they recognized that somehow the metal had been transformed.

southwestern part of the island that witnessed the first arrival of the Greek colonists.

The influence of these Greek colonists can be seen in the pottery and the architecture as well as in the iron artifacts of 12th century Cyprus. Contemporaneous iron objects from Cyprus and from the Aegean suggest a common cultural and ironworking heritage for that area. For instance, consider the one-edged curved knife of iron having a hilt of bone or ivory fastened with three bronze rivets, examples of which have been found at numerous eastern Mediterranean sites. The combination of metals may be a result of the fact that bronze rivets, unlike iron ones, could be cold-worked, thus preventing damage to the delicate ivory hilt. But the combination suggests a certain conti-

nuity between bronze and iron cultures and supports the contention that iron technology developed in areas where Bronze Age culture, including a bronze metalworking industry, survived.

Such iron knives with bronze rivets have been found in 12th to early 11th century contexts throughout the Aegean and the eastern Mediterranean, from Perati in Attica to Hama in Syria, almost always* uncovered in association with typical Mycenaean IIIC1 pottery of the 12th century B.C. (or its local imitations). Such an iron knife was recently found at the Philistine site of Tell Qasile, again in a

*The exception is an iron knife from Hama which was not found in this Mycenaean IIIC1 context.

A crucible *in which bronze was heated to molten temperatures. Found at Ayia Irini, a Late Bronze Age (15th century B.C.) site on the island of Kea, Greece, this clay crucible still bears flakes of pale green bronze. Under its thick rim at right is a spout through which the bronze was poured into a mold.*

12th century B.C. context and at a site having very strong connections with Cyprus, especially Kition, and with the Aegean.

From the so-called "500" cemetery at the Philistine site of Tell el-Far'ah (south), another site with strong Aegean connections, come several 12th century B.C. iron objects, including a dagger from Tomb 542. We have not studied this dagger, but an iron knife with one bronze rivet from Tomb 562, dating from the 11th century B.C., proved to be made of carburized iron presenting a metallurgical structure that strongly suggested deliberate carburization.

From Cyprus we have even better evidence for the development of a sophisticated iron technology. In 1971 the Swedish metallurgist Erik Tholander analyzed a curved iron knife from a tomb at Idalion and found it to be made of quench-hardened steel. We have now confirmed Tholander's results, working with another sample from the same knife, and have at the same time greatly expanded the evidence for the use of carburized iron from sites scattered all over the southern half of the island, including Kouklia-Skales (Palaepaphos), Amathus, Idalion and Kition, as well as from Lapithos in the north. All this evidence for carburization comes from 11th century B.C. contexts.

We have very little metallurgical evidence for the state of ironworking technology in the 12th century B.C. We do have a number of surviving iron objects from Canaanite, Philistine, and Israelite sites,[4] but with two exceptions, no scientific studies have been carried out on any of these 12th century pieces. One exception is a knife from Tell Qasile which proved, unfortunately, to be totally corroded. The other exception is somewhat extraordinary—an iron pick found in 1976 by a young Israeli archaeologist, David Davis, excavating on behalf of the Israeli Department of Antiquities at Har Adir, near Sasa in the Upper Galilee. The iron pick is in a remarkable state of preservation and clearly dates to the early 12th, perhaps even the 13th century B.C. We are working with the excavator on the publication of this pick, which to date remains unpublished, but even now we can state that our metallurgical analysis of the iron indicates that the manufacturer of the pick had knowledge of the full range of ironworking skills associated with the production of quench-hardened steel. The pottery from the site associated with the pick reflects close connections with the island of Cyprus.

Thus the 12th and 11th century iron objects that have been found throughout the eastern Mediterranean all come from sites that have in common an international milieu, and more particularly some sort of contact with the Aegean and Cyprus. The archaeological evidence also indicates some degree of continuity, perhaps even the survival of metalworking traditions, from the more sophisticated world of the Late Bronze Age. The only exceptions to these general propositions are the Early Israelite sites located just to the north of Jerusalem: Ai, Khirbet Raddana, and Tell el-Ful (ancient Gibeah where an 11th century iron plowshare was found). At these sites iron appears in a context independent of any evidence for contact with the outside world. They also represent new settlements with no Bronze Age metalworking traditions.

An essentially Bronze Age culture continued to survive in the Aegean at a number of sites—the Ionian islands, the southeastern part of the Greek mainland (eastern Attica and Euboea), and in some of the larger islands such as Crete, Rhodes and Naxos. This was also true in Cyprus. In Palestine this same continuity can be seen in the northern Canaanite cities, like Megiddo (stratum VIIA) and Taanach (period IB) in the Jezreel Valley, and at Beth-Shean (stratum VI).*

Both in the northern and central parts of Palestine, the Israelites were initially limited to the occupation of isolated sites in the hills (such as Izbet Sartah)** because they could not conquer the rich cities in the plain below. The sons of Joseph complained to Joshua that:

"The highlands are not enough for us, and what is more, all the Canaanites living in the plain have iron chariots, and so have those in Beth-Shean and its dependent towns, and those in the plain of Jezreel." (Joshua 17:16, *Jerusalem Bible* translation)

Joshua replied that:

"A mountain shall be yours; it is covered with woods, but you must clear it, and its boundaries shall be yours, since you cannot drive out the Canaanite because of his iron chariots and his superior strength." (Joshua 17:18, *Jerusalem Bible* translation)

This tradition is found throughout the Conquest narratives. The Israelites, as a loose confederation of tribes, lacked the military technology necessary to conquer the fortified Canaanite cities of the plain. The technological superiority of the Canaanites is dramatized in this passage from Joshua by the emphasis upon their possession of "chariots of iron." Jabin, the king of Canaan who reigned at Hazor, is said to have possessed a force that included 900 chariots of iron. (Judges 4:3)

These passages from Joshua and Judges referring to "iron chariots" and "chariots of iron" present some problems—both metallurgical and chronological. No one actually had chariots of iron. The *Jerusalem Bible* translates one passage of Judges 4 as chariots "plated with iron." In Joshua, it translates simply "iron chariots." The translation "plated with iron" is really an interpretation without textual support. The words "plated with" were simply supplied by the translator. It is extremely difficult to plate with iron. These "chariots of iron" must be regarded as a poetical and psychological description of the latest in military hardware, combining chariots, the most formidable aspect of all Late Bronze Age armies, with iron, the latest addition to the military arsenal and a metal that was just starting to make its impact upon the military world of the Early Iron Age. The actual use of iron must have been confined to fittings, such as the hubs of the chariot's wheels, perhaps even parts of the wheel itself. (The same explanation probably applies to the iron bedstead of Og, king of Bashan, in Deuteronomy 3:11.) Such iron chariot fittings have been recovered at Taanach, but unfortunately in an uncertain archaeological context.

The chronological problem unsolved in these Biblical references to chariots of iron is that they appear to date to the 12th century at the latest. The excavator of Hazor, Yigael Yadin, dates the Israelite destruction of Hazor to about 1230 B.C. A 13th century date for this destruction is

now universally accepted.† Yet the use of iron for offensive weapons cannot be documented before the 12th century, and really not before the 11th. Perhaps in one way or another, the Conquest Narratives describe the world of the 12th to early 11th century B.C., although some events may have occurred earlier.

In any event the present evidence indicates that iron technology developed in Palestine in the 12th century at the earliest, stimulated by the arrival of the Philistines and other Sea Peoples who brought with them the inspiration, and perhaps even the new technology from the Aegean area. We have already examined the evidence for the development of iron technology in the Aegean area as well as the impressive recent evidence for the extensive use of iron in 12th to early 11th century Cyprus.

Trude Dothan has recently examined in these pages the Aegean origins of the Philistines.†† We may therefore be brief here: According to the Bible the Philistines came from Caphtor (Amos 9:7), long identified as the Biblical name for the island of Crete. Other traditions (Zephaniah 2:5 and Ezekiel 25:16) link the Philistines with the Cherethites, identified as Cretans. The connections between Cyprus and the Philistines are most apparent in the characteristic Philistine style of pottery. The Aegean elements in Philistine pottery, long recognized as being influenced by Mycenaean IIIC1 ceramic traditions, clearly

†† See Dothan, "What We Know About the Philistines," **BAR** July/August 1982.

Two fragmentary tuyeres, *or hollow clay nozzles through which blasts of air entered a Late Bronze Age furnace, flank a crucible fragment. Industrial debris like this found at Bamboula on Cyprus is often discovered during the course of an excavation; it is evidence that some metallurgical operation was conducted at the site, probably involving the melting and casting of copper or bronze.*

Robert Maddin, courtesy Dr. Vassos Karageorghis, Episkopi Museum, Cyprus

*See "The Israelite Occupation of Canaan," by Yohanan Aharoni, **BAR**, May/June 1982, p. 15.

See "An Israelite Village from the Days of the Judges," by Aaron Demsky and Moshe Kochavi, **BAR, September/October 1978.

†See Aharoni, **BAR,** May/June 1982, p. 19.

Limestone molds. *In about 1740 B.C., metal workers at Tell el-Daba in the Eastern Nile Delta cast a variety of copper tools and weapons in these molds. In the stone at left, two chisels and an axe head are clearly outlined. The stone at right includes a knife, a saw and a chisel, and at bottom are two thin harpoons and an adze. Harpoons were used to catch fish and hippopotamus, a popular local dish.*

The metal craftsmen at Tell el-Daba were Canaanites originating most likely from the area of Byblos, an eastern Mediterranean port with a long tradition of copper tool production. In the late Middle Kingdom (c. 1750–1700 B.C.), intensive trade linked the two harbor cities of Byblos and Tell el-Daba and led to the establishment of a major settlement of Byblites at Tell el-Daba. (The dates and interpretation used in this caption are those of the excavator of Tell el-Daba, Manfred Bietak.)

came not from Greece itself, but from the local imitations of Mycenaean wares produced at 12th century B.C. sites in Cyprus. Amihai Mazar has recently excavated three superimposed Philistine temples at Tell Qasile dating from the first half of the 12th century to the middle of the 11th century. (Drawings of plans of these temples appear in **BAR** July/August 1982, pp. 34-35.) He also uncovered a *favissa* of cult objects associated with the second of the three temples. There are very close connections between these Philistine temples and the Philistine cult objects, on the one hand, and a series of so-called shrines or temples excavated recently in Cyprus (Kition), the Greek Islands (Phylakopi or Melos) and the Greek mainland (Mycenae), on the other

hand. Thus it seems reasonable to conclude that the Philistines introduced advanced iron technology into Palestine. What still remains unclear is the formative history of that technology.

In a recent issue of **BAR**, Yohanan Aharoni argued that "thus far no substantial archaeological evidence indicates that iron had been widely used in Philistia before it was widely used at Israelite sites."* This statement in fact misses the point. Aharoni failed to distinguish between the *kinds* of iron artifacts found at Philistine and Israelite sites. Philistine political control of the area of southern Palestine dates from the end of the 12th century B.C. at the earliest. Iron artifacts from the 11th century are to be found at Israelite as well as Philistine sites, but *all of the weapons*— swords, daggers, spearheads—are found at Philistine sites.

This archaeological picture is entirely consistent with the literary tradition preserved in 1 Samuel 13:19-22, quoted at the beginning of this article. In this passage we are told that there were no smiths in the land of Israel because the Philistines were fearful that the Hebrews might make swords or spears. So the Israelites had to come to the Philistines to get their farm implements repaired.

Aharoni rightly points out that the Biblical passage makes no mention of iron—nor of an ironworking monopoly for that matter. But the Israelites obviously had metal

*See Aharoni, "The Israelite Occupation of Canaan," **BAR**, May/June 1982.

farm implements that needed repairing. On the basis of the surviving artifactual evidence, it is reasonable to assume that, by the end of the 11th century B.C. (the time of the reign of Saul), these farm implements were made of iron.

In contrast to the farm implements found at Israelite sites, an important collection of 11th century iron objects, including three daggers and five knives, has been found at Tel Zeror, a site with strong Cypriot connections in the Late Bronze Age. Tel Zeror also had close connections with the Sea Peoples at nearby Tell Dor, known from the Wenamun tale to have been inhabited by the Tjekker (one of the Sea Peoples). Indeed, the inhabitants of Tel Zeror may well have been Sea Peoples (perhaps Philistines).

Aharoni has argued that the absence of iron artifacts in Philistine levels at Ashdod, the most important Philistine site to be excavated in modern times, indicates that the Philistines had no role in the development of early iron metallurgy. This overlooks the fact that at Tel Mor, which served as the harbor for ancient Ashdod, Moshe Dothan (who also excavated Ashdod) found extensive evidence for 12th century B.C. metalworking activity, including tuyères, crucibles and copper spatter, the bits and droplets of copper that fall out when molten copper is poured into a crucible.** True, this all relates not to iron, but to the casting of molten copper, but it indicates the sort of background usually associated with the development of iron metallurgy. Dothan also found iron slag from the 10th century B.C. In addition, at Ashdod itself, Dothan found a single-edged knife from about 1000 B.C. and a large blade-like object and an axe from the end of the 10th century B.C.

What is puzzling—and still difficult to understand—is the distribution of carburized as opposed to noncarburized iron. For example, the iron objects from Philistine Ashdod mentioned above are not carburized at all.

We have analyzed iron objects from several other sites in Palestine, but unfortunately these objects do not include the 12th to early 11th century iron objects from Megiddo. At Taanach, we did extensive work on 10th century iron objects; most showed some degree of carburization. Yet the evidence was not consistent and objects that one would have expected to be made of steel, such as a chisel, were made of wrought iron. Of the two plowshares from Taanach that we examined, one was made of carburized iron, the other was not. We have no explanation for this inconsistency. At Tell Jemmeh, near Gaza, a site we would naturally associate with the Philistines, iron objects probably dating to the 10th century (although some modern investigators date them later) show little or no evidence of carburization. These objects, along with the ones from Ashdod, certainly provide no support for any claim to Philistine superiority in the technology of ironworking. Yet the 11th century iron knife from Tomb 562 at Tell el-Far'ah (south)

showed evidence for carburization, while two others from the contemporaneous Tomb 220 did not—again the same inconsistency as at Taanach. From Tomb 240, probably of the 10th century, an iron dagger presented excellent evidence for carburization.

Clearly, our sample base is still too small to provide data for meaningful conclusions. We can present good arguments for the role of the Philistines in the early development of iron technology, but these arguments can, at present, only be supported, not substantiated by the existing analytical evidence.

Having looked at the objects themselves, let us now consider what little evidence we have relating to iron-working installations. It is sad but true that until the last 20 or 25 years most field archaeologists focused their attention on the excavation of monumental public and administrative buildings, on religious and ceremonial centers, and on cemeteries where there was a good chance of finding rich burial goods. Thus, we still know little about domestic architecture and the routine of daily life, and practically nothing about the industrial centers of the ancient world. Moreover, sometimes what are in fact pottery kilns for firing pottery have been mistakenly described as metalworking installations. Published examples of this error include the so-called "furnaces" from Beth Shemesh stratum IV (room 490) and stratum III (room 441), and from Tell Deir Alla (phase B).†

In the early part of this century, Sir Flinders Petrie excavated some "furnaces" at Tell Jemmeh near Gaza. These furnaces probably date to the 9th to 8th centuries B.C. As Petrie correctly observed, they were forging furnaces, not smelting furnaces. It would be helpful to know more about these discoveries, but unfortunately Petrie published only the briefest account and nothing is left of the remains at the present time.

During the first excavations at Megiddo, 1903-1905, Gottlieb Schumacher identified a blacksmith's workshop consisting of a small room very likely from the Solomonic period. Again, few details were published, apart from references to the discovery of ash and slag and a substance

---

**Our analysis of this material led to the conclusion that Tel Mor served as a recycling or reprocessing center for the impoverished bronze industry of the 12th century B.C.

---

†The "furnaces" at Tell Deir Alla have been related to the passage in 1 Samuel 13: 19-22, as representing one of the places where the Israelites went down to have their metal implements repaired, but the published plans indicate that what was excavated there were pottery kilns of the channel type, best known from second millennium sites on the island of Crete.

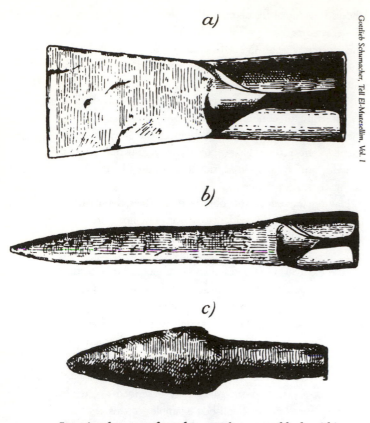

a)

b)

c)

Gottlieb Schumacher, *Tell El-Muessellim, Vol. I*

Iron implements found *in a 10th century blacksmith's workshop at Megiddo: a) a hoe, b) a plowshare, and c) an ox-goad.*

identified as iron ore. Associated with the workshop was a hoard of iron artifacts including a hoe (a), a plowshare (b), and an ox-goad (c). This hoard is very similar to the one from Taanach that we have studied, but, alas, the Megiddo hoard seems to have vanished, so there is no possibility of subjecting it to metallurgical analysis.

To summarize and conclude, the evidence is strong that iron technology developed in the Aegean and was probably brought to Palestine by the Sea Peoples, and perhaps by the Philistines themselves. Based on excavated evidence, it appears that the Philistines did have a monopoly of sorts on ironworking, as reflected in the passage from 1 Samuel. Iron weapons are found at Philistine sites only; at Israelite sites we find iron agricultural implements, as reflected in the literary tradition preserved in the Bible.

In my view, however, the Philistine ironworking monopoly was political, not technological. What is described in the passage from 1 Samuel is not a Philistine technological monopoly supported by metalworking secrets known only to the Philistines. At least at the present, we have no evidence of Philistine ironworking technological superiority; indeed, the evidence regarding deliberate carburization of iron at Philistine sites is inconsistent, some artifacts showing deliberate carburization and others, quite late,

showing no carburization. The restrictions imposed on the Israelites could thus only have been accomplished as a result of Philistine political control. In order to overthrow Philistine political domination, the tribally organized Israelites finally agreed to band together, to elect Saul as king, and to present a united front against the Philistine pentapolis. Finally, in the early 10th century, King David broke the dominion the Philistines had exercised over much of Palestine.

Our analysis indicates that a common typology of iron artifacts is found throughout Palestine, dating at the latest to the end of the 10th century B.C. But at this point in our research we cannot say whether there was a common ironworking technology. At present, the scientific evidence for the early history of ironworking technology is confined to Cyprus and Israel, and even there it is incomplete and inconsistent. We know much more than we did five years ago, but we still have much to learn. We know nothing, for example, about the early period of ironworking in Greece, Turkey or Syria. We have not examined a single piece of iron from Lebanon and we are just beginning to learn something about iron technology in Jordan.

Clearly what is needed is a major international research project designed to explore all facets of the history of early ironworking throughout the ancient world. Until now, our group at the University of Pennsylvania has supplied the entire body of existing scientific evidence relating to ironworking in the eastern Mediterranean during the years 1200-800 B.C. We have, I believe, demonstrated the enormous potential of this research. Whether our project will grow and expand, whether our efforts will encourage other scholars to undertake work in this field remains to be seen.

But we have already advanced beyond the time when Biblical scholars could analyze passages like 1 Samuel 13:19-22 in blissful ignorance of everything except philology. The Biblical authors had a multi-faceted view of their world—of its domestic and industrial life as well as its monuments and ceremonies. It is time that modern scholars attempt to reach the same level of competence. We must strive to recreate, through all the means at our disposal, a world that was taken for granted by its contemporary inhabitants.

[1] Ernst Weidner, "Ausden Tageneines assyrischen Schattenkonigs," *Archiv fur Orientforschung*, Vol. X, pp. 1-48.

[2] W.G. Lambert, *Babylonian Wisdom Literature*, Oxford University Press, 1960, pp. 146-147, lines 51-52.

[3] R.J. Forbes, "The Coming of Iron," *Jaarbericht . . . Ex Orient Lux*, 9-10 (1944-48 [1952]), pp. 207-14.

[4] Trude Dothan, *The Philistines and Their Material Culture* (Yale University Press, 1982), p. 92, Table 1; and Jane Waldbaum, *From Bronze to Iron* (Gotebörg, Sweden: 1978).

How Water Tunnels Worked

Jerusalem, Megiddo, Hazor, Gezer and Gibeon all had systems to bring water safely within their city walls during time of siege—Cole offers new suggestions on how this technology developed.

By Dan Cole

"A CITY SET ON A HILL cannot be hidden," said Matthew (5:14). Neither can it easily be supplied with water.

Cities were built on hilltops because of the obvious defensive advantages. These advantages were somewhat offset by the disadvantage that the city's springs or wells were normally at the base of the hill, outside the city walls. As the size of urban populations grew and the height of the cities themselves grew through successive rebuildings—creating higher and higher "tells"—the water supply moved progressively farther away.

In peacetime, this distance was merely an inconvenience for women and slaves; in time of war, it could be a fatal weakness. Under siege the city could be deprived of its water supply. No city can last for long without water.

Because almost no rain falls from March until October Palestinian cities were particularly vulnerable to prolonged sieges. Cisterns and other rain collectors inside the city walls were not replenished for six months or more.

Some ancient Departments of Defense solved the problem of bringing fresh water inside the city walls by means of massive engineering projects involving tunnels and shafts hewn through bedrock beneath their cities.*

Over the past century archaeologists have uncovered a dozen examples of such ambitious projects at various cities in ancient Israel. Now, a sufficient number of these engineering operations have been revealed to enable us to begin to reconstruct the

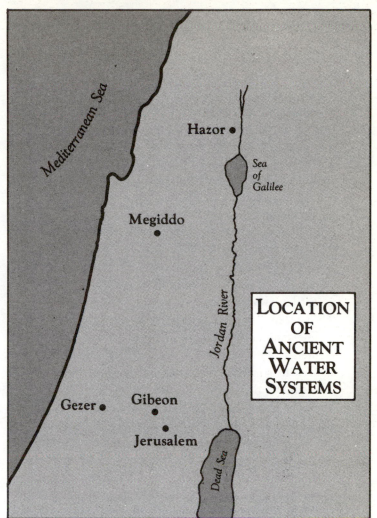

LOCATION OF ANCIENT WATER SYSTEMS

---

* For the sake of clarity, the term "tunnel" will be reserved for *horizontal* cuttings, "shaft" for *vertical* ones, and "stepped tunnel" for *angling* ones.

Hazor—*A young workman stands near the rubble-filled entrance of the great 9th century B.C. tunnel.*

Archaeologist Yigael Yadin came to Hazor expecting to find a water system comparable to the one discovered at Megiddo: that is, a vertical shaft, inside the city walls, connected to a tunnel leading to a spring outside the city.

Yadin found the Hazor water shaft and tunnel, but instead of leading toward a water source outside the city wall, the tunnel descended to the water table beneath the city. The confident tunneling of these ancient Israelite engineers suggests that they knew that by heading toward the water table, they could create a water system which would be completely enclosed and secure within the city walls.

development of hydraulic technology in ancient Palestine.

Probably the most famous of these water systems are the two cut into the Ophel Hill of Jerusalem (the so-called City of David). The earlier system is "Warren's Shaft" (named for Charles Warren, who discovered it in 1867); it is also referred to as the "Jebusite Shaft" on the common assumption that it dates to the pre-10th century B.C. Jebusite city.* This system consisted of four elements. 1. A *tunnel* which was cut to direct water from the plentiful Gihon Spring (in the Kidron Valley east of the city hill), into a chamber deep within the hill. 2. A *stepped tunnel* which was cut downward from the street level behind the city's defense wall and which led to 3. *an almost horizontal tunnel ramp* running out under the city wall to a point directly above the water chamber where 4. *a shaft* connected the end of this upper tunnel to the water chamber. A jar could then be lowered down the shaft by a rope and filled from the

---

* There are reasons to question this early a dating, but they need not concern us here.

spring-fed chamber below.*

Later—in the 8th century B.C.—King Hezekiah replaced this earlier water system with a 1750-foot tunnel under the city which was cut by two crews starting at either end (see p. 255). This underground tunnel was graded or slanted so that it carried the water from the Gihon Spring, located outside the walls, to a pool inside the city. (See "How the Blind See the Holy Land" BAR May/June 1979; "Queries & Comments," BAR November/December 1979, pp. 8-9, and Hershel Shanks, The City of David, (The Biblical Archaeology Society, 1975).)

Next to Jerusalem, the best-known Israelite water system is the shaft and tunnel at Megiddo,[1] which writer James Michener incorporated into his fictional "Tell Makor" in his novel The Source (see p. 256).

The famous Megiddo water system involved two elements (see plan on p. 249): First, a large vertical shaft with steps cut down around its sides was sunk through the debris layers of earlier periods into the bedrock, going down 115 feet to the level of an already-known nearby spring. Second, a horizontal tunnel, 200 feet long, was dug, running from the bottom of the shaft out under the city wall to connect

---

* This shaft and tunnel system has been described and illustrated in "Digging in the City of David," July/August 1979 BAR.

How to Read Plans and Sections

The plans and sections printed with this article are the tools of professional archaeologists. We have attempted to use them to give the reader a three-dimensional picture of a site.

A plan is a picture which shows what is seen when looking straight down at the site. The limitation of a plan is that it cannot show depth: thus the height of two walls cannot be compared.

The function of a section drawing is to show the vertical relationship of the structures excavated at a site. A section drawing takes a vertical slice through an area. This slice may be taken through any two points on the plan at any angle. This means there are an infinite number of possible section drawings. That is why it is important to indicate on the plan where the slice or section was made.

On our plans of Hazor and Gezer the points marked A-A on the plan show the position of the section. The slice is taken from one A to the other A.

Jerusalem—Before the 10th century B.C. the Jebusites settled near the plentiful water supply of the Spring Gihon (1) on the Hill of Ophel. They constructed a water system with four elements: a tunnel (3) cut into the hill to direct water from the spring into a chamber (4) within the hill; a stepped or sloping tunnel (8) cut downward from street level (9) behind the Jebusite city wall (10); an almost horizontal tunnel (7) passing under the city wall to a point above the spring filled chamber (4), and a shaft (5) connecting the end of the upper tunnel to the chamber below. Water carriers could stand at the top of the shaft (6) and lower buckets to bring up water.

In the 8th century B.C. King Hezekiah built a graded 1750 foot tunnel (14) under the city. It carried the water of the Spring Gihon (1), located outside the city wall, to a pool (16) located inside the city. A portion of this tunnel (15) nearest to the spring was part of the earlier Jebusite system.

---

with the spring. As at Jerusalem, this tunnel was cut by two teams of pick men working toward each other, one from the bottom of the shaft and the other from the spring.

Dating an ancient water system which is cut into bedrock is no easy task. The pottery and other objects found in it can only suggest when it went out of use, not when it was originally constructed. The most reliable indication of the date of construction comes from the stratigraphy at the entrance to the system inside the city. It is a safe assumption that a shaft was cut after the latest stratum of the tell through which it cuts. This is not helpful, however, for dating a later system where ancient erosion has destroyed the uppermost strata.

The University of Chicago team which excavated Megiddo in the late 1920's dated its water system to the 12th century B.C. because the latest stratum clearly cut by the shaft dated to that time. Unfortunately, several later occupation levels had eroded from around the top of the shaft, as we now know from other areas of the mound; the shaft should have been connected stratigraphically with the so-called "Solomonic stables" which the excavators uncovered immediately to the east of the shaft and with the inset-offset* city wall which they traced around the

---

* An "inset-offset" wall is one which has periodic zigzag vertical cutbacks along its face. This device gave defenders a line of fire against attackers at the base of their wall; it became popular in Israel in the 9th century B.C.

JEBUSITE *(pre-10th century B.C.)* AND HEZEKIAH'S *(8th century B.C.)* WATER SYSTEMS

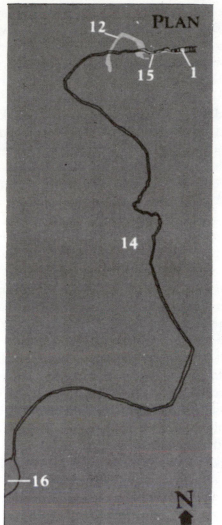

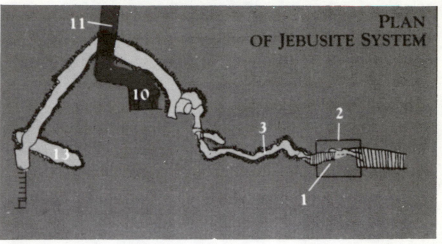

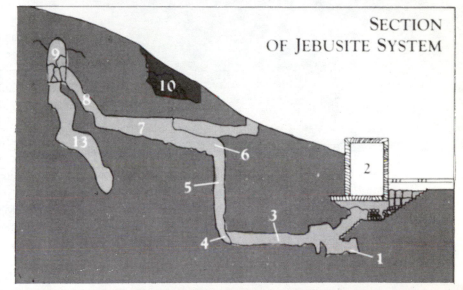

1. Spring Gihon
2. Modern house
3. Spring-filled tunnel
4. Water chamber
5. Shaft
6. Place from which bucket was lowered to water below
7. Horizontal tunnel
8. Stepped-tunnel

9. Entrance to Jebusite tunnel
10. Jebusite wall
11. Probable course of Jebusite wall
12. Successful shaft and tunnel system
13. First unsuccessful Jebusite shaft
14. Hezekiah's Tunnel (8th century B.C.)
15. Tunnel common to Hezekiah's and Jebusite systems
16. Pool of Siloam

Megiddo— *The water gallery is a narrow passage made of well-dressed ashlar stones. It is just over three feet wide and up to six feet tall and originally was roofed. The gallery started inside the city, then cut through the 10th century B.C. Solomonic casemate wall, and ended at a point above the spring outside the city wall on the southwest slope of the mound. From there, stairs, which were probably hidden with a covering of wood and earth, linked the gallery to the spring chamber entrance.*

In the 9th century B.C. the Solomonic gallery was blocked and covered over by a solid "inset-offset" wall— probably at the same time that the shaft-and-tunnel water system was engineered.

mound from the Solomonic gateway on the north. Had Chicago's excavators correctly connected the water shaft to the "Solomonic stables" and to the inset-offset wall, they would have dated the water shaft not to the 12th century B.C., but to the Solomonic period (10th century B.C.). This dating however, would also have been wrong, because the "Solomonic stables" and the inset-offset wall with which it was associated proved not to be Solomonic at all, but in fact dated to the 9th century B.C. In the late 1950's Yigael Yadin became suspicious of the Megiddo excavators' date for the inset-offset city wall and the buildings (including the "Solomonic stables") related to it. Digging at Hazor, Yadin had found that the 10th century Solomonic gateway (strikingly similar to Megiddo's) had been connected to a casemate wall* *over which* a solid inset-offset wall had been laid in a 9th century rebuilding of the city (presumably by King Ahab).[2] Yadin reasoned that if at Hazor a Solomonic gateway was connected to a casemate wall over which a solid inset-offset wall was built a century later, the same thing was probably true at Megiddo.

Yadin re-investigated the Megiddo walls in the 1960's and clearly demonstrated that the inset-offset wall (and the so-called "Solomonic stables") belonged to a rebuilding of the city after Solomon. Yadin uncovered at Megiddo, as he had at Hazor, beneath the inset-offset wall, a casemate wall from King Solomon's time (10th century B.C.) which connected to the Solomonic gate in its initial phase.[3]

The Megiddo water system was not, however, the only water system in evidence at the site: the Chicago excavators found earlier, less technically developed water systems at Megiddo. One, just north of the 9th century B.C. water shaft is known as the "gallery"—a narrow passage leading from inside the city, through the earlier Solomonic casemate city wall. This gallery was directly above an old entrance to the same spring which the later shaft and tunnel system served. Steps descended from the end of the gallery, down the slope to this old spring entrance. A wood and earth roofing originally concealed the steps leading down the slope to the spring entrance.[4]

---

* A casemate wall consists of two parallel walls connected by periodic cross walls. The effect is to create a line of narrow rectangular rooms, but the main purpose probably was to provide a wall system with sufficient space on the top for defenders to maneuver easily. We know that this wall style was most characteristic of Israel in the 10th century B.C.

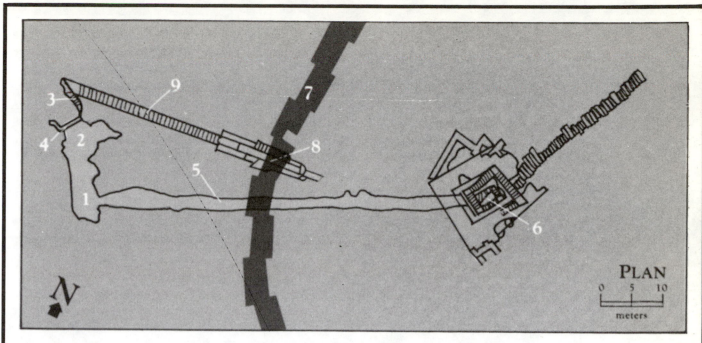

THE MEGIDDO WATER SYSTEMS

1. Spring
2. Spring chamber
3. Pre-10th century B.C. stairs to spring chamber
4. 9th century B.C. blocking wall at entrance to chamber

5. 9th century B.C. tunnel
6. 9th century B.C. stepped shaft
7. 9th century B.C. inset-offset wall
8. Solomonic (10th century B.C.) gallery
9. Solomonic (10th century B.C.) covered stairway

At the base of the slope, this covered stairway had connected with an even earlier set of steps. These steps descended into the face of the hillside to a water chamber cut out of bedrock around the spring.

Thus we can now reconstruct three stages of the water system at Megiddo: 1. Sometime in the Late Bronze or Early Iron Age—surely before the 10th century B.C. gallery—steps were cut into the base of the slope down to a natural spring; the area of the spring was enlarged by a chamber cut out of the bedrock. 2. When Solomon fortified the city in the 10th century, a narrow passageway or gallery led from inside the city, through the Solomonic casemate wall to a point above the spring; from there stairs, which were probably covered, led down the slope and connected the gallery to the old spring chamber entrance. 3. In the 9th century B.C., King Ahab replaced this system with the huge vertical shaft inside the city and the horizontal tunnel system leading from the shaft to the spring.

After King Ahab's shaft and tunnel were cut, the old stepped entrance to the spring could be blocked

Megiddo—The first of three water systems at this site was constructed before the 10th century B.C. It was very simple. It consisted of a stairway (3) at the base of the tell descending to the spring chamber (2) which was filled by a spring (1). To obtain water, one had to go outside the city walls.

King Solomon constructed the second water system in the 10th century B.C. as part of his large fortified city. He cut a gallery (8) through the casemate city wall extending from inside the city to the outside. (Here the casemate is covered by the later inset-offset wall (7).) Camouflaged with a dirt and wood roof, the gallery led to a set of stairs (9) which were also covered. These stairs joined the earlier set of stairs (3) which in turn connected with the spring at the base of the tell.

The latest water system at Megiddo was constructed by King Ahab in the 9th century B.C. A shaft (6) 115 feet deep was sunk inside the city. At the bottom of the shaft, a 200-foot long tunnel (5) led to the spring chamber (2) at the base of the hill. To prevent entrance into Ahab's water system from outside the city walls, the earlier hillside entrance to the spring chamber was blocked by a wall (4).

Megiddo— *The 9th century B.C. water tunnel is part of the latest and most technologically advanced of Megiddo's three water systems. To create this 200 foot long passageway, two teams of workers, one starting at the bottom of a 115 foot deep shaft behind the city walls, and one starting at the base of the hill by the spring, dug toward one another through the hill. By descending the shaft and walking through this underground tunnel, the residents of the city could reach the spring. Thus, during times of siege, water could be drawn without going outside the city walls.*

Hazor—*An aerial view of the shaft and stairs. The three people standing on the stairs provide a scale for the massive shaft.*

up to prevent access from the outside. In fact, the excavators found this entrance blocked by a wall of huge stones.*

The steps of this outside entrance are now unblocked, so the modern visitor to Megiddo can enter the water system from inside the city, climbing down the 9th century shaft and follow the tunnel to the spring and then exit by way of the much earlier steps leading out to the base of the hill.

As we have seen, Yadin used what he had learned on his Hazor excavations to redate at Megiddo the inset-offset wall, the "stables" and therefore the water system with which it was associated, all to the 9th century B.C. Conversely, when Yadin returned to Hazor for renewed excavations in 1968, he was able to use the Megiddo water system to help him find a similar water system at Hazor.[5]

Yadin reasoned that Israelite Hazor *should* have had a comparable water system to Megiddo's because of Hazor's strategic military position controlling major highways and because of its strong fortifications in the 10th and 9th centuries B.C. Having already exposed a palace within the walls at the western end of the mound and having found the Iron Age city gate on the east, Yadin deduced that the only available place for a water shaft (and the most likely place based on the mound's present topography) was midway along the south side of the tell.

A shallow depression in the mound at this point confirmed this reasoning. The depression was comparatively close to a wadi below, where water still flows today. In addition, earlier soundings in the depression had revealed no structures, only a deep fill. In short, it seemed the perfect place for an Iron Age water shaft.

Removing the tons of debris which had gradually filled the shaft after the 8th century B.C. destruction of Israelite Hazor was a mammoth operation and something of an act of faith on Yadin's part. But his hunch was right. The water shaft was there. In the upper portion it was similar to the water shaft at Megiddo. As at Megiddo, it proved to have been dug *after* Solomon's time, since the ramp leading down to

---

* Sometime after the 9th century B.C. shaft/tunnel system was cut, the tunnel was deepened and graded so that the water then flowed from the spring to the base of the shaft inside the city. This saved steps for the water carriers who no longer had to walk through the tunnel, but the arrangement apparently proved unsatisfactory. Perhaps the water became fouled at the shaft end since it had no place to flow off. So the tunnel floor was again recut and regraded so the spring water no longer flowed to the base of the shaft.

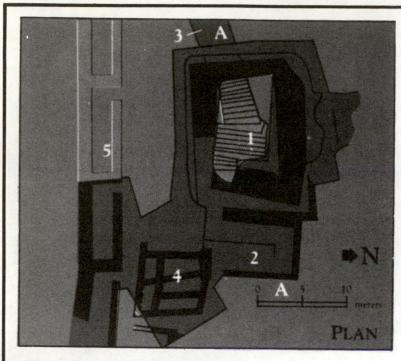

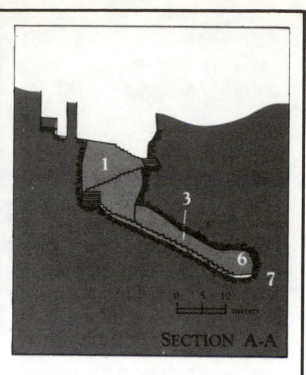

THE HAZOR SHAFT/TUNNEL

A-A mark position of the section

1. Rock-hewn shaft with steps
2. Entrance structure
3. Stepped (or sloping) tunnel leading to water table
4. 9th century B.C. 4-room Israelite house
5. 10th century B. C. Solomonic casemate wall
6. Chamber on water table
7. Pool on water table

Hazor— *This water system was built in the 9th century B.C. some time after the completion of the Gibeon water system.*

Five flights of stairs encircling the shaft (1), led to the entrance of a stepped sloping tunnel (3) at the bottom of the shaft. The tunnel descends an additional 65 feet before reaching the water table chamber (6) 125 feet deep under the Hazor streets.

The Hazor engineers may have learned the stepped-tunnel-to-water-table technique from Gibeon where the latest water system used this technology. The engineering at Hazor appears confident and purposeful—not accidental.

the shaft and the retaining walls around it cut through buildings containing 10th century pottery. Moreover, these buildings were clearly associated with the 10th century casemate wall along the south slope of the mound. So the water shaft must have been dug *after* the 10th century.

More than 95 feet below the surface, Yadin finally reached the bottom of the shaft. Next he expected to find a tunnel branching off from the shaft to the south, in the direction of the water source *outside* the city, as was the case at Megiddo. This time his expectation proved wrong. Instead, he found a stepped tunnel leading *down* to the west, going 80 feet farther into the heart of the bedrock beneath the tell. There, indeed, Yadin found water—as had Ahab's engineers 2800 years before: the natural water table over 130 feet below the city street!

Ahab's engineers at Hazor apparently knew in advance that if they dug deep enough into the hill they would strike water; there is no evidence of false starts or fumbling on the part of Ahab's diggers.

The Hazor shaft and stepped tunnel system was completely secure from an enemy because it was all inside the walls. It was thus a considerable improve-

Hazor — In this aerial view, the reader can appreciate the bottleshape of the tell. As seen here, the "bottle" is upside down. The dark depression in the light excavated area of the tell is the entrance to the shaft which was carved from bedrock in the 9th century B.C. At times of siege, the inhabitants of Hazor could draw water, without emerging from the protective city walls, by descending this shaft to a connecting tunnel which led underground to the water chamber.

At the narrow end of the "bottle" is a small part of the glacis which enclosed the "lower city," inhabited only in the Middle Bronze Age (18th through 13th centuries B.C.); to the left of the glacis is a dark area which was once a moat.

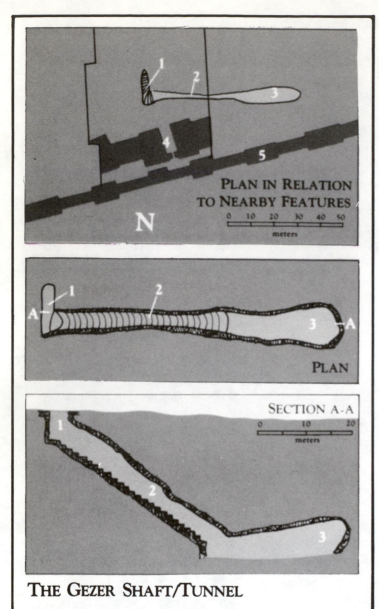

In the 14th or 9th century B.C., a shaft (1) was sunk 35 feet into the ground. From it a sloping stepped tunnel (2) 48 feet long was carved. The tunnel terminated in a chamber (3) on the water table. The engineers of the Gezer water system probably knew before they began this project that they would find water if they dug deeply enough, suggesting that the people of Gezer may have learned the stepped-tunnel-to-water-table technology from other Mediterranean civilizations or from a similar discovery at another Israelite site such as Gibeon.

PLAN IN RELATION TO NEARBY FEATURES

0 10 20 30 40 50
meters

N

PLAN

SECTION A-A

0 10 20
meters

THE GEZER SHAFT/TUNNEL

1. Rock-cut shaft
2. Stepped (or sloping) tunnel
3. Chamber on water table
4. Southern Gate in Middle Bronze wall
5. Late Bronze wall (initial phase built c. 1400 B.C.)

ment over the water system at Megiddo (and at Jerusalem, for that matter).

A military man himself, Yadin was immediately aware of the strategic importance of this ancient technological advance. He realized that as soon as hydraulic engineers at one city discovered the water table beneath their city, this type of water system would be copied and used elsewhere if conditions permitted. (It is unlikely that the discovery was made at Hazor because the Hazor engineers seemed to know ahead of time just what they were doing). This realization led Yadin to reexamine the date which had been assigned to still another water tunnel, one that R.A.S. Macalister had discovered at the beginning of this century at Gezer.

Macalister excavated at Gezer from 1902 to 1909. There he found a step-lined shaft which led into a tunnel, also stepped, which sloped downward into the heart of the hill until it ended in a long chamber at the water table level.[6] All this was inside the city wall. Macalister dated the tunnel to his "Second Semitic" period—which we now call the Middle Bronze Age—about 1650 B.C. Macalister's dating was based principally on some Mycenaean sherds from his "Third Semitic" period (the Late Bronze Age, 1550 B.C.—1200 B.C.), which he had found in the debris from the tunnel. He thought the tunnel must have pre-dated the pot sherds debris found in the tunnel. He was, however, wrong. We now realize that in the erosion that occurs after the breakdown of the retaining walls around the top of a shaft, sherds from almost any period can and often do make their way into the shaft cavity.

Yadin's excavation of the Hazor shaft suggested to him that Gezer's tunnel really belonged to a later period. He argued that the Gezer shaft and stepped tunnel, like the Hazor shaft and stepped tunnel,

Jerusalem — *Waist deep in the water of the Spring Gihon, a young man stands between the well-hewn walls of Hezekiah's Tunnel. Carved in the 8th century B.C. this impressive engineering project carried the water of the Spring Gihon which is outside the city to a pool within the defensive walls of the city.*

reflected the engineer's knowledge that the water table could be reached inside the city. Since this technology, once discovered, was likely to be copied at various sites, Yadin expected that the Gezer tunnel should be dated close to the period of the Hazor water system, which he had clearly dated to the 9th century B.C.[7]

William Dever, who directed renewed excavations at Gezer from 1965 to 1971, maintained, however, that the Gezer water system probably dated to the Late Bronze Age.[8] He thought the Middle Bronze city gateway too close to the shaft head to date the construction that early. On the other hand, Dever pointed out, Iron Age walls appear on Macalister's plans above the area of the shaft, suggesting the water

system had gone out of use before that time.* Therefore he thought the Late Bronze Age the most likely candidate for the Gezer water system.

Because Macalister had cut through all the building layers around the head of the water shaft at Gezer, there is no way to obtain new stratigraphic evidence to determine the last stratum through which the shaft was originally cut. This, unfortunately, is the only way to confidently date the system.

But whether the Gezer water system dates from the Late Bronze Age, as Dever argues, or from the Iron II

---

* I am not convinced by Dever's argument against a 9th century date. One of the Iron Age walls which on Macalister's plan appears above the shaft looks as if it could have been a retaining wall around the top of the shaft steps.

255

Age, as Yadin aruges, Yadin's basic thesis still remains viable. Perhaps the stairs-to-water-table concept was known as early as the Late Bronze Age at such a major Canaanite city as Gezer. The Late Bronze II Age was a period of active trade among eastern Mediterranean cultures. Fine Mycenaen pottery from this period has been found in Palestine and Egypt and large Canaanite storage jars have turned up in Greece. Ideas as well as merchandise travel the same trade routes. We know that in this period Mycenae, Athens, and other cities in Greece had water stairs inside their walls which cut directly to the water table rather than out to springs. Thus, the Canaanites could well have learned from the Mycenaeans this technique of digging down to the water table inside the city walls.

The Gezer water system could have been dug at Canaanite Gezer in the Late Bronze II Age; it could then have been abandoned and choked with rubble at the end of the Bronze Age and have remained that way through the 12th-11th century B.C. Philistine occupation. Perhaps the top of the water shaft was still visible during later periods, but Israelite engineers of the 10th or 9th century B.C. would not have known about the water table concept on which this underground water system was based. In short, Israelite engineers may have had to rediscover this knowledge. Yadin may therefore still be correct in stating that once the stairs-to-water table concept was discovered (or rediscovered) by the Israelites in Iron II, this idea was likely to be quickly copied in other

Gibeon — *Jar handles inscribed with the word "Gibeon" were found in the debris of the water shaft. Written from right to left in 7th century B.C. Hebrew script, many of the inscriptions on the handles have next to the word "Gibeon" the phrase, "the enclosed vineyard" and the name of the owner of the vineyard. The discovery of an extensive wine production and storage complex at Gibeon confirmed that the Gibeonites stored wine in the jars to which the inscribed handles were once attached.*

Megiddo — *The tell overlooks the Jezreel Valley where ancient and modern armies clashed and where today fields of wheat, corn, cotton, and sugar beets blanket its well-watered plains. The fortified 20-acre site protects the outlet of the Wadi 'Ara, a pass connecting the Mediterranean coastal road with routes continuing to the north and east.*

The dark depression at the base of the light-colored excavated areas (right, center) is the 115-foot-deep shaft King Ahab constructed in the 9th century B.C. This shaft connects to an underground tunnel which leads to the spring at the base of the hill. Directly below the shaft is a short incision which is the 10th-century B.C. Solomonic water gallery (see p. 248). Directly below the gallery is a spring, the ancient city's life supply.

In the upper right half of the picture and directly behind the depression of the water shaft is another round depression marking an Iron II Israelite grain silo.

Israelite cities of the period. Thus, other Israelite water systems of this type probably should be dated to about the same time as Hazor's 9th century B.C. system.

Naturally, it would be interesting to know where the Hazor engineers got their stairs-to-water-table concept. In other words, where was this type of water system *first* used by the Israelites?

A re-study of the complicated water systems and associated excavations at Gibeon (modern el-Jib) suggests to me that it was at Gibeon that Israelite engineers discovered—or re-discovered—the possibility of locating a source of fresh water inside the city, safe from enemy control during a siege.

The discovery of a huge pool-like shaft at Gibeon in 1956 came as a complete surprise, both to the excavators (led by James B. Pritchard of the University

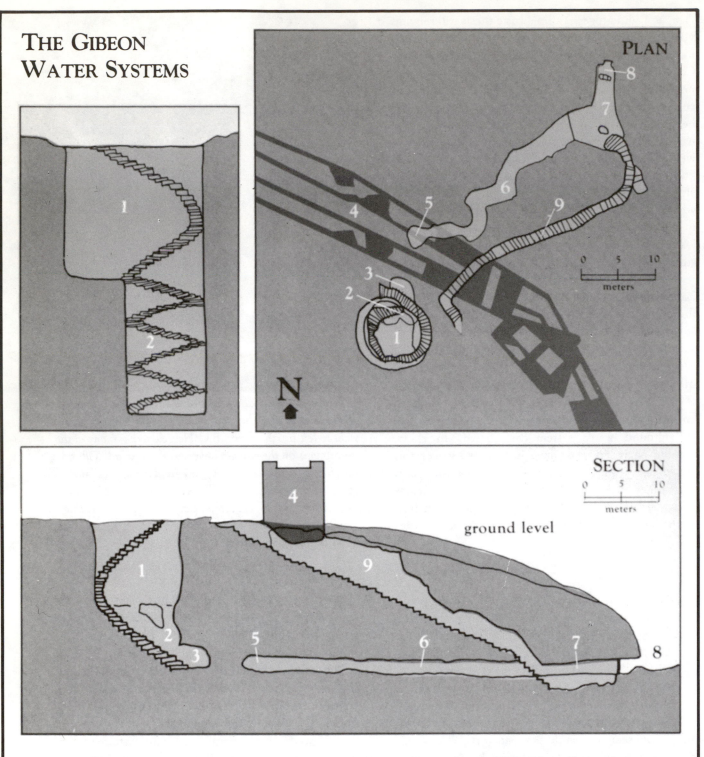

THE GIBEON WATER SYSTEMS

PLAN

N

SECTION

ground level

1. Pre-10th century B.C. "Pool"
2. Stepped shaft to water table
3. Chamber at water table
4. City wall constructed in 12th-10th centuries B.C.
5. Spring
6. Feeder tunnel to increase flow of spring to water chamber
7. Water chamber
8. Outside entrance to water chamber
9. Stepped (or sloping) tunnel from inside city to water chamber

Gibeon — *The earliest of three water systems was the pool, a large cistern which stored rain water (1). The pool was carved from solid rock some time before the 10th century B.C. During the long rainless summers this cistern probably stored an inadequate amount of water for the city.*

The Gibeonites then constructed a second system to increase their water supply. This system consisted of a stepped sloping tunnel (9) leading from just inside the city wall to a water chamber (7) outside the city at the base of the hill. In order to avoid the pool, the upper portion of the stepped tunnel abruptly turned 90 degrees, flush with the city wall after it passed under it. The water chamber at the lower end of the stepped tunnel was filled by fresh water from the spring (5) under the hill. The water flowed from the spring to the water chamber through a feeder tunnel (6) which increased the flow.

After completing this feeder channel, the Gibeonite engineers may have realized that they had tunneled to a point almost directly under their cistern pool. They then decided to dig below the cistern pool to the level of the spring (2), intending to dig a tunnel to the spring. Before reaching the spring they hit the water table, thus discovering an abundant source of water without tunneling to the spring. There they carved out a kidney shaped water chamber (3).

of Pennsylvania), and to the local villagers. It had been completely sealed from view under tons of fill and debris for over two and one-half millennia.[9]

When Pritchard and his colleagues began excavating the site, they were already inclined to identify it as ancient Gibeon, as Edward Robinson had proposed in 1838[10] based on his explorations of the area and the similarity of the modern name (el-Jib) to Gibeon. This identification was confirmed dramatically during the first season of Pritchard's excavation with the discovery of storage jar handles inscribed with the name of Gibeon.[11] (see p. 257).

Pritchard naturally knew about the famous "Pool of Gibeon" which is referred to in 2 Samuel 2:13-17. For a period after King Saul's death (c. 1000 B.C.) David reigned over Judah while Saul's son Ishbosheth ruled over Israel. David's army led by Joab, and Ishbosheth's army led by Abner met at the Pool of Gibeon. Each side appointed 12 young champions who faced each other on either side of the Pool of Gibeon. They were evenly matched, however, and in the bloodbath that ensued all 24 were killed — deciding nothing.

Despite this famous Biblical reference to the Pool of Gibeon, the discovery of the great shaft surprised Pritchard because another plausible candidate for the Pool of Gibeon had already been suggested.

Robinson had noticed on the northeast slope of the hill a large rectangular reservoir (37 x 60 feet across and 8 feet deep) which caught the overflow from a nearby spring. It seemed to him likely that this was the "Pool of Gibeon" mentioned in the Bible. Most scholars who accepted Robinson's identification of the site as Gibeon also accepted his suggestion about the location of the pool. When Pritchard later excavated part of the reservoir, however, he found that none of the pottery sealed beneath the plaster lining pre-dated the Roman period, so the reservoir could not have been a "pool" from King David's time.

Pritchard spent his first days at el-Jib investigating a long-known stepped tunnel which went from the spring at the base of the mound upward into the side of the hill. (This was the same spring which fed the as-yet unexcavated reservoir from the Roman period).

Pritchard had no reason, therefore, to suspect that the site would yield a second water system. The spot where he decided to begin digging on the summit of el-Jib, in fact, was dictated by his desire to uncover the upper end of the stepped tunnel which led from the spring. He found the upper entrance exactly where he expected it, directly inside a massive fortification wall.

He did not, however, expect that less than ten feet beyond the entrance to the stepped tunnel he would encounter the top of another water system, one so ambitious that it would take the rest of that first summer and all of the next to clear. The upper portion alone spanned some 37 feet in diameter and extended 35 feet down. To construct it required the cutting and hauling away of approximately 1100 cubic feet (almost 3,000 tons!) of limestone bedrock. This second water system is now almost universally identified as the Biblical "Pool of Gibeon."

When fully cleared, the "Pool" revealed two distinct segments. The upper portion consisted of a 35-foot-deep cylindrical shaft with almost vertical sides and a relatively flat floor. One descended into the shaft by 40 steps which spiraled down around its side. All but the top three of these steps are cut from the living rock and are approximately five feet wide. They are well cut and not very worn. A low balustrade effect is created by a rim about 20 inches wide and

Hazor — *After completing excavation of the water shaft and tunnel, the archaeologists constructed heavy wooden scaffolds to prevent rocks from falling on visitors. Because they were often immersed in spring water, the steps at the end of the sloping stepped tunnel were made of hard basalt rather than of the softer and faster weathering limestone. These steps are visible in the foreground.*

averaging a foot or so high which was left on the inside edge of the steps. Pritchard suggests that this balustrade might represent the level of the initial workmen's steps cut during the original quarrying out of the shaft.[12]

But the stairs do not end at the floor of the shaft. The steps continue downward for another 45 feet through a narrow, slanted tunnel which spirals down as if following the outline of the broad shaft above. This slanted, stepped tunnel reaches the water table within the hill at step 79, 80 feet below street level. There, a kidney-shaped water chamber had been hollowed out, about 22 feet long and 11 feet wide. (In addition, two small vertical shafts extend down from the floor of the pool shaft to the stepped tunnel, at its mid-point and near its termination. Presumably these had the function of providing light on the tunnel steps (see p. 264).

This shaft/stepped-tunnel system leading to the water table inside the city should not be confused with the other water system at Gibeon. That water system consists of three elements: (1) a 146-foot-long stepped tunnel[13] from inside the city down to a water chamber outside the city walls; (2) the cave-like water chamber with an entrance from outside the hill slope (similar to the earliest system at Megiddo); during times of siege, the entrance to the water chamber could be blocked; (3) a horizontal zigzag tunnel, 110 feet long, following the natural fissures in the bedrock leading to the spring—the source. By following the natural fissures in the rock, the flow from the source to the water chamber would be greatly increased. The source of the spring lies almost directly under the city wall.

Just before the stepped tunnel ends inside the city, it takes a sharp right-angle turn. This brings the entrance of the tunnel and its top steps parallel to and flush with the inside of the city wall. If the stepped tunnel had not taken this right-angle turn, it would have extended into the huge pool-shaft, barely 10 feet away.

Pritchard reasoned that the seemingly inconvenient 90-degree turn at the top of the stepped tunnel was probably necessary to avoid the rim of the pool-shaft. The pool-shaft, Pritchard concluded, must therefore have pre-dated the stepped tunnel system which he dated to the 10th century B.C.

Pritchard's dating of the stepped tunnel was based on the following evidence: just outside the city walls, the stepped tunnel appears to have been deliberately

Gibeon — *The zigzag feeder tunnel was cut from the cave-like water chamber at the base of the tell to the spring under the city wall, so that the spring water would flow more freely into the water chamber. Although the spring is only 94 feet from the water chamber, the feeder tunnel covers about 110 feet. The meandering path of the tunnel suggests that the original diggers followed a trickle of water as it flowed through fissures in the rock.*

opened to the ground slope surface during the cutting, perhaps to make it easier to steer the picking teams. (After completion, the exposed portion of the stepped tunnel was covered with huge slabs and concealed from sight.) The city wall at this point shows two phases. The inner wall is dated, by the latest pottery beneath it, to the Iron I Age (12th-11th centuries B.C.); the outer wall appears to be a strenghtening of the fortifications in the 10th century. Since the stepped tunnel to the spring was cut through the bedrock beneath both *walls* (apparently in order *not* to undermine them), Pritchard concluded that the stepped-tunnel-to-spring system was built after the second of those walls, but probably not by much—i.e., late in the 10th century.

But if the Gibeonites already had a completely secure stairway down to the water table inside the city (the pool-shaft system), why would they later have built a more vulnerable stepped tunnel leading under and outside the city wall? Pritchard answered that perhaps the water flow in the pool-shaft system was not sufficient to meet the city's needs. Such circumstances might have required the cutting of the second stepped tunnel directly to the spring outside the city wall, after which the pool-shaft and its stepped tunnel continued in use only as a supplementary system.

Pritchard recognized that the huge pool-shaft and its lower stepped tunnel represent two distinct phases of construction, but he argued that they are part of a single construction project. He believed that the engineers' intention from the beginning was to cut a broad stairwell to the water table, but that a change in political or economic conditions (a new king? an increase in labor costs?) caused the Gibeonites to alter their plan and to complete the project along less ambitious lines, i.e., by the narrower stepped tunnel instead of by extending the broad and vertical pool-shaft. The threat of an enemy attack could have had the same effect, impelling the Gibeonites to change design in order to speed up the pace of their descent to a secure water source.

Gibeon — *The stepped tunnel, with its 93 steps cut from solid rock, leads underground from a spring chamber at the base of the hill up to the city; it passes beneath the city wall, then opens within the city. Worn stone treads and polished walls are vivid evidence of the nameless carriers of Gibeon who climbed the steps and touched the walls for support as they carried water up into the city.*

Whatever the reasons for the differences between the upper pool-shaft and its lower stepped tunnel, Pritchard was convinced that the two phases of the project were executed relatively closely in time because the steps in the pool-shaft show no more wear than the steps in the stepped tunnel below.

I should like to propose another solution to the Gibeon puzzle. Perhaps the pool-shaft and its continuation, the stepped tunnel that goes to the water table, were two distinct projects separated by a century or more. I suggest that the pool-shaft was originally dug only as a cistern for the collection of rain water—that in David and Abner's time it was indeed a "pool" and nothing more than a pool.[14]

Following this suggestion further, the other stepped tunnel, leading to the spring outside the walls, was built after the pool-shaft in order to supplement the water supply by making the fresh water of the spring accessible inside the city (that is, through the stepped tunnel to the spring).

When, as part of that second project, the Gibeonites cut the horizontal feeder tunnel back into the hill from the spring to increase the flow of water, they certainly must have realized that they had reached a point almost underneath the earlier cistern shaft, which we have been calling the pool-shaft. Note the proximity of the inner end of the feeder tunnel to the area of the pool-shaft. The engineers might have thought that they were closer than, in fact, they were. Because of its zigzag course, the horizontal feeder tunnel extended some 16 feet less in actual distance than its 110-foot length.

The Gibeonites might have decided to cut a stairway tunnel down from the base of their earlier cistern (the pool-shaft) with the intention of reaching the level of the horizontal feeder tunnel and then cutting out horizontally to connect with it. The water chamber at the base of the pool/stepped-tunnel system does, in fact, extend in the direction of the feeder tunnel. Before reaching that goal, however, the Gibeonites hit the water table! They thus discovered a fresh water supply wholly secure inside the city walls. This project—and the discovery it led to—should be dated *after* the 10th century stepped-tunnel-to-spring system. An early 9th century date would be quite plausible.

The news of this remarkable discovery would have quickly spread. It could easily have become the model for Hazor, whose engineers opted for this system instead of the Megiddo shaft and tunnel system which

Gibeon — *Carved completely from bedrock, the steps and curving balustrade lead to the bottom of the great pool. The lowest portion of the balustrade at the bottom of the pool-shaft may originally have been part of a platform. At that time the pool may have been used as a cistern in which the water carriers stood on the platform while they drew water.*

Later, after the feeder tunnel had been dug from the base of the hill to the spring, the Gibeonites may have realized that the spring was almost directly below the floor of the cistern. A stepped tunnel was then dug below the cistern floor (the opening is seen on the left) to try to reach the spring. The tunnel struck the water table—on the same level as the spring—where abundant water was found, providing a reliable water supply completely within the city walls.

Under the ladder are two vertical shafts through which light entered the tunnel.

led to a spring outside the city wall. This could explain why the Hazor system reflects such confidence in the result. After the Gibeon experience, the Hazor engineers would have known precisely what they were doing. (If Yadin's dating of the Gezer water system is correct, Gibeon could have served also as the model for Gezer where the engineers also proceeded to their goal with confidence.)

My theory about the Gibeon water system assumes that the pool-shaft was first built as a cistern. Pritchard considered this possibility but rejected it because the fissured bedrock would probably not have retained water for long without plaster, and he found no trace of plaster in the pool shaft. But the Gibeon engineers may not have known this when they dug it. Perhaps they hoped that the bedrock would be as impermeable as it is in some other places in the region. Or

perhaps the Gibeonites inhibited percolation out of the pool by periodically applying a clay mortar lining, all traces of which would have been washed away over time.[15]

Pritchard also argued that the pool-shaft and its lower stepped tunnel could not have been separate projects because of the balustrade left on the steps. The balustrade alongside the pool-shaft steps seems to continue as a rim around the top of the stepped tunnel cavity. According to Pritchard, "The balustrade left in the live rock at the point where the steps go below the floor of the pool indicates that the circular stairway into the [stepped] tunnel was a part of the plan of construction when the floor of the pool was leveled off. The floor on the east side is carefully smoothed, while on the south and southwest provision was obviously left for the descent of the stairway into the [stepped] tunnel."[16]

But this same evidence might be used to argue the opposite interpretation. Why plan for a balustrade around the top of the tunnel steps? The water carriers on the steps would hardly need it at that point. If it was to protect persons standing on the pool floor from falling into the stepped tunnel, why wasn't a similar rim left around the two holes in the pool-shaft which provide light to the stepped tunnel below? Why finish off the bottom of the pool-shaft at all if the intention had been to tunnel deeper?

Perhaps the balustrade at the bottom of the pool-shaft represents the lowest level of the earlier cistern steps, which had terminated in a platform slightly above the cistern floor to allow water carriers to fill their jars without stepping into the water when the water was at its lowest levels. Pritchard found a shallow, almost square basin hollowed out of the pool-shaft floor alongside the bottom segment of the balustrade. This might have been an installation to facilitate filling jugs when the water level was low. Perhaps when the stepped tunnel project was initiated below the pool-shaft, the earlier pool stairs were sufficiently worn to lead the pickmen to re-cut them, creating the balustrade effect in the process as an afterthought. The stepped tunnel which extended the line of the steps down through the earlier platform was made narrow enough to leave the outer edge of the platform as an incidental rim—not necessary, but also not in the way.[17]

One cannot say for certain that the stepped tunnel beneath the pool-shaft provides the specific "missing link" which prepared the way for the Hazor shaft-to-water-table system. But it is clear that the Hazor project presupposes an awareness of the subterranean water table deep beneath the Israelite city. The Gibeon water system, on the other hand, does *not* demand such prior knowledge. The groping of the diggers who accidently found the water table under the city is apparent. Gibeon it seems, then, is the most likely model for the Hazor engineers who, with sure and steady picks, dug directly through bedrock beneath the city streets to the water table level, 146 feet below.

The water tunnels of ancient Israel—whether in Jerusalem, Megiddo, Gezer, Gibeon or Hazor—are records through which modern day tourists may wander. They are unique archaeological remains—testimony to the engineering prowess of the ancient inhabitants of Israel.

1 For fullest description see Robert Scott Lamon, *The Megiddo Water System* (Chicago, 1935).
2 Yigael Yadin, *Hazor: the Rediscovery of a Great Citadel of the Bible* (New York, 1975), pp. 168, 187-193.
3 Yadin, *Hazor*, pp. 207-220.
4 A stairway of similar concept was excavated by James G. Pritchard at Tell es-Sa'idiyeh in the Jordan Valley in 1964; see *Biblical Archaeologist* XXVIII:1 (Feb., 1965), 12-14.
5 Yadin, *Hazor* pp. 233-247.
6 R.A.S. Macalister, *The Excavation of Gezer* (London, 1912), II, 256-265; III, Plate LII.
7 *Biblical Archaeologist* XXXII, 3 (September, 1969), 70.
8 Ibid., 71-78.
9 For the fullest description of the Pool and its discovery, see James B. Pritchard's *Gibeon. Where the Sun Stood Still* (Princeton, 1962), pp. 64-74.
10 Edward Robinson, *Biblical Researches in Palestine* (London, 2nd ed. 1860), Vol. I, pp. 454-456.
11 Pritchard, *Gibeon*, pp. 45-52.
12 James B. Pritchard, *The Water System of Gibeon* (Philadelphia, 1961), p. 8. See this volume for the most complete technical description of both the Pool and the stepped tunnel to the spring at el-Jib.
13 The same general concept (stepped tunnel through bedrock to already-known spring source) is exhibited in modified form in "Warren's Shaft" at Jerusalem. An even closer analogy may be the tunnel at Khirbet Bel 'ameh (ancient Ibleam) near Jenin, but it has not been fully exposed or dated (see G. Schumacher in *Palestine Exploration Quarterly*, 1910, 107-112, Pl. 2).
14 If the pool had been used originally as a cistern, we should not necessarily find traces today at the top of the shaft of the channels which led water into the reservoir. When it was converted to its later use the channel endings would have been dismantled to *prevent* water from flowing into the cavity.
15 Alternately, the upper shaft may have been a grain silo. A silo of similar shape, complete with spiraling steps, is preserved at Iron Age Megiddo. The installation at Megiddo, however, only entailed cutting through earlier earthen debris layers and then lining the silo walls with small stones. It seems unnecessarily ambitious of the Gibeonites to have hewn through solid bedrock merely for grain storage.
16 Pritchard, *The Water System of Gibeon*, p. 10.
17 A secondary cutting of the upper stairs would explain why they appear less worn than those of the stepped tunnel to the spring in spite of the fact that the pool appears to predate the stepped tunnel and yet to have been still in use right up until the city's destruction at the end of the Iron Age.

There is a further reason to suggest that the upper shaft may have been originally a reservoir. The Hebrew word identifying the early 10th century installation at Gibeon in 2 Samuel 2 and translated "pool" (*berekah*) seems to be used elsewhere in the Bible for places where water is *collected*: basins into which water flows, natural pools in which rain water collects and so forth, for instance Isaiah 22:9,11; Ecclesiastes 7:5. I find no place where the meaning is clearly a *source* of water or a place *from which* water flows. One verse is particularly striking. In Nahum 2:8 the prophet writes, "Nineveh is like a pool (*berekah*) whose waters run away." The implication, of course, is that the waters should *not* run away from a *berekah*; they should be held by it. ∎

Both these articles are examples of what we might call synthetic analysis. That does not mean something that is artificial as opposed to real; "synthetic" here refers rather to the process of *synthesizing* different kinds of evidence from different sites in order to reconstruct a larger picture of ancient society. As the isolated bits and pieces of archaeological evidence gradually accumulate from separate enterprises, occasionally it becomes possible to step back and ask questions about the activity behind the artifacts, to look for the larger patterns that help us better understand whole facets of an ancient culture at work.

Muhly's study would have been impossible if he had not been able to draw on evidence of destructions and population migrations from dozens of sites spread across the eastern Mediterranean at the end of Late Bronze/beginning of Iron I, on technical knowledge of bronze and iron metallurgy, on geological surveys of the location of sources for tin and iron ore, as well as on the evidence from different sites and periods for the occurrence or nonoccurrence of particular artifacts (e.g., weapons vs. tools) made of different metals (copper, bronze, wrought iron or forged carburized iron).

The article on Israelite water systems is less far-ranging, but its conclusions also depend on the accumulation of evidence from a half-dozen or more different Iron Age water systems, as well as on a willingness to look back over the evidence and ask anew the questions of how and why.

Note that Muhly and his colleagues not only synthesized previously uncovered evidence, they conducted their own new analyses of selected Iron I metal artifacts. To do this required two things: First, they needed to articulate a clear research design. That is, they needed to determine what remaining questions they might be able to answer by gathering further data (such as, were iron objects from datable Iron I Philistine and Israelite contexts made of wrought iron or of forged carburized iron?). Second, they needed to make use of recently developed scientific techniques for analyzing such things as metal composition and hardness.

In "How Water Tunnels Worked," note the creative and ongoing dialogue between archaeologist and object, as well as between different archaeological interpreters. Yadin's reexamination of the Megiddo walls led to a revised dating of the Megiddo water tunnel. This, in turn, led him eventually to search for a similar system at Hazor. The different character of the Hazor system then led him to suggest that the Hazor tunnel-to-water-table system was a technological advance over the Megiddo tunnel-to-outside-spring system. Out of these developments, the question of where the Hazor engineers might have gotten the confidence to dig down to the water table emerged. The answer suggested in the article came from engaging in a new dialogue with the archaeological evidence uncovered years before at Gibeon.

In the wake of the article on Israelite water systems, Walter Zanger of Jerusalem, who describes himself as "a working guide in Israel," wrote a letter published in **BAR**, January/February 1981:

> What surprises me is [Dan Cole's] enthusiasm for the Hazor system. I certainly agree that Ahab designed and built confidently at Hazor, but in my judgment that system can't hold a candle to the one he built at Megiddo.
>
> Megiddo's waterworks is not only deeper and more complicated, but it boasts what I think to be the most extraordinary technical accomplishment of Biblical antiquity—the dead straight tunnel from the bottom of the shaft to the pool. I've been through it a hundred times, and to this day am lost in wonderment. How did he know how to make it so straight? Although more than a hundred years earlier than Hezekiah's tunnel in Jerusalem, the Megiddo system managed what Jerusalem couldn't—a straight beeline to the source. If ever the idea of "confident" engineering seemed called for, Megiddo is the place. I have literally no idea how on earth Ahab managed it, but in my judgment it far surpasses the Hazor waterworks in engineering skill.

The author's response, published in **BAR**, March/April 1981, was as follows:

> Walter Zanger expressed surprise that in my recent article . . . I was so enthusiastic about the Hazor water system in comparison with that at Megiddo. He is, of course, quite right that the Megiddo system is more monumental in size (the Hazor shaft is 95 feet deep and leads to an 80 foot long tunnel while the Megiddo shaft descended 115 feet and was connected to a 200 foot tunnel). My enthusiasm for the Hazor water system, however, was not because it was bigger but because it was better—better at achieving its purpose. The Israelite engineers were trying to reach fresh water from inside their city walls. The Hazor engineers did this in a more secure and efficient manner than the Megiddo masons by digging down to the water table. Had the Megiddo engineers known that they could reach water by digging *down* from their shaft another 25-50 feet instead of digging *out* 200 feet, I'm sure they would have done so, and would have gladly spared themselves approximately one-half of the time and effort they expended.
>
> Mr. Zanger also expressed awe at the engineering skill reflected in the Megiddo tunnel since it was cut on so straight a line between the bottom of the shaft and the spring. He writes "I have literally no idea how on earth Ahab managed it. . ." This raises an interesting question I did not take time to deal with in my article. The engineering feat at Megiddo might, indeed, appear even more

impressive than Mr. Zanger has remarked when we note that the tunnel was cut by two teams who started at either end and dug towards each other, seemingly straight as an arrow. James Michener suggested fifteen years ago, however, exactly how such a tunnel project might have been engineered. The water system at his fictional Tell Makor (on "Level XII" of *The Source*) was modelled after the shaft and tunnel at Megiddo, and he reconstructed the process in the following way. After the vertical shaft was dug, flag poles were set up on the hill across the valley from the city mound beyond the spring to mark the line between the shaft head and the spring. Other flag poles were then set up on roof-tops in the city to extend that line beyond the shaft in the other direction. Sighting along the line of these poles, the engineers were then able to lay a pole across the head of the shaft which was aimed straight for the spring. Strings weighted with stones were lowered from this pole at the opposite corners of the shaft down to the shaft floor to provide a guide to the team cutting toward the spring from that end, while a similar arrangement at the spring end guided the team starting from there. The diggers cut their tunnels as small as possible at first until they came near enough to each other to be further guided by the sounds of each other's picks, adjusting as necessary in the last few feet to connect their tunnels. They knew they would eventually need a tunnel high enough for the townswomen to walk through with water jugs on their heads and wide enough to allow the women to pass each other going in opposite directions. After the initial tunnels were joined, any irregularities in the alignment of the two segments could be removed as the tunnel was enlarged.

Michener's reconstruction is conjectural, but quite plausible.

For Further Reading

Concerning Philistine and Israelite Cultures in Iron Age I

Trude Dothan, "What We Know About the Philistines," **BAR**, July/August 1982

Trude Dothan, *The Philistines and Their Material Culture*; reviewed by Michael Coogan, **BAR**, July/August 1982

George L. Kelm and Amihai Mazar, "Excavating in Samson Country—Philistines & Israelites at Tel Batash," **BAR**, January/February 1989

Concerning Israelite Water Systems

Yigal Shiloh, "Jerusalem's Water Supply During Siege—The Rediscovery of Warren's Shaft," **BAR**, July/August 1981

Ze'ev Herzog, Miriam Aharoni and Anson F. Rainey, "Arad—An Ancient Israelite Fortress with a Temple to Yahweh," **BAR** March/April 1987 (*see Section D*)

Concerning Siege Warfare Tactics in Iron Age II

Hershel Shanks, "Destruction of Judean Fortress Portrayed in Dramatic Eighth-Century B.C. Pictures," **BAR**, March/April 1984 (*see Section C*)

David Ussishkin, "Defensive Judean Counter-Ramp Found at Lachish in 1983 Season," **BAR**, March/April 1984 (*see Section C*)

Notes

Voices from the Biblical Dust —
Inscriptions from the Israelite Period

Inscriptions are rare finds in Iron Age Palestine; the scraps preserved for us do not begin to compare with the royal archives and monumental inscriptions from contemporary Egypt, Assyria or Mesopotamia. Aside from the occasional names inscribed in seal impressions on jar handles and bullae (clay document sealings), the few examples of Hebrew or related texts that, until recently, had come to light from the period could be counted on the fingers of one hand. They included the Gezer calendar (a listing of the agricultural seasons), the Mesha Stele (a proclamation on stone of the Moabite king Mesha's accomplishments), the Siloam Tunnel inscription (describing how the tunnel was cut) and a couple of collections of ostraca (personal notes on potsherds).

One of those ostraca collections, the Lachish letters, has recently been reassessed (see p. 314). The other articles in this section focus on new inscriptional materials uncovered since the 1960s. The finds continue to be modest in size and number, but they bring a dramatic human immediacy, as well as some fresh insights, to facets of Biblical history and religion.

In the first selection, André Lemaire reports on an unusual discovery at Deir Alla, east of the Jordan River. This text, written in the eighth century B.C. on a plastered wall, recounts an oracle of doom by the prophet Balaam, son of Beor, who appears in the Bible in Numbers 22-24. Lemaire notes similarities between formulaic statements in the Deir Alla inscription and in the Numbers account that suggest that the Biblical writers were acquainted with the same local literary tradition reflected in the inscription.

The second and third articles, dealing with inscriptions of a startling nature, should be read together.

In the second article, Ze'ev Meshel focuses on some enigmatic ninth- or early eighth-century B.C. inscriptions found on wall plaster and on two large storage jars at Kuntillet Ajrud in the Sinai wilderness. The inscriptions refer by name to Israel's god, Yahweh, but also mention an "asherah" that seemed to Meshel to refer to a consort of Yahweh, a female deity who may also have been depicted on one of the jars. If these inscriptions have been properly interpreted they are unprecedented evidence for the early worship (and depiction!) of a female deity as a consort of Yahweh, expressing an idea familiar in Canaanite and other Near Eastern religions. Meshel observes that the evidence should not surprise us because Biblical accounts of the period give vivid witness to Israelites resorting to Canaanite gods and religious practices.

Next, André Lemaire reports on several other inscriptions discovered near Hebron that also invoke "Yahweh and his asherah," prayers etched in the walls of eighth-century B.C. tombs. Lemaire examines these prayer texts as well as the similar Kuntillet Ajrud inscriptions. He takes issue with Meshel and argues that neither set of inscriptions refers to a separate female deity as a consort of Yahweh.

The fourth article carries us to the last generation before the fall of Judah. Hershel Shanks describes discoveries in Jerusalem since 1975 of over 250 bullae (wads of clay used to seal documents) with names impressed in them from officials' seals. The names include two known to us from the Bible: Baruch, Jeremiah's faithful scribe, and (ironically) Jerahmeel, King Jehoiakim's son, who was sent to arrest Jeremiah and Baruch.

The last two articles bring us to the final days of the Israelite Iron Age period. Both articles deal with notes written on potsherds (ostraca) to military officers (one from Lachish; the other from Arad) during the days just before the fall of Judah to the Babylonians in 586 B.C.

Oded Borowski summarizes a study by Yigael Yadin of the Lachish letters, 21 ostraca found in a guardroom of the outer gate of Lachish. The letters reflect the last days of Lachish, when it was already under siege from Nebuchadnezzar's Babylonian armies, shortly before it fell in the campaign that would end with Jerusalem's destruction. Yadin made some ingenious suggestions about the letters' character and about the translation of a critical Hebrew phrase that could tell us definitely whether Tell ed-Duweir is really Lachish.

Anson Rainey describes a collection of ostraca that help us reconstruct Arad's last days. Most of the notes appear to be instructions sent to Eliashib, probable commander of the garrison at Arad. One ostracon instructs Eliashib to rush reinforcements to another fort in the region in anticipation of an imminent Edomite attack. Shortly thereafter an attack came, either from Edomites or Babylonians, which destroyed the final Israelite fort at Arad. That ostracon, found by an American volunteer, may be the last voice to speak to us from the dust of ancient Israel before its fall.

The destruction of Jerusalem and the Babylonian Exile would shortly alter for all time the character of the Biblical community.

FRAGMENTS
from the Book of Balaam
FOUND
at Deir Alla

TEXT FORETELLS COSMIC DISASTER

André Lemaire

THE DATE WAS March 17, 1967, a Friday. A Dutch expedition led by Professor Henk J. Franken of the University of Leiden was excavating a mound named Tell Deir Alla in the middle Jordan Valley, east of the river, in Jordan. The site lay halfway between the Sea of Galilee and the Dead Sea, barely a mile north of what was known in Biblical times as the Jabbok River and now is called the Zerqa, a tributary of the Jordan.

Some scholars have identified Deir Alla with Biblical Succoth, where Jacob built a house for himself and booths (*succoth*) for his cattle (Genesis 33:17). My own view, as I shall explain, is that the tell is Biblical Penuel, where Jacob wrestled with the angel (Genesis 32:25-32). Of one thing we may be certain: During the eighth to seventh centuries B.C., long after Jacob's time, Deir Alla was an important city, probably more than ten acres in size. It was in the archaeological levels from this city that the Dutch expedition was digging on that fateful Friday in 1967. An Arab foreman named Ali Abdul-Rasul suddenly noticed traces of letters on tiny pieces of plaster among the debris the workers were cleaning up.

Excitement spread like wildfire through the camp. Excavation stopped, and the entire team concentrated on taking all possible steps to preserve whatever was left of the writing.

Unfortunately, the weather had been bad. It had rained frequently on the days before the discovery, and the clay the excavators were digging had absorbed considerable moisture. The site of the inscription was immediately covered with a plastic sheet, as the excavators report, "to prevent any increase in the soil's water content." On the other hand, their report continues:[1]

> "it soon became apparent that drying the mortar quickly would have disastrous consequences ....From the first day onwards it was known that the text was written in red and black ink. It was not clear whether the red ink would still be able to withstand light. To make both rapid drying in dry weather, and

Tell Deir Alla. *Archaeologists have sliced into this artificial hill—created by layer upon layer of earth-covered settlements—to reveal a prominent city from Biblical times. Sometime during the eighth century B.C. there may have been an important religious school here at Deir Alla in the Jordan Valley; in one building from that period excavators discovered a wall that had been inscribed in Aramaic with a religious text mentioning "Balaam, son of Beor," the same Balaam famous from the story in the Book of Numbers, chapters 22-24.*

271

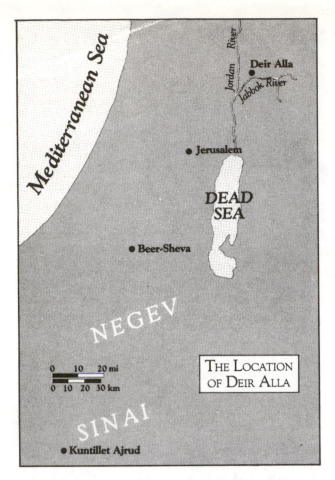

THE LOCATION
OF DEIR ALLA

began to circulate, and a photograph of the largest inscribed fragment was published with a preliminary announcement in the international Biblical scholars review, *Vetus Testamentum*.[2] The excitement in the Biblical community mounted with a rumor (that was later confirmed) that the inscribed plaster fragments contained a reference to "the seer Balaam, son of Beor," so well known from the Bible (Numbers 22-24).

Following these sensational reports, slow, careful work began, to restore and conserve all the very brittle plaster fragments, some of them tiny. The restoration, conservation and analysis of the fragments was undertaken at the Central Research Laboratory for Objects of Art and Science in Amsterdam. After several years this work was completed. It took several more years to study, draw, reassemble and begin to read and understand the often faint traces of black and red letters. This work was done at the Institute of Palestinian Archaeology of the Rijksuniversiteit in Leiden. Then, in 1976, a magnificent

Ali Abdul-Rasul, *foreman of the workers excavating at Tell Deir Alla, found the first eighth-century B.C. inscribed wall fragments. In this photo, taken just after the discovery, a plastic sheet just behind Abdul-Rasul's left shoulder covers the moist clay in which the fragments were found. Soon after this photo was taken, a Bedouin tent was raised to prevent sunlight from drying out the fragile plaster fragments lying in the clay soil.*

the absorption of more moisture on wet days impossible, the plastic sheet was replaced by a Bedouin tent. Owing to this, there was never any direct sunlight on the mortar fragments during the excavation."

From the moment of discovery, each plaster fragment was carefully picked up, gingerly cleaned of any remaining clay, either by hand or with a very soft fine brush, and then put in a tin with a number. As soon as possible, infrared photographs of each fragment were taken; these made clearer the traces of organic ink on the plaster. The discovery seemed so important that, for the last two weeks of the season, the normal work of excavation ceased while everyone concentrated on the inscribed plaster fragments.

The news of the discovery spread quickly. One of the first visitors to the site was Lancaster Harding, director of the Jordanian Department of Antiquities. Paul Lapp, director of the American Schools of Oriental Research, and Père Roland de Vaux of the French École Biblique et Archéologique, prominent scholars from what was then Jordanian Jerusalem also came to participate in the excitement. Eminent scholars from abroad, such as Germany's Martin Noth and Holland's P. A. H. de Boer also made their way to Deir Alla.

Soon, the first preliminary drawings of the inscriptions

book with facsimiles and pictures, both black-and-white and color, was published.[3]

By 1972, the inscribed plaster fragments had been arranged in two principal groups or combinations; scholars refer to these as Combination I and Combination II. Each of the two assembled combinations was strengthened by mortar on the back and put into a wooden frame. The frames were then sent to Jordan, where they are now on exhibit at the Amman Archaeological Museum.

Readers of **BAR** will not be surprised to learn that the publication of the 1976 book with facsimiles and pictures, what scholars call an *editio princeps*, was just the beginning, not the end, of the analysis of the inscriptions. Even now, nearly ten years after the *editio princeps* appeared, it is clear that there are still many problems with the inscription. However, little by little, as scholars have proposed various solutions, many aspects of the inscription and its importance to our understanding of Biblical literature are becoming clearer.

The time has now come for a more general treatment of the inscription, although many conclusions must remain somewhat tentative.

The first question concerns the date of the inscription. On this matter, a scholarly consensus is developing within a surprisingly narrow range. In the preliminary announcement, the inscription was inexplicably dated to the Persian period (from the end of the sixth century to the fourth century B.C.). However, subsequent excavations on the tell itself by Moawiyeh Ibrahim of the Jordanian Department of Antiquities and Gerrit van der

Bright red and black letters *painted on plaster wall fragments relate a 2,600-year-old religious text. Shown here soon after they were excavated, the fragments have been reassembled and strengthened on the back with paraffin wax.*

Most of the text of the inscription was written in black ink, with red ink reserved for titles, important passages and straight lines that framed the top and left edge of each column of text. Part of a horizontal line of one such frame can be seen here.

One sentence partially seen here in the top line of text begins "The gods came to him at night." The scribe forgot to write the word for "to him," and so added it above the line.

Kooij of the University of Leiden demonstrated that the archaeological stratum in which the inscribed plaster fragments were found was to be dated, on the basis of pottery, "in the eighth century B.C."[4] This eighth-century dating agrees with the results of radiocarbon dating tests. According to these tests, the inscriptions were to be dated c. 800 B.C., plus or minus 70 years, with a probability of 66% that the dating was within this range.[5] Paleographical analysis—based on the shapes and forms of the letters—performed by Professor Joseph Naveh of Hebrew University supported this eighth-century B.C. conclusion. Professor Naveh classified the writing as a cursive Aramaic script to be dated "to the middle of the eighth century or even earlier (by one or two decades)."[6]

Recently, a few scholars have suggested lowering the date to the beginning of the seventh century B.C.[7] Their

273

suggestion is based on an alleged connection between the handwriting of the Deir Alla inscription and certain Ammonite inscriptions of the seventh century. However, the arguments for the mid-eighth-century dating seem to fit the evidence far better.

A mid-eighth-century date also provides an attractive historical context for the inscription. It is clear, even from the preliminary excavation report, that the archaeological stratum in which the inscribed plaster fragments were found was destroyed by an earthquake. This is hardly surprising in the Jordan Valley, where so many earthquakes have been recorded in historical periods. But this earthquake appears to have been particularly severe, producing numerous cracks and shifts in the archaeological strata. These cracks and shifts stopped, however, at the top of the stratum in which the fallen inscribed plaster fragments were found.

If this major earthquake is dated to the eighth century

B.C.—more specifically, to the middle of the eighth century—it is very tempting to identify it with the famous earthquake that occurred about 750 B.C., during the reigns of King Uzziah of Judah and King Jeroboam II of Israel, mentioned in the book of the prophet Amos (Amos 1:1) and by Zechariah (Zechariah 14:4-5). Chapter one, verse one of the Book of Amos tells us that the "words of Amos" were given during the reigns of Uzziah and Jeroboam, "two years before the earthquake." Zechariah, writing in the sixth century B.C., predicts that a day will come when the earth will shift and split and the valley of the Hill of Jerusalem will be stopped up as it was "as a result of the earthquake in the days of King Uzziah of Judah." The eighth-century B.C. earthquake, probably felt throughout Palestine, may well account for the destruction encountered in strata of this date at a number of sites, for example, at Hazor and Samaria. Indeed, this same earthquake may have crumbled the plaster of the

Deir Alla in the eighth-century B.C. was a large city, perhaps even a center of religious instruction. On the walls of a room in one building (photo, opposite) that may have stood near a temple, a professional scribe copied the text of an important religious manuscript. First he drew four red frames. Then he filled the frames with text, adding a drawing here and there for adornment. An artist's reconstruction (top) shows how this inscribed wall may have looked.

Sometime in the eighth century B.C. Deir Alla was leveled by an earthquake, perhaps the very earthquake mentioned in the Book of Amos, and also spoken of by Zechariah as "the earthquake that stopped up the valley in the days of King Uzziah of Judah." In the Deir Alla disaster, the inscribed wall fell, crumbling into a myriad of fragments that scattered over an area of more than 20 square feet. The author observes that most of one section of the wall seems to have fallen in a pit, while another section fell at the corner of the original wall (plan, bottom).

Telescoping into one drawing (top) details of the Deir Alla building both before and after the earthquake, the artist shows us the two areas where most of the inscribed fragments probably fell. Many inscribed fragments from these two toppled sections have now been reassembled into two groups, called Combination I and Combination II.

walls on which the inscriptions at Deir Alla were originally painted. In any event, the earthquake was of such magnitude that it was remembered two centuries later, as the quotation from Zechariah demonstrates.

Although the *editio princeps* suggested that the inscription was originally written on a stele, that is, a freestanding monument, a detailed analysis of the archaeological reports and of the shape of the plaster fragments seems to indicate that the inscription was written on white plaster that covered a mudbrick wall.[8]

The loci, or exact locations, of the inscribed plaster fragments were carefully recorded by the excavators. This is important not only for dating purposes, but also because this helps to divide the fragments into two groups or combinations. One group was found in a pit in the middle of the floor of a room identified as locus 34. These fragments are designated Combination I. The other group was found outside the northeastern corner of the wall of the room (locus 57 on the plan), about ten feet from the first group. The second group is called Combination II. In dividing the fragments into two groups, the archaeologists considered not only each locus but also the possibility of fitting the pieces together. The fragments in Combination II are generally larger and in relatively better condition than those in Combination I. The inscription itself was probably originally painted on the eastern side of the wall identified on the plan as Wall

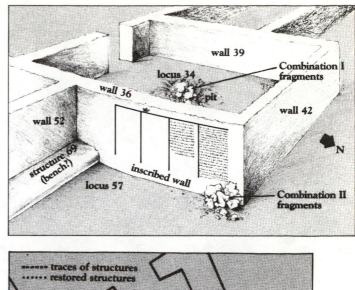

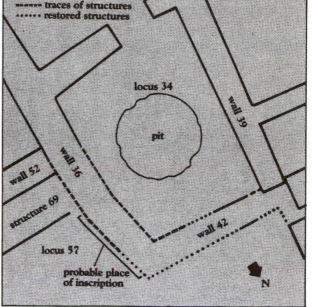

36, in the room adjoining locus 34, a conclusion based on the orientation of the fragments as they were found in the excavation. Although the fragments in Combination I were found on the other side of Wall 36, it is likely that they, too, were part of the inscription painted on the eastern face of Wall 36. Although the two major combinations lay at extreme ends of the excavation area containing the inscribed fragments, smaller groups and single pieces[9] were scattered throughout the intervening area, so all fragments probably originally came from the same wall. Apparently when the wall on which the inscription was written collapsed, part of the wall fell into the adjoining room.

The very regular, careful handwriting of the inscription is easily identified as that of a professional scribe. The scribe followed guiding lines and used beautiful thick and thin strokes in his letters. The general aspect gives us the feeling that we are standing before a column of a manu-

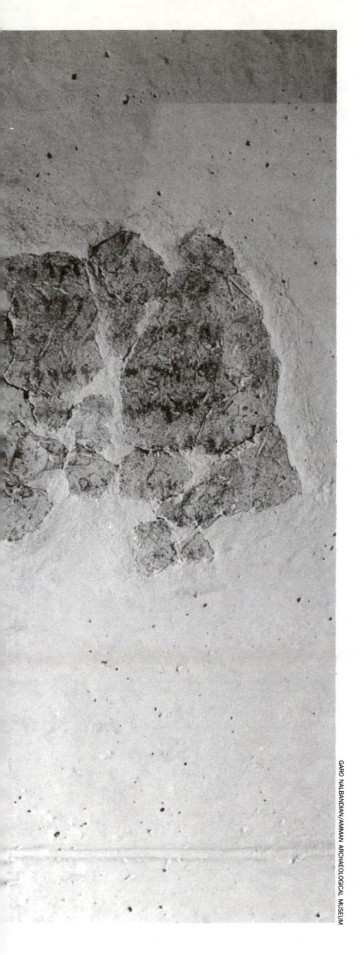

"Balaam, son of Beor," the name of a Biblical prophet, appears, incompletely, in the plaster wall fragment enclosed in the rectangle, left. The four groupings of fragments called Combination I are seen here as they were published in 1976, forming 18 lines of text. At that time the excavators did not connect these four groups. Over the last decade, however, various scholars have realigned the groups and have painstakingly filled in gaps with a few of the hundreds of original fragments.

Now André Lemaire has proposed a restoration of Combination I based on these scholars' work. Tiny fragments, sometimes a single letter here and another letter there, have been placed in the puzzle, which has been tightened to 16 lines.

Above the first line of Combination I, the scribe painted a thick straight line, part of a red frame that originally enclosed the column of text on its top and left sides. A few words were also written in red (shown here as gray) because they form the title of this portion of text: "[Ba]laam [son of Beo]r, the man who was a seer of the gods." This is undoubtedly the famous Balaam, son of Beor, who figures so prominently in Numbers 22-24.

Below, top, shows the four groupings as pictured left. Below, bottom, shows the four groupings as compressed, forming 16 instead of 18 lines. Other fragments, not shown, have also been added in Lemaire's reconstruction, p. 278.

   Comparing Lemaire's restoration of Combination I (above) with pages 276 and 277 demonstrates that Lemaire has added some fragments to his reconstruction. Restored letters are drawn with dotted lines.

   Lemaire says that, even though there are still a few gaps, the first nine lines of Combination I can now be read with considerable certainty:*

1. Inscription of [Ba]laam [son of Beo]r, the man who was a seer of the gods. Lo, the gods came to him at night and [spoke to] him.

2. According to these wor[ds], and they said to [Balaa]m, son of Beor thus: "There has appeared the last flame, a fire of chastisement has appeared!"

3. And Balaam arose the next day [. . . several?] days [. . .] and he cou[ld not eat] and he wept

4. Intensely and his people came to him and s[aid] to Balaam, son of Beor: "Why do you fast and why do you weep?" and he

5. Said to them: "Sit down! I shall show you how gre[at is the calamity!] and come, see the deeds of the gods! The gods have gathered

6. And the Mighties [Shaddayin**] have fixed a date, and they said to Sha[ma]sh [/the sun]: 'Sew shut the skies with your cloud! let there be darkness and no shi-

7. ning . . . ? . . . , for you will provoke terror [by a clo]ud of darkness, and do not make noise forever but [in its place?] the swift,

8. The bat, the eagle and the peli[can,] the vultures, the ostrich and the s[tork and] the young falcons, and the owl, the chicks of the heron, the dove, the bird of prey,

9. The pigeon and the sparrow, [every bird of the s]kies, and [on the earth] down, in the place where the [shepherd's] crook was leading the ewes, hares eat

10. [Alto]gether free[ly . . .].

* André Lemaire, "L'inscription de Balaam provenant de Deir 'Alla: aspects épigraphiques," *Proceedings of the International Congress on Biblical Archaeology,* April 1-10, 1984.

** See endnote 13.

script. This feeling is heightened by the fact that the scribe used red ink for the title and for the most important sentences of the text he was copying, and black ink for the rest of the text. And he wrote within a frame: A large red horizontal line marks the upper limit of the inscription, and another vertical red line on the left side of the inscription marks the end of the column. (Remember that this inscription is written from right to left.) This frame at the top and on the left of the inscription brings to mind the preparations scribes customarily made before copying a column of manuscript. The use of red ink for the framing, the title and the principal passages of a manuscript was already well known by this time in Egypt; this cultural influence was no doubt clearly felt in Palestine. Indeed, the etymology of the word rubric includes the meaning red, a meaning that derives from the use of red ink in antiquity to mark off topical sentences, as was done in the Deir Alla inscriptions.

Although we cannot be sure, several details hint that four red frames had been painted on this wall, but at the time of the earthquake only one and a half frames had been partially filled. Combination II was written at the bottom of the first column and Combination I at the top of the second column, counting the columns from right to left.

Each column was about 15½ inches wide, as indicated by the width of surviving lines of writing (12¼ inches) plus surviving margins between the writing and the red frame (3 to 3½ inches). Each line of writing contained about 48 letters. It appears from the vestiges of the red framing that the height of the columns was probably between two and three feet. All of these factors suggest that the writing on the wall was a copy of a manuscript writ large.

This inscription, as we have reconstructed it, provides us with what is probably the best example we have of the appearance of an eighth-century B.C. northwest Semitic manuscript in Aramaic, Phoenician or Hebrew. At that time, the differences among these three scripts were minimal, so the Deir Alla inscription allows us to visualize in a very concrete way the appearance of original Biblical books, for example, the books of the prophets Amos and Hosea, who lived in the eighth century B. C.

What about the content of this inscription? What does it say? To read the inscription, we must first decide how its pieces should be fit together. The *editio princeps* provided a major first step in solving the puzzle. The large pieces of Combination II found near the wall were easily put together; however, this did not result in restoring a single complete line. Even today, we can read but a few words and phrases of Combination II. The reading of the text and its interpretation are still very uncertain. We can only conjecture about the general ideas the text covers, and these ideas vary from commentator to commentator.

Combination I consists of numerous small fragments, many of them tiny. As a result, restoration work is more difficult than with the larger pieces of Combination II. Despite the difficulty, however, restoration of Combination I has been far more successful. In the *editio princeps*, Professor van der Kooij succeeded in restoring four groups that made up different parts of Combination I. He could not, however, position these groups in relation to one another; that is, he could not connect any of his four groups. Shortly after the *editio princeps* was published, Professor André Caquot of the Collége de France, Paris, and I[10] successfully demonstrated the vertical connection between these four groups. Other studies, including one by P. Kyle McCarter, Jr.,[11] and another by Jo Ann Hackett,[12] helped to place other small fragments. Thus it is now possible to restore the beginning of the first line, a restoration with which all scholars now agree.

These first words, written in red ink, were actually the title of that part of the text:

SPR [B]LʻM[.BR Bʻ]R. ʼŠ.ḤẒH. ʼLHN

"*Inscription/text/book of [Ba]laam [son of Beo]r, the man who was a seer of the gods.*"

(The italics indicate that the letters are damaged; consequently, the proposed reading is probable, but given with some caution. The letters in brackets are probable restorations of missing letters.)

There is little doubt that this is the same Balaam, son of Beor, whose oracles are preserved in Numbers 22-24! Here we have the title of the inscription written in red. Although the name Balaam, son of Beor, in the title is partially reconstructed ("Ba" in "Balaam" and most of "son of Beor" are missing), the second line does much to confirm this reconstruction; nearly the full name appears in line 2 ("son of Beor" is complete and the "m" in "Balaam" has survived [see p. 278]). In line 3, "Balaam" is complete, and in line 4 "Balaam son of Beor" is complete.

The text goes on to describe a divine vision that came to Balaam at night, probably in a dream: "Lo, the gods came to him at night" and spoke to him (line 1). The content of the vision is frightening: his people are to be chastised, punished by a "fire of chastisement" that appeared to Balaam in his vision (line 2). The next day Balaam arose. "He could not eat and he wept" (line 3). "His people came to him and said to Balaam, son of Beor: 'Why do you fast and why do you weep?' " (line 4).

Balaam describes for his people the calamity that is to come (line 5); the gods "have fixed a date" (line 6a).

What is foretold next is not entirely clear. It appears that the gods[13] have instructed Shamash,[14] the sun god, to "shut the skies" (the rays of the sun) with a "cloud":

Balaam in the Bible

Balaam, son of Beor, was a seer from the land of Aram—perhaps in Mesopotamia—who was famous for the power of his blessings and curses. As the Israelites were poised for battle with the Moabites, Balak, king of Moab, summoned Balaam to aid his side by cursing Israel.

As the Biblical account begins, the Israelites are on their way from Egypt to the Promised Land. They have already defeated the Ammonites east of the Jordan and are camping on the steppes of Moab. Balak, seeing that their forces are great, fears for his own kingdom. He therefore sends emissaries to Balaam to bring him back to Moab and curse the Israelites. With Balaam's curse, Balak hopes to defeat the Israelites. In the end, Balaam comes to Moab, but, to Balak's surprise and anger, Balaam blesses the Israelites and foretells the subsequent victory of Israel over her adversaries.

Balaam is one of the most enigmatic figures in the Bible. Although clearly a foreigner, Balaam was subject to the command of the God of Israel and openly acknowledged that his prophetic powers derived from God. However, his reputation as an effective diviner throughout the ancient world was such that Balak, speaking to Balaam, could confidently state: "I know that he whom you bless is blessed indeed, and he whom you curse is cursed" (Numbers 22:6).

A detailed account of Balaam's blessing of the Israelites appears in Numbers 22-24.

When Balak's emissaries first ask for his help, Balaam immediately tells them he will do only as the Lord instructs him. In a dream, God tells Balaam not to go with Balak's emissaries, but Balak's emissaries offer Balaam further pleas and rich reward, so Balaam agrees to go with them, after first obtaining God's permission.

Although Balaam has God's permission to go to Moab, his departure nevertheless incenses God. As Balaam rides on his she-ass with Balak's emissaries on their way back to Moab, an angel sent by God obstructs the road. The she-ass, who alone sees the angel with a sword drawn in his hand, tries to swerve every which way to avoid the angel, and, finally, when she cannot, lies down in the road, refusing to go further. Angered, Balaam beats the creature with his staff. At this point, God grants the gift of speech to the she-ass: "Look, I am the ass that you have been riding all along until this day," she says. "Have I been in the habit of doing thus to you?" Balaam must humbly reply, "No." God thereupon opens Balaam's eyes to the angel. Balaam admits his error, and offers to return home. But the angel tells him to go on with Balak's emissaries.

This is the only animal in the Bible—with the exception of the serpent in the Garden of Eden—that speaks; the story of the exchange between Balaam and the ass has since been immortalized in literature and in art.

Once in Moab, Balaam is taken by King Balak to a high place, Bamoth-Baal, where Balaam can see a group of

"Balaam and His Ass," 1626, *a youthful work by Rembrandt van Rijn (1606-1669).*

Israelites encamped below. Balaam warns the king that he can speak only the words that God puts into his mouth. To Balak's displeasure, Balaam pronounces the following oracle:

"From Aram has Balak brought me,
  Moab's king from the hills of the East:
  Come, curse me Jacob,
  Come, tell Israel's doom!
  How can I damn whom God has not damned,
  How doom when the Lord has not doomed?
  As I see them from the mountain tops,
  Gaze on them from the heights,
  There is a people that dwells apart,
  Not reckoned among the nations;
  Who can count the dust of Jacob,
  Number the dust-cloud of Israel?
  May I die the death of the upright,
  May my fate be like theirs!"

(Numbers 23:7-10)

Balak then leads Balaam to another height from which he can see another group of Israelites and again asks him to curse them. But instead Balaam pronounces another oracle of blessing.

In exasperation, Balak asks Balaam neither to curse the Israelites nor to bless them, but to remain neutral. Balaam replies, "Did I not tell you, 'All that the Lord says, that I must do?'" (Numbers 23:26).

Finally, Balak guides Balaam to the top of Peor. From this

height overlooking the desert, Balaam turns his face to the wilderness and again blesses Israel:

"Word of Balaam son of Beor,
 Word of the man whose eye is true,
 Word of him who hears God's speech,
 Who beholds visions from the Almighty,
 Prostrate, but with eyes unveiled:
 How fair are your tents, O Jacob,
 Your dwellings, O Israel!
 Like palm-groves that stretch out,
 Like gardens beside a river,
 Like aloes planted by the Lord,
 Like cedars beside the water;
 Their boughs drip with moisture,
 Their roots have abundant water.
 Their king shall rise above Agag,
 Their kingdom shall be exalted.
 God who freed them from Egypt
 Is for them like the horns of the wild ox.
 They shall devour enemy nations,
 Crush their bones,
 And smash their arrows.
 They crouch, they lie down like a lion,
 Like the king of beasts; who dare rouse them?
 Blessed are they who bless you,
 Accursed they who curse you!"

(Numbers 24:3-9)

Balak, in impotent anger, declares, "I called you . . . to damn my enemies, and instead you have blessed them these three times! Back with you at once to your own place!" Balak orders Balaam to go home, but before Balaam leaves, he pronounces yet another oracle in which he foretells the future victory of Israel over its enemies.

"Word of Balaam son of Beor,
 Word of the man whose eye is true,
 Word of him who hears God's speech,
 Who obtains knowledge from the Most High,
 And beholds visions from the Almighty,
 Prostrate, but with eyes unveiled:
 What I see for them is not yet,
 What I behold will not be soon:
 A star rises from Jacob,
 A meteor comes forth from Israel;
 It smashes the brow of Moab,
 The foundation of all children of Seth.
 Edom becomes a possession,
 Yea, Seir a possession of its enemies;
 But Israel is triumphant.
 A victor issues from Jacob
 To wipe out what is left of Ir."

(Numbers 24:15-19)

What we know about Balaam in the Bible comes principally from this story of Balaam's blessing of the Israelites in Numbers. The episode was interpreted as signifying God's mercy toward Israel because God turned a curse into a blessing; the episode is referred to in Deuteronomy 23:4-5; Joshua 13:12, 24:9-10; Nehemiah 13:2 and Micah 6:5. The account of Balaam's oracular gift reflects the extraordinary powers attributed to the spoken word in ancient Israel.

"There, let there be darkness" (line 6b). The darkness will "provoke terror" (line 7). A variety of birds in the sky will multiply as the sun disappears. The text becomes obscure, and then breaks off. Perhaps by execrations or other forms of magic, Balaam attempted to avert the disaster. One commentator, Baruch Levine,[15] has suggested that Balaam was successful and that therefore his deeds were memorialized in the manuscript copied on the wall.

Balaam's vision recalls several prophetic texts in the Bible that announce and describe the coming of the "day of the Lord," a day of judgment accompanied by a final disaster. See, for example, Isaiah 13:9-11:

"Lo! The day of the Lord is coming
 With pitiless fury and wrath,
 To make the earth a desolation,
 To wipe out the sinners upon it.
 The stars and constellations of heaven
 Shall not give off their light;
 The sun shall be dark when it rises,
 And the moon shall diffuse no glow.
 And I will requite to the world its evil,
 And to the wicked their iniquity;
 I will put an end to the pride of the arrogant
 And humble the haughtiness of tyrants."

Another example may be found in Joel 2:1-3:

" Blow a horn in Zion,
 Sound an alarm on My holy mount!
 Let all dwellers on earth tremble,
 For the day of the Lord has come!
 It is close—
 A day of darkness and gloom,
 A day of densest cloud
 Spread like soot over the hills.
 A vast enormous horde—
 Nothing like it has ever happened.
 And it shall never happen again
 Through the years and ages.
 Their vanguard is a consuming fire,
 Their rearguard a devouring flame.
 Before them the land was like the Garden of Eden,
 Behind them, a desolate waste:
 Nothing has escaped them."

In the Deir Alla text, we read that "The gods came to him [Balaam] at night and spoke to him." In Numbers, we also read that "God came to Balaam [after he had invited his visitors to spend the night] and . . . God said to Balaam" (Numbers 22:9, 12).

In the Deir Alla text, we read that, after receiving his night vision, "Balaam arose the next day." In Numbers 22:13, we read that "Balaam arose in the morning." The Biblical author was no doubt familiar with the Transjordanian Balaam tradition and even used what appears to be

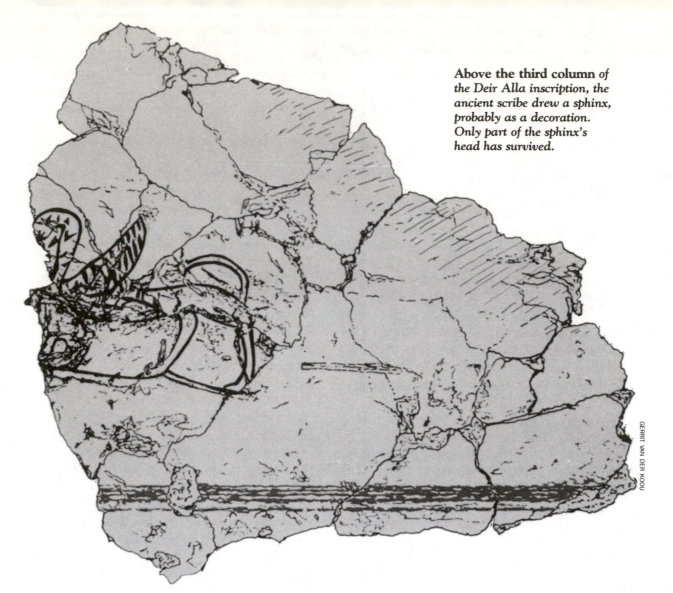

Above the third column *of the Deir Alla inscription, the ancient scribe drew a sphinx, probably as a decoration. Only part of the sphinx's head has survived.*

the same stereotyped narrative formulas that appear in the Deir Alla inscription.

The language or dialect of the Deir Alla text is still a matter of dispute among scholars. The language is clearly northwest Semitic, but which one? The identification is made more difficult by the fact that the inscription is probably a copy of a manuscript that was already decades or perhaps centuries old when it was copied on the wall at Deir Alla. Moreover, the text itself had been edited, or redacted, over a period of time, incorporating linguistic characteristics from the period of redaction.

Some commentators think the language is a Canaanite dialect close to Hebrew and Ammonite. Others, with whom I agree,[16] believe it to be an old Aramaic dialect probably used in southern Syria and in northern Transjordan. The many archaic features of old Aramaic revealed in the text suggest that it was edited hundreds of years before this version was copied on the plaster wall at Deir Alla.

If we are right in thus classifying the language, the Deir Alla inscription provides us with the earliest literary text in old Aramaic. Indeed, we have two such texts, Combination II as well as Combination I. I believe these are two different texts. The story of Balaam begins only with Combination I, with its explicit title at the beginning of line 1. Combination II, which was written on the wall before Combination I, does not mention Balaam and is probably a copy of another literary text that, unfortunately, we cannot yet understand.

Why were these literary, probably religious, texts copied on the plaster wall of a room at Deir Alla? Maybe because the building was close to a temple or cult place. Although, as I noted earlier, Deir Alla has often been identified, especially in rabbinical tradition, as Succoth, a close analysis of the topographical geography of this part of the country suggests that Deir Alla should be identified with Penuel,[17] where Jacob wrestled with the angel and where there was probably some cultic tradition (see Genesis 32:25-32). This same identification is supported by the references to Penuel in the story of Gideon in

Judges 8.

Another reference in the Gideon story indicates that some people of the middle Jordan Valley were literate at least from the 11th century B.C.—a young man at Succoth wrote down a list of 77 elders and officials (Judges 8:14).

But this demonstrates literacy; it does not explain why the inscription was written on a wall. If someone wanted to write a very important inscription to be kept in a sanctuary or official place, he would likely put it on a freestanding stele. A famous example of such a freestanding stele is the Moabite Stone, inscribed by the Moabite king Mesha in the ninth century B.C. Apparently, however, writing on walls was not uncommon at this time. We have another example at Kuntillet Ajrud,[18] a site recently discovered in Sinai. Religious inscriptions found there date from the first half of the eighth century B.C.,[19] roughly the same time as the Deir Alla inscription. At Kuntillet Ajrud, in addition to inscriptions and drawings on storage jars, several inscribed plaster fragments written in Phoenician and Hebrew, in black and red ink, were discovered on a wall of a building at this desert site. At Deir Alla, a sphinx was drawn above the frame of one of the inscriptions (part of the head of this sphinx has not survived). At Kuntillet Ajrud, too, the inscriptions are sometimes accompanied by drawings. Several abecedaries (alphabets) were written on the storage jars at Kuntillet Ajrud; a fragmentary abecedary incised on a pottery sherd was discovered at Deir Alla. All this probably means that Kuntillet Ajrud and Deir Alla were both sites where some kind of teaching, writing and drawing occurred, that is, where some kind of religious "school" was maintained. At Deir Alla we have literary and probably classical texts that could well have been used for teaching purposes in this room.

This interpretation is supported by allusions in several Biblical passages. For example, in a famous passage in Deuteronomy (6:9), the Israelites are directed to write the commandments of the Lord "on the doorposts of your house and on your gates." (Jews still fulfill this instruction by attaching *mezuzahs*—pieces of parchment inscribed with this Biblical passage, and enclosed in cases—to the doorposts of their homes.) In Joshua 8:32 we learn that Joshua inscribed the teachings of Moses on plastered stones beside the altar he built on Mt. Ebal in fulfillment of the directions previously given by Moses and the elders in Deuteronomy 27:2-3. In the passage from Deuteronomy, the people are instructed to "set up great stones and plaster them over" before inscribing them. A kind of school for prophets is alluded to in 2 Kings 6:1-2, where the prophet Elisha's students complain about their cramped quarters.

Despite these difficulties, the inscription from Deir Alla, dated to about the middle of the eighth century B.C. and written on the wall of what may have been some kind of religious teaching center, is very likely the earliest extant example of a prophetic text. The principal personage in the Deir Alla text is the seer Balaam, son of Beor, well known to us from the stories in Numbers. Balaam clearly appears as a foreigner in these Biblical stories; the ancient Hebrew scribes who wrote the Biblical stories about Balaam no doubt had some familiarity with old Aramaic literature, including the Aramaic book of the seer Balaam, son of Beor. Unfortunately, the Deir Alla fragments allow us to restore only a very small part of this book. ▨

[1] Extract from the archaeological notes published in Jacob Hoftijzer and Gerrit van der Kooij, *Aramaic Texts from Deir 'Alla (ATDA)*, (Leiden, 1976), p. 18.

[2] Henk J. Franken, "Texts from the Persian Period from Tell Deir 'Alla," *Vetus Testamentum (VT)* 17 (1967), pp. 480-481.

[3] Hoftijzer and van der Kooij, *ATDA*.

[4] Moawiyeh Ibrahim and van der Kooij, "Excavations at Tell Deir 'Alla, Season 1979," *Annual of the Department of Antiquities of Jordan* 23 (1979), p. 50.

[5] Hoftijzer and van der Kooij, *ADTA*, p. 16.

[6] Joseph Naveh, "The Date of the Deir 'Alla Inscription in Aramaic Script," *Israel Exploration Journal* 17 (1967), pp. 256-258.

[7] Cf. Jo Ann Hackett, *The Balaam Text from Deir 'Alla* (Chico, California, 1984), p. 19.

[8] Cf. André Lemaire, "La disposition originelle des inscriptions sur plâtre de Deir 'Alla," to be published in *Studi epigrafici e linguistici (SEL)* 2 (1985).

[9] In the *editio princeps*, 13 other groups of very fragmentary pieces are listed.

[10] André Caquot and Lemaire, "Les textes araméens de Deir 'Alla," *Syria* 54 (1977), pp. 189-208.

[11] P. Kyle McCarter, Jr., "The Balaam Texts from Deir 'Alla: The First Combination," *Bulletin of the American Schools of Oriental Research* 239 (1980), pp. 49-60; cf. also Baruch A. Levine, "The Deir 'Alla Plaster Inscriptions," *Journal of the American Oriental Society* 101 (1981), pp. 195-205.

[12] Hackett, *The Balaam Text*, pp. 4, 7, 21, 31, etc.

[13] The word is *shaddayin*, the plural of the related Hebrew word *shadday*, which is usually translated "Almighty" as in El-Shadday, "God Almighty." The philological evidence seems to indicate that *shadday* originally meant "the one of the mountains"; that is, a mountain god. The plural used at Deir 'Alla may refer to a divine council where major decisions were made.

[14] Only the initial phoneme *sh* is extant. I have reconstructed Shamash on the basis of the disappearance of the sun suggested in the text. Another reconstruction, suggested by P. Kyle McCarter, Jr., is Sheol, goddess of the underworld and, in rabbinic literature, the realm of the underworld.

[15] Levine, "The Deir 'Alla Inscriptions." See note 11.

[16] Cf. Lemaire, "La langue de l'inscription sur plâtre de Deir 'Alla," to be published in *Comptes Rendus du Groupe Linguistique d'Etudes Chamito-Sémitiques*.

[17] Cf. Lemaire, "Galaad et Makir," *VT* 31 (1981), pp. 39-61, esp. 50-52.

[18] Cf. Ze'ev Meshel, *Kuntillet 'Ajrud*, Israel Museum Catalog 175 (Jerusalem, 1978).

[19] Cf. Lemaire, "Date et origine des inscriptions hébraïques et phéniciennes de Kuntillet Ajrud," *SEL* 1 (1984), pp. 131-143. See "Who or What Was Yahweh's Asherah?" by André Lemaire, **BAR**, November/December 1984.

Did Yahweh Have a Consort?

The New Religious Inscriptions from the Sinai

By Ze'ev Meshel

THE BOOK OF KINGS describes a time during the 9th-7th centuries B.C. when the land was divided into two kingdoms—Judah in the south and Israel in the north. Phoenicia and Israel were linked by commerce and royal marriages and Hebrew monotheism struggled to resist the attraction of pagan gods. The prophets Elijah, Elisha, Amos and Isaiah inveighed against transgressions. At Kuntillet Ajrud, a remote desert way-station in the wilderness of northern Sinai, we found evidence of the multiplicity of religious practices which provoked the prophets' fury.

The ruined walls of the rectangular west building at Kuntillet Ajrud occupy most of the summit of the hill. Closest to the observer is the entryway and immediately beyond it is the bench-room with its small square storage room at either end (seen most clearly on the right side). In the foreground are fragments of walls and all that remains of another building which disappeared when the hill eroded.

In three short seasons of excavation in 1975 and 1976 we uncovered a remarkable (and completely unexpected) collection of ancient Hebrew and Phoenician inscriptions painted on plaster walls and large storage jars, and incised on stone vessels. When the inscriptions were read, we discovered that they provided clear evidence that Kuntillet Ajrud was not merely a resting place for desert travelers but was principally a religious center. The inscriptions contain the names of *El* and *Yahweh*, words for God used in the Hebrew Bible. *Yahweh* (spelled *YHWH* in Hebrew consonantal writing) is the holy name of the Hebrew God as it appears in the Bible. *El*, a generic term for God, is also used in the Bible to refer specifically to the Hebrew God.

But the religious inscriptions from Kuntillet Ajrud also contain the names of pagan gods and goddesses, like Baal and Asherah. Both the travelers who stopped at this desert religious center and its few inhabitants were not all dedicated to the pure monotheistic principles espoused by the Hebrew prophets of their day. Some of these people may have been syncretistic Israelites mixing their Yahwistic principles with pagan influences. Others may have been Phoenicians—we also found some Phoenician inscriptions. Still others may have been pagans of other religious beliefs.

The most spectacular of the finds were two large pithoi (singular: pithos) or storage jars (see p. 288). Each of these storage jars is over three feet high and

weighs (empty) almost thirty pounds. Although both pithoi were found in fragments, they proved to be almost completely restorable. On the outside of each of these pithoi were several crude, folk-art drawings in red and black ink as well as a number of religious inscriptions. Two of these pictures may even be Yahweh and his consort—a blasphemous concept never before suggested by an archaeological discovery!

The first announcement and photographs of the Kuntillet Ajrud finds were published in the March 1976 issue of **BAR**. This early account promised **BAR** readers a more complete report in the future. Here is that report—including some pictures never before published.

The report has been longer in coming than I expected because the words and drawings are faded and enigmatic. What I present here are tentative conclusions and alternative hypotheses about material which I, and other scholars, will be studying for years to come.

Kuntillet Ajrud is located about forty miles south of Kadesh-Barnea and sits on a hill which rises beside the Wadi Quraiya*. Old maps reveal that the site is a crossroads of desert tracks: one leads from Gaza through Kadesh-Barnea to Eilat; another traverses the

*A wadi is a dry river bed which flows only one or two days each winter when it rains. Then the water flows with furious and dangerous intensity.

Three people, arms upraised in a gesture of prayer, were drawn on the outside of one of two large, almost complete, pithoi, or storage jars, found at Kuntillet Ajrud. Both pithoi contain inscriptions as well as drawings. The three praying figures are part of a group of five people, too faded to illustrate in their entirety. The drawing technique is crude and personal, probably that of an unskilled, local artist. The numerous inscriptions on this pithos include blessings and an incomplete Hebrew alphabet with the letter peh preceding ayin, an alphabetic order known from the Bible in Lamentations and Proverbs. Drawings and inscriptions from the other pithos may be found on pages 292 and 295.

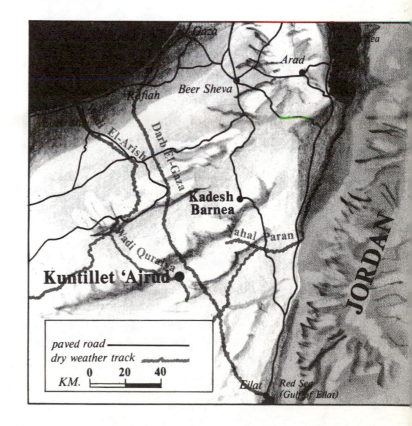

Sinai along the Wadi Quraiya; and a third branches off to the south via Temed, a well-known way station in later times, to the center of southern Sinai.

The site was discovered by the famous English explorer Edward Palmer who surveyed the Sinai Peninsula in the 1860's and visited Ajrud in 1869. There he carried out a small sounding into the ancient remains and subsequently identified the site as Gypsaria, a site known from Roman sources as a station on the Roman road from Gaza to Eilat.

But since Palmer's day archaeologists have learned a great deal about pottery dating. After the 1967 Six-Day War we came to the site and by examining the sherds which lay strewn about we were able to detect Palmer's error easily and to date the site to Iron Age II or the Israelite period. This new date identified the site as the southernmost outpost of the Judean kingdom, and it became a prime candidate for excavation. A few years later I led the archaeological expedition to Kuntillet Ajrud on behalf of Tel Aviv University (Institutes of Archaeology, and of Nature Conservation Research); the Israel Department of Antiquity; the Department for Holy-Land Studies in the Kibbutz Movement, and the Israel Exploration Society.

The top of the hill comprising the site is an oblong plateau extending east-west, with the ruins located at its western end (see p. 285). Wells in the vicinity—in use even today—gave the site its ancient importance.

The two large pithoi, bearing drawings and inscriptions, on display in the Israel Museum next to the 400 pound stone bowl.

The modern Arabic name Kuntillet Ajrud means "Solitary Hill of the Wells," a name which accurately reflects its character.

The site contains the remains of only two structures: a main building at the western extremity of the plateau and a smaller building east of it (see plan on p. 289). The two buildings are in very different states of preservation. Almost nothing is left of the small building on the east, and there is little to say of it. The main building, whose walls have survived to a height of five feet, measures approximately 75 x 45 feet, and takes up the whole width of the narrow plateau.

The entrance to this building is from the east, through a small court (1)* with stone benches along the walls. Fragments of frescoes found amidst the debris on the floor of the entrance indicate that parts of the walls were painted with colorful floral motifs and linear designs. An entryway (2) led from the small entrance court to a broad, narrow room, which we call the "bench-room" (3). Both the bench-room and the entry had benches along the walls and were plastered all over with white, shiny plaster.

The bench-room extends across the width of the building. The benches along the walls on each side of the entrance-way take up most of the floor space, leaving only a narrow passage between them. At either end of the bench-room is a window-like opening into a small room. The sills of these windows are formed by the benches immediately adjacent; the windows are the only openings or entrances into the small rooms (4 and 5) at the ends of the bench-room.

Strangely enough, the inner courtyard (6) of the building—to which we pass from the bench-room—was empty except for three ovens (7) found in each of the southern corners, indicating that this was probably the cooking area. The three ovens could not have been used simultaneously because the floor level of each oven overlapped the dome of the one below. It is hard to tell how long each oven was in use, but together, the three ovens probably functioned as long as the total life of the site, which may have been no more than one generation. Steps (8) were found in the southern corners and probably formed part of staircases leading to the roof.

To the south and west of the courtyard were two long rooms (9 and 10). In the floor, bases of pithoi, or storage jars, were firmly embedded and so closely

*Numbers in parentheses refer to the plan on p. 289.

spaced that it must have been difficult to pass between them. There is no doubt that these rooms were used for storing food.

Tower-like corner rooms (11 and 12) were found in the western corners of the building. Access to these rooms is from the courtyard. At the rear of each room is a small compartment. Not much is left of the south-western room, most of which had collapsed into the valley, but the room in the northwestern corner is fairly well preserved and contained some flat limestone slabs of unknown purpose, stone bowls, and red- and black-painted pottery vessels.

The relatively well-preserved condition of these tower-like rooms revealed some interesting construction details: the walls were built of rough unhewn stones, quarried from local limestone; branches—mainly of the tamarisk tree which grows abundantly in the Wadi Quraiya—were placed between the stone courses, some lengthwise and others crosswise, forming an intermediate course which acted as a binder for the wall. Incorporating tree branches in construction is well-known from various countries and was used over long periods. In 1 Kings 7:12, it is said that in the court of the Temple in Jerusalem there were "three courses of hewn stone ... and a course of cedar beams." At Kuntillet Ajrud there were no hewn stones and no cedar beams, but the interlaced tamarisk branches seem to be a less refined version of the Temple construction technique. Wood of any kind is a rare find in such an ancient building in Israel.

With the exception of the bench-room, the entry-way and the entrance court (which were covered with white plaster), the walls of this building were coated with a plaster of mud mixed with straw. Ceilings were made of branches, many of which were found in the debris of the rooms.

The most remarkable finds of the excavation, however, were the inscriptions and drawings. Most of these were found in the bench-room and in the two side rooms entered from the bench-room.

A fragment of a Phoenician inscription was found in situ on the north jamb of the doorway leading from the bench-room to the courtyard. Unfortunately, it is so faded that it cannot be read. Near the entrance to the western store room (10), fragments of another inscription on plaster were found. It too had originally been written on the jamb of the entrance to this store room. It resembles the other inscription in its poor state of preservation and fragmentary condition. It

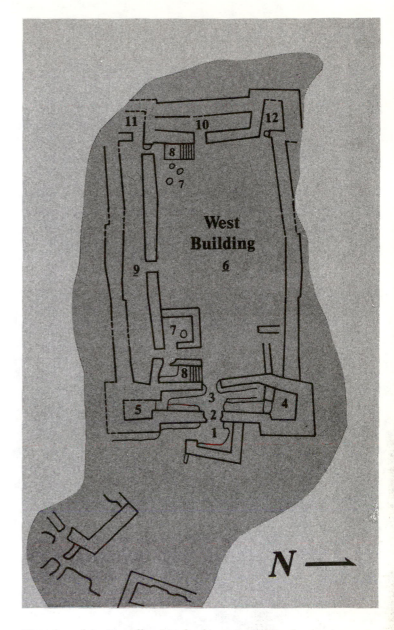

This plan of the Kuntillet Ajrud cult center enables the reader to identify (1) outer court, (2) entrance, (3) bench-room (4) and (5) small rooms entered from windows at either end of the bench-room, (6) inner court, (7) ovens, (8) stairs, (9) and (10) storage rooms, (11) and (12) tower-like corner rooms.

Bench-room at Kuntillet Ajrud   *Most of the plaster and pottery bearing inscriptions and drawings were found here. Travelers probably deposited their offerings here when they stopped at this desert way-station and religious center. The entryway to the building is in the middle of the bench-room, on the right, and the entrance to the inner courtyard is opposite, on the left. At either end of the white-plastered bench-room was a doorless storage room, where old offerings were placed when the bench-room became overcrowded.*

can, however, be read partially. The words which we have been able to decipher include:

> *wbᵢrh.'l.b...* "and in the (just) ways of El"
> *brk.bʿl.bym.ml...* "blessed be Baʾal in the day of ..."
> *šm.'l.bym.ml...* "the name of El in the day of ..."

(The dots are word dividers).

The original location of these inscriptions—on the door jambs—recalls the Biblical verse: "And you shall write them on the doorposts of your home and one your gates" (Deuteronomy 6:9).

Another inscription was found on a plaster fragment which had dropped off the wall of the bench-room. It reads: *...brk.ymm.wyšbʿw/hytb.yhwh....* (The slash indicates a new line.) The religious content is clear. *Brk.ymm* means "blessed be their day" and *hytb.yhwh* means "Yahweh favored." Although these texts are extremely incomplete and difficult to decipher, they are clearly religious in nature and appear to consist of requests, prayers and blessings.

The most dramatic discoveries were on two pithoi, previously mentioned, which were restored from sherds found in the bench-room. Both pithoi were densely covered with drawings as well as inscriptions. The drawings and inscriptions frequently overlapped. Most were executed in red ink and all are in early Hebrew script. Because of their very poor condition, we used a special photographic technique to bring out the script to help us decipher it.

The first large pithos contains two drawings, one on either side. One of the drawings includes three figures (see p. 295): a seated woman playing the lyre; —————————— the god Bes in the center with his genitals (or tail) exposed between his legs; and another unidentified deity on the left similarly exposed. Bes stands in his characteristic stance, arms akimbo with his customary feathered headdress. Originally an Egyptian demi-god, in the course of time Bes was adopted by most other countries in the ancient Near East and figures depicting him have been found frequently in Syria, Phoenicia, and the Mediterranean islands.

The inscription written across the top of the drawing and over the unusual headdress of the god (goddess?) on the left reads as follows:

> *'mr.'...h. k. 'mr.lyhl...wlywʿsh.w...brkt.'tkm. lyhwh.smrn.wl'srth.*

The first portion of the inscription seems to be a statement in the form "X said to Y and Z" but only the word 'mr "said" and the name yw'sh "Yo'asah" are legible.

The words following can be read in several ways. It is clearly a blessing which begins "May you be blessed by Yahweh." Then come the two final words smrn and wl'srth*. The former, pronounced "shomrenu" in Hebrew, may have the meaning "protect us" or "guard us." The same letters can also be read as "Shomron," a proper name referring to the Biblical city of Shomron (Samaria), the capital of the Northern Kingdom. Which of the two interpretations is preferable? We cannot be sure. It would seem at first that the translation of smrn as "protect" is clearly preferable to "Shomron" because, in the Bible, Yhwh "Yahweh" is never followed by a proper name (with the exception of the title tsebaot, usually translated "God of Hosts"). However, there is an argument for the translation "Shomron" which we will present below.

The meaning of the last word 'srth (pronounced "Asherato") is even more enigmatic. Asherah is a pagan female diety mentioned frequently as the consort of Baal. But the "to" ending is a possessive form and this form is not used in Hebrew in connection with a proper name. However, if Asherah had the generic meaning of a female deity who was Yahweh's consort, then the possessive form could have been used. Asherah or Asherat also has two other meanings: one, it is an object, usually a tree, which symbolizes a deity, and the second, cella or holy of holies (or shrine). With either of these two meanings the possessive ending "o" would be grammatically correct. Thus it would be proper to say, "his (Yahweh's) holy of holies," or "his (Yahweh's) tree symbol or "his (Yahweh's) consort."

It is enticing to try to find a connection between the inscription and the drawings below it. One notices that the faces and ears of the two figures on the left resemble a cow or a calf. The calf may have had a holy meaning in the northern kindgom of Israel—suggested by the fact that Jeroboam erected a statue of a golden calf in the sanctuary at Bethel and at Dan (1 Kings 12:29). Therefore, the depiction of deities with cow-like faces suggests that perhaps the inscription above them may be read "Yahweh of Shomron." It is also possible that two of the three figures, (the lady with the lyre, the Bes or the other standing person) may be depictions of "Yahweh and his consort" if the final phrase is read in this way—a thoroughly blasphemous notion, but one which seems consistent with the diverse religious influences at Kuntillet Ajrud.

On the other side of this same large pithos is a drawing of a "tree-of-life," sprouting lily flowers, and flanked on either side by ibexes (see p. 292). Below the tree of life is a majestic lion in motion. This pithos also contains a drawing of a cow, head turned back, suckling its calf. ——————————— These motifs are well known in the Syro-Phoenician world, and we found many close comparisons to the Ajrud drawings. It is easy to see that the artistic execution at Ajrud is not refined; we may be quite sure that the drawings were by local artists who, although isolated in the desert, were influenced by the Syro-Phoenician cultural environment.

The second pithos contains a number of drawings, most of them poorly executed. These include the figure of a man drawing a bow, a cow (this time without a calf) and a striking scene of five figures standing in a row with arms upraised in a gesture of prayer (see p. 286).

This pithos also contains a number of inscriptions and four Hebrew abecedaries*. In these abecedaries the letter pe precedes the ayin, rather than the reverse, as is usually the case in the later Hebrew alphabet. This reversal of letters is also found in four acrostic paragraphs in the Bible (Lamentations 1-3 and Proverbs 31). Recently a Hebrew alphabet from the 11th century B.C. was discovered at Izbet Sartah (see A. Demsky and M. Kochavi "An Alphabet from the Days of the Judges" BAR, September/October 1978, p. 23) in which the same letter reversal occurred. Apparently, the alphabetic order preserved in the 8th century Kuntillet Ajrud inscription is not an error, but a continuation of a much earlier alphabetic tradition.

Another inscription on this pithos contains a blessing:

'mryw 'mrl.'dny h. . .brktk.lyhwh. . .
wl'srth.ybrk.wysmrk wyhy 'm.'dnu. . .

---

*The w which precedes the final word and two other words in the full transcription of the inscription is the particle which is translated "and."

*An abecedary is an alphabet.

A tree of life sprouting lilies is flanked by two ibexes. Below is a lion. The cow and suckling calf drawing also appears on this pithos, as does the Bes scene (p. 295).

"Amaryau said to my lord . . . may you be blessed by Yahweh and by his Asherah. Yahweh bless you and keep you and be with you. . ."

A similar inscription was incised on the rim of an enormous stone bowl found in the bench-room (see p. 293). The bowl was apparently dedicated to the site for use there by its donor. What the use was we do not know. Given the fact that the bowl weighs over 400 pounds, it is safe to say that the donor, one "Obadyau," was not only wealthy but also believed in the sanctity of the site.

The inscription on the rim of the bowl reads as follows:

l'bdyw bn 'dnh brk h'lyhw

"(Belonging) to 'Obadyau son of 'Adnah, may he be blessed by Yahwe(h)."

The donor's name "Obadyau", like most of the other private names, has the ending "yau" (common in the northern kingdom and known from the Samaria Ostraca* and other finds) and not "yahu"

*The Samaria Ostraca are a collection of inscribed sherds found in excavations at Samaria, capital of the northern kingdom. The ostraca were commercial documents from about 800 B.C.

(the common form in Judah). Does this show that the people who wrote the inscriptions came from the northern kingdom of Israel? This is another problem yet to be solved. A second stone bowl found in the bench-room also contains a "yau" name. It reads:

sm'yw bn 'zr

"Shema'yau son of 'Ezer"

Adnah (the father of Obadyau who gave the large stone bowl to the site) bears a name that appears in 2 Chronicles 17:14. This Biblical Adnah commanded 300,000 men under King Jehosaphat, who reigned in Judah between 867 and 851 B.C. If the donor of the bowl was the son of the Biblical Adnah, this would date the bowl and the site a generation after Jehosaphat—that is—to the late 9th century B.C. This fits well into our dating of the site to a period between the mid-9th century and the mid-8th century B.C.

Another group of secular inscriptions are those which were incised on vessels before and after firing. Those incised after firing include three personal names. They also include the inscription *lsr'r* which

This stone bowl weighing more than 400 pounds was an offering found in the bench-room at Kuntillet Ajrud. The inscription on the rim reads "(Belonging) to 'Obadyau son of 'Adnah, may he be blessed by Yahwe(h)".

was found scratched four times on storage jars. *lsr'r* is similar to two inscriptions on recently found bullae (sealings) which were stamped *lsrh'r* (lesar ha'ir) "(belonging) to the governor of the city." These sealings have been attributed by Professor Nachman Avigad to the governor of Jerusalem. According to this hypothesis, the Kuntillet Ajrud inscription should be read *lesar 'ir* (without the article *ha*-the) — "(belonging) to the governor of a city." The term would then refer to the person who was in charge of the site. The presence of a governor who received supplies shows that Ajrud was organized as a small administrative unit.

Finally, we should mention short inscriptions which were incised on storage jars before firing. Most of the large storage jars had one or two letters incised on the shoulder. The most common single letter was *'alef*. Less common was the letter *yod*. The combination *qof resh* occurred twice. The purpose of these signs is not clear. Perhaps they were marks of capacity, quantity or quality, destination or use. In any case, the markings were decided on at the place of manufacture of the vessels, and before they were finished; this place could not have been Kuntillet Ajrud.

These letters may indicate that the content com-

plied with religious law or was intended for religious use. At Masada, some storage jars were found marked with the letter *taw* as well as many small sherds with the letter *yod* and other initials. Yigael Yadin notes that in the Mishna (a second century A.D. compilation of what was previously oral law) the use of letters on vessels is explained: "If a vessel was found on which is written a *qof*, it is *qorban* (offering); if a *mem*, it is *ma'aser*(tithed); if a *dalet*, it is *demai* (tithing is uncertain); if a *tet*, it is *tebel* (untithed); if a *taw*, it is *terumah* (heave-offering)." The vessels from Masada date about 800 years later than the storage jars at Kuntillet Ajrud and the Mishna is still later, but perhaps the tradition recorded in the Mishna and preserved at Masada is based on a custom already prevalent in the days of the Monarchy. If so, then do the letters *qof resh* at Kuntillet Ajrud stand for *qorban* (sacrifice) and does the letter *yod* signify *ma'aser* (tithed)? Do the letters indicate that the site was inhabited by a group of priests who, as in Jerusalem and other centers, received and lived on tithes and offerings?

Additional support for the hypothesis of a group of priests living at Kuntillet Ajrud is the large quantity of finely woven linen fabric found there. Linen fabrics must have had some special meaning for the inhabitants. According to the Bible, linen had cultic significance. Ezekiel stresses that when the priests enter the gates of the inner court, "they must wear linen garments; they must have nothing of wool on them while they minister at the gates of the inner court and within. They shall have linen turbans upon their heads and linen breeches upon their loins ..." (Ezekiel 44:17-18).

Over 100 pieces of textile fragments were found in our excavations, preserved by the dry desert air. Most of the fabric was linen, but there was some wool too. All the fabric was made from good quality yarn and was evenly woven, although the thickness and density of the weave varied. Pieces of cloth were woven together so neatly and carefully and with such a fine needle that it resembles today's so-called "invisible mending." Some of the fabrics have colored yarn woven into them as decorations.

We found some fabric made of mixed wool and linen. In one instance the red threads are wool and the blue linen. Garments made of a mixture of linen and wool are expressly forbidden in the Bible (Leviticus 19:19; Deuteronomy 22:11), but it may be that the prohibition was for ordinary people and not priests. The description of the garments of Aaron shows that they were especially splendid. The rich colors could probably be obtained only by dying woolen threads, thus indicating that part of the garments were of wool as they were at Ajrud.

It would be tempting to call the building at Kuntillet Ajrud a temple, but it bears none of the architectural features we customarily associate with a temple. The plan of the building does not contain a holy of holies, nor does it conform to the plan of other temples known from excavations in the Near East. Moreover, we found the remains of no cult objects, such as animal altars or incense burners or cult altars.

On the other hand, although the building was probably not a temple, we think that it was a religious center of some kind where people deposited their offerings in the bench-room.

The site represents, in our opinion, a religious center which had some connection with the journeys of the Judaean kings to Eilat, Ezion-Geber and perhaps even to southern Sinai. The establishment of this center may have come about through identification of the site with one of the Israelite traditions concerning Sinai. Travelers could pray here, each man to his god, and ask the divine blessing for his journey, much as is done today at holy places, or at sheikhs' tombs.

After the Exodus, the only Biblical personality who went to Mt. Horeb (identified with Mt. Sinai) was Elijah (1 Kings 19:8), who lived during the reign of King Jehosaphat (867-851 B.C.). Following Elijah, did a tradition of pilgrimage to Mt. Horeb (Sinai) develop, and was Kuntillet Ajrud a station on the pilgrims' route?

The pagan elements, so tangibly represented at Kuntillet Ajrud, are also vividly portrayed in Biblical descriptions of the period. Elijah himself vented his fury at King Ahab (871-852 B.C.) of Israel who took for himself a Phoenician queen, Jezebel (1 Kings 17-18). Jezebel propagated Baal worship in Israel and her husband built her a temple of Baal (1 Kings 16: 31-32). Jezebel's daughter, Athaliah, became queen of Judah after the death of her son Ahaziah, who ruled only one year. Athaliah built a temple of Baal in Jerusalem and murdered all living descendents of the Davidic line (except for Joash—her grandson—who was hidden from her for seven years).

It is tantalizing to try to date Kuntillet Ajrud, to pinpoint in whose reign this religious center was established. The pottery and the form of the script suggests the end of the 9th to the beginning of the 8th centuries. But to be more precise, we must look for a time when these "facts" which we have discovered at Kuntillet Ajrud could have occurred together: the use of Phoenician script, the mixture of religious practices, priests in residence, names with *yau* endings (a northern rather than a Judaean influence), tools made of wood from trees in southern Sinai, and the location of the site on a route linking Judah with Eilat.

Perhaps Kuntillet Ajrud was established during the short reign of the half-Phoenician queen, Athaliah, whose Phoenician lineage, whose hatred of the priests of the house of David, and whose worship of Baal is all documented in the Book of Kings. Perhaps she sent *her* priests to live and serve at Ajrud. Perhaps it was she who gave the Phoenicians from the north their much sought passage through Judah on their way to the Red Sea. Perhaps this traffic explains why we find wood from the south and *yau* names from the North. Perhaps in the Phoenician inscriptions they left behind, these Phoenician travelers left evidence of their respite at Kuntillet Ajrud.

A large cow-eared figure stands on the left and a seated lyre-player on the right. In the center is a drawing of the god Bes. Bes, originally an Egyptian demi-god, is recognized by his arms akimbo and by his characteristic feathered head-dress. The figures on the left have exposed genitals or tails. The inscription above the two left hand figures includes the two enigmatic words asherah ("consort," "holy of holies" or "tree-symbol") and shomron ("guard" or the city of Shomron). If the correct reading is "consort," two of the three figures may represent Yahweh and his consort.

WHO OR WHAT WAS
Startling New Inscriptions from Two Different Sites

André Lemaire

NEW INSCRIPTIONS from two different sites have reopened the debate about the meaning of asherah, a term often used in the Bible. Is it—or she—a goddess? Is it a holy place? Or perhaps a sacred tree? Or a pole? Or possibly a grove of trees? All these suggestions have been proposed at one time or another by scholars.

The question is especially intriguing because, as a result of these new inscriptions, the inquiry now arises in connection with the sacred unpronounceable name of Israel's God, usually written YHWH, or Yahweh.* Whatever an asherah is, Yahweh had one!

The first of these inscriptions came to light, as seems to be the case so often, as a result of an illegal excavation by Bedouin or by Arab farmers. A few months after the Six-Day War of June 1967, when Old and New Jerusalem were reunited, some Iron Age material, including a short Hebrew inscription on limestone cut from a tomb wall, was offered on the Jerusalem antiquities market. All this material, including about 125 pieces of eighth-century B.C. pottery and a collection of iron and bronze implements as well as the inscription, was acquired by Dr. William G. Dever for Hebrew Union College, with which he was then associated. After considerable intrigue, the material was traced to a small Arab village named Khirbet el-Kom, just eight miles west of Hebron in the territory of Judah. There Dever located a group of Iron Age tombs that gave evidence of having been recently robbed on a very large scale. The materials Dever had purchased obviously came from this site. Dever immediately undertook a salvage excavation of the site.

In the course of his excavation, Dever not only located the tomb from which the inscription had been cut, he

WILLIAM G. DEVER

also found two other Hebrew inscriptions carved on the limestone walls of the tomb-cave. All the inscriptions could be dated on epigraphic grounds* to the eighth century B.C. Two of the three inscriptions are short and simple. One reads as follows: "Belonging to Ophai, the son of Nethanyahu, (is) this tomb-chamber." The second, written in ink, reads nearly the same: "Belonging to Ophai, the son of Nethanyahu."

The longest and most interesting inscription, however, is what appeared to Dever to be a four-line inscription carved on a pillar between two tomb chambers. Unfortunately, some of it is very difficult to read because it was

---

* In Hebrew, the name consists of the four letters YHWH, *yod, he, waw, he,* and is known as the Tetragrammaton. In many English translations of the Bible, YHWH is translated LORD. *Elohim,* by contrast, is translated as the generic name God; YHWH, however, is the name of Israel's God. No one is sure how these four Hebrew letters were pronounced (in Biblical Hebrew, the vowels are not generally indicated), but by scholarly convention, the name is vocalized as Yahweh.

* That is, by the shape, stance, and form of the letters.

YAHWEH'S ASHERAH?

Reopen the Debate about the Meaning of Asherah

"Blessed by Yahweh *and by his asherah." This Hebrew blessing on the wall of a tomb near Hebron may have been as popular in the eighth century B.C. when it was carved as "May he rest in peace" is today. A similar inscription found in Sinai appears on p. 299.*

What or who was Yahweh's asherah? Some scholars suggest that asherah was the name of a goddess, the consort or wife of Yahweh. Others say that an asherah was a holy place or sanctuary. But the author proposes that an asherah was a sacred tree or group of trees that was an integral part of a hilltop sanctuary.

incised as a graffito* in the soft chalky rock of the tomb. Line three's meaning is especially difficult to determine; most of the letters on this line were incised twice, but the second time the engraver did not scratch them exactly on the same line, so that most of the letters are doubled and the general aspect is very confusing. In 1970, Dever published the inscription together with his reading and interpretation of it,[1] recognizing that "line 3 is most difficult." Although Dever gave what he called a "tentative translation," he conceded that "perhaps the whole last line [line 3] is to be divided [into words] and under-

stood quite differently." (The letters are not divided into words but simply run on in a continuous sequence; moreover, since Hebrew is written for the most part without vowels, interpretation can be quite difficult.)

In these circumstances, I decided it would be desirable to attempt my own reading of the inscription, which, after a careful study of the incisions, I published in 1977.[2] In general, I was in accord with Dever with respect to much of the inscription, but I disagreed with him significantly in the reading of line 3. By dividing the letters into words differently, I discovered a reference to an asherah. Both Dever and I read Yahweh at the end of line 2, so in my reading this was to become an asherah of Yahweh.

In addition, at the end of the inscription there were

---

* A graffito is an incised or scratched inscription or drawing on a wall or on a rock.

some scratchings that Dever did not identify as part of the inscription. He recognized the Hebrew letters לשרת (LŠRTH), but he did not offer a translation. In my examination of the inscription, I concluded that these letters were the fifth line of the inscription and read them as לאשרת (L'ŠRTH), another reference to asherah. Finally, I saw at least the hint of a sixth line of the inscription that Dever did not see at all. This line too may contain a reference to asherah.

My reading and translation of the inscription is as follows:

1. Uryahu *the wealthy man had it written:*
2. Blessed be Uryahu by Yahweh
3. and *by his asherah; from his enemies he saved him!*
4. *(written) by Onyahu.*
5. . . . . . *and by his asherah*
6. . . . . . *(and by) his (ashe)r(ah)*

The words and letters in parentheses are reconstructions not actually in the inscription. In addition, I have changed the position of "by his asherah" in line 3; in the original it appears after "enemies." I believe that the engraver, working in the dark of the tomb with only an oil lamp for light, made a mistake, perhaps forgetting to carve "by his asherah" at the beginning of the line and then writing it after "from his enemies."

In any event, the reading of asherah now seems quite certain.* It is confirmed by the undoubted reference to asherah in line 5 and the probable reference in line 6.

When we transpose the reference to asherah in line 3 to the beginning of the line, as I believe we must do, we are able to resurrect what was probably an old popular blessing formula from the middle of the eighth century B.C., the date of this inscription as indicated by an analysis of the letters and spellings. Although this blessing formula—"Blessed by Yahweh and his asherah"—appears only once in the inscription and despite some uncertainty in the transposition, it seemed to me very likely that this formula was extremely common at that time.

It is not hard to imagine the excitement and satisfaction with which I greeted the news—just when my translation was being printed—that another inscription bearing this very same formula had been found in an excavation in Sinai.

In fact, the archaeologists working in Sinai had excavated their inscription shortly before my publication of the Khirbet el-Kom inscription. This Sinai excavation, in

* This has been confirmed by two other epigraphists, J. R. Engle, *Pillar Figurines of Iron Age Israel and Ashérah-Ashérim*, Diss. 1979 (Ann Arbor, 1981), p. 82, and K. Jaroš, "Zur Inschrift Nr. 3 von Hirbet el-Qôm," *Biblische Notizen* 19 (1982), pp. 30-41, although they do not transpose the reference to asherah to the beginning of the line as I do.

1975 and 1976 at a site known as Kuntillet Ajrud, was directed by Ze'ev Meshel of Tel Aviv University (see "Did Yahweh Have a Consort?" **BAR**, March/April 1979, pp. 24-35 [284-295]).[3] The site lies about 40 miles south of Kadesh Barnea and about 55 miles northwest of Eilat, almost on the border of the Negev. The major building on the site was apparently a kind of caravansary for travelers and traders. It was perhaps also a guard station protecting the desert crossroads connecting the Nile Delta with Gaza and Eilat. Dozens of crudely painted inscriptions were found on the plastered walls and on large storage jars.

Many questions have been raised about these intriguing and highly important inscriptions from Kuntillet Ajrud, and they have already been the subject of numerous scholarly articles.[4] But at least one thing is clear: *asherah* after *Yahweh* in a blessing formula is repeated several times. Thus, for example, on one storage jar we find: "I bless you by Yahweh of Samaria and by his asherah" (*brkt 'tkm lyhwh šmrn wl'šrth*)(pithos 1, lines 1-2).

Another reads: "I bless you by Yahweh of Teiman and by his asherah" (*brktk lyhwh tmn wl'šrth*)(pithos 2, lines 4-6).

Similar blessing formulas seem to appear in the Phoenician inscriptions painted on the plaster walls of Kuntillet Ajrud, which, like the Old Hebrew inscriptions on the storage jars, can be dated on paleographical grounds to the first half of the eighth century, about 776-750 B.C.,[5] during Jeroboam II's reign. The mention of "Samaria" and the way the personal names are written with the ending *-yw* seem to indicate that these Kuntillet Ajrud inscriptions were written by people from the northern kingdom of Israel, rather than the southern kingdom of Judah.

The inscriptions from Kuntillet Ajrud of course strongly reinforce my reading of the inscription from Khirbet el-Kom.

It is now clear that we must confront blessing formulas mentioning Yahweh's asherah. These blessing formulas were used by people from Judah (as at Khirbet el-Kom) as well as by people from Israel (as at Kuntillet Ajrud) in about the middle of the eighth century B.C., that is, during the period before Hezekiah's reign (c. 719-699 B.C.) and during the religious reforms associated with his reign.

In understanding these blessing formulas, we must start with the fact that Yahweh had an asherah. The asherah is clearly associated with Yahweh. It is, of course, tempting to conclude that asherah is a goddess—more precisely, Yahweh's consort. And indeed, this interpretation has been urged by several commentators,[6] especially by scholars who are familiar with the texts from Ugarit and are also experts in other ancient non-Hebrew Semitic religions. It is these materials that most strongly suggest

Yahweh and his consort? *Fragments from a broken storage jar excavated at Kuntillet Ajrud reveal an enigmatic drawing. The inscription across the top of the drawing reads: "I bless you by Yahweh of Samaria and by his asherah."*

At first, the excavator of Kuntillet Ajrud, Ze'ev Meshel, thought that the word *asherah* on this sherd could mean a goddess, consort of Yahweh, and that the three crudely drawn figures could be interpreted as Yahweh, far left; his consort, the seated lyre player, far right; and, in the center, the Egyptian demigod Bes, identifiable by his feathered headdress and his pose of arms akimbo. But now, a recently published interpretation by Pirhiya Beck concludes that both standing figures are representations of Bes, while the lyre player is not a goddess, but just a musician. Both Bes and the lyre player are common iconographic motifs on Syro-Phoenician artifacts such as seals and ivories, especially those dating to the eighth century B.C.

Thus, it seems that a meaningful relationship between the inscription and the figures on the Kuntillet Ajrud vessel is unlikely, although one scholar, William G. Dever, who initially published the Khirbet el-Kom inscription discussed in the text, is reportedly about to publish an article defending the identification of the seated lyre player in the picture as Yahweh's Asherah.

299

that asherah is in fact a goddess.

The famous site of Ugarit, on the Syrian coast, yielded a cache of 14th- to 13th-century B.C. cuneiform tablets that are a primary source for understanding pre-Israelite, Canaanite religion.* Included in the cache are several ritual texts and at least three religious epic myths. Among the many goddesses who appear in the Ugaritic texts is Athirat, the consort of the great god El. Athirat is the Ugaritic linguistic equivalent of Hebrew asherah.** One of Athirat's epithets is "Athirat-of-the-Sea (aṭrt ym)." As El's consort, she is also called "creator (or begetter) of the gods (qny ilm)." The cult of Athirat was especially strong in Late Bronze Age Tyre (15th to 13th centuries B.C.). In one Ugaritic myth, the Story of Keret, we learn of a sanctuary dedicated to "Athirat of the Tyrians."[7]

It is well-known that in Israelite religion Yahweh replaced the great god El as Israel's God. If Yahweh replaced El, it would seem logical to suppose that under Canaanite influence asherah replaced Athirat, and that, at least in the popular religion of ancient Israel if not in the purer form of that religion reflected in the Bible, asherah functioned as the consort or wife of Yahweh.

Moreover, a number of Biblical texts seem consistent with this interpretation. In Judges 3:7, we read that during Joshua's time (c. second half of the 13th century B.C.), "The Israelites did what was offensive to Yahweh; they ignored Yahweh their God and worshipped Baalim (plural of Baal) and Asherot (plural of asherah)." Here the asherot are worshipped in association with a god.

In 1 Kings 18:19, the prophet Elijah, in the ninth century, asks King Ahab to summon on Mount Carmel "450 prophets of Baal and 400 prophets of Asherah." Again asherah is associated with a god (Baal); this time the asherah even has prophets, apparently about as many as Baal.

Asherah is again associated with Baal during the religious reform of King Josiah (c. 622 B.C.) when Josiah ordered "the objects made for Baal and Asherah" removed from the Temple and burned (2 Kings 23:4).

In the Iron Age (12th to 6th centuries B.C.) levels of excavations all over Israel, one of the most common finds are small female fertility figurines. We now have hundreds of these figurines.[8] Several archaeologists and Biblical scholars have identified these figurines as representa-

tions of a goddess Asherah.[9]

Moreover, on one of the large storage jars (called pithoi) from Kuntillet Ajrud, some commentators believe they see asherah as a goddess depicted in a drawing, standing beside a figure identified as Yahweh.[10]

Despite what may appear to be the formidable case I have summarized above, I do not believe that asherah is a goddess-consort to Yahweh either in the Khirbet el-Kom inscription or in the Kuntillet Ajrud inscriptions. Neither do I believe that asherah refers to a goddess in the Biblical texts I have cited. Let us look at the evidence more closely.

First, we return to the drawing on the storage jar from Kuntillet Ajrud, which supposedly features asherah standing beside a figure representing Yahweh. The middle figure on the storage jar, in a group of three with two standing on the left and one seated on the right, is clearly the Egyptian god Bes, easily recognized by his arms akimbo and his feathered headdress. Additional study of the figure standing on the left reveals that it too is clearly a depiction of Bes. There is no reason to believe that the left figure is Yahweh or that the middle figure is a depiction of Yahweh's consort, an asherah.[11] In short, there is no figure here that could possibly be Yahweh. This leaves us with the figure of a seated female lyre player on the far right. She is simply a lyre player accompanying the standing figures of Bes. The storage jar does contain an inscription referring to Yahweh's asherah, but the drawing on the jar in no way suggests that the word asherah as used in the inscription means a goddess or a consort.

Upon careful study, the Ugaritic texts are no more persuasive than the drawing on the storage jar from Kuntillet Ajrud. We are considering whether references to Yahweh's asherah in the eighth century B.C. are intended to refer to a female consort. In assessing what light is shed on this question by the Ugaritic texts, we must remember that they were written at least 500 years earlier, in a different country (on the northern Syrian coast) and in a different language (Ugaritic). The use of Ugaritic parallels in this instance is probably an example of excessive use of religious comparativism to reach an extreme and invalid conclusion. Phoenician texts of the first millennium, which are much closer in time to our references to Yahweh's asherah than the Ugaritic texts of the second millennium, make no mention of a goddess asherah.[12] Baal is often mentioned in these texts, especially in votive inscriptions and as part of personal names,* but no reference is ever made to his asherah.

* See "An Appreciation of Claude Frederic-Armand Schaeffer-Forrer (1898-1982)" by James M. Robinson, "The Tablets from Ugarit and Their Importance for Biblical Studies" by Peter C. Craigie, and "The Last Days of Ugarit" by Claude F. A. Schaeffer, translated by Michael D. Coogan, **BAR**, September/October 1983.

** The Ugaritic t (th) is equivalent to the Hebrew s (sh), and the Ugaritic feminine ending -t is equivalent to the Hebrew -h.

* As in 'dnb'l, "Adonibaal," 'zrb'l, "Azorbaal,"/"Azdrubal," b'lhn' "Baalhano." F. L. Benz, Personal Names in the Phoenician and Punic Inscriptions (Rome, 1972), pp. 280, 288-290.

This brings us to the Biblical references to Baal and asherah. Without the support of the Ugaritic texts referring to asherah as a goddess and without the depiction of an asherah goddess on the storage jar from Kuntillet Ajrud, there is no reason to interpret asherah in the Biblical references cited above as a goddess. Nor is there any special or peculiar reason to interpret the common fertility figurines of the Iron Age as depictions of a goddess Asherah.

Moreover, a knowledge of Hebrew grammar reveals that there is an insuperable grammatical obstacle to interpreting these Biblical passages as references to the name of a goddess. This argument is not hard to understand, but it does require a little background. In English we use the definite article "the" to make a noun definite or, as the scholars say, determinated. In Hebrew, the prefix *ha* is used for this purpose. But in Hebrew (as in English), proper names *are* determinated;[13] they do not normally take the prefix *ha*. You would no more say "the asherah" or *ha-asherah* if it were the name of a goddess than you would say "the Susie." (A rare exception is when the Hebrew name is used not as a personal name but as an appellative; that is, when it has become a common noun, for example, when Baal is used to denote not the name of a particular god, but simply *lord*.) Asherah is used in the Bible, however, with the definite article ("the" or *ha-*). There are many examples of this, for example, Judges 6:25,26,30 and 1 Kings 16:33. Thus, these Biblical references to asherah preceded by the definite article indicate that asherah is *not*, in these references, a personal name.

Moreover, personal names in Hebrew never have a pronominal (or pronoun) suffix, such as *-y* meaning "my." The new inscriptions from Khirbet el-Kom and Kuntillet Ajrud show that asherah can be constructed with a pronominal (or pronoun) suffix, in this case, *-h*, meaning "his."

Thus, it is clear that neither in these Biblical passages

Text continues on p. 304

Fertility figurines *(below left). Excavated in Israel, stylized sculptures with perforations indicating physical features were in common use both in the Late Bronze Age (13th and 14th centuries B.C.) and in the following Iron Age. At many tells in Israel dating to the Iron Age (ninth to seventh centuries B.C.), archaeologists have uncovered a profusion of pillar figurines, such as those pictured below right. Some scholars, but not the author, identify these figurines as the goddess Asherah.*

ISRAEL DEPARTMENT OF ANTIQUITIES AND MUSEUMS/© ERICH LESSING

SACRED TREES IN ANCIENT ART

In antiquity, sacred trees, or asheroth, were associated with cult places throughout the Near East, from Egypt to Mesopotamia and Syria-Palestine. A sacred tree (left) stands taller than King Esarhaddon in the upper register of this black basalt stele. To the right of the tree is a bull and to the left of the ruler is an altar at which the king worships. A seed plow in the lower register is flanked on the right by a date palm tree and on the left by an object that may be a hill or a stylized ear of grain. This stele dates from the reign of Esarhaddon, Sennacherib's son, who ruled Assyria and Babylonia from 680 to 669 B.C.

A plaque from Sumer (below), with its black and red painted designs still bright, shows two rearing goats on either side of a sacred tree. This relief, now in the British Museum, dates to the third millennium B.C. The same motif is seen on an orthostat (drawing, far left) from the "palace of Kapara" in Northern Mesopotamia at Tell Halaf (c. 10th century B.C.). The trunk of this tree is stylized, but the palm fronds and date clusters at the top are naturalistic. Sometimes this motif varied to show two human figures flanking the asherah, as in the drawing (left) of an early first-millennium B.C. orthostat from Carchemish in Turkey.

On an exquisitely carved ivory plaque (opposite), a bearded man grasps a sacred tree. Dating to the eighth century B.C., the plaque from Nimrud stands ten inches high.

ISRAEL DEPARTMENT OF ANTIQUITIES AND MUSEUMS

Cylinder seal (bottom) of bluish-gray chalcedony and an impression of it in clay (top). A stylized and schematically rendered sacred tree is flanked by two figures that are half man and half bull. The bull-men support a winged sun disk from which emerge three stick-like figures, identified as deities. To the right, a worshipping priest towers over the cultic scene. Faintly etched Aramaic letters, LSLM, to the left of the scene tell us that the late eighth-century B.C. seal "belongs to Shallum."

303

nor in the Old Hebrew inscriptions from Khirbet el-Kom and Kuntillet Ajrud is asherah a personal name of a goddess. It is a generic noun referring to something else.

Another possibility is that an asherah is simply a holy "place." This interpretation is suggested by comparisons with other Semitic languages. In Akkadian, *asirtu* indicates a holy "place," a "sanctuary."[14] Cognates from eighth-century B.C. Old Aramaic[15] have the same meaning, as do cognates in Middle (roughly 500 B.C.) and Late (third century B.C.) Punic Phoenician.[16] On this basis, one prominent scholar has suggested that we understand the Hebrew word asherah as a holy place or sanctuary.[17]

Even though asherah is often associated in the Bible with a sacred place, especially the so-called "high places" or *bamot* (singular: *bamah*), the context seems to indicate that the asherah is not the high place itself or the whole sanctuary but rather a cultic object which is part of the high place. In short, asherah is more specific.

Let us look more closely at a few of the Biblical references. (There are too many to cite them all.)

Asherot are mentioned most prominently in connection with the two great religious reforms of the Old Testament, the first by King Hezekiah of Judah at the end of the eighth century B.C. and the second by King Josiah of Judah toward the end of the seventh century B.C.

Hezekiah's reform is described in 2 Kings 18:4:

"He [Hezekiah] abolished the *hill-shrines* (bamot) and smashed the *sacred pillars* (massebot) and cut down the asherah. He also broke into pieces the bronze serpent which Moses had made."

The book of Deuteronomy is usually associated with the Josianic reform of the next century. It was then, many scholars believe, that most of Deuteronomy was written. In this passage from Deuteronomy, the Lord commands the Israelites through Moses:

"You shall not plant a tree as an asherah beside the altar of Yahweh your God that you shall build; you shall not set up a sacred pillar (massebah) which Yahweh your God hates" (Deuteronomy 16:21-22).

In the first quotation above (the one from 2 Kings), asherah is preceded by the definite article "the" (the Hebrew letter *he*), an indication that asherah is not the personal name of a goddess.

Both these passages make clear that the suppression of Yahweh's asherah was one of the principal aims of both Hezekiah's religious reform and Josiah's.

These passages also reflect the fact that an asherah is a wooden object associated with the cult of the high places (*bamot*). From other Biblical passages we learn that an asherah can be planted (*nt'*, Deuteronomy 16:21), pulled down (*ntš* Micah 5:13), cut (*krt*, Exodus 34:13) and burned (*srp*, Deuteronomy 12:3), but generally it stands up ('*md*,

cf. 2 Kings 13:6).

In rabbinic commentaries as well as in some ancient translations into Greek (like the Septuagint of the third century B.C.) as well as in the King James Version, asherah is translated *grove*. Others suggest it should be translated as a wooden pole. Either is possible, but I prefer to think of it as a sacred tree or possibly a group of trees, as in a grove. Some commentators who see the term as referring to a sacred pole suggest that this pole was a symbol—or possibly a wooden statue—of a goddess Asherah.[18]

Interpreting asherah as a sacred tree or grove conforms very well with what we know generally about the cultic places of the ancient Near East (Egypt, Mesopotamia and Syria-Palestine). A sacred tree, or grove, or garden is frequently associated with a sanctuary or cult place (see for instance Judith 3:8). The tradition of the sacred tree is found as late as the 19th century A.D. in a few Palestinian villages.

Nevertheless, it must be conceded that the references to asherah associated with Baal could point in the direction of an asherah's being a goddess. But all the references to asherah in association with Baal are relatively late (in terms of when the Biblical text was actually written down)—that is, beginning in the late eighth century B.C.

In the late eighth century B.C., about the time of Hezekiah's religious reformation and his centralization of the cult in Jerusalem (which is why all outlying cult centers were destroyed), we notice the beginnings of some transformation in the attitude toward the asherah. This transformation appears not only in the context of Hezekiah's religious reformation in the eighth century but also in the context of the religious reformation associated with the writing of the book of Deuteronomy, led by King Josiah, in the late seventh century B.C. The latter occurred, of course, after a certain amount of Israelite backsliding following Hezekiah's reforms.

During these two major religious reformations, asherot were officially and definitively expelled from Israelite religion. What had been acceptable in the patriarchal age was no longer acceptable. The outlying cult places—the high places (bamot) with their sacred pillars (massebot) and asherot were no longer tolerated. They had to be destroyed. The Bible, especially those passages containing historical accounts attributed to the so-called Deuteronomic historian (that is, to the same tradition that produced the book of Deuteronomy), preserves polemical texts directed against these cult centers scattered about the country.

To argue more effectively against these outlying cult centers, the Biblical polemicist sought to associate them and their constituent parts with the debased Canaanite religion and the cult of Baal. The message to the people of Israel was that they must reject the outlying cult centers, including the asherot, just as they must reject the cult of Baal (and other gods).

The objectification of aspects of the divine and the personification of cultic objects is a common phenomenon in the history of religions.[19] We find it, for example, in Ugarit and in Aram.* Among a polytheistic people, such an evolution is unobjectionable. But to people of a monotheistic or monolatric** religion, such an evolution is a very serious threat, raising the specter of an anathema. The eighth-century prophet Hosea inveighs against the high places (bamot), although they were acceptable in the patriarchal age. The prophet tells us that the Lord will destroy the high places; thorns and thistles will then grow on the altars (mizbehot), and the mountains where once these cult places stood will humiliate the people (Hosea 10:8).

Amos, from about the same period, prophesies that for the transgressions of the people, the Lord will destroy the altars (mizbehot) of Beth-el and cut off their horns (Amos 3:14); the high places (bamot) of Isaac will be desolate (Amos 7:9).

We may assume that the asherot were similarly condemned (Deuteronomy 16:21-22). The prophets were fearful that these cultic objects might become sacred in themselves, as a god, and so become rivals of Yahweh.

The recent inscriptions from Khirbet el-Kom and Kuntillet Ajrud help illuminate the prophet's messages. They help us understand why the asherah was rejected from official Israelite religion at the end of the eighth century B.C. In these inscriptions, asherah is still a generic name, as shown by the pronominal (or pronoun) suffix, but it is on the way to being personified, as reflected in the way the asherah is associated with Yahweh in blessing. In a more subtle psychological or theological way, we are witnessing a kind of birth of a hypostasis in which the essence of the divine is bound to a cultic object; that is, an aspect of the divine is becoming concretized or reified—and may soon rival God himself.

Thus these recently recovered inscriptions do more than give us direct evidence of an eighth-century blessing formula; they also illuminate an important chapter in the history of Israelite religion. They help us to understand the nature of popular Israelite religion before Hezekiah's reforms. They also help us to understand why the prophets and kings (or at least some of them) sought to suppress the traditional local sanctuaries, which very probably contained sacred trees known as asherot.

---

* See the Ugaritic goddesses "Qudshu" (qds, etymologically "sanctuary") and "Athirat" (atrt, etymologically "[holy] place") and the Aramaic god "Bethel" (byt-'l, etymologically "house of god," "temple").

** A monolatric religion has one god but admits the possibility of other gods for other nations or peoples.

[1] W. G. Dever, "Iron Age Epigraphic Material from the Area of Khirbet el-Kom," *Hebrew Union College Annual* 40/41 (1969-1970), pp. 139-204.

[2] A. Lemaire, "Les inscriptions de Khirbet el-Qom et l'ashérah de YHWH," *Revue Biblique* 84 (1977), pp. 595-608.

[3] See also Ze'ev Meshel, *Kuntillet 'Ajrud, A Religious Centre from the Time of the Judaean Monarchy on the Border of Sinai*, Israel Museum Catalog 175 (Jerusalem, 1978).

[4] Cf. J. Naveh, "Graffiti and Dedications," *Bulletin of the American Schools of Oriental Research* 235 (1979), pp. 27-30; J. R. Engle, *Pillar Figurines of Iron Age Israel and Ashérah-Ashérim*, Diss. 1979 (Ann Arbor, 1981); M. Weinfeld, "A Sacred Site of the Monarchic Period," *Shnaton* 4 (1980), pp. 280-284 (Hebrew); D. A. Chase, "A Note on an Inscription from Kuntillet 'Ajrud," *Bulletin of the American Schools of Oriental Research* 246 (1982), pp. 63-67; J. A. Emerton, "New Light on Israelite Religion: The Implications of the Inscriptions from Kuntillat 'Ajrud," *Zeitschrift für die alttestamentliche Wissenschaft* 94 (1982), p. 2-20; P. J. King, "The Contribution of Archaeology to Biblical Studies," *Catholic Biblical Quarterly* 45 (1983), pp. 1-16, especially 12-13; A. Lemaire, "Abécédaires et exercices d'écolier en épigraphie nord-ouest sémitique," *Journal Asiatique* (1978), p. 221-235; id., *Les écoles et la formation de la Bible dans l'ancien Israel* (Orbis biblicus et orientalis [a series]) 39 (Fribourg, 1981), pp. 25-32.

[5] A. Lemaire, "Date et origine des inscriptions hébraïques et phéniciennes de Kuntillet 'Ajrud," to be published in *Studi Epigrafici e Linguistici* 1, 1984.

[6] Cf. R. Patai, "The Goddess Asherah," *Journal of Near Eastern Studies* 24 (1965), pp. 37-52; id., *The Hebrew Goddess* (1967), pp. 29-52.

[7] 1 *Keret* 197-199.

[8] J. B. Pritchard, *Palestinian Figurines in Relation to Certain Goddesses Known through Literature* (American Oriental Series 24: London, 1943); K. M. Kenyon, *Jerusalem* (London, 1967), pp. 101-103; T. A. Holland, "A Study of Palestinian Iron Age Baked Clay Figurines...", *Levant* 9 (1977), pp. 121-155.

[9] Cf. J. R. Engle, *Pillar Figurines*.

[10] M. Gilula, "To Yahweh Shomron and his Asherah," *Shnaton* 3 (1978/9), pp. 129-137 (Hebrew).

[11] Pirhiya Beck, "The Drawings from Horvat Teiman (Kuntillet 'Ajrud)," *Tel Aviv* 9 (1982), pp. 29-31.

[12] None of the references proposed by J. R. Engle (*Pillar Figurines*) is certain; more probably, each one is to be explained otherwise; cf., for instance, Z. Zevit, *Israel Exploration Journal* 27 (1977), p. 115.

[13] *Gesenius' Hebrew Grammar* (Oxford, 1970), pp. 401-403.

[14] *The Chicago Assyrian Dictionary* (CAD) A/II (1968), pp. 436-439.

[15] Sfiré I B 11, 'srthm, "their sanctuaries": See A. Lemaire and J. M. Durand, *Les inscriptions araméennes de Sfiré et l'Assyrie de Shamshi-ilu*, Hautes études orientales (Geneva, 1984), pp. 114, 123.

[16] Pyrgi 1, 1, 'sr; Umm el-Amed 4, 4: See J.C.L. Gibson, *Textbook of Syrian Semitic Inscriptions III, Phoenician Inscriptions* (Oxford, 1982), pp. 119-120, 154-155.

[17] E. Lipinski, "The Goddess Atirat in Ancient Arabia, in Babylon and in Ugarit," *Orientalia Lovaniensia Periodica* 3 (1972), pp. 101-119.

[18] W. L. Reed, *The Nature and Function of the Asherah in Israelite Religion According to Literary and Archaeological Evidence*, Diss. 1942 (Ann Arbor, 1982); T. Yamashita, *The Goddess Asherah*, Diss. 1963 (Ann Arbor, 1982); A. L. Perlman, *Asherah and Astarte in the Old Testament and Ugaritic Literatures*, Diss. 1978 (Ann Arbor, 1979).

[19] Cf., for instance, J. Teixidor, *The Pagan God, Popular Religion in the Greco-Roman Near East* (Princeton, 1977), pp. 31, 86-87.

Jeremiah's Scribe and Confidant Speaks from a Hoard of Clay Bullae

HERSHEL SHANKS

SELDOM DOES ARCHAEOLOGY come face to face with people actually mentioned in the Bible. When that happens, the discovery takes on a unique immediacy, touched with awe.

When a hoard of inscribed Hebrew bullae surfaced on the antiques market and was found to contain a bulla impressed with the name of Baruch, son of Neriah, known from the Bible as secretary and faithful companion to the prophet Jeremiah, the scholarly community was stunned.

That was more than ten years ago. Even now, however, the mysteries surrounding this hoard are as great as the revelations. So much is unknown about these little pieces of clay—so much that we intuitively feel should be knowable.

Like where they came from.

A bulla is a small lump of clay impressed with a seal that served as a kind of signature. Bullae were attached to ancient documents to secure them and to identify the sender. The backs of bullae often bear the impress of the papyrus on which the documents were written and the string with which the documents were tied (see photo, p. 311).

The first four bullae in this particular hoard—a hoard

DAVID HARRIS

impressions—made from the same seal—were found in the hands of different collectors who brought their purchases to Professor Avigad for evaluation. On several occasions, one lot of bullae contained a fragment that fit together with a fragment from another lot.

Apparently, the Arab villagers who found the hoard, either accidentally or as a result of illicit excavation, divided up the loot and sold their various shares to different antiquities dealers.

Eventually, a Jerusalem collector named Yoav Sasson acquired nearly 200 of the bullae. Another collector, philanthropist Reuben Hecht, who owns Haifa's famous Dagon Tower and the shipping company associated with it, acquired 49 pieces. Hecht donated his collection to the Israel Museum, and Sasson made his collection available for scholarly publication. The entire collection has now been published by Professor Avigad in a beautiful volume entitled *Hebrew Bullae from the Time of Jeremiah* (Israel Exploration Society, 1986).

Professor Avigad has wrung more information from these bullae than was imaginable—at least to this observer—but the mystery remains: Where was this hoard of bullae found? As we shall see, it is a question of some importance.

In contrast to the mystery as to where the bullae were found, the date of the bullae can be fixed with certainty. Usually, bullae that come on the market in this way are dated by the shapes of the letters in the script. Here, however, we have not one, but two, Biblical figures whose seals have been impressed in the bullae—and we know when they lived. In addition to Baruch, son of Neriah, the hoard contains the seal of King Jehoiakim's son Yerahme'el (Jerahmeel), who, together with two other police types, was sent to arrest Jeremiah and Baruch because of Jeremiah's politically unpalatable prophecies (Jeremiah 36).

Jeremiah prophesied shortly before the Babylonian destruction of Jerusalem in 586 B.C., as well as during

that would ultimately number over 250—came to light in October 1975 in the shop of an Arab antiquities dealer in East Jerusalem. The four bullae were purchased by a collector who took them for evaluation to the leading Israeli expert on ancient seals and sealings, Nahman Avigad of the Hebrew University.

That was only the first of many visits to Professor Avigad by a series of collectors who had purchased bullae from several Arab dealers—in Jerusalem, in Bethlehem and in the village of Beit Sahour. It was obvious to Professor Avigad that all the bullae had come from the same hoard: Bullae bearing identical seal

Nebuchadnezzar's First Campaign 605-604 B.C.

Haran
Carchemish
Euphrates River
Cyprus
Hamath
Byblos
Damascus
Tyre
Mediterranean Sea
Sea of Galilee
Jordan River
Samaria
Jerusalem
Ashkelon
Dead Sea
Nile River
Brook of Egypt
Noph

0 20 40 mi
0 25 50 km

Jeremiah by Michelangelo, *from the Sistine Chapel ceiling. Jeremiah decried Judah's alliance with Egypt, predicting that it would bring destruction from the Babylonians. As Nebuchadnezzar thrashed the Egyptians at Carchemish (c. 605 B.C.), the Lord told Jeremiah to write his prophecies on a scroll, "and Baruch wrote in the scroll, at Jeremiah's dictation, all the words which the Lord had spoken to him" (Jeremiah 36:4).*

Nebuchadnezzar's first campaign. *The Egyptian army under Pharaoh Neco marched (solid line) to Carchemish in 609 B.C. to help the Assyrians try to reconquer Haran. The invasion failed, but the Egyptians retained possession of Palestine and Syria and installed Jehoiakim as king of Judah. In the fourth year of Jehoiakim's reign (c. 605 B.C.), Nebuchadnezzar's Babylonian army (dotted line) defeated the Egyptians twice in succession at Carchemish and Hamath. These events confirmed Jeremiah's warnings—dictated to his scribe, Baruch—against Judah's alliance with Egypt. Nothing stood between Judah and the onslaught of the Babylonians now that the Egyptians were in full retreat. Nebuchadnezzar's forces swept through the Holy Land a year later, conquered Ashkelon, and in 586 B.C. turned east to Jerusalem and destroyed the Temple and the city.*

the Exile thereafter. Professor Avigad dates these bullae to the very end of the seventh century and the beginning of the sixth century B.C., just before Jerusalem's conquest and destruction.

In the summer of 605 B.C., Nebuchadnezzar, king of Babylonia and the most powerful political figure in the entire world, crushed the Egyptian army at Carchemish and began to advance into Syria. It was clear that tiny Judah would be next on the line of march. The northern kingdom of Israel had already been conquered by the Assyrians (in 721 B.C.) and was no more. Judah was obviously no match for the Babylonians, who had assumed the position of world superpower after defeating the Assyrians. The Egyptian defeat at Carchemish made it plain that Judah was relying on a weak reed if she expected any protection from her alliance with Egypt.

For some time Jeremiah had been lashing out against Judah's alliance with Egypt and had been predicting Judah's destruction at the hands of the Babylonians.

In the fourth year of the reign of King Jehoiakim (c. 605 B.C.), as the Bible tells us (Jeremiah 36:1), the Lord spoke to Jeremiah and instructed him to write his prophecies on a scroll. "Perhaps," Yahweh* told Jeremiah, "if the house of Judah hears all the disasters I intend to bring upon them, they will turn back from their wicked ways, and I will pardon their iniquity and their sin" (Jeremiah 36:3).

"So Jeremiah called Baruch son of Neriah; and Baruch wrote down in the scroll, at Jeremiah's dictation, all the words which the Lord had spoken to him" (Jeremiah 36:4).

Jeremiah himself was in hiding, so he told his friend and confidant to take the scroll and read it aloud in the Temple on a fast day.

"Baruch son of Neriah did just as the prophet Jeremiah had instructed him, about reading the words of the Lord from the scroll in the House of the Lord" (Jeremiah 36:8).

When Baruch did this, it was reported to high officials at the king's palace not far away. Baruch was sent for and was told to read the scroll to the palace

* Yahweh is the common vocalization of the personal name of the Hebrew God represented in the Bible by four Hebrew consonants YHWH, referred to by scholars as the tetragrammaton.

officials. The officials, showing some courage, advised Baruch to go into hiding with Jeremiah.

The scroll—apparently confiscated from Baruch at the palace—was then taken to King Jehoiakim himself. Each time a few columns was read to the king, he would take those columns and burn them in the winter fire that was warming him.

Then the king ordered three courtiers, including his son Yeraḥme'el, to go and "arrest the scribe Baruch and the prophet Jeremiah." But the courtiers could not find the pair: "The Lord hid them" (Jeremiah 36:26).

When Jeremiah heard that the king had burned the scroll, he dictated to Baruch a second copy (Jeremiah 36:32). Then the Lord instructed Jeremiah to prophesy to King Jehoiakim:

"Thus said the Lord: You burned that scroll, saying, 'How dare you write in it that the king of Babylon will come and destroy this land and cause man and beast to cease from it?' Assuredly, thus said the Lord concerning King Jehoiakim of Judah: He shall not have any of his line sitting on the throne of David; and his own corpse shall be left exposed to the heat by day and the cold by night. And I will punish him and his offspring and his courtiers for their iniquity; I will bring on them and on the inhabitants of Jerusalem and on all the men of Judah all the disasters of which I have warned them—but they would not listen" (Jeremiah 36:29-31).

The hoard of bullae contained not only a seal impression of Baruch, son of Neriah, but also of King Jehoiakim's son Yeraḥme'el, who was sent on the unsuccessful mission to arrest Baruch and Jeremiah. Baruch's seal impression reads as follows:

(Belonging) to Berekhyahu	לברכיהו
son of Neriyahu	בן נריהו
the scribe	הספר

The inscription is in three lines, as printed above. A double line separates the first from the second and the second from the third line of text. The letters, in the old Hebrew script used in pre-Exilic Israel and Judah, are all clear and easily readable. A linear frame encloses the seal.

Baruch's full name was apparently Berekhyahu, a fact not previously known. The common suffix -yahu in ancient Hebrew names, especially in Judah, is a form of Yahweh. Baruch means "the blessed." Berekhyahu means "blessed of Yahweh."

An equivalent form to -yahu is -yah, traditionally rendered as "-iah" in English translations. Neriah is really Neri-yah or Neriyahu.

Eighty of the 132 names represented in the hoard (many names appear more than once on the 255 bullae) include the theophoric element -yahu. Yeraḥme'el's bulla bears the inscription:

(Belonging) to Yeraḥme'el	לירחמאל
son of the king	בן המלך

Yeraḥme'el's seal is very similar to Baruch's, except that it is in two lines, instead of three.

Baruch and Yeraḥme'el are not the only important persons whose names appear on the bullae in this collection. They are the only two who are known to us from the Bible; but a number of other people whose seals are impressed on the bullae were important high officials. We know this because we have their titles—just as Baruch is identified as "the scribe" and Yeraḥme'el is identified as the "king's son."

The "son of the king" or "king's son" is itself an important position, equivalent to a title. Whether it actually refers to the king's son, however, is a matter of debate. Some scholars believe that it does refer to the king's physical son, both when we read of the king's son in the Bible and on seals and bullae. (Incidentally, the title has now been found on four seals and on four other seal impressions.) Of course, in addition to his paternal tie, the king's son played a significant role in the royal service.

Other scholars, however, argue that "son of the king" simply refers to the title of a high royal official unrelated to the king. Professor Avigad holds a middle position: His view is that the title was held by male members of the king's family. Thus, while bearers of the title were of royal blood, they were not necessarily the king's son in a literal sense. Of course, many scions of the royal family (king's sons) held high official positions and used seals in the performance of their duties.

Another title that appears in this collection of bullae is "servant of the king." The title is referred to in the Bible (2 Kings 22:12; 2 Chronicles 34:20) and is known from numerous seals and seal impressions. According to Professor Avigad, "This title was apparently a rather general one and was not indicative of the type of office held, beyond the fact that its holder was a high-ranking official of the circle close to the king." Apparently, it was a somewhat lower title than "son of the king."

(Belonging) to 'Elishama^c **לאלשמע**
servant of the king **[ע]בד המלך**

One of the seal impressions in the hoard of bullae contains the name " 'Elishama^c, servant of the king." A man by the name of Elishama figures in the episode already described from Jeremiah 36. After Baruch read aloud the seditious scroll in the Temple, he was ordered to appear before high court officials at the palace where he again read the scroll dictated to him by Jeremiah. These officials, apparently somewhat sympathetic, or at least respectful of Jeremiah's message, advised Baruch to go into hiding with Jeremiah. One of those officials is identified in the Bible as Elishama (Jeremiah 36:12).

Professor Avigad rejects the identification of the seal of 'Elishama^c with the Elishama mentioned in this passage, because in the Bible, Elishama bears the title of scribe ("Elishama the scribe"), and on the bulla he is identified as "servant of the king." I would not reject the identification so easily. Elishama may well have held more than one title. A scribe might also be the servant of the king.* We know that many people had more than one seal. Perhaps the seal impressed in the bulla reflected Elishama's work as "servant of the king," while in Jeremiah 36 where he is called "the scribe" he is listening to the work of another scribe, Baruch. Or the bulla may have been stamped with Elishama's name at a different time in his life than the episode described in Jeremiah 36. In the course of his royal service, Elishama could well have occupied different positions at different times.

* Professor Avigad rejects the possibility because if 'Elishama^c of the seal had also been a scribe, "It is unlikely that the royal scribe would put aside his own title for another, less specific one which did not reflect his function."

Still another official title contained on the bullae in this hoard is one "who is over the house," as in "(Belonging) to 'Adoniyahu who is over the house." Incidentally, 'Adoniyahu had at least two seals. The hoard contains three bullae stamped with his seals, two with the the same seal and one with a second seal. One of 'Adoniyahu's bullae appears as follows:

(Belonging) to 'Adoniyahu **לארניהו ·**
who is over the house **אשר על הבית**

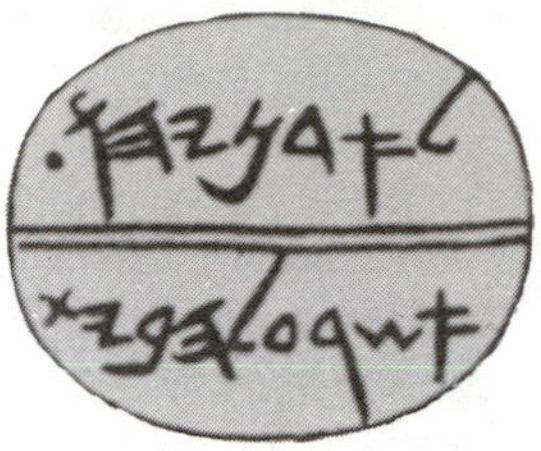

The title "who is over the house" was reserved, as Professor Avigad tells us, for the highest office at the royal court after the king. In the Bible this title is held by the senior members of the royal bureaucracy (1 Kings 4:6, 16:9, 18:3). In the eighth century B.C., one Shebna held this position under King Hezekiah, until Shebna was reduced to the rank of scribe (Isaiah 22:15ff, 36:3; 2 Kings 18:18).

Finally, a unique seal impression in the hoard bears the title "Governor of the city" (*sar ha-ir*). Instead of the typical form, which would lead us to expect "(belonging) to x, governor of the city," this seal impression contains only the title, not the name of the person who bore the title. Moreover, the title appears only in tiny letters enclosed in an oval (or cartouche, to use the scholar's term). Most of the seal is taken up with two figures facing one another, in pseudo-Assyrian style. Both are bearded, with long hair, and are dressed in long garments. One holds a bow and three arrows. The other has his right hand raised as if giving a blessing to the man with the bow and arrows. Based on parallels on Assyrian reliefs and cylinder seals, it would appear that the figure with the bow and arrows—he is depicted somewhat larger than the other man—is the king. The slightly smaller figure is probably the governor of the city. According to Professor Avigad, the governor is raising his hand to indicate his submission and loyalty to the king, a common theme in Assyrian glyptic art.

Since this seal did not bear the owner's name, perhaps it was used by successive governors of the city,

This unusual seal impression ***contains only the title "Governor of the city," without the name of the person who possessed the title. The two figures in pseudo-Assyrian style probably depict the governor, with his hand raised, indicating his submission and loyalty to the king. This seal may have been handed down with the office, rather than belonging to a single individual.***

as a kind of seal of office. Although it was obviously used as late as the end of the seventh century B.C., it may have been carved in the first half of the century, during the reign of Manasseh, when Israel was a loyal vassal of Assyria and strongly influenced by her.

The title "governor of the city" is known from the Bible (Judges 9:30; 1 Kings 22:26; 2 Chronicles 34:8; 2 Kings 23:8). There it appears that the title was held only by rulers of capital cities. Accordingly, Professor Avigad concludes that this seal belonged to the governor of Jerusalem:

> "The city [referred to in the seal impression] was surely the capital and not an outlying, secondary town, and the anonymous official was certainly the mayor of Jerusalem."[1]

All of this leads us to ask what kind of documents these bullae secured and where the document collection was stored.

These bullae survived for the most part because they came from a site destroyed in a great conflagration. As Professor Avigad notes, "Bullae of dried clay do not generally survive in good condition in the presence of damp soil." The fire that destroyed the documents to which the bullae were attached assured the preservation of the bullae, however, by baking the clay. The bullae

were fired unevenly, with the result that they contain variations in color from reddish-brown to yellowish and shades of gray and black. Sometimes the clay was overfired, resulting in clay that is fragile and friable.

While none of the papyrus documents from this collection survived (although the impress of the payrus weave and of the string or cord that tied the documents can often be seen on the backs of the bullae), we know a great deal about how the bullae were used and how the documents were sealed and stored. Our evidence comes from the Bible and from other archaeological discoveries as well.

While no papyri sealed with bullae have survived from as early as the seventh century B.C. (the date of this hoard), a collection of Jewish documents from Elephantine (an island in the Nile in Upper Egypt) dating to the fifth and fourth centuries B.C., was discovered largely intact with their bullae. The

Imprints of papyrus *documents and strings scar the backs of the bullae (right). Although no documents survived with this collection, the marks impressed on the damp clay confirm that these bullae were used to seal papyri. Documents with bullae still attached have been preserved from later periods, however, and show us how the bullae were employed.*

A collection of Jewish letters, deeds and financial documents, sealed with bullae and dating to the fifth and fourth centuries B.C., were found on Elephantine, an island in the upper Nile. Typical of this collection, the papyrus shown (below, bottom) has been folded several times, bound with a string and sealed with a bulla. The word "deed" written in ink appears on the papyrus.

Several bullae were used to seal the fourth century B.C. papyrus fragments discovered at Wadi Daliyeh, near Jericho. One of these documents (below, top) was tied with seven strings, each sealed with its own bulla.

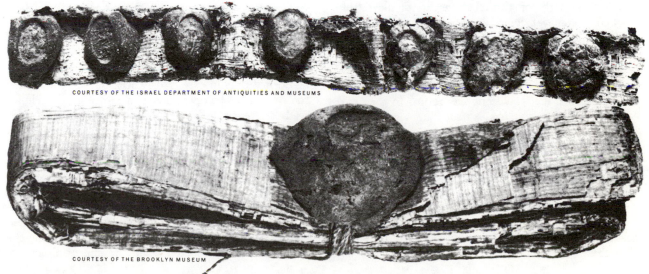

COURTESY OF THE ISRAEL DEPARTMENT OF ANTIQUITIES AND MUSEUMS

COURTESY OF THE BROOKLYN MUSEUM

collection included letters, deeds of sale, marriage deeds and documents concerning finances. The papyri had been folded several times and tied with string, and then sealed with a single bulla.

In a cave in the Wadi Daliyeh near Jericho, some papyrus fragments from the fourth century B.C. were discovered in the 1960s.* There each document was sealed with *several* bullae. One document had seven bullae attached to seven strings that tied it (see p. 311).

One wonders whether this is the reason for some of the duplicate bullae in the hoard from the time of Jeremiah. The hoard contains several examples of two and four bullae stamped with the same seal. In one case, 14 bullae are stamped with the same seal: "(Belonging) to Neriyahu (son of) 'Asherḥai."

In addition, some people whose names are contained in the hoard had two, three and, in one case, six different seals.

The documents themselves were undoubtedly archival documents—important letters, permits, contracts and perhaps deeds for the purchase of land.

Which brings us back to the Book of Jeremiah. Chapter 32 of the Book of Jeremiah contains the clearest description we have of the way property was transferred in pre-Exilic Judah, including the preparation of the deed, its form and the steps taken to preserve it. Moreover, this description is not in reference to just any land, but to land purchased as a symbol of Jeremiah's faith in God and a sign of his confidence that someday things would return to normal.

It was during Nebuchadnezzar's siege of Jerusalem. Zedekiah, then king of Judah, had had Jeremiah arrested—confined in the court of the palace guards—because of his prophecies.

Then the Lord came to Jeremiah and told him that his cousin Hanamel would offer to sell Jeremiah a field Hanamel owned in Anathoth. Jeremiah, it was explained, had a kinsman's right of redemption on the land. Just as God had said, Hanamel came to Jeremiah and offered to sell him the land. Apparently Hanamel was selling in despair, bereft of any hope for the future. The kinsman's right of redemption (see Leviticus 25:25) was a kind of right of first refusal. Jeremiah bought the field in Anathoth for 17 shekel weights of silver (this was before coinage). Jeremiah, who one might suppose was in the depths of despair, thereby expressed his hope for the future. Jeremiah knew that God was instructing him to buy the land (Jeremiah 32:8). God was thus symbolically telling him that, beyond the impending tragedy, normal life would one day return to the land. As one commentator has stated: "In view of this passage, the authenticity of which is unquestionable, one need not ask whether or not Jeremiah held out hope for the future."[2]

To memorialize the sale, a deed was signed, sealed and delivered, and then placed in storage. The Bible

A double deed *from Avroman in Kurdistan (third century B.C.), probably similar to the one Jeremiah used when he bought a field in Anathoth from his cousin Hanamel (Jeremiah 32). As Nebuchadnezzar besieged Jerusalem, Zedekiah, king of Judah, arrested Jeremiah for prophesying the fall of the city. In this time of little hope, God told Jeremiah that the despairing Hanamel would offer to sell him the field in Anathoth. When this came to pass, Jeremiah bought the land as a symbol of his faith and hope for the future. The Bible refers to "copies of the deed of purchase, the sealed and the unsealed" (Jeremiah 32:14), which Baruch deposited in a jar. This may indicate a double deed. One text on the scroll would be rolled up and sealed with strings and bullae, to be opened in the event of a legal dispute; and a copy or abstract of the deed would be written on the scroll's unsealed portion for the purpose of casual consultation. Or, as Professor Avigad suggests, in Jeremiah's case, the two copies may have been written on separate sheets.*

describes the transaction in some detail, which, as one might expect, was handled by Jeremiah's faithful friend, Baruch.

"I wrote out a deed [says Jeremiah], sealed it, and had it witnessed; and I weighed out the silver on a balance. I took the deed of purchase, the sealed text and the open one according to rule and law, and gave the deed to Baruch son of Neriah son of Mahseiah in the presence of my kinsman Hanamel, of the witnesses who were named in the deed, and all the Judeans who were sitting in the prison compound. In their presence I charged Baruch as follows: Thus said the Lord of Hosts, the God of Israel: 'Take these documents, this deed of purchase, the sealed text and the open one and put them into an earthen jar, so that they may last a long time.' For thus said the Lord of Hosts, the God of Israel: 'Houses, fields, and vineyards shall again be purchased in this land' " (Jeremiah 32:10-15).

The deed was in writing, witnessed and sealed. It was apparently a so-called double deed. There were two copies, "the sealed text and the open one." The sealed text was rolled up and sealed with a bulla or bullae. The sealed text contained the original deed, and would be opened only in case of a judicial dispute concerning the contents. The open, unsealed copy was available for ready reference. It is not clear whether the open deed contained the entire text of the original or just an abstract of the provisions in the original.

Examples of documents in two copies are known from Elephantine, where the two texts were written on a single sheet of papyrus. One half of the sheet was then rolled up, tied with cord running through holes in the middle of the sheet, and then sealed. The other half was then loosely rolled but not sealed. In this way the sealed copy was protected against fraudulent alteration,

---

* See Paul W. Lapp, "Bedouin Find Papyri Three Centuries Older than Dead Sea Scrolls" and Frank M. Cross, "The Historical Importance of the Samaria Papyri," **BAR**, March 1978.

while the open copy remained available for inspection. Similar documents from the third century B.C. have been found in Avroman in Kurdistan. Such documents were also used in Roman times when the closed, rolled-up portion was known as *scriptura interior*, and the open portion as *scriptura exterior*. In the Talmud, double documents are referred to as "tied deeds." These deeds were common in the Hellenistic period as well.

In early Mesopotamia, scribes writing in cuneiform on clay tablets often enclosed the document in a clay envelope. The clay envelope bore on its outside a copy of the original document inside the envelope.

In order to, as it were, file the deed to the Anathoth land, Jeremiah instructed Baruch to put the copies "into an earthen jar so that they may last a long time" (Jeremiah 32:14).

This was apparently the method of storing important documents. The Elephantine documents were found in earthen jars, and so were the Dead Sea Scrolls.

Of course, one can't help wondering if one of the documents to which one or more of the bullae in this hoard was attached—perhaps the bulla bearing Baruch's name—was the very deed transferring the field at Anathoth from Hanamel to Jeremiah. It's possible, but there is no evidence either way.

There is an even more intriguing question, however—more intriguing because it is perhaps answerable: Where did this hoard of bullae come from?

If we knew, we could excavate and perhaps find other remains that might tell us more about the bullae and the documents that they originally sealed. We might also learn more about the people who sealed them, what kind of archive they came from and what relationship the archive had to the Jerusalem court.

The presence of so many bullae bearing the titles of high-ranking royal officials—from the king's son to the governor of, according to Professor Avigad, Jerusalem—strongly suggests that this was a royal administrative archive or depository that originated in Jerusalem. Professor Avigad speculates that the archive was destroyed in the final conflagration that consumed Judah in 586 B.C.

According to the antiquities dealers through whose hands the bullae passed, the hoard was found about 44 miles southeast of Jerusalem, near Tell Beit Mirsim. As soon as this was learned, several archaeologists, including Professor Avigad, searched the area and located a hill near Tell Beit Mirsim that revealed traces of recent illegal digging, but not at a sufficient depth to suggest that this was the findspot of the bullae. Professor Avigad admits, however, that the search was "brief" and "not very thorough."

Why wasn't a more thorough search of the area conducted by the Department of Antiquities? Why didn't someone offer $5,000 to the antiquities dealers and another $5,000 to any person who would anonymously lead the archaeologists to the findspot?

The answer will no doubt be that there was no money for this—or even enough to make a thorough search. But imagine the value of what could have been learned if the findspot had been located. The reward could easily have been paid from the antiquities that would surely have been uncovered.* Unfortunately, a petrifying inertia seems to characterize the archaeological establishment when faced with a problem like this. No one even thinks of trying to solve it, or weighs the cost against the likely benefits, or brings any imagination to the task.

So, in the end, we are left with speculation, with more or less likely possibilities.

Professor Avigad considers the possibility that the bullae may actually have been found in the oldest inhabited part of Jerusalem, known as the City of David. Digging here, archaeologist Yigal Shiloh recently found a hoard of 51 bullae, contemporaneous with the hoard we have been considering. Shiloh's bullae too were preserved by having been baked in a conflagration—the burning of Jerusalem in 586 B.C.

Professor Avigad rejects the possibility that his bullae came from the City of David because, he says, illicit diggers would probably have been quickly discovered if they had been digging in that well-observed area. (What if they had been digging in the basement of a house?)

So the bullae probably came from a site outside Jerusalem. Perhaps in anticipation of the Babylonian destruction of Jerusalem, the archive was removed to what was considered—incorrectly, as it turned out—a safer location.

We may close with one final question, a question about Baruch, Jeremiah's friend, confidant and loyal supporter—Baruch, Jeremiah's secretary and recorder of his life and prophecies—Baruch the professional scribe:

Was he an official who bore this title as part of his royal administrative duties, or was he simply Jeremiah's personal scribe?

Professor Avigad suggests this appealing scenario: From the Bible, we know that Baruch was of a noble family. His brother Seriah was a minister at King Zedekiah's court and was sent on an important mission to Babylonia (Jeremiah 59:64). Baruch's seal impressed on a bulla in this collection, which included so many important royal officals, suggests that at the time Baruch pressed his seal into this lump of clay, he too was serving as an official royal scribe. Later, Professor Avigad suggests, he left the royal employ and joined his friend Jeremiah in his struggle against the pro-Egyptian, anti-Babylonian foreign policy of the court. That struggle, alas, proved unsuccessful, and Jerusalem in all its glory was destroyed soon thereafter. ◈

Photos of the individual bullae are by Zev Radovan; the drawings are by Nahman Avigad.

* See Hershel Shanks, "A Radical Proposal: Archaeologists Should Sell Ancient Artifacts," **BAR**, January/February 1985.

1 Nahman Avigad, *Hebrew Bullae from the Time of Jeremiah* (Jerusalem: Israel Exploration Society, 1986), p. 32.

2 John Bright, *Jeremiah*, Anchor Bible (Garden City, NY: Doubleday, 1965), p. 239.

YADIN PRESENTS NEW INTERPRETATION OF THE FAMOUS LACHISH LETTERS

By Oded Borowski

Scholars Corner

ON JANUARY 29, 1935, during the third season of excavations at Tell ed-Duweir, a site thought to be Biblical Lachish, archaeologists discovered a collection of 18 ostraca, or inscribed potsherds. The ostraca had been covered by a thick layer of destruction debris on the floor of a guardroom in the upper gate. The archaeologists credited the Babylonians, led by Nebuchadnezzar, with this destruction layer. In about 588 B.C., Nebuchadnezzar attacked Lachish just before he assaulted Jerusalem in 586 B.C., totally destroying that city and the First Temple. Later, three more ostraca were found at Lachish, making a total of 21.

The Lachish ostraca, or "The Lachish Letters" as they were called by Professor N. H. (Harry) Torczyner (Tur-Sinai), who was the first to decipher and interpret them, made an immediate splash in the scholarly world. Less than one month after their discovery, Sir Charles Marston, writing from Jerusalem to the *Palestine Exploration Quarterly*, proclaimed: "It is premature to suggest the precise effect that this find will have on old [sic!] Testament scholarship . . . But it already seems quite evident that further important evidence has been found that will tend to confirm the Old Testament . . . "

The letters clearly constituted some kind of correspondence and name lists. According to another scholar, J. W. Jack, who studied them, they were written in "iron-carbon ink with a reed or wood pen, the nib part of which must have been broad but not split."[1] Since the ostraca were inscribed in different handwritings, it is safe to assume that several scribes were involved. Some of the ostraca are inscribed on both sides, starting on the outer side of the jar. According to Jack, the handwriting is "fluent cursive, resembling in some signs the Samaria Ostraca."[2] The ink is still so clear on most of the Lachish ostraca that they can be read without difficulty. It is almost as if they had been written the day before their discovery. However, only seven of the 21 are long enough to produce a coherent translation.

A reading of the ostraca suggests that they belong to an exchange of letters between two military commanders. Unfortunately, only one side of this exchange has survived. The sender of the letters, Hosha'yahu, is mentioned in Ostracon III but not in the others—a strange fact. The addressee, Ya'ush, is mentioned in three of the ostraca (II, III, VI), but not in the others. Together, the ostraca seem to describe certain events the sender wishes to bring to the attention of the addressee.

Over the years most scholars have accepted the interpretation that Hosha'yahu, the sender, was commander of an outpost and reported to Ya'ush, the commander of Lachish and its region. We can conclude that the addressee, Ya'ush, is Hosha'yahu's superior by the way Hosha'yahu addresses Ya'ush: "Who is thy servant (but) a dog"[3] (Ostraca II, V, VI). This expression was also used by vassals addressing their overlord, Pharaoh, in the Amarna Letters.*

*The Amarna letters are 14th-century B.C. missives written in Akkadian cuneiform by feudal princes of Canaan to their Egyptian overlords. The clay tablets were discovered in the diplomatic archive of two 18th-dynasty Pharaohs at Tell el-Amarna near Cairo.

Lachish Letter Number IV, *written just before the Babylonians completed their conquest of Judea in the early sixth century B.C. Most scholars have considered this ostracon, or inscribed pottery sherd, the final form of a letter, which was sent from a military outpost in Judea to the garrison at Lachish. But now, renowned archaeologist-scholar Yigael Yadin is countering both elements of this theory. Yadin calls this ostracon a rough draft for a letter that was later written on papyrus. He further claims that the sender, Hosha'yahu, wrote this letter from Lachish to his superior officer Ya'ush, who may have been stationed at Jerusalem.*

The Lachish ostraca constitute the only collection of Hebrew letters from the time of the First Temple and have thus been scrutinized and argued about almost continuously since their discovery about 50 years ago.

Hosha'yahu is a direct voice from the past, speaking to Ya'ush, and now to us, with an urgency that reflects the precariousness of his position at Lachish. From his vantage point on the tel, Hosha'yahu cannot see signal fires from Tel Azekah less than seven miles away. Hosha'yahu no doubt fears that Azekah has fallen to the Babylonians and Lachish is in direct danger. The text of this sherd, shown clearly in the drawing, reads (from right to left) according to Yadin's new interpretation:

". . . but (I will send him) tomorrow morning./ And let (my lord) know that we are watching over the beacon of Lachish, according to the signals which my lord hath given, for Azekah is not to be seen."

Some of the reports sent by Hosha'yahu to Ya'ush describe events taking place just before the letters were written. In Ostracon II, Hosha'yahu the sender seems to be trying to quell a rumor about himself. As he tells the story, the rumor is untrue. Hosha'yahu invokes Yahweh to "afflict those who re[port] an (evil) rumor about which thou art not informed!" In Ostracon V a humble Hosha'yahu asks Ya'ush: "How can thy servant benefit or injure the king?" In Letter VII: "Truly I lie not—let my lord send thither!" Has Hosha'yahu been charged with plotting rebellion or treason against Jerusalem?

In Ostracon III Hosha'yahu refers to a letter from Ya'ush received by him on the previous day in which he, Hosha'yahu, had been accused of some misdeed. In the same letter, Hosha'yahu makes a reference to a delegation going to Egypt: "The commander of the host, Coniah son of Elnathan, hath come down in order to go into Egypt." Hosha'yahu ends the letter by mentioning another letter he has received; this passage contains an intriguing reference to "the prophet": "And as for the letter of Tobiah, servant of the king, which came to Shallum son of Jaddu'a through the prophet, saying 'Beware!', thy servant hath sent it to my lord." Apparently, Hosha'yahu has been accused of reading a letter sent to someone else. Some scholars also saw here a reference to an event described in Jeremiah 26:20-23, in which the prophet Uriah flees to Egypt. In this Biblical text, Elnathan son of Achbor is sent to Egypt to capture Uriah. In the Lachish ostracon, Coniah son of Elnathan goes down to Egypt.

Although it's not easy to project the full contents of the Lachish Letters, most scholars concluded that they were describing the final days of Judah, when she was defending herself against the Babylonian onslaught in the early sixth century B.C.* The mention of a prophet and a delegation to Egypt perhaps referred to the prophet and delegation mentioned in the Book of Jeremiah.

The case for a connection with the Biblical text became even stronger in Ostracon IV. Hosha'yahu reports: "And let (my lord) know that we are watching for the signals of Lachish, according to all the indications which my lord hath given, for we cannot see Azekah." To many scholars this sentence seemed to refer to the war situation in Judah just before the fall of Jerusalem. At the time Ostracon IV was written, Azekah had fallen to the Babylonians, and Lachish alone (except for Jerusalem) remained unconquered. A report in the Bible written, as it were, almost the day before this Lachish letter, refers to the fact that at one point in the battle only Lachish *and*

---

*This should be distinguished from the attack of the Assyrian king Sennacherib a little more than 100 years earlier, in 701 B.C., described in the two articles on pages 148 and 166.

City gate *of ancient Lachish. Most of the Lachish letters, 21 ostraca inscribed with messages from one Judean military commander to another, were found on the floor of a guardroom in this gate. They were buried by destruction debris when the Babylonians attacked this fortified gate and took the city in about 588 B.C.*

Azekah were left (again, except for Jerusalem). By the time Ostracon IV was written, Azekah too had fallen. As we read in the book of Jeremiah: "The prophet Jeremiah spoke all these words to King Zedekiah of Judah in Jerusalem, when the army of the king of Babylon was waging war against Jerusalem and against the remaining towns of Judah, against Lachish and Azekah, for they were the only fortified towns of Judah that were left" (Jeremiah 34:6,7).

Several of the Lachish Letters make references to similar events and occurrences. They also contain a number of repetitions. Some scholars explain these similarities and repetitions by suggesting that these messages were urgent. The military commander who sent them was unsure that any particular letter would reach its destination, so he sent several letters with the same information. The urgency of the situation was emphasized by the fact that the style of the letters was that of dictation. In addition, five of the letters were written on sherds from the same jar.[4] The sender apparently needed to repeat the message because delivery was so uncertain.

Since some letters seem to allude to accusations against Hosha'yahu, some scholars suggested that the letters were collected at the gatehouse as part of a court martial dossier against Hosha'yahu. Perhaps Hosha'yahu was accused of conspiracy or at least of not following the policy of the administration. In Ostracon V, he tries to defend himself, "How can thy servant benefit or injure the king?"

As the only collection of Hebrew letters from the time of the First Temple, the Lachish Letters are an extraordinarily important find. They are in a very real way a direct voice from the past. Although there have been arguments concerning their interpretation, most scholars have accepted, with only occasional hesitations, Tur-Sinai's view that the Lachish Letters were original documents sent to Ya'ush, the commander of Lachish, by Hosha'yahu, a commander of an outpost, most likely Qiryat-Ye'arim. Nevertheless, many questions remained:

1. Why are these documents written on potsherds and not on papyrus? Official correspondence at the time was written on papyrus.

2. Are the ostraca original letters or copies?

3. Since most of the ostraca do not bear the names of both the sender and the addressee, do they all belong to the same correspondence?

4. How can we explain the fact that for some of the letters, the text is fragmentary although the ostracon itself seems to be complete?

5. Why was this correspondence placed in the guardroom of the gateway?

These are only some of the questions raised by the Lachish Letters.

A recent paper by Yigael Yadin of The Hebrew University in Jerusalem* suggests a dramatically new hypothesis that may answer these questions and suggests a new interpretation of the letters themselves.

According to Yadin, the ostraca are drafts (or "trial versions"), not actual letters. That is why they are written on potsherds rather than papyrus. (The actual letters were later written for dispatch on papyrus and sealed with the signet of the sender.) That is also why five of the ostraca come from the same storage jar. That is also why the ostraca were written in such a short space of time. The ostraca are various drafts intended to be incorporated into no more than two or three letters, says Yadin. That is the reason for the frequent repetitions. That is also why the sender or addressee is so frequently omitted. This also explains the fragmentary nature of some of the ostraca.

The most startling aspect of Yadin's hypothesis is that if the Lachish ostraca are drafts, then they must have originated *at* Lachish and were not sent *to* Lachish. That is why five sherds from the same vessel were found in the guardroom of the gateway at Lachish; the drafts were written there by the scribes who were on duty at the gate bastion.

If Yadin is correct, the sender Hosha'yahu is the commander of the garrison at Lachish. He writes to his supe-

*"The Lachish Letters—Originals or Copies and Drafts?" *Recent Archaeology in the Land of Israel* (Biblical Archaeology Society: Washington, D.C., 1984), pp.179-186.

Yigael Yadin *suggests a new interpretation of the Lachish Letters.*

rior Ya'ush who is located elsewhere. But where? Yadin suggests that Ya'ush may well have been stationed at headquarters in Jerusalem. Ya'ush may even have been one of the king's sons.

One key to Yadin's hypothesis involves a new interpretation of a phrase in Ostracon IV relating to "the beacon of Lachish." Ostracon IV contains the following sentence: "And let (my lord) know that we are watching for (*shomerim 'el*) the beacon of Lachish, according to the signals which my lord hath given, for Azekah (or: the signal of Azekah) is not to be seen (lines 10-13).

The question Yadin asks is, Does *shomerim 'el* really mean "watching for"? If it does, the Lachish ostraca could not have been written *at* Lachish. The sender Hosha'yahu could not be *in* Lachish if he is watching for the beacon of Lachish.

But, says Yadin, *shomerim 'el* does not mean "watching for." The sender Hosha'yahu is reporting that he is "watching over" the beacon of Lachish to make sure that it still burns brightly as a signal that the city is still undefeated. If this is the meaning of *shomerim 'el*, then the letter was sent *from* Lachish, not *to* Lachish, and Hosha'yahu was loyally *tending* the beacon of Lachish.

Yadin's interpretation of *shomerim 'el* as "watching over" rather than "watching for" is based on several references in the Bible (1 Samuel 26:15-16; 2 Samuel 11:16) where a similar phrase clearly means "watch over."

With this reorientation in our thinking about the Lachish letters, Yadin is able to offer a new interpretation of the situation reflected in the letters.

According to Yadin, the sender Hosha'yahu is defending himself against a libelous charge. This theme, says Yadin, "runs like a scarlet thread through most of the ostraca."

The false charge against Hosha'yahu seems to be that he read a classified letter. In Ostracon VI, he states: "As the Lord thy God liveth, that . . . thy servant hath no[t] read the [le]tter . . . " And again in Ostracon III: "As the Lord liveth, no one hath ever dared to read a letter for me; moreover, nor any letter that hath come to me, I did not

read it . . . " As Yadin observes: "These are essentially two different, albeit similar versions of one and the same matter." These are simply different trial drafts of replies to the libelous charge.

The classified letter that Hosha'yahu is charged with having read apparently advised that the commander-in-chief was going to Egypt on a secret journey.

Hosha'yahu defends himself vigorously. "May the Lord afflict the utterers of a thing of which I was not aware" (Ostracon II). "As the Lord thy God liveth, . . . thy servant hath not read the letter" (Ostracon VI). Hosha'yahu says he learned of the commander-in-chief's journey to Egypt by other means ("And thy servant was told: 'The commander-in-chief, Coniah son of Elnathan, hath gone to Egypt'") (Ostracon III).

Hosha'yahu proclaims his loyalty, and as evidence cites all that he has done: "Thy servant hath done according to all that my lord hath instructed" (Ostracon IV). This letter then lists all that he has done.

Apparently Hosha'yahu is also warning Ya'ush about a statement made by "the prophet."

Finally Hosha'yahu reports that he is tending (*shomerim 'el* "watching over") the beacon of Lachish, as he was ordered.

Yadin's new interpretation also clinches the identification of Tell ed-Duweir as Biblical Lachish. Several scholars who interpreted the expression *shomerim 'el* as "watching for" Lachish suggested that Tell ed-Duweir, where the ostraca were found, could *not* be Lachish. Other doubts were also raised about the identification of Tell ed-Duweir as Lachish.[5] If Yadin's interpretation is correct, however, and *shomerim 'el* should be read as "watching over," the identification of the site with Lachish cannot be doubted anymore, for these are drafts of correspondence by the commander at Lachish, saying he is watching over the beacon of Lachish.

Yadin's striking new theory about the nature of the Lachish ostraca and their place of origin is both imaginative and attractive. It stands on solid ground. Yadin has indeed made a very strong case for his hypothesis. The Lachish Letters will now return to the forefront of scholarly debate.

[1] J. W. Jack, "The Lachish Letters; Their Date and Import; An Examination of Professor Torczyner's View," *Palestine Exploration Quarterly* 70 (1938), p. 167.
[2] Ibid.
[3] Translated by William F. Albright, in *Ancient Near Eastern Texts Relating to the Old Testament*, Third Edition with Supplement, ed. James B. Pritchard (Princeton University Press: Princeton, N. J., 1969).
[4] J. W. Jack, op. cit.
[5] G. W. Ahlström, "Tell ed-Duweir: Lachish or Libnah?" *Palestine Exploration Quarterly* 115 (1983), pp.103-104; idem, "Is Tell ed-Duweir Ancient Lachish?" *Palestine Exploration Quarterly* 112 (1980), pp. 7-9; G. R. Davies, "Tell ed-Duweir=Ancient Lachish: A Response to G. W. Ahlström," *Palestine Exploration Quarterly* 114 (1982), pp. 25-28.

OVER 20 YEARS AGO, I was excavating a room on the south side of the Israelite fortress at Arad—it was the 1964 season—when Miriam Aharoni, wife of the director of the dig, came rushing over to warn us to be especially careful. We were uncovering an archive of old Hebrew letters, she shouted excitedly.

Mrs. Aharoni knew this—and we didn't—because she had been "dipping" the potsherds from the previous day's excavation of this area. The "dipping method," now common on excavations in Israel, was originated by her husband Yohanan Aharoni at Arad. Each sherd is doused in water and examined to see whether it contains an inscription that cannot otherwise be observed because of the dust and dirt clinging to it. If no inscription appears, a light brush is then applied to see whether such an inscription is under dirt still stuck to the sherd. Dipping requires an extraordinary effort, because any Near Eastern dig will uncover thousands of sherds, but the results are often worth the effort. That was certainly true at Arad.

Thanks to dipping, a rich collection of epigraphic materials was unearthed at Arad, including political, administrative and cultic documents. We have already described one of two bowls incised with two Hebrew letters, q and k (see p. 221), probably standing for $q\bar{o}de\check{s}$ $k\hat{o}han\hat{i}m$, "set apart [holy] for the priests"; the bowls were used in the Israelite temple at Arad.

Over 80 other Hebrew inscriptions were found at Arad because of the special care taken to insure that none was overlooked. Moreover, unlike the rare collections of inscriptions found at other sites in Israel, the Arad inscriptions range over a period of 350 years,

"[Belonging] to Eliashib, *son of Ehiyahu" is the simple inscription on these seals found in the stratum VII (seventh century B.C.) Arad fortress.*

Other Arad documents, including a military order (p. 320) from the stratum VI (605-595 B.C.) archive are addressed to Eliashib. Thus we know that he probably served as commander during the time of both stratum VII and stratum VI.

The materials from which the seals were made are unknown and would be difficult to determine without harming the seals. Two were found with string threaded in them, indicating that they may have been hung on a wall. Eliashib probably used them to seal official documents and consignments from the fortress's storerooms. The fortress may have been a very busy place—the commander may have needed three seals so that his subordinates could help share his workload.

IASHIB

Office Files Found of Commander of the Fort at Arad

ANSON F. RAINEY

covering six different strata. As a result, we can study the development of cursive Hebrew script—so-called old Hebrew (as opposed to the later square Hebrew script)—from the United Monarchy, say about 950 B.C., to the Babylonian conquest of Judah in the early sixth century B.C.

We were excavating in stratum VI on that day in 1964 when Mrs. Aharoni came running over to tell us that we had uncovered an archive. It turned out to be the largest collection of inscriptions found at Arad—18 different documents. Stratum VI was the last stratum before the fort was destroyed in the early sixth century, just before the Babylonians destroyed Jerusalem. Without knowing it, we had been digging in the office of the Israelite commander of the Arad fort.

His name was Eliashib son of Eshiyahu. Three of his

YOHANAN AHARONI

seals were found on the floor of a room on the south side of the fort in stratum VII (c. 620-597 B.C.). They are beautifully preserved seals that simply read "[Belonging] to Eliashib son of Eshiyahu" in two lines. Remnants of a string were even found threaded in two of the seals. It is interesting that they are "private" seals, although we now know from the archive that Eliashib was not a private citizen, but was in fact a responsible officer of the fort. This suggests that other so-called private, as opposed to royal, seals probably belonged to important government officials even though they did not bear titles.

Eliashib may have been commander of the fort. He not only served there during stratum VII, as we know from the seals, but also in stratum VI, as we know from the archive found in his office.

Yohanan Aharoni believed the fort was occupied by the Egyptians in stratum VII because in the same room of stratum VII where the Eliashib seals were found, an ostracon was found written entirely in Egyptian hieratic (cursive) script. The ostracon appears to record an inventory of stock stored at Arad. In 609 B.C. Pharaoh Necho attacked Judah, cutting a swath from south to north, finally killing the Judahite king Josiah at the battle of Megiddo (2 Kings 23:29-35; 2 Chronicles 35:20-36:4). Aharoni assumed the Egyptians occupied the fort at Arad in connection with Necho's campaign in Judah and that an Egyptian scribe wrote the ostracon. However, a very similar ostracon in Egyptian hieratic was found at the contemporaneous Judahite fort at Kadesh-Barnea.*

But the Kadesh-Barnea ostracon also contains a word written in Hebrew. This shows that the Arad ostracon, like the one at Kadesh-Barnea, was written by a Hebrew-speaking scribe. Indeed, Egyptian symbols for numerals and measures, as well as for commodities, are found in Hebrew inscriptions not only from the southern kingdom of Judah but even from the northern kingdom of Israel.

In my view, stratum VII at Arad was destroyed not by Pharaoh Necho, but by the "bands of raiders" sent

* See Rudolph Cohen, "Did I Excavate Kadesh-Barnea?" **BAR**, May/June 1981.

319

Letters, supply vouchers, *inventory lists and important military orders were among the documents discovered in Eliashib's archive. This document, found outside the fortress, may have originally been part of the archive, for it is addressed, on the obverse (not shown) to Eliashib. Its urgent message, on the reverse seen here, orders soldiers to be sent as reinforcements from Arad to Ramat-Negeb.*

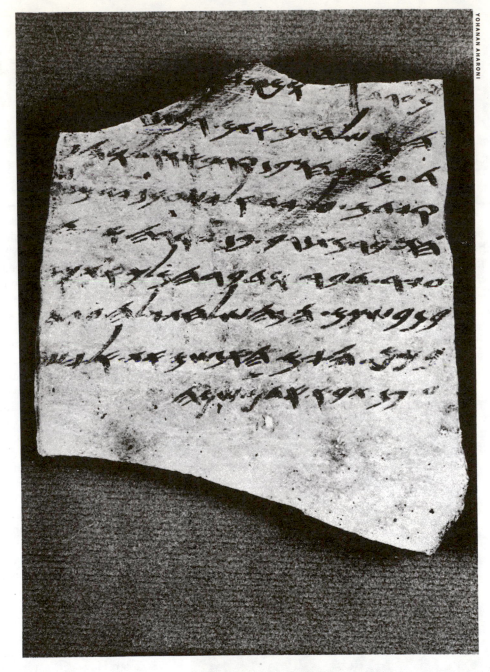

by Nebuchadnezzar, the Babylonian ruler who later destroyed Jerusalem in 587 B.C. These raiders probably destroyed stratum VII at Arad in a softening up operation against Judah in 598/597 B.C. (2 Kings 24:1-2, 12; Jeremiah 13:18-19).

The fort was then rebuilt by Eliashib, who continued as commander. The most likely historical background to account for the reconstruction of the Arad fortress (stratum VI) is this: After Nebuchadnezzar captured the Judahite king Jehoiachin and took him back to Babylonia in chains in 598 B.C., Nebuchadnezzar placed a puppet king, Zedekiah, on the throne of Judah. Apparently, Nebuchadnezzar decided to trust Zedekiah despite some diplomatic hanky-panky and political unrest in the early years of Zedekiah's rule (594 B.C.).

Accordingly it was probably Zedekiah who directed the rebuilding of the fortress (the stratum VI fortress) under the supervision of the old commander Eliashib.

The archive from Eliashib's office in the stratum VI fortress gives a graphic picture of life in a major Judahite fortress at the end of the monarchy. First of all, this archive demonstrates that the maintenance of such an archive was neither extraordinary nor unique. Indeed, writing was common at administrative and military centers in Judah and Israel. Discovering Eliashib's archive was not left to chance: Arad was small enough to be excavated in its entirety, and we took special care to find inscriptions at the site. In addition, the dry, desert environment of Arad for the most part preserved the carbon ink on the sherds.

Most of the Eliashib archive displays a uniformity of script and a fine form that indicate the documents were written by professional scribes. The few crude exceptions only emphasize this conclusion. It seems that a professional scribe was included in the cadre stationed at Arad.

A number of ostraca in the archive appear to be vouchers presented to Eliashib as commander of the fortress for the issuance of supplies from the fortress storehouses. Unfortunately, the vouchers do not contain the names of the senders. But it is clear from other letters that various groups passed through Arad and were provisioned there. For this purpose, at the beginning of their journey they were given vouchers addressed to Eliashib with specific instructions as to the amount and type of provisions they were to be issued.

The vouchers thus authorized the release of provisions from the fortress storehouses. The administrators of Arad then kept the vouchers as receipts. Apparently, Eliashib was instructed, according to standard practice, to write on the back the date he satisfied the voucher; one of the vouchers states: "To Eliashib: And now [the standard opening], give the Kittiyim three baths* of wine, and write the name of the day." The voucher goes on to list the amount of flour to be issued. On the back of one of the vouchers, the date is written in a handwriting different from that on the front.

The usual provisions kept in the storehouses, as indicated on the voucher referred to above, were wine and flour or bread. These are the basic provisions mentioned in the Bible as provisions for the road (compare Genesis 14:18; Joshua 9:4-5; Judges 19:19; 1 Samuel 10:3, 16:20, 25:18; 2 Samuel 16:1-2).

Kittiyim, referred to in the voucher discussed above, are mentioned frequently in the ostraca. These are the Kittim of the Bible. The name comes from Kition, a city on the Mediterranean island of Cyprus where the population was mainly of Phoenician origin. The Kittim thus spoke a language closely akin to Hebrew, and could easily converse with Eliashib. These Kittim or Kittiyim might have been mercenaries in the service of Judah.

In one ostracon the Kittim are given provision for "*the* four days": "To Eliashib: And now give the Kittiyim two baths of wine for the four days, and 300 [loaves of] bread." The voucher obviously came from a person of higher rank than Eliashib for it also admonishes him somewhat testily, "Don't delay." The use of the definite article "the" in "the four days" suggests that there must have been a definite organized route and way stations through the desert based on units of distance per day. This was not provision for "a" four-day journey, but for "the" four-day journey, probably with specific stopovers and a final destination, in this case, probably Kadesh-Barnea, where the unit of Kittiyim would be reprovisioned.

We can also draw some conclusions as to the size of the military unit from the amount of the provision.

When Zedekiah imprisoned the prophet Jeremiah, Jeremiah was allotted a ration of one loaf of bread a day (Jeremiah 37:21), no doubt a minimal portion, which is why it is specifically mentioned. Military units traveling in the desert were also minimally supplied—say two loaves a day for each man. If this is accurate, 300 loaves of bread for four days indicates a unit of about 35-40 men (who would be given two loaves of bread each for four days).

One of the letters in the Eliashib archive refers to "the Temple of Yahweh." It is a cryptic reference addressed to Eliashib from one of his subordinates: "To my lord Eliashib, May Yahweh seek your welfare. And now: . . . as to the matter which you commanded me— it is well; he is in the Temple of Yahweh." The reference could not be to the temple at Arad for that had long ago been destroyed. The reference must be to the Temple of Jerusalem. Apparently, Eliashib sent one of his subordinates on a mission to Jerusalem and this is his report. Alas, the details of this mission to Jerusalem were not given.

The most chilling episode in Eliashib's career came to light three years after the discovery of the archive in his office. I was supervising the excavation of the slope outside the fortress on the western side. An American volunteer from the University of North Carolina came running over with an inscribed sherd she had just found. It was a letter to Eliashib, but unfortunately only the back side was well preserved. From the script, we could tell that it had come from the stratum VI fortress. It was an order to rush troops from Arad and from neighboring Kinah to strengthen the defenses of Ramat-Negeb (probably Tel 'Ira, southwest of Arad on a hill overlooking the entire Beer-Sheba Valley): "To Eliashib . . . king . . . troop . . . from Arad 50 and from Kin[ah] . . . and you shall send them to Ramat-Negeb . . . ." The message is stringent—not to say hard-boiled: "The word of the king is incumbent on you for your very life! Behold I have sent to warn you today." Ramat-Negeb had to be defended, "lest Edom should come there."

When the Edomites to the south and east saw that Judah was under heavy pressure from the Babylonians, the Edomites invaded the Negeb, occupied southern Judah and even cheered when Nebuchadnezzar destroyed Jerusalem (Obadiah 1:10, 14; Psalm 137:7).

It was in this probable context that Eliashib was ordered to rush troops from Arad and Kinah for the defense of Ramat-Negeb. This defense probably failed.

Eliashib's office (where the archive was found) and his dwelling quarters were destroyed by fire, probably the work of these same Edomite troops.

Another sherd found elsewhere mentions the "Son of Eliashib." But nothing is known of the son's fate— or of Eliashib's.

The Eliashib letters and the other inscriptions discovered at Arad now comprise the most valuable corpus of ancient Hebrew inscriptions from the period of the Israelite monarchies.

---

* A liquid measure equal to about 22 liters (six gallons).

The materials treated in this section are diverse. They range in time over a 350-year period; they range in character from formal texts written carefully on plastered walls to hasty notes scribbled on potsherds; they range in content from prophecy to prayers to battlefield communiques.

Taken together, they dramatically illustrate how fragmentary and how few are the epigraphic finds from the Israelite period. These reports also help us appreciate the painstaking processes necessary to recover, preserve and transcribe the few traces of ancient writing that do occasionally come to light.

André Lemaire's description of the condition of the Deir Alla fragments and how carefully they had to be treated, Anson Rainey's description of the "dipping method" of treating pottery that Yohanan Aharoni had introduced at Arad—these accounts underscore how ephemeral and fragile the epigraphic materials are. The Deir Alla fragments, the Kuntillet Ajrud inscriptions and drawings, the Khirbet el-Kom inscription faintly scratched into the chalk of a tomb wall—all these help us appreciate what patience is required to extract a readable text from most ancient inscriptions.

By their very sparseness these inscriptions also help us appreciate how amazingly extensive are the ancient archives that have been drawn together and preserved for us in the Bible.

Indeed, the inscriptions examined here would not make much sense if we could not draw on information from the Biblical texts to help interpret them and to reconstruct the context out of which they were produced. What we know of the history, culture and religion of the region from the Biblical records has been invaluable in different ways in the analysis of each of these inscriptions.

In return, these inscriptions help to sharpen our understanding and appreciation of facets of the Biblical experience. The Deir Alla inscriptions help us better to sense the cultural atmosphere out of which the early Biblical prophets arose and from which the early Biblical historians drew. The Kuntillet Ajrud and Khirbet el-Kom inscriptions—however they are interpreted—help us to appreciate firsthand something of the diversity of religious belief and practice in early Israel, which also helps us to better understand the fervor of the prophets'

calls for reform. The scraps of military correspondence from Lachish and Arad bring into dramatic focus the Biblical accounts of the military campaigns that ultimately engulfed the Israelite nation in the early sixth century B.C.

Perhaps it would be appropriate to close this section—and this volume—with a reader's comment. It appeared in **BAR**, March/April 1985:

> Because I am a non-scholar, one of the many reasons I so much enjoy reading **BAR** is that once I have read an article by one of your scholars, I can sit back and think about what I read, and then try to reason in my own unscholarly mind what might have occurred millennia ago. You gave me a good opportunity to do just that in "Who or What Was Yahweh's Asherah?" My belief is that Asherah was all those things (including Yahweh's consort) André Lemaire mentions. It is well-known that many pagan practices and rites have been carried over into revealed religions. It is therefore not unreasonable to expect that in the beginning of the Jewish tradition, there was a mental carry-over from the Canaanite Astarte (the consort of Baal) to Asherah (the consort of Yahweh). To go from a fertility goddess to a holy place, a sacred tree, a pole or possibly a grove of trees, to Deuteronomy (considerably longer than a millennium) is not surprising.
>
> I know scholars want proof. I don't have it. I simply enjoy logic and my knowledge of the working of the human mentality, which is no different today than it was thousands of years ago.
>
> Hy Grober, Teaneck, New Jersey

For Further Reading

Concerning Iron Age Inscriptions

"Cache of Hebrew and Phoenician Inscriptions Found in the Desert," **BAR**, March 1976 (Kuntillet Ajrud inscriptions)

"Did the Philistines Write?" **BAR**, July/August 1982

Rodney Wright, " 'Lachish and Azekah Were the Only Fortified Cities of Judah that Remained' (Jeremiah 34:7)," **BAR**, November/December 1982 (Lachish letters)

Gabriel Barkay, "The Divine Name Found in Jerusalem," **BAR**, March/April 1983

Contributors

Hershel Shanks, co-editor of this volume, is editor of *Biblical Archaeology Review* and *Bible Review*. He is the author of *The City of David, A Guide to Biblical Jerusalem* and *Judaism in Stone*, on the history and archaeology of ancient synagogues. He edited *Ancient Israel, A Short History from Abraham to the Roman Destruction of the Temple* and *Recent Archaeology in the Land of Israel*, both published by the Biblical Archaeology Society.

Dan P. Cole, co-editor, is professor of religion at Lake Forest College in Illinois. He wrote the booklets of descriptive captions accompanying three Biblical Archaeology Society slide sets: Biblical Archaeology, Jerusalem Archaeology and New Testament Archaeology. Cole has excavated at Tell Halif, Gezer and Shechem, and is the author of *Shechem I: Middle Bronze II B Pottery*. He serves on the Editorial Advisory Board of *Biblical Archaeology Review*.

Miriam Aharoni has excavated, with her late husband, archaeologist Yohanan Aharoni, at Hazor, Ramat Rahel, Beer-sheba and Arad. She edited *The Archaeology of the Land of Israel*, written by Yohanan Aharoni. With Ze'ev Herzog and Anson Rainey, she is preparing the final excavation report on the Israelite fortress at Arad.

Itzhaq Beit-Arieh, professor of archaeology at Tel Aviv University, directed the Ophir Expedition to Sinai from 1972 to 1980, and since 1979 has directed excavations in the eastern Negev. He is a member of the Israel Archaeological Council, the Council of the Israel Exploration Society and the Israel Survey Committee.

Oded Borowski is chairperson of the department of Near Eastern and Judaic languages and literatures at Emory University and senior staff member of the excavation at Tell Halif in the northern Negev. A frequent contributor to **BAR**, he is the author of *Agriculture in Iron Age Israel: The Evidence From Archaeology and the Bible* and serves on **BAR**'s Editorial Advisory Board.

Joseph A. Callaway directed the archaeological expedition at Ai between 1964 and 1976; he also excavated at Jericho, Shechem and Bethel. He served as president of the William F. Albright School of Archaeological Research in Jerusalem and was a trustee of the American Schools of Oriental Research. Callaway was professor of Biblical archaeology at Southern Baptist Theological Seminary, in Louisville, Kentucky, until 1982. Before his death in 1988, he authored or edited eight books and numerous articles.

Ze'ev Herzog, senior lecturer on archaeology at Tel Aviv University, has excavated at Beer-sheba, Megiddo, Hazor, Tel Michal, Tel Gerisa and Arad. He is the author of *Beer-Sheba II: The Early Iron Age Settlements* and co-editor of *Excavations at Tel Michal*.

Aharon Kempinski teaches archaeology and ancient Near Eastern history at Tel Aviv University and has been a visiting lecturer at the University of Tübingen and at Harvard University. He has excavated in Turkey and at many sites in Israel, including Tell Erani, Tell Kabri, Ein Gedi, Achziv, Megiddo and Beer-sheba. Kempinski is the author of *The Rise of Urban Culture—Palestine in the 3rd Millennium BC* and serves on **BAR**'s Editorial Advisory Board.

André Lemaire is *chargé de recherche* at the Centre National de la Recherche Scientifique in Paris. He has excavated at Lachish and Tel Keisan in Israel and is the author of a history of Israel in French. He is the editor of a collection of ancient Hebrew ostraca and is preparing a full corpus of paleo-Hebrew inscriptions from the First Temple period.

Amihai Mazar, associate professor of archaeology at the Hebrew University in Jerusalem, has excavated extensively in the Judean Hills and in the Shephelah, directing the excavations at Tell Qasile, Tel Batash and Tel Beth-Shean. He is the author of *The Archaeology of the Land of the Bible*.

Ze'ev Meshel, senior lecturer in archaeology at Tel Aviv University, has been a visiting research fellow in the United States, England and Australia. Meshel excavated the northern Sinai desert site of Kuntillet Ajrud and has continued to study its important inscriptions. He has also reevaluated the pottery of Tell el-Kheleifeh, on the northern shore of the Gulf of Eilat. Meshel serves on **BAR**'s Editorial Advisory Board.

James D. Muhly, professor of Oriental studies and chairman of the ancient history program at the University of Pennsylvania, directs excavations at Tel Michal and Tel Gerisa. Since 1965 he has researched the development of metallurgical technology, production and trade throughout the ancient world. He is co-editor of *Coming of the Age of Iron* and the author of *Copper and Tin* and *The Nature of the Metals Trade in the Bronze Age*. Muhly is a member of **BAR**'s Editorial Advisory Board.

Anson F. Rainey teaches Semitic languages at Tel Aviv University and historical geography of Biblical lands at the Institute for Holy Land Studies in Jerusalem. He has excavated at Lachish, Arad, Beersheba, Tel Michal and Tel Gerisa.

David Ussishkin is professor of archaeology at Tel Aviv University. He has directed the Lachish excavations since 1973 and is the author of *The Conquest of Lachish by Sennacherib*. Ussishkin is on the executive committee of the Israel Exploration Society and a member of the Israel Archaeological Council and **BAR**'s Editorial Advisory Board. He edits *Tel Aviv*, the journal of Tel Aviv University's Institute of Archaeology.

Yigael Yadin was Israel's most celebrated archaeologist until his death in 1984. A former Chief of Staff of the Israeli army, Yadin led the excavations at Hazor and Masada. He also discovered the Bar-Kokhba letters near the Dead Sea and helped obtain four of the Dead Sea Scrolls for the state of Israel. He was the author of *The Message of the Scrolls, Art of Warfare in Biblical Lands, The Temple Scroll, Masada* and *Hazor, the Head of All Those Kingdoms*.

Adam Zertal teaches archaeology at Haifa University. In 1978 he organized and led the Survey of the Hill Country of Manasseh and continues to excavate on Mt. Ebal, the subject of his articles in this volume. He is the author of *The Plain of the Wilderness*, a novel.